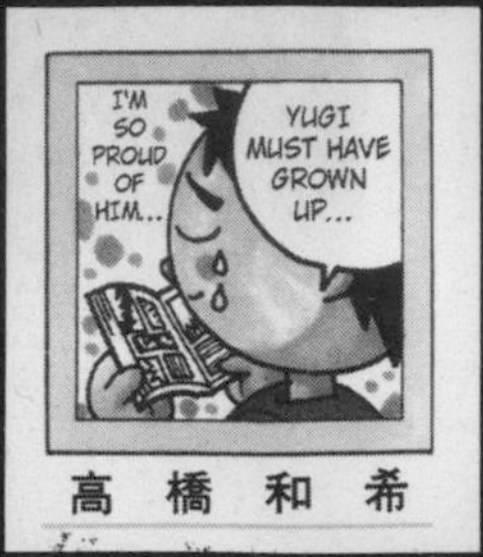
YUGI MUST HAVE GROWN UP...
I'M SO PROUD OF HIM...
高橋和希

WHEN I WAS IN ELEMENTARY SCHOOL, THERE WAS A BOOK RENTAL STORE IN MY NEIGHBORHOOD. I WOULD BORROW MANGA EVERY DAY AND READ IT BEFORE GOING TO BED. SOMETIMES I WOULD READ TEN VOLUMES IN ONE NIGHT. ONE DAY I THOUGHT TO MYSELF, "WHAT'S WRONG WITH THIS MANGA? THE MAIN CHARACTER'S FACE SLOWLY CHANGES FROM THE FIRST VOLUME!"

TIME PASSED...

NOW, WHEN I LOOK AT *YU-GI-OH!* VOLUME 1, IT'S UNBELIEVABLE! THE MAIN CHARACTER'S FACE IS SLIGHTLY DIFFERENT FROM NOW. AND THAT'S HOW MY CHILDHOOD QUESTION WAS ANSWERED.

-KAZUKI TAKAHASHI, 2002

Artist/author Kazuki Takahashi first tried to break into the manga business in 1982, but success eluded him until **Yu-Gi-Oh!** debuted in the Japanese **Weekly Shonen Jump** magazine in 1996. **Yu-Gi-Oh!**'s themes of friendship and fighting, together with Takahashi's weird and wonderful art, soon became enormously successful, spawning a real-world card game, video games, and two anime series. A lifelong gamer, Takahashi enjoys Shogi (Japanese chess), Mahjong, card games, and tabletop RPGs, among other games.

YU-GI-OH!: DUELIST VOL. 22
The SHONEN JUMP Manga Edition

STORY AND ART BY
KAZUKI TAKAHASHI

Translation & English Adaptation/Joe Yamazaki
Touch-up Art & Lettering/Eric Erbes
Design/Andrea Rice
Editor/Jason Thompson

Editor in Chief, Books/Alvin Lu
Editor in Chief, Magazines/Marc Weidenbaum
VP of Publishing Licensing/Rika Inouye
VP of Sales/Gonzalo Ferreyra
Sr. VP of Marketing/Liza Coppola
Publisher/Hyoe Narita

In the original Japanese edition, YU-GI-OH!, YU-GI-OH! DUELIST and
YU-GI-OH!: MILLENNIUM WORLD are known collectively as YU-GI-OH!.
The English YU-GI-OH!: DUELIST was originally volumes 8-31
of the Japanese YU-GI-OH!.

Printed in the U.S.A.

Published by VIZ Media, LLC
P.O. Box 77010
San Francisco, CA 94107

SHONEN JUMP Manga Edition
10 9 8 7 6 5 4 3 2 1
First printing, August 2007

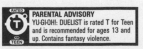

PARENTAL ADVISORY
YU-GI-OH!: DUELIST is rated T for Teen
and is recommended for ages 13 and
up. Contains fantasy violence.

www.viz.com

THE WORLD'S
MOST POPULAR MANGA

www.shonenjump.com

SHONEN JUMP MANGA

Vol. 22
SLIFER VS. OBELISK!
STORY AND ART BY
KAZUKI TAKAHASHI

THE STORY SO FAR...

YUGI MUTOU/
YU-GI-OH

When 10th grader Yugi solved the Millennium Puzzle, another spirit took up residence in his body...Yu-Gi-Oh, the King of Games, a dark avenger who challenges evildoers to "Shadow Games" of life and death!

YUGI FACES DEADLY ENEMIES!

Using his gaming skills, Yugi fights ruthless adversaries like Maximillion Pegasus, multimillionaire creator of the collectible card game "Duel Monsters," and Ryo Bakura, whose friendly personality turns evil when he is possessed by the spirit of the Millennium Ring. But Yugi's greatest rival is Seto Kaiba, the world's second-greatest gamer—and the ruthless teenage president of Kaiba Corporation. At first, Kaiba and Yugi are bitter enemies, but after fighting against a common adversary—Pegasus—they come to respect one another. But for all his powers, there is one thing Yu-Gi-Oh cannot do: remember who he is and where he came from.

| HIROTO HONDA | ANZU MAZAKI | KATSUYA JONOUCHI |
| MARIK | ISHIZU ISHTAR | SETO KAIBA |

  THE TABLET OF THE PHARAOH'S MEMORIES

Then one day, when an Egyptian museum exhibit comes to Japan, Yugi sees an ancient carving of himself as an Egyptian pharaoh! The curator of the exhibit, Ishizu Ishtar, explains that there are seven Millennium Items, which were made to fit into a stone tablet in a hidden shrine in Egypt. According to the legend, when the seven Items are brought together, the pharaoh will regain his memories of his past life.

  THE EGYPTIAN GOD CARDS

But there is another piece of the puzzle—the three Egyptian God Cards, the rarest cards on Earth. To collect the God Cards, Kaiba announces "Battle City," an enormous "Duel Monsters" tournament. Attracted by the scent of blood, the most powerful God Card wielder comes to Tokyo: Ishizu's insane brother Marik, who wants to murder the pharaoh to satisfy a grudge. Using his sadistic torture deck, Marik climbs to the tournament semi-finals, where he defeats Yugi's friend Jonouchi, leaving him in a deathlike state. Now, only one semi-finals match remains. Now, Yugi and Kaiba must fight their final duel…and the winner will face Marik in the ultimate battle of the gods!

Yu-Gi-Oh! Duelist

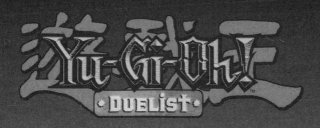

Vol. 22

CONTENTS

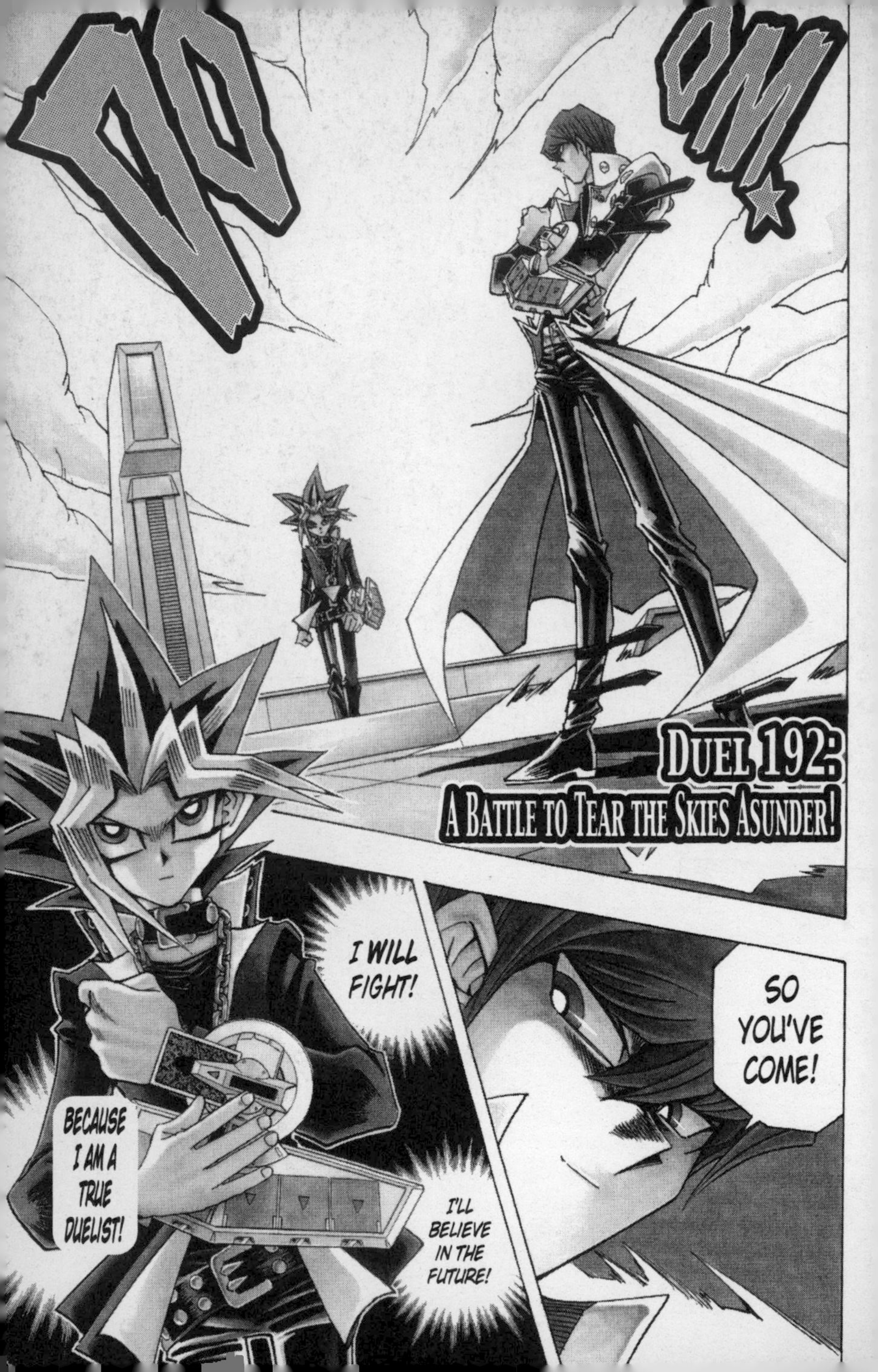
DOOM
DUEL 192:
A BATTLE TO TEAR THE SKIES ASUNDER!
SO YOU'VE COME!
I WILL FIGHT!
BECAUSE I AM A TRUE DUELIST!
I'LL BELIEVE IN THE FUTURE!

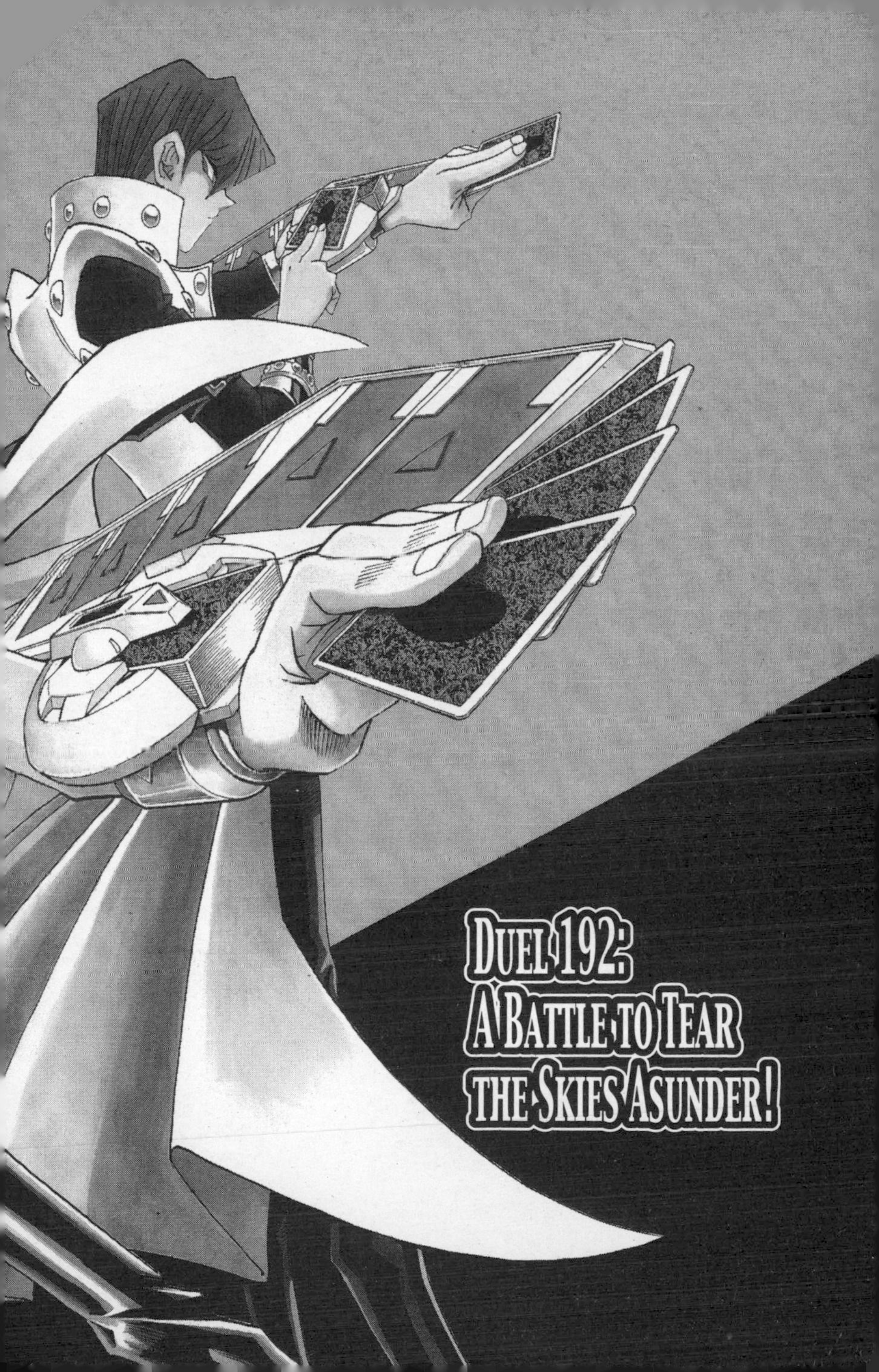
DUEL 192:
A BATTLE TO TEAR
THE SKIES ASUNDER!

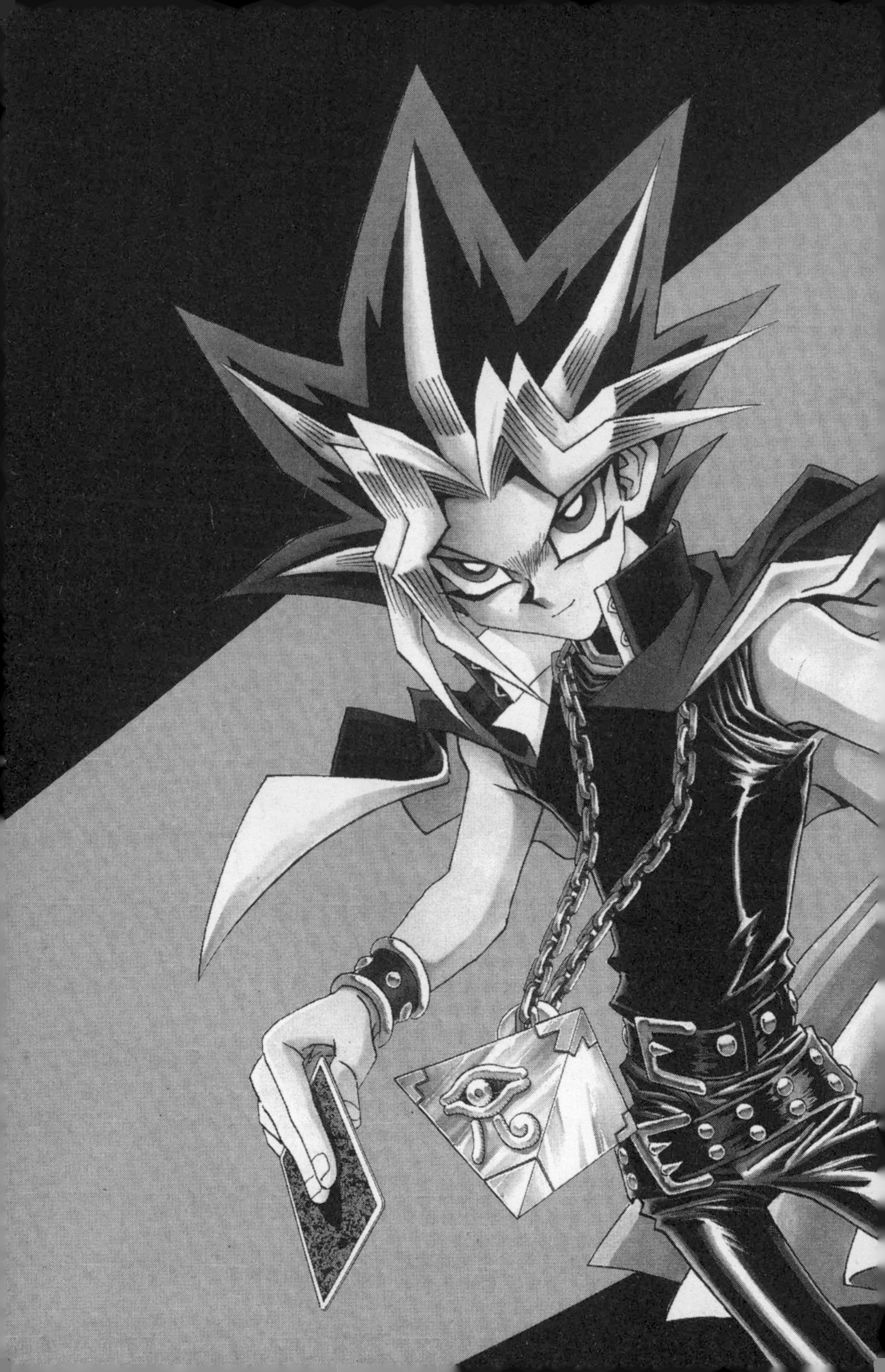

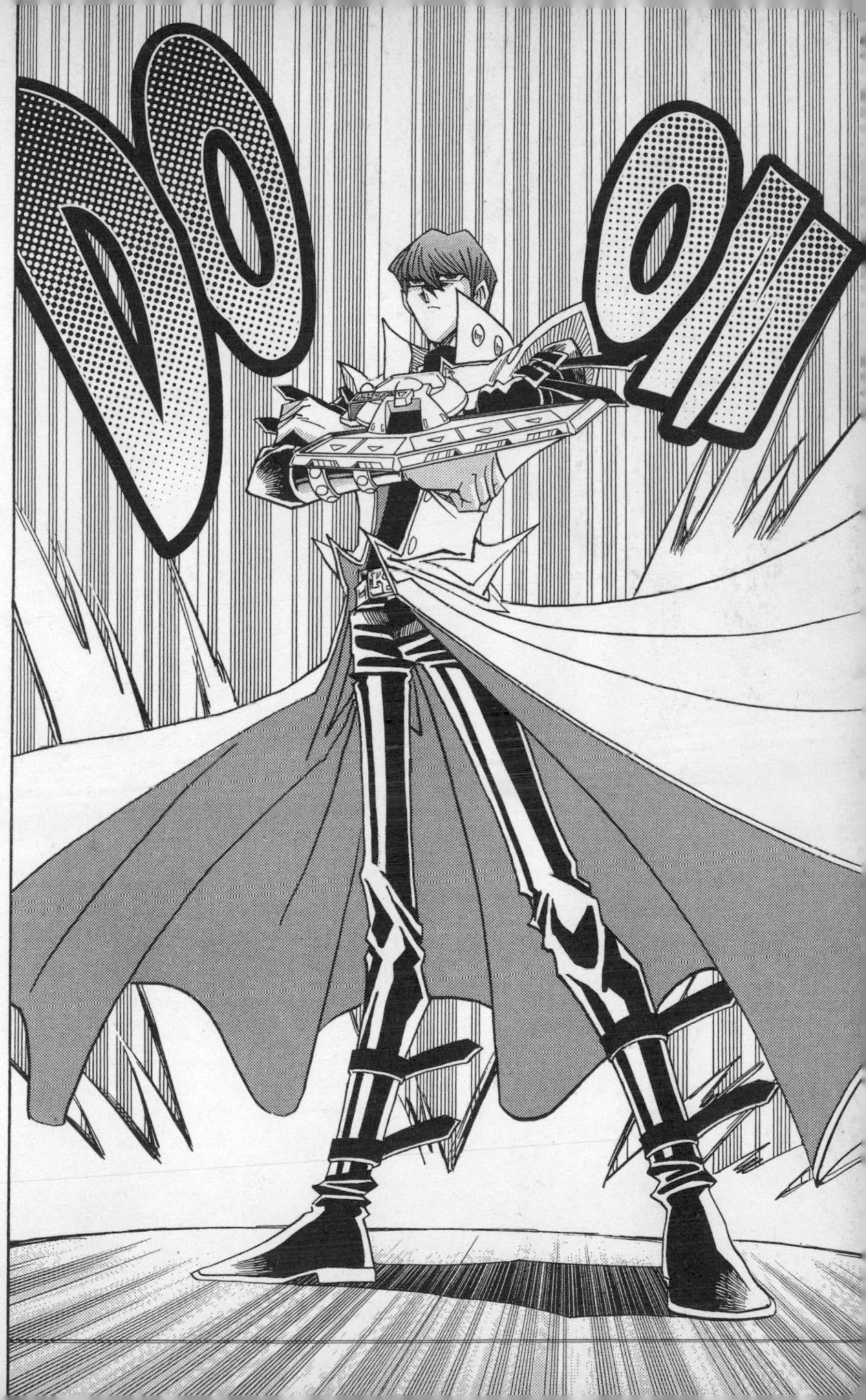
DOON!!

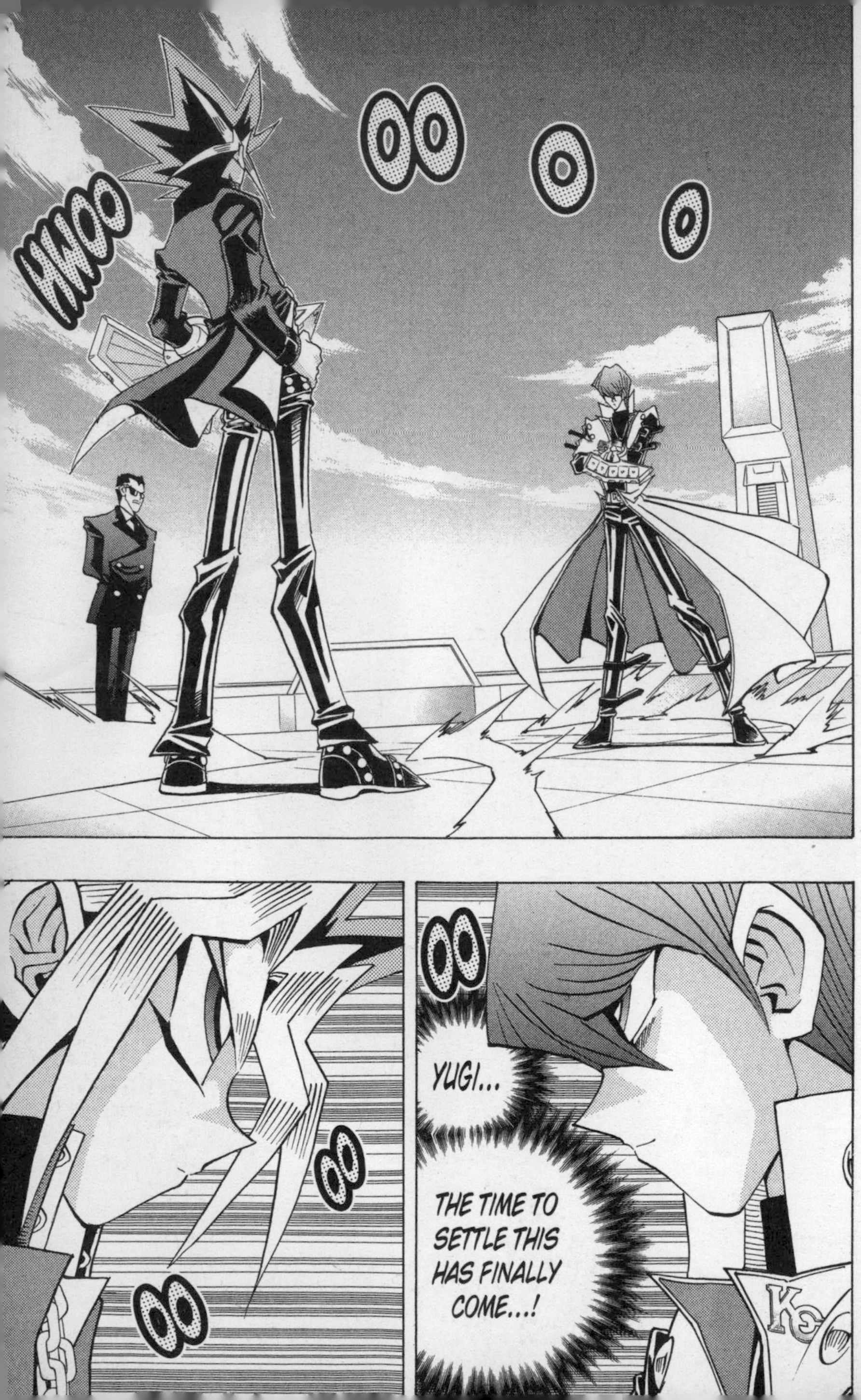
WHOO
YUGI...
THE TIME TO SETTLE THIS HAS FINALLY COME...!

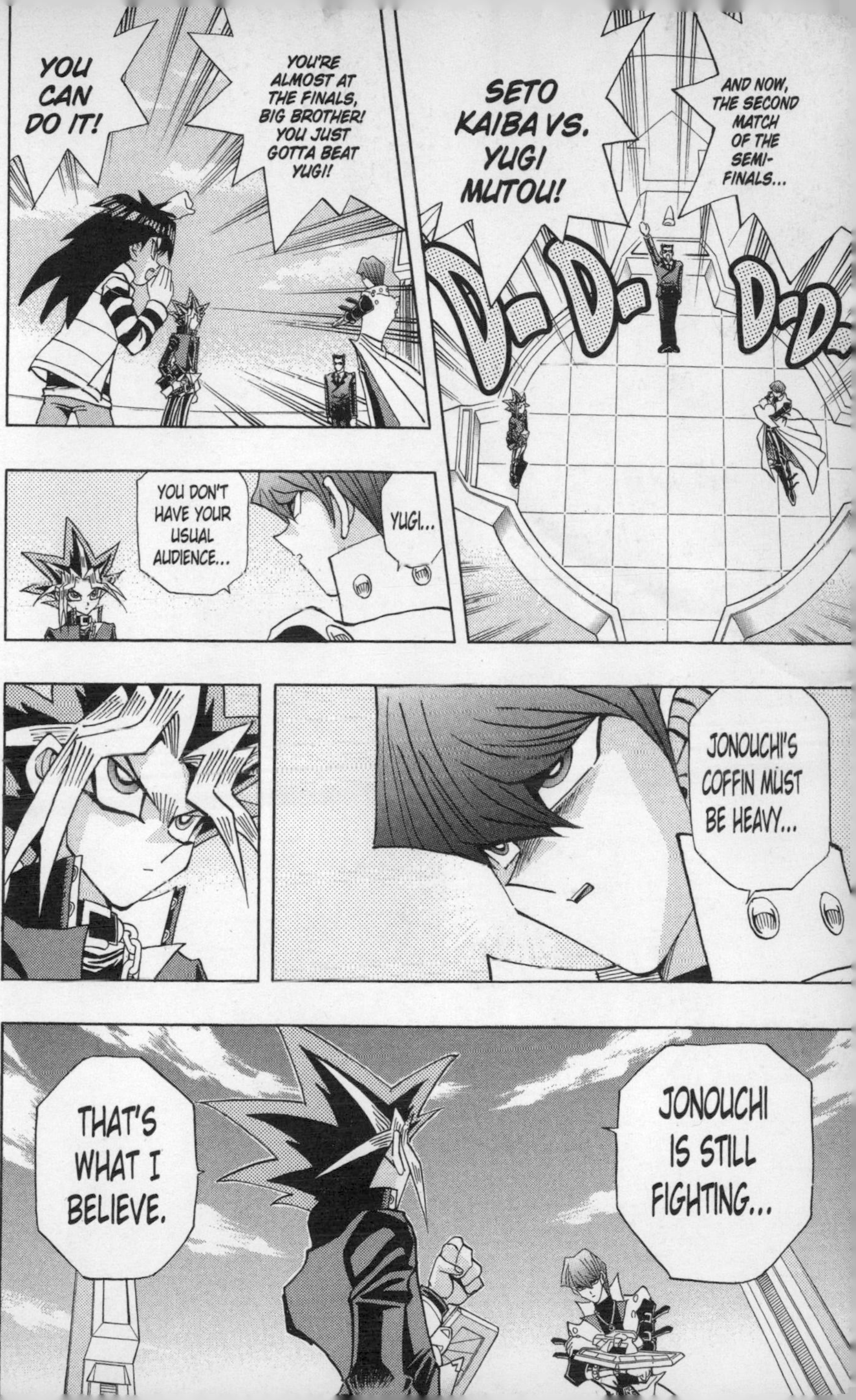
AND NOW, THE SECOND MATCH OF THE SEMI-FINALS...
SETO KAIBA VS. YUGI MUTOU!
D-D-
D-D-
YOU'RE ALMOST AT THE FINALS, BIG BROTHER! YOU JUST GOTTA BEAT YUGI!
YOU CAN DO IT!
YUGI...
YOU DON'T HAVE YOUR USUAL AUDIENCE...
JONOUCHI'S COFFIN MUST BE HEAVY...
JONOUCHI IS STILL FIGHTING...
THAT'S WHAT I BELIEVE.

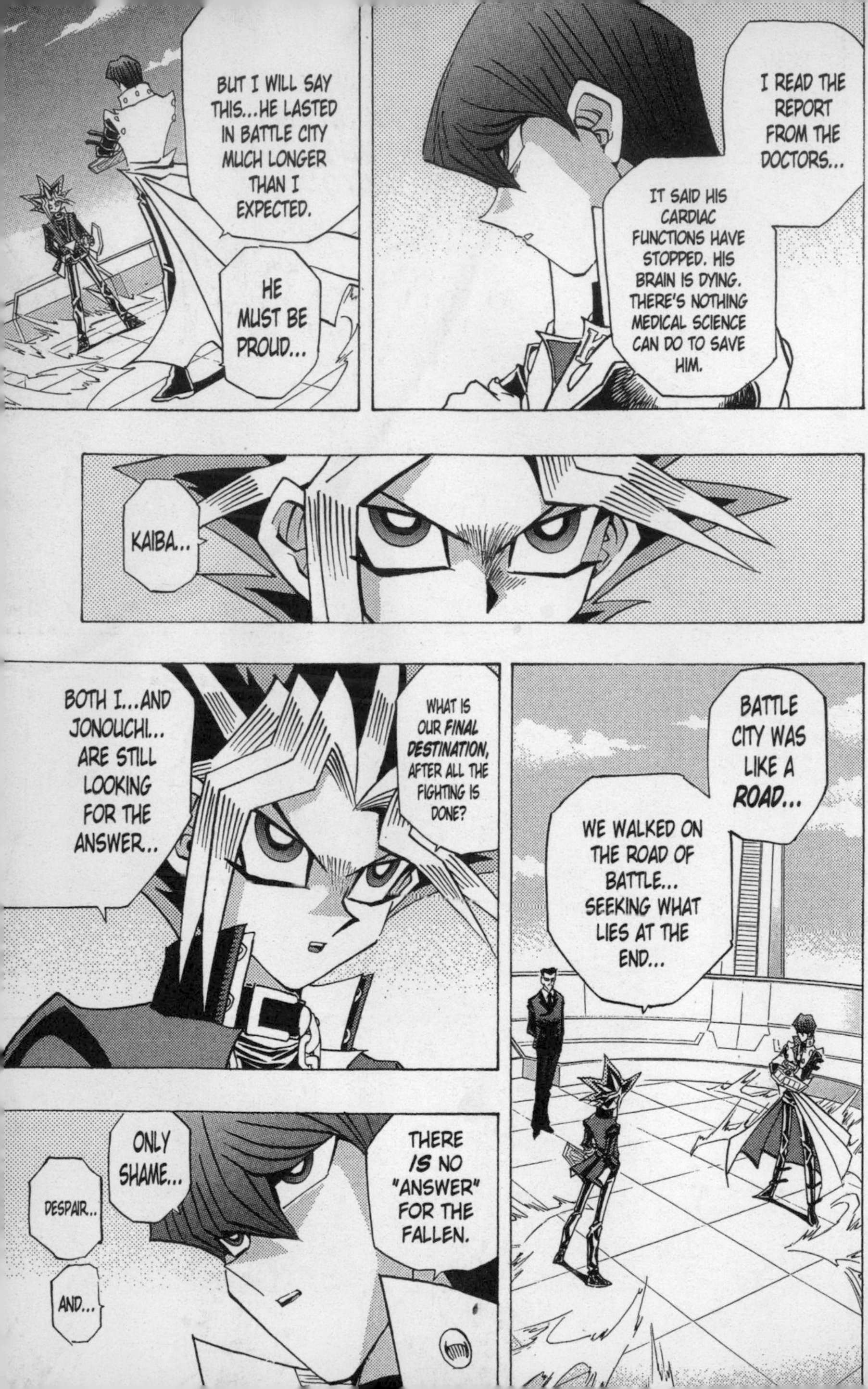
I READ THE REPORT FROM THE DOCTORS...
IT SAID HIS CARDIAC FUNCTIONS HAVE STOPPED. HIS BRAIN IS DYING. THERE'S NOTHING MEDICAL SCIENCE CAN DO TO SAVE HIM.
BUT I WILL SAY THIS...HE LASTED IN BATTLE CITY MUCH LONGER THAN I EXPECTED.
HE MUST BE PROUD...
KAIBA...
BATTLE CITY WAS LIKE A **ROAD...**
WE WALKED ON THE ROAD OF BATTLE... SEEKING WHAT LIES AT THE END...
WHAT IS OUR *FINAL DESTINATION,* AFTER ALL THE FIGHTING IS DONE?
BOTH I...AND JONOUCHI... ARE STILL LOOKING FOR THE ANSWER...
THERE *IS* NO "ANSWER" FOR THE FALLEN.
ONLY SHAME...
DESPAIR...
AND...

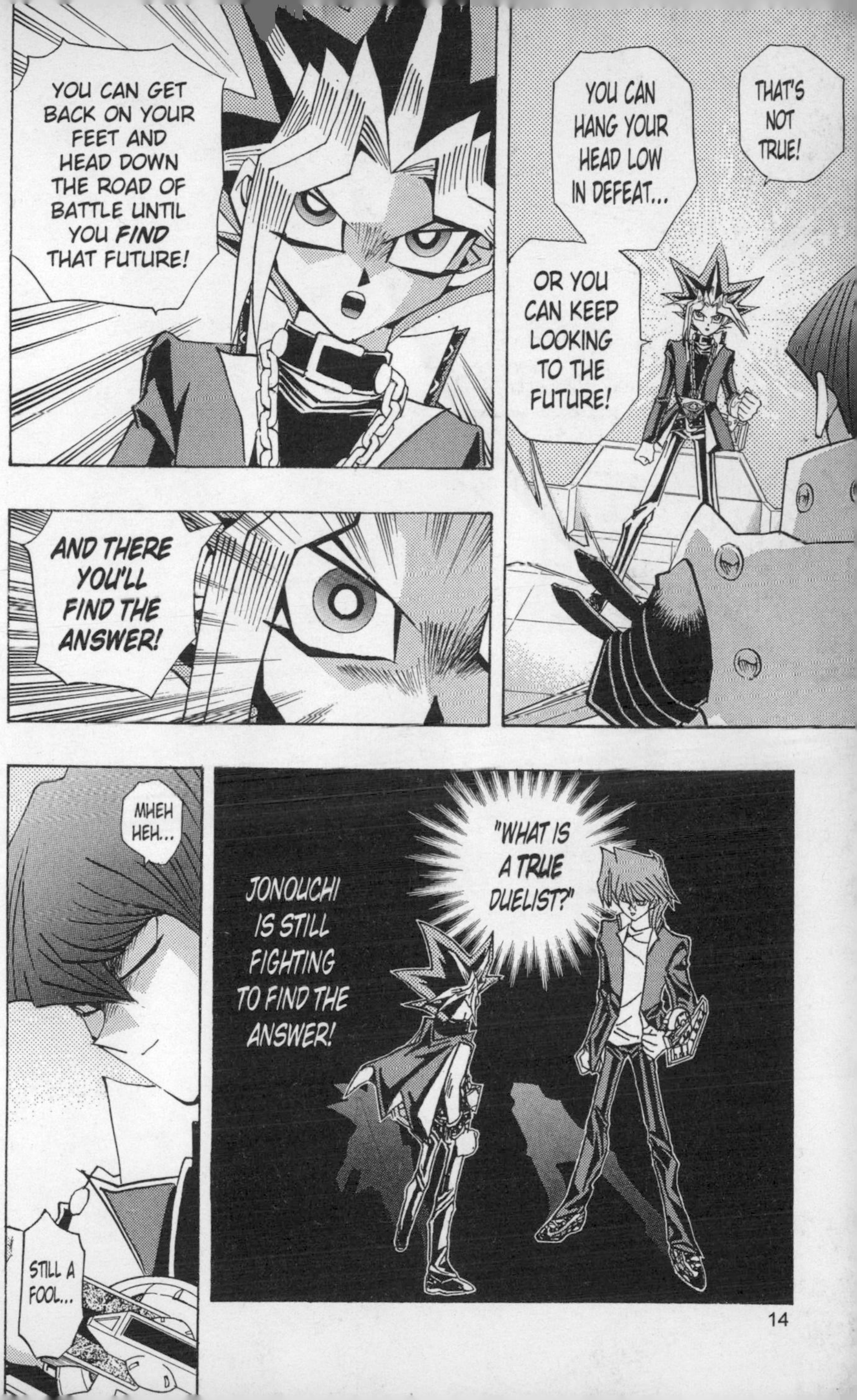
THAT'S NOT TRUE!
YOU CAN HANG YOUR HEAD LOW IN DEFEAT...
OR YOU CAN KEEP LOOKING TO THE FUTURE!
YOU CAN GET BACK ON YOUR FEET AND HEAD DOWN THE ROAD OF BATTLE UNTIL YOU FIND THAT FUTURE!
AND THERE YOU'LL FIND THE ANSWER!
"WHAT IS A TRUE DUELIST?"
JONOUCHI IS STILL FIGHTING TO FIND THE ANSWER!
MHEH HEH...
STILL A FOOL...

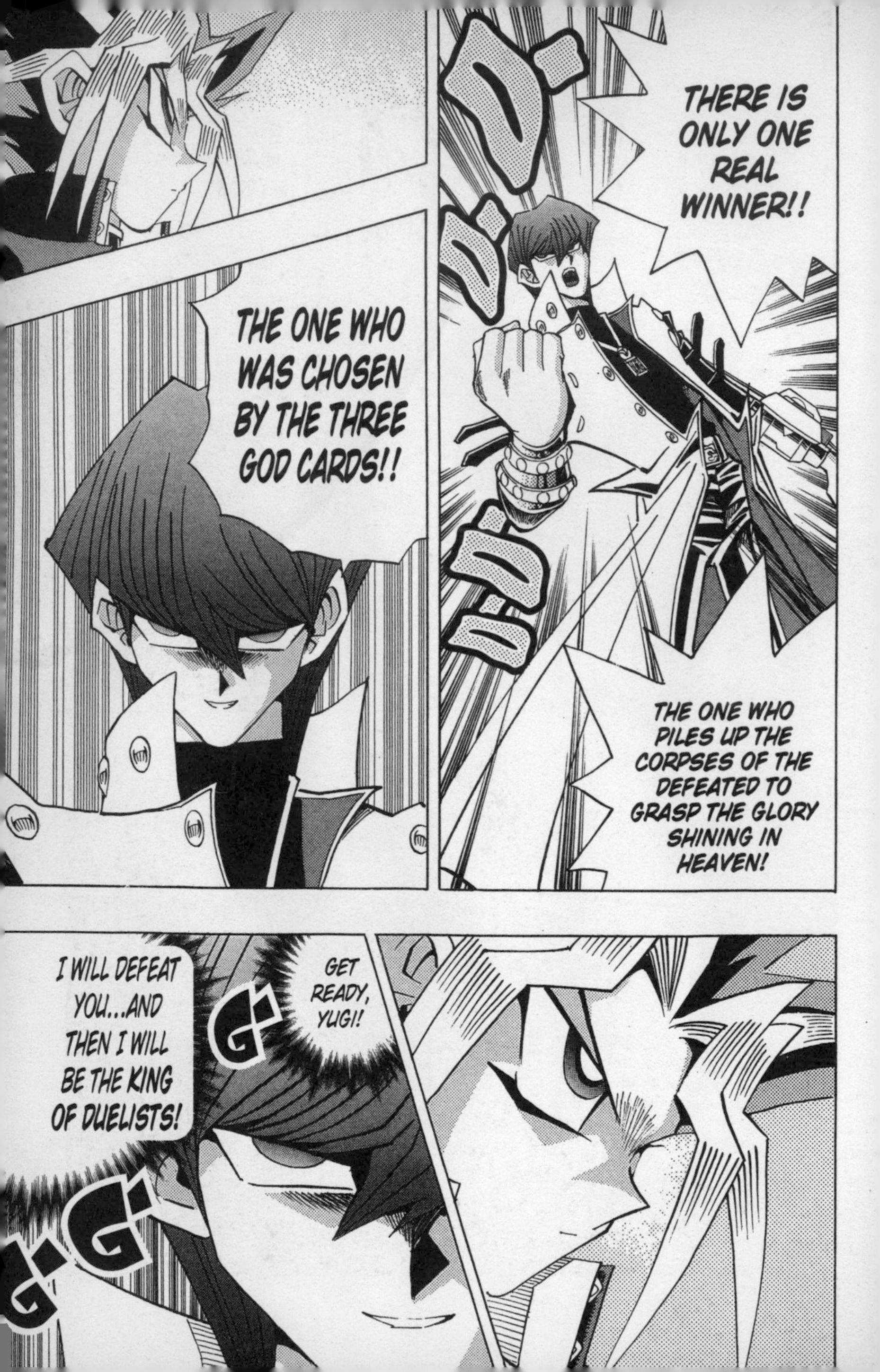
THERE IS ONLY ONE REAL WINNER!!
THE ONE WHO PILES UP THE CORPSES OF THE DEFEATED TO GRASP THE GLORY SHINING IN HEAVEN!
THE ONE WHO WAS CHOSEN BY THE THREE GOD CARDS!!
GET READY, YUGI!
I WILL DEFEAT YOU...AND THEN I WILL BE THE KING OF DUELISTS!

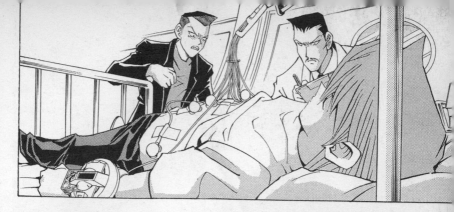

HEY...
DIDN'T THE ECG MOVE JUST NOW?
NO... I DON'T THINK SO...
C'MON!
IF YOU'RE A DOCTOR, DO SOME-THING!
I TRIED ...!
IT'S TOO LATE!
...
KATS-UYA...
JONOUCHI... YUGI'S DUEL IS ABOUT TO START...

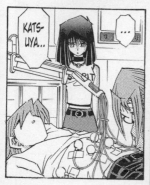

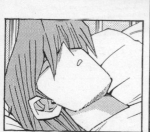

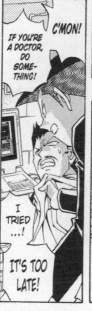

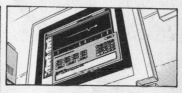

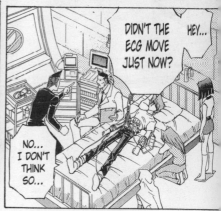

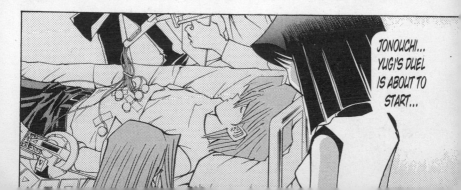

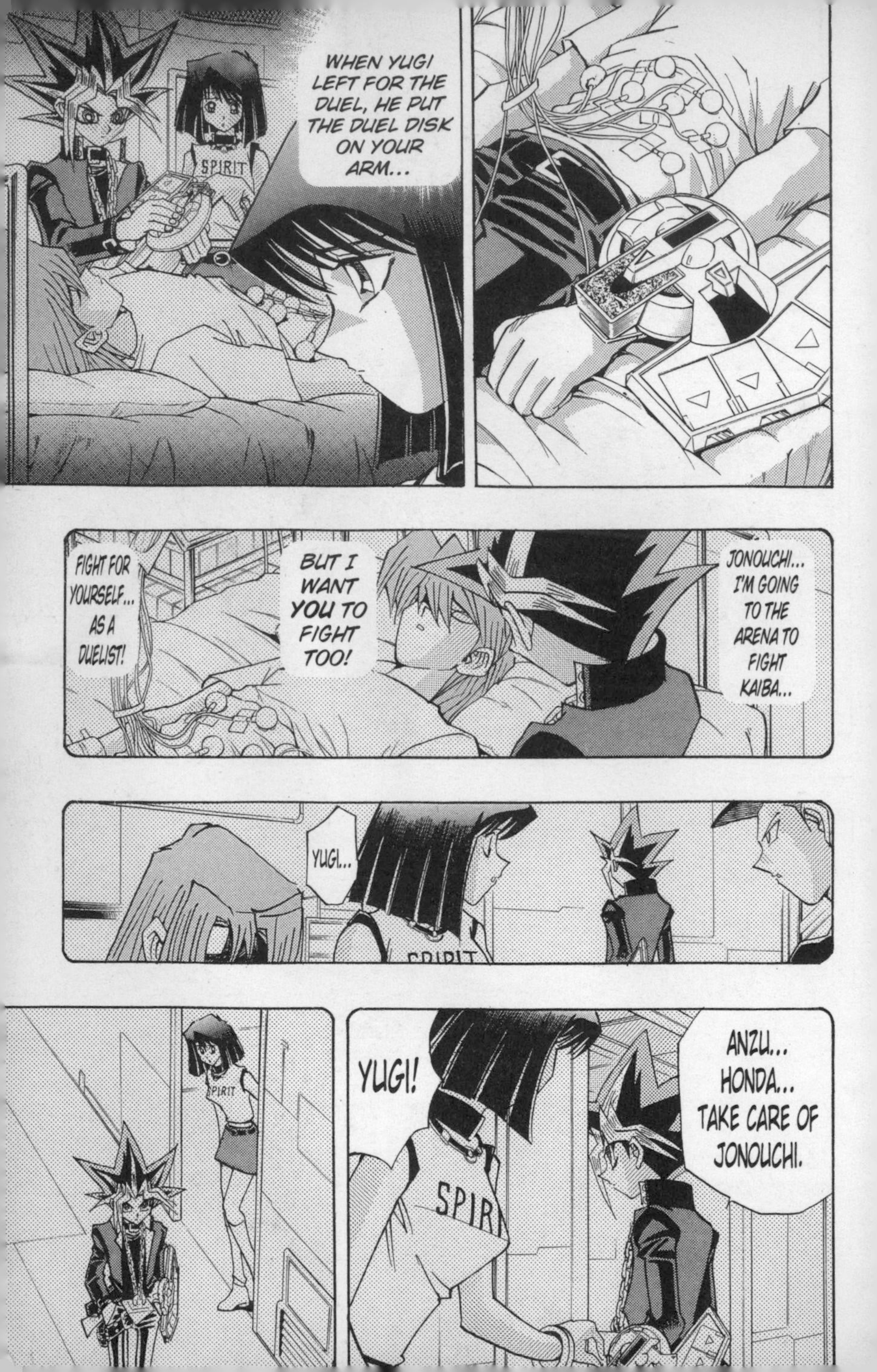
WHEN YUGI LEFT FOR THE DUEL, HE PUT THE DUEL DISK ON YOUR ARM...
SPIRIT
JONOUCHI... I'M GOING TO THE ARENA TO FIGHT KAIBA...
BUT I WANT YOU TO FIGHT TOO!
FIGHT FOR YOURSELF... AS A DUELIST!
YUGI...
ANZU... HONDA... TAKE CARE OF JONOUCHI.
YUGI!
SPIRIT

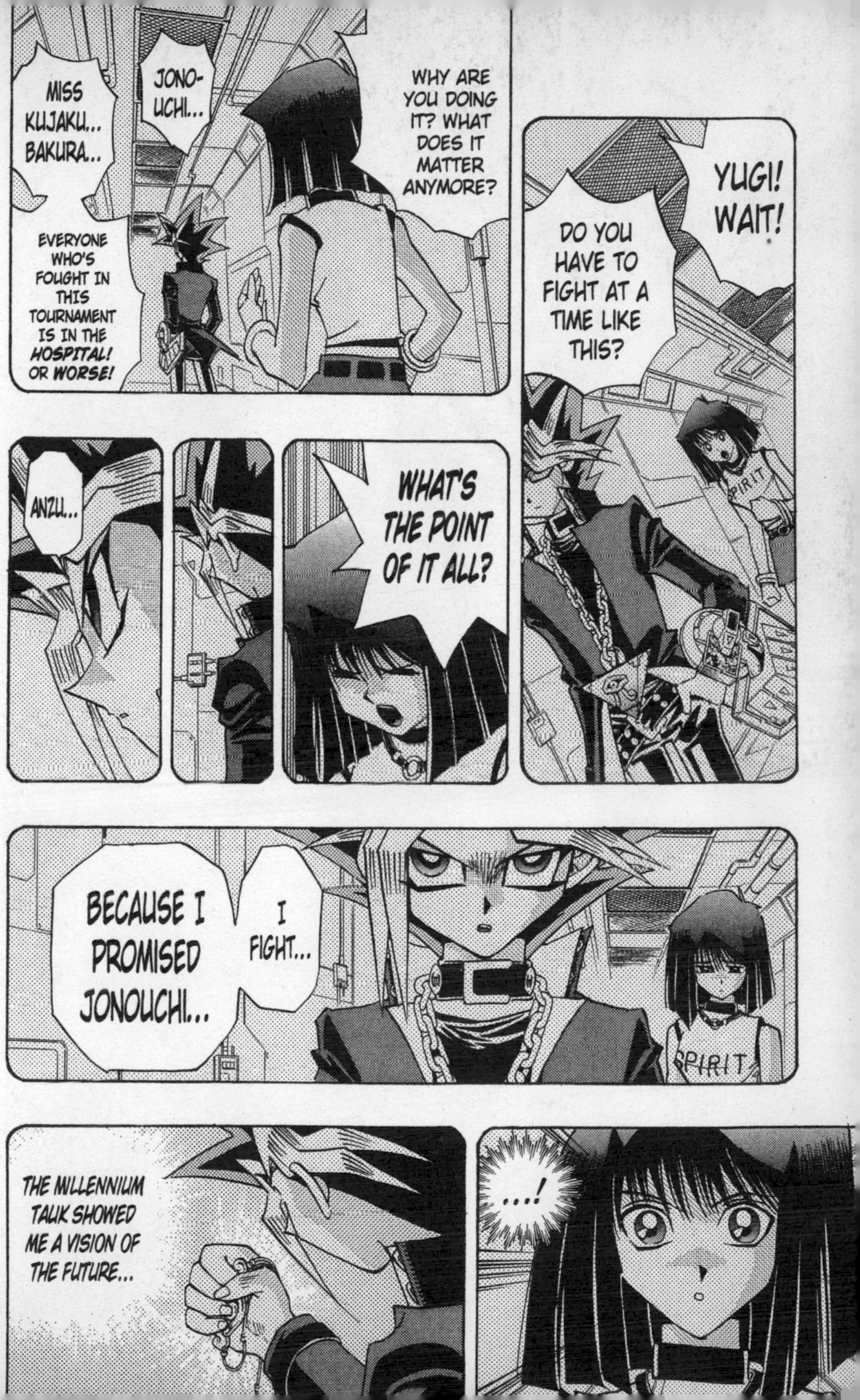
YUGI! WAIT!
DO YOU HAVE TO FIGHT AT A TIME LIKE THIS?
WHY ARE YOU DOING IT? WHAT DOES IT MATTER ANYMORE?
JONO-UCHI...
MISS KUJAKU... BAKURA...
EVERYONE WHO'S FOUGHT IN THIS TOURNAMENT IS IN THE HOSPITAL! OR WORSE!
WHAT'S THE POINT OF IT ALL?
ANZU...
I FIGHT...
BECAUSE I PROMISED JONOUCHI...
...!
THE MILLENNIUM TAUK SHOWED ME A VISION OF THE FUTURE...

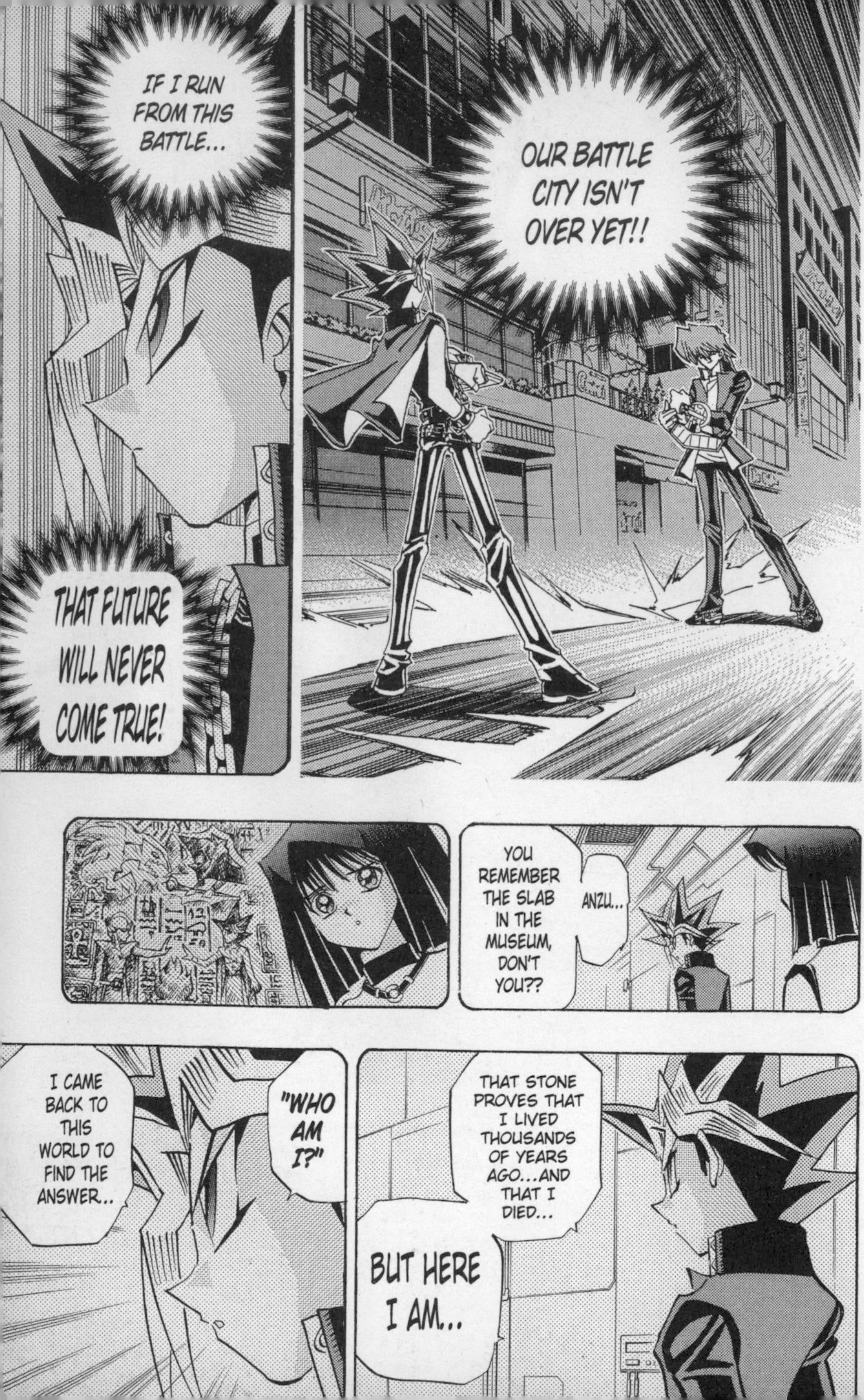
OUR BATTLE CITY ISN'T OVER YET!!
IF I RUN FROM THIS BATTLE...
THAT FUTURE WILL NEVER COME TRUE!
ANZU...
YOU REMEMBER THE SLAB IN THE MUSEUM, DON'T YOU??
THAT STONE PROVES THAT I LIVED THOUSANDS OF YEARS AGO...AND THAT I DIED...
BUT HERE I AM...
"WHO AM I?"
I CAME BACK TO THIS WORLD TO FIND THE ANSWER...

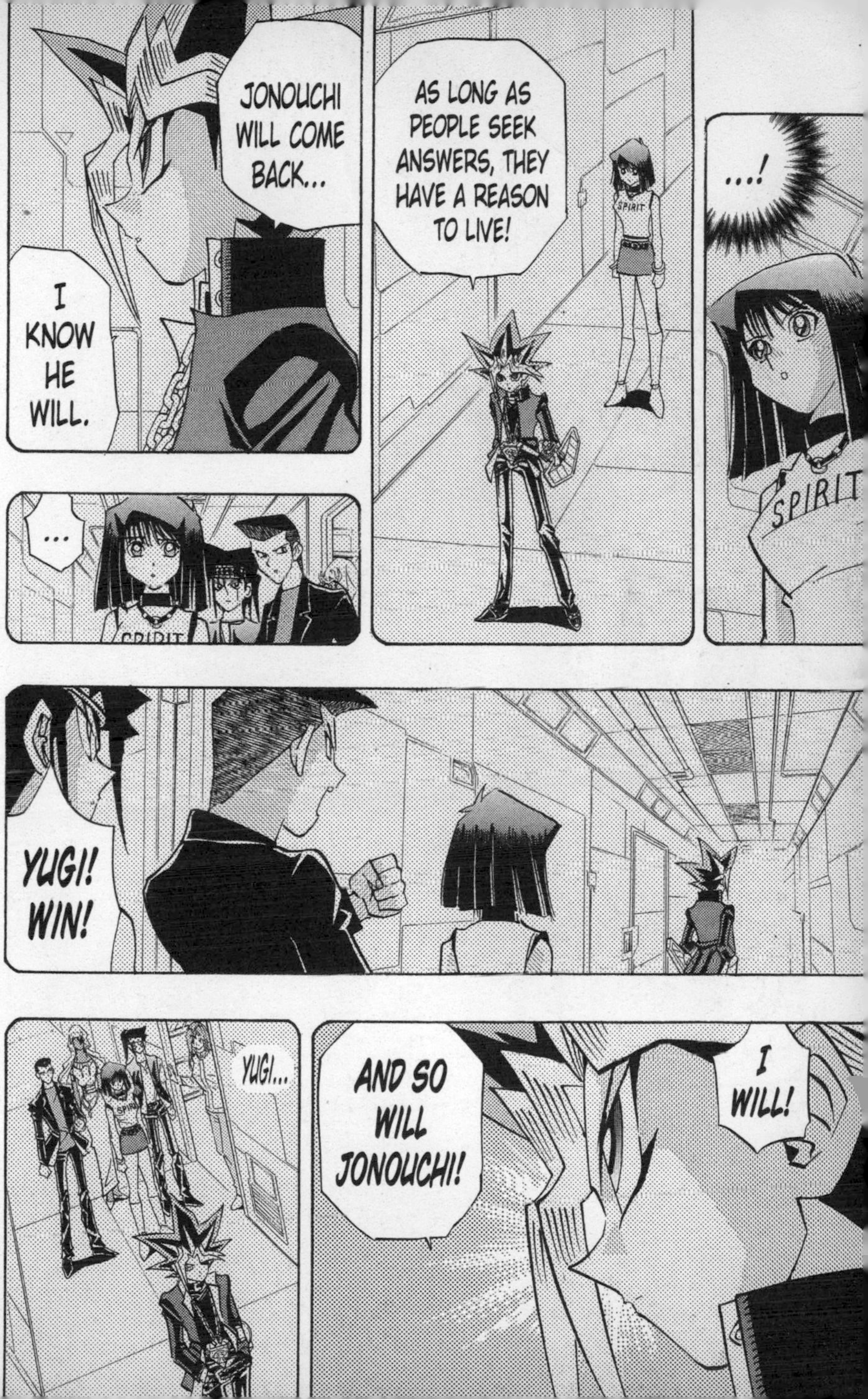
...!
SPIRIT
AS LONG AS PEOPLE SEEK ANSWERS, THEY HAVE A REASON TO LIVE!
SPIRIT
JONOUCHI WILL COME BACK...
I KNOW HE WILL.
...
YUGI! WIN!
I WILL!
AND SO WILL JONOUCHI!
YUGI...

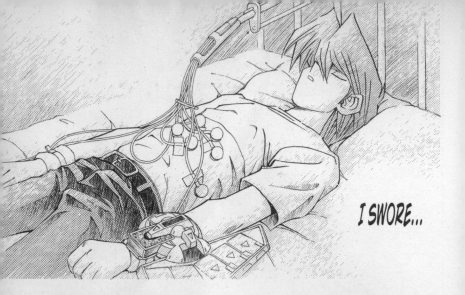

I SWORE...

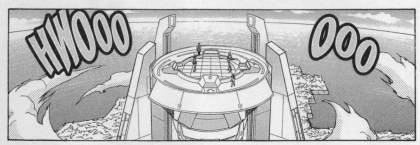

...I'D BECOME A TRUE DUELIST...

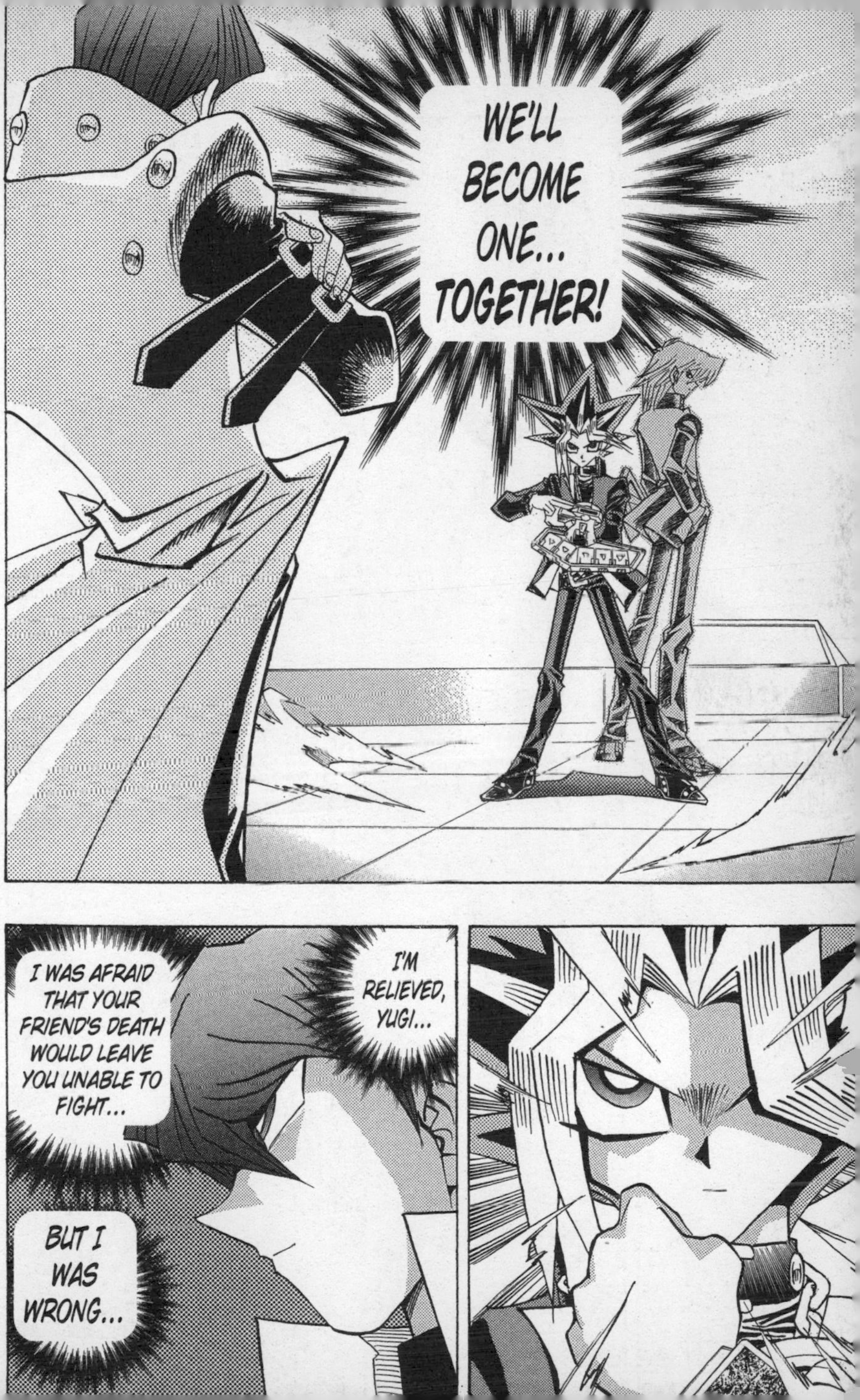
WE'LL BECOME ONE... TOGETHER!
I'M RELIEVED, YUGI...
I WAS AFRAID THAT YOUR FRIEND'S DEATH WOULD LEAVE YOU UNABLE TO FIGHT...
BUT I WAS WRONG...

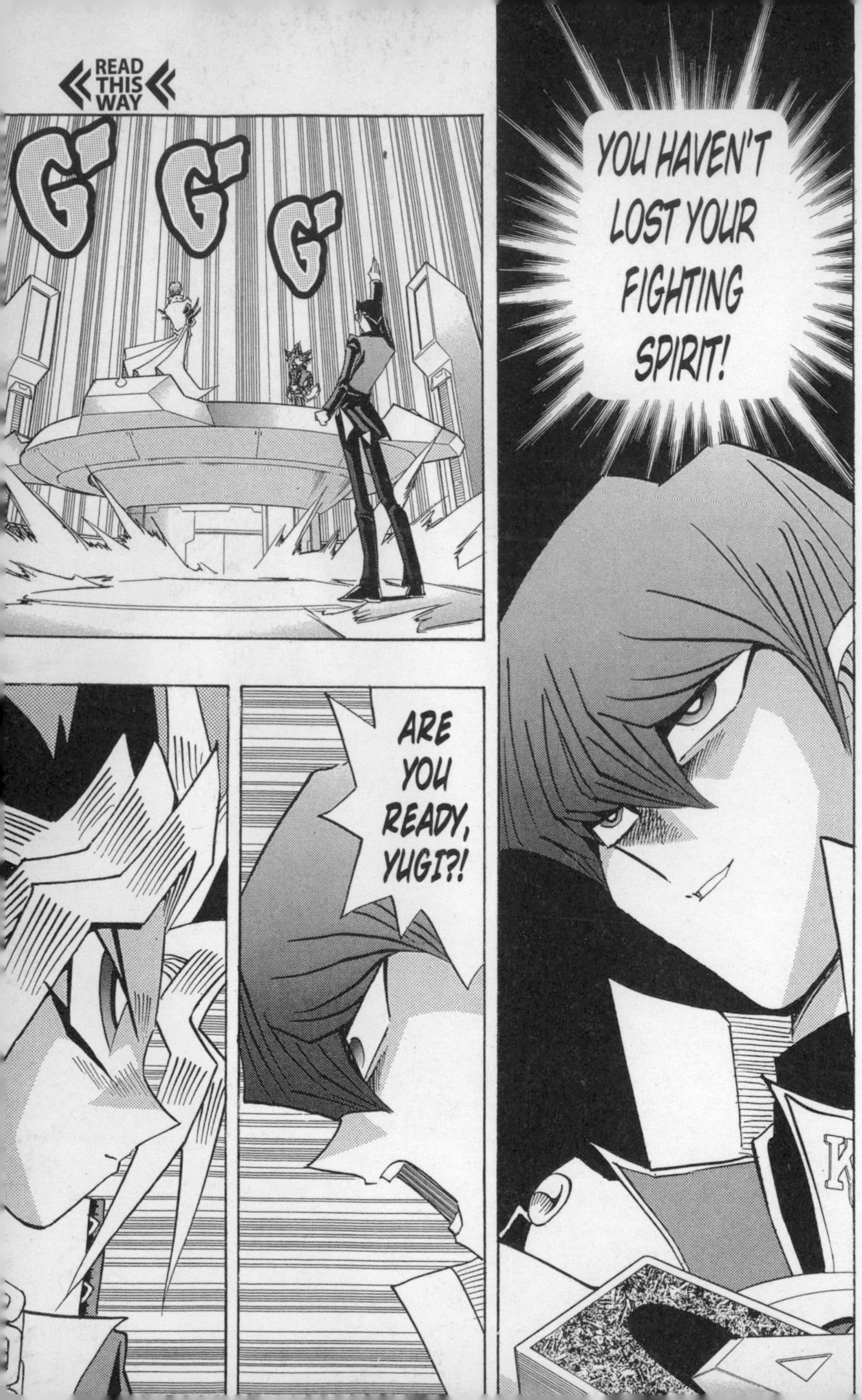
READ THIS WAY
YOU HAVEN'T LOST YOUR FIGHTING SPIRIT!
G G G
ARE YOU READY, YUGI?!

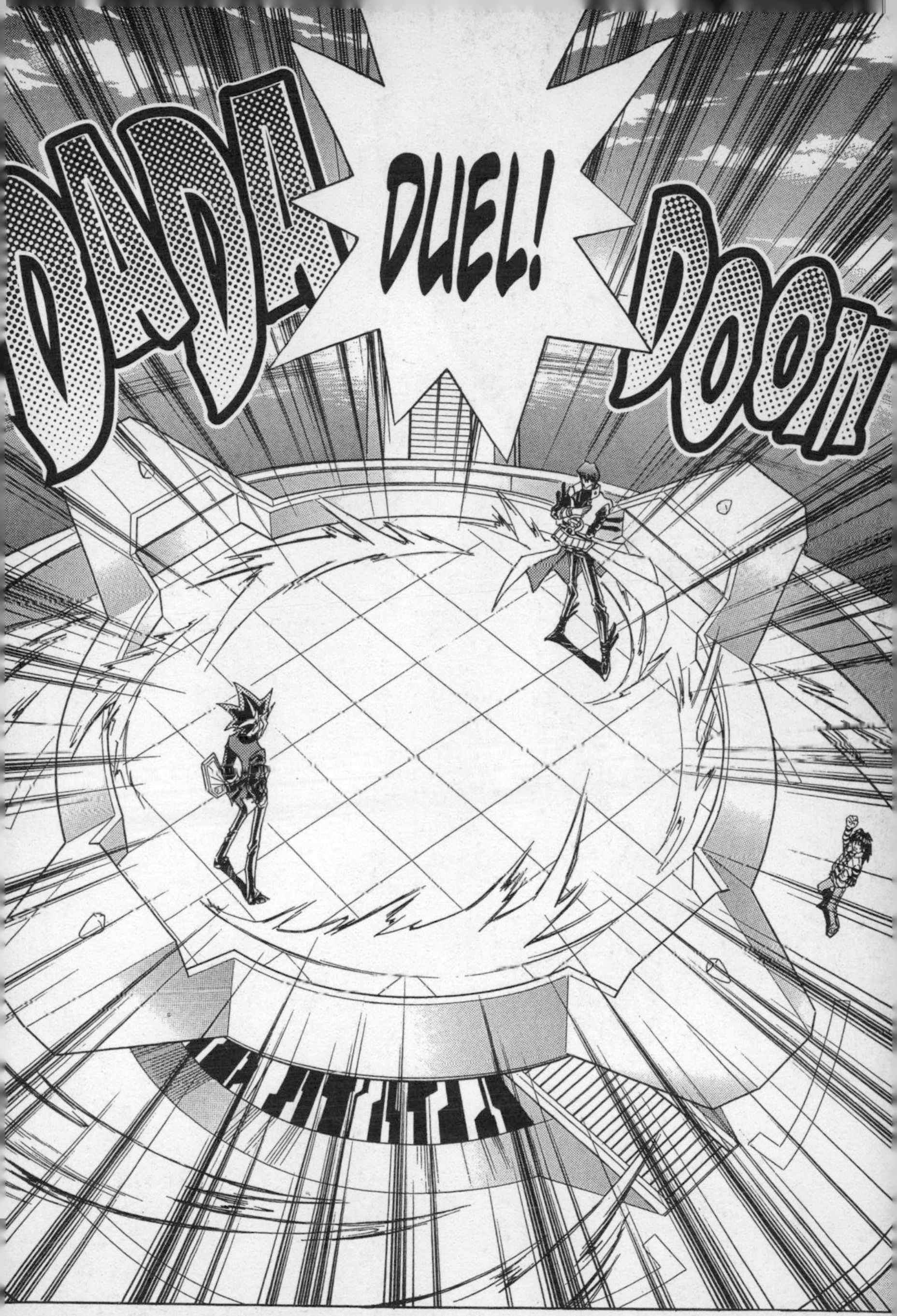
DOOM
DUEL!
DADA

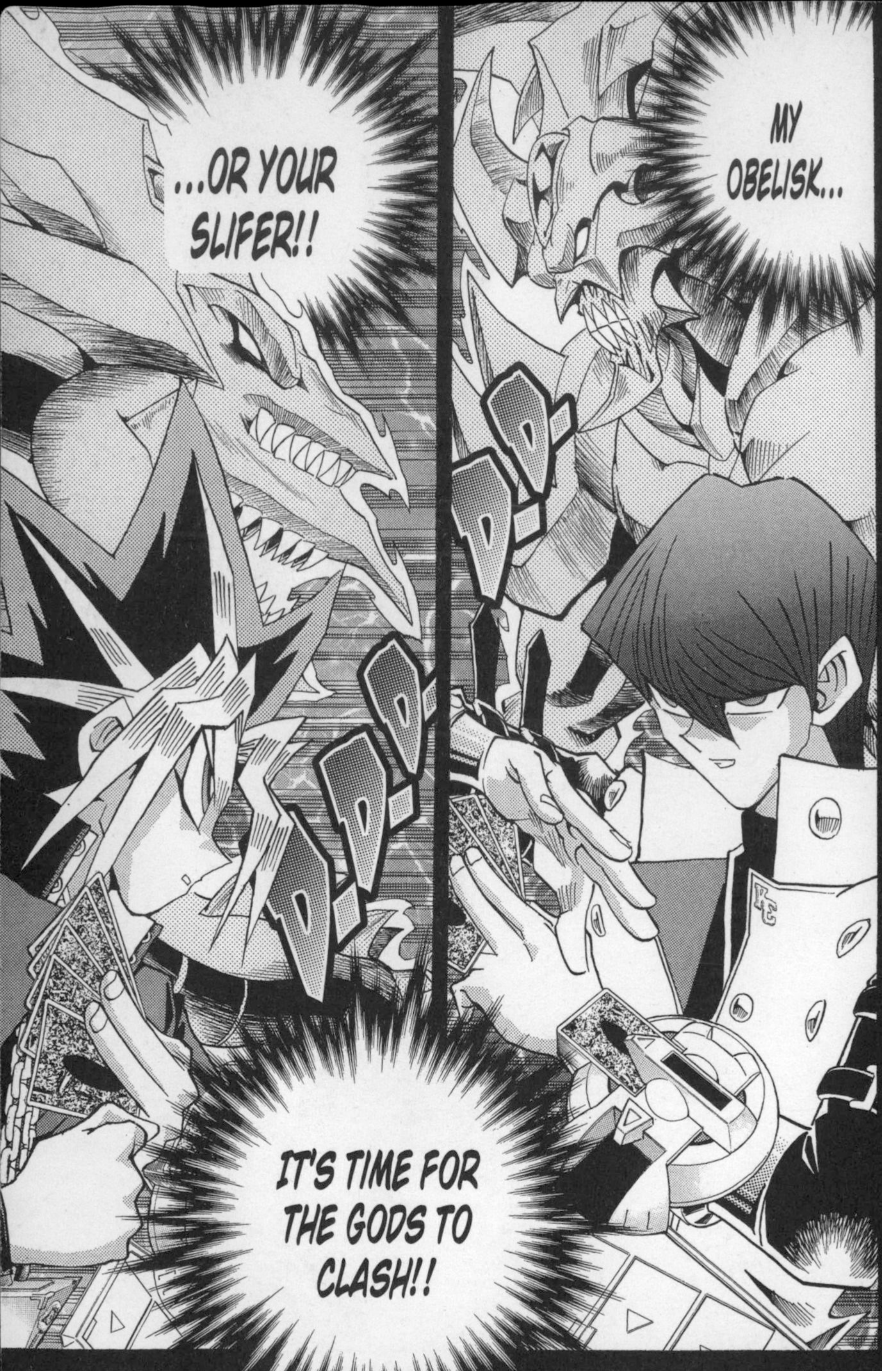
MY OBELISK...
...OR YOUR SLIFER!!
IT'S TIME FOR THE GODS TO CLASH!!

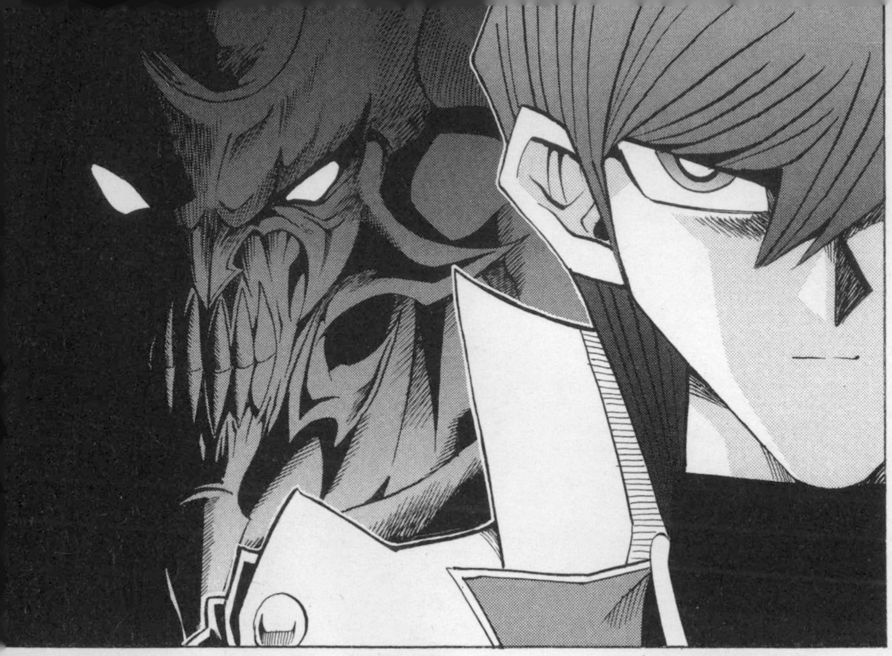

Duel 193: Sky Duel Coliseum!

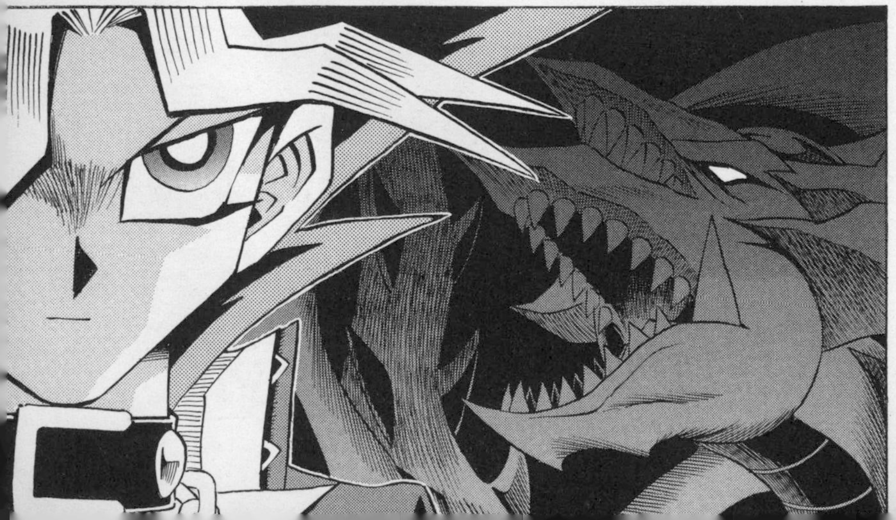

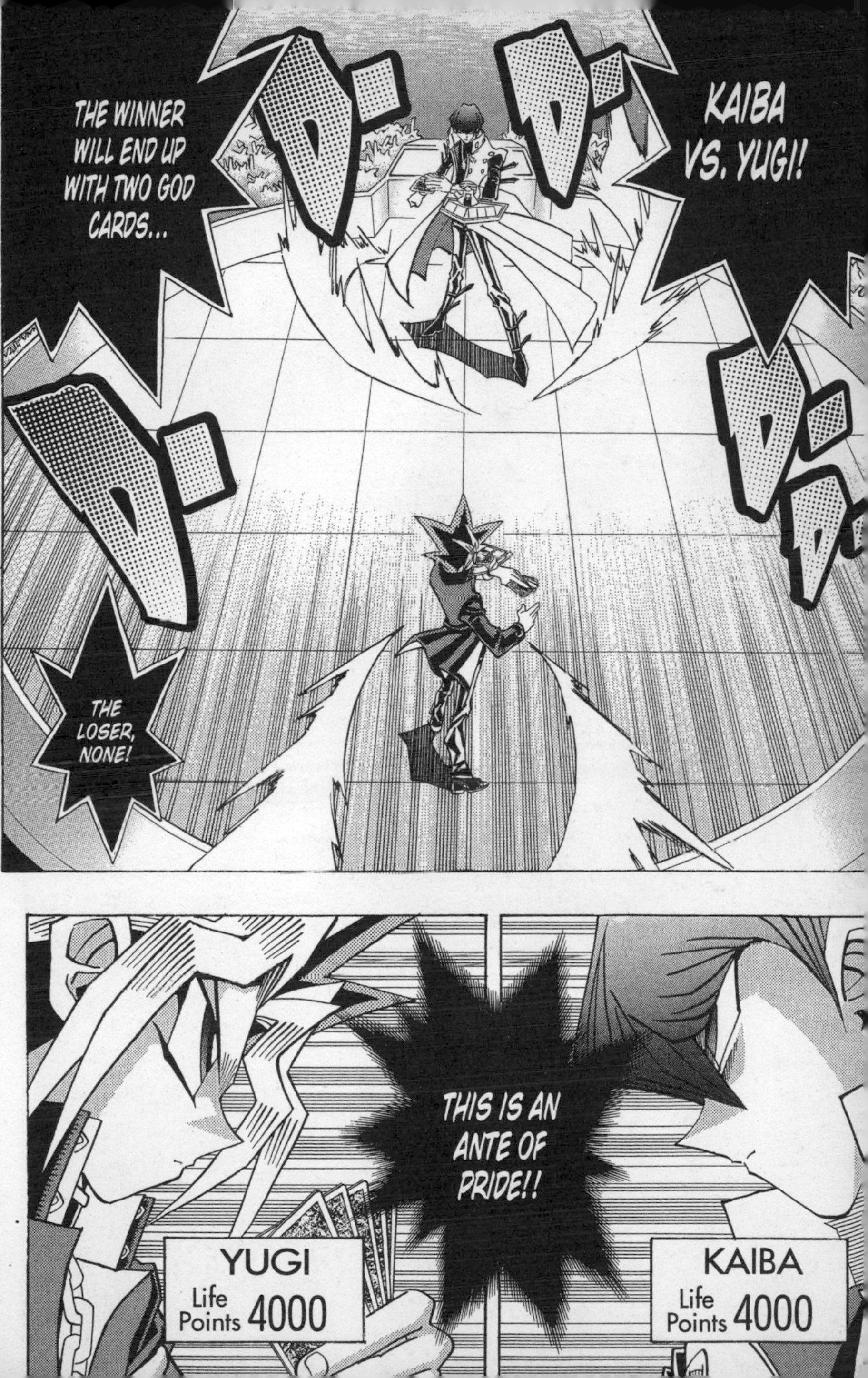
KAIBA VS. YUGI!
THE WINNER WILL END UP WITH TWO GOD CARDS...
THE LOSER, NONE!
THIS IS AN ANTE OF PRIDE!!
KAIBA Life Points 4000
YUGI Life Points 4000

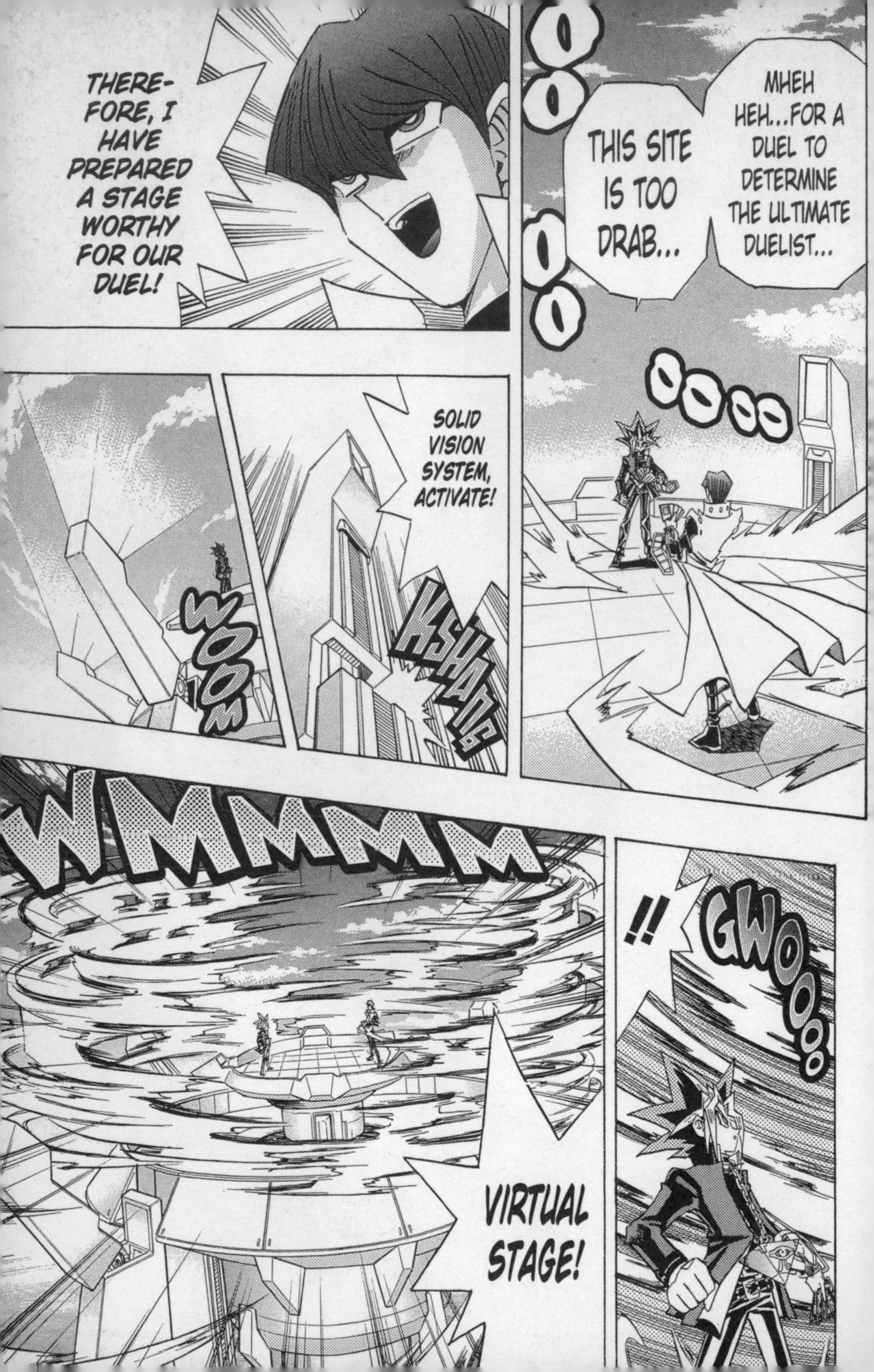
MHEH HEH...FOR A DUEL TO DETERMINE THE ULTIMATE DUELIST...
THIS SITE IS TOO DRAB...
THERE-FORE, I HAVE PREPARED A STAGE WORTHY FOR OUR DUEL!
SOLID VISION SYSTEM, ACTIVATE!
KSHANG!
WOOM
!!
GWOOOOO
WMMMMM
VIRTUAL STAGE!

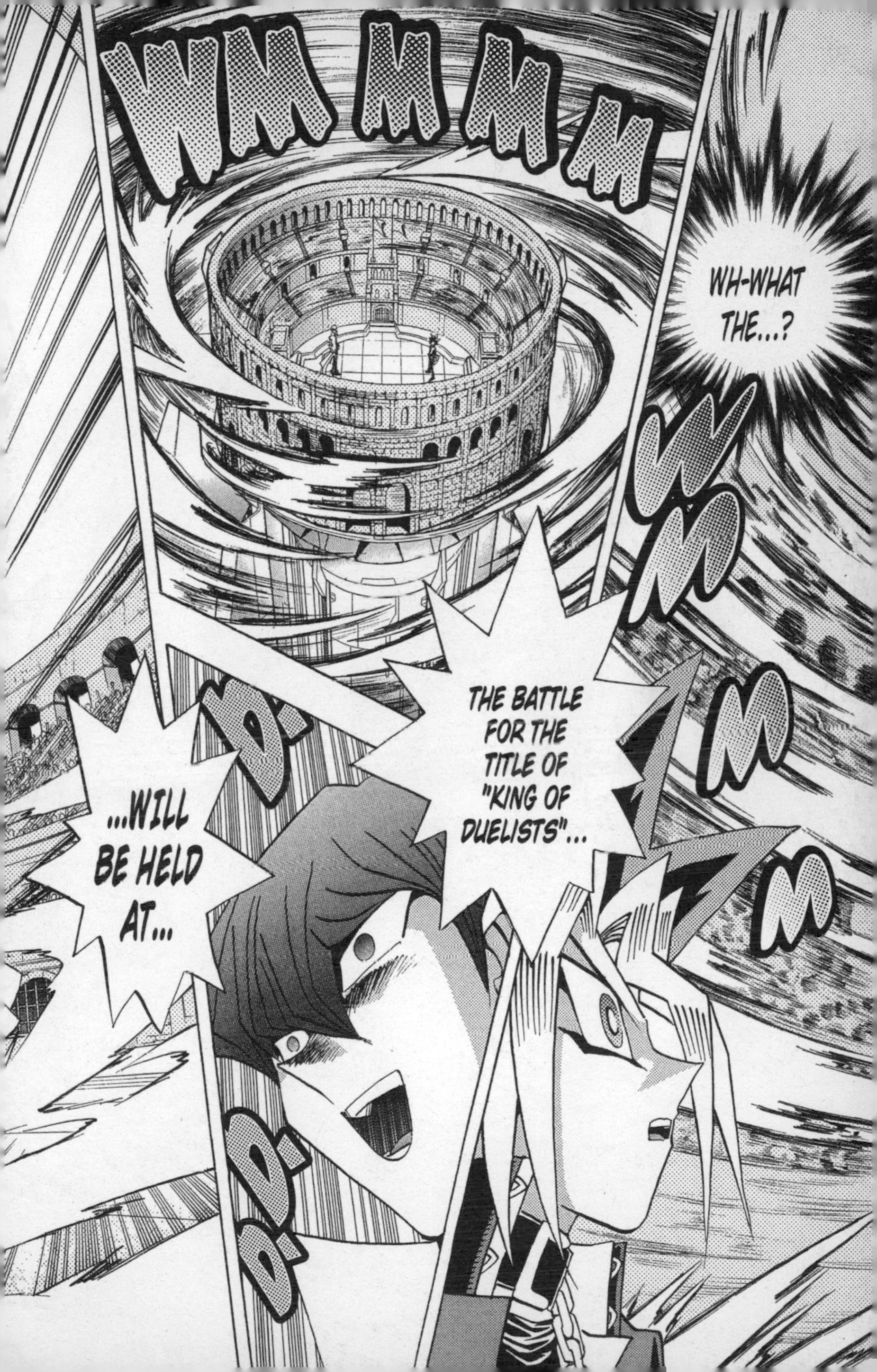
WMMMMM
WH-WHAT THE...?
THE BATTLE FOR THE TITLE OF "KING OF DUELISTS"...
...WILL BE HELD AT...

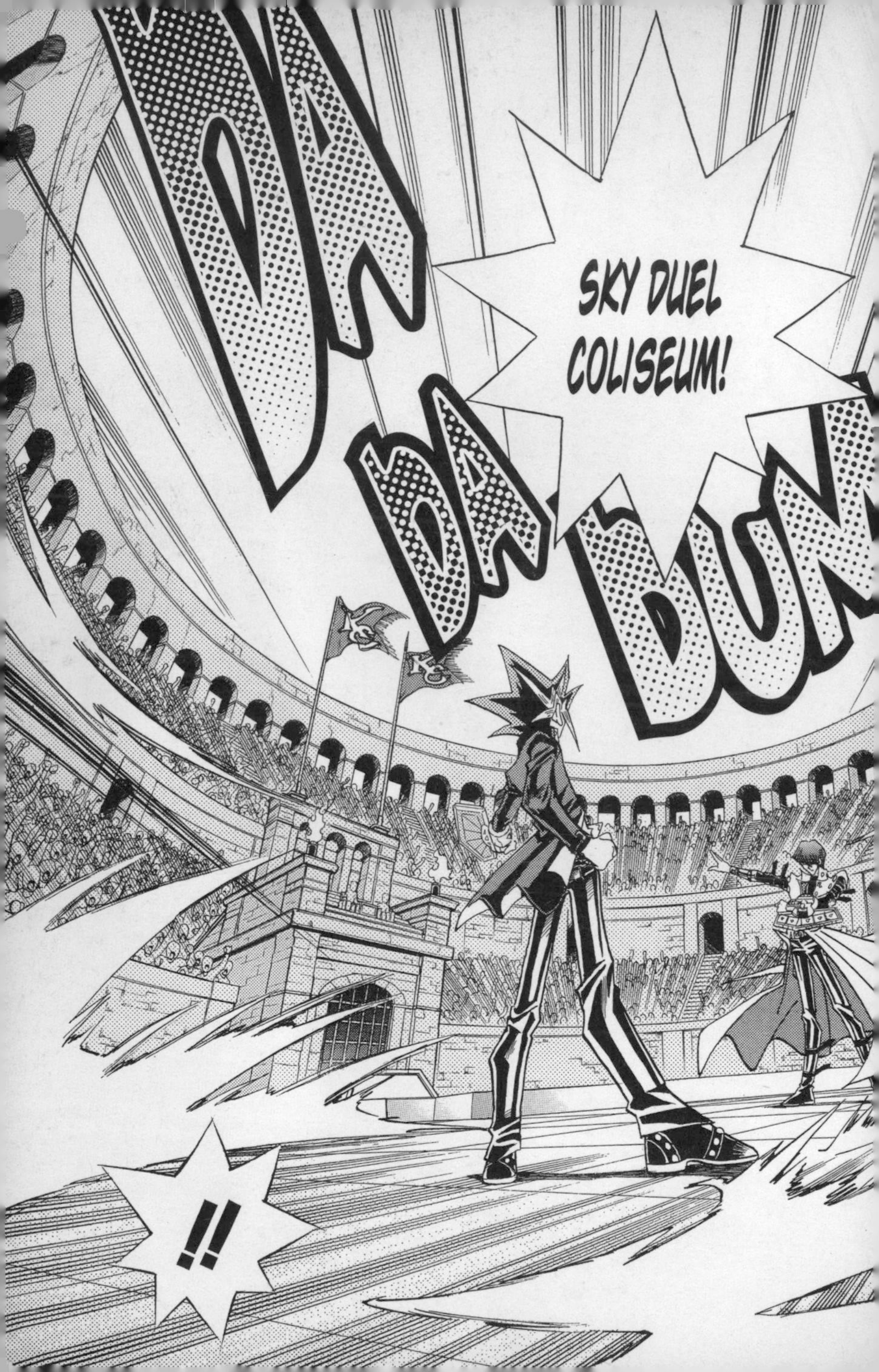
SKY DUEL COLISEUM!
DA DA DUN
!!

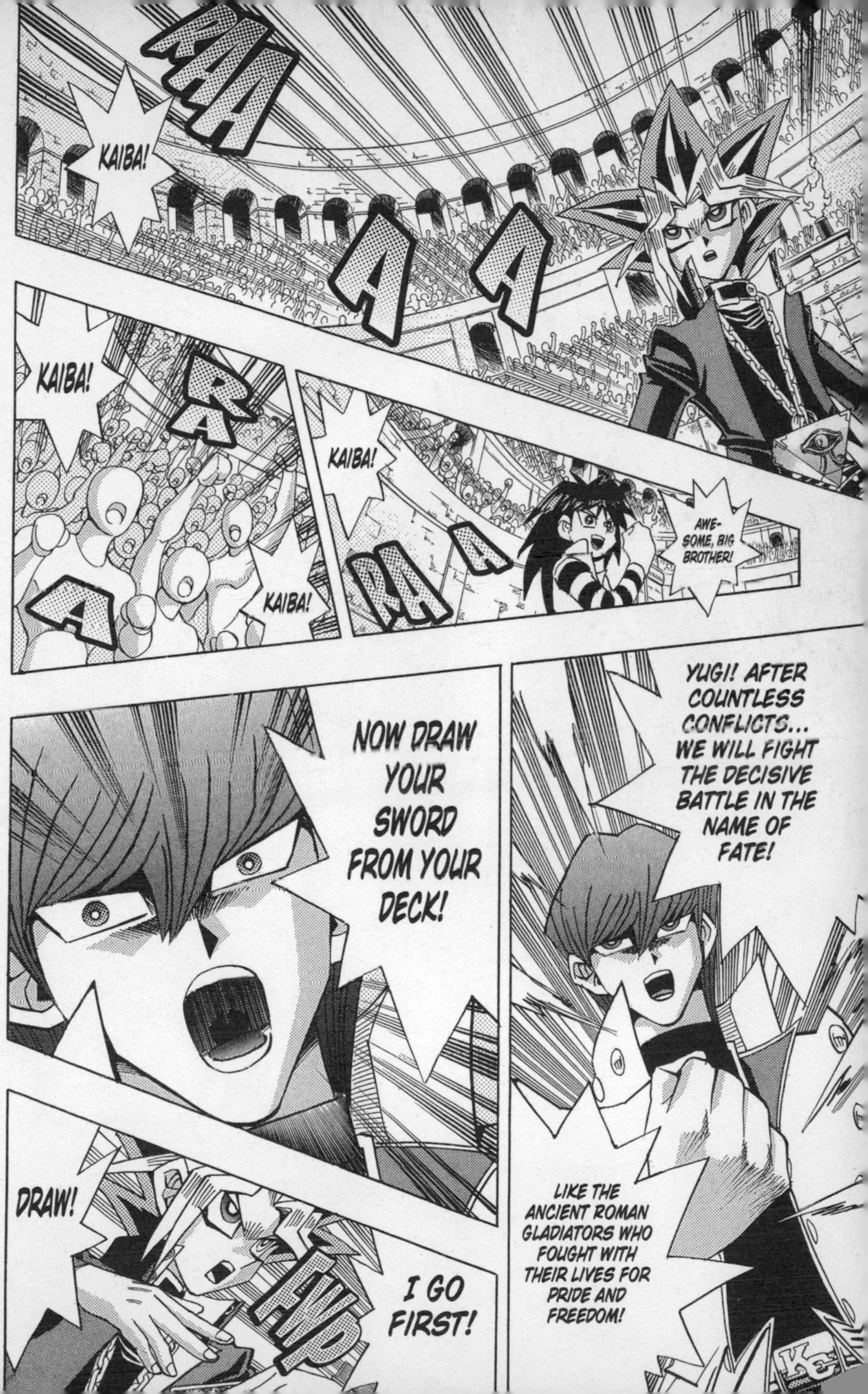
RAA
KAIBA!
A
A
AWE-SOME, BIG BROTHER!
KAIBA!
RA
A
KAIBA!
RA
A
KAIBA!
YUGI! AFTER COUNTLESS CONFLICTS... WE WILL FIGHT THE DECISIVE BATTLE IN THE NAME OF FATE!
LIKE THE ANCIENT ROMAN GLADIATORS WHO FOUGHT WITH THEIR LIVES FOR PRIDE AND FREEDOM!
NOW DRAW YOUR SWORD FROM YOUR DECK!
DRAW!
I GO FIRST!
FWIP

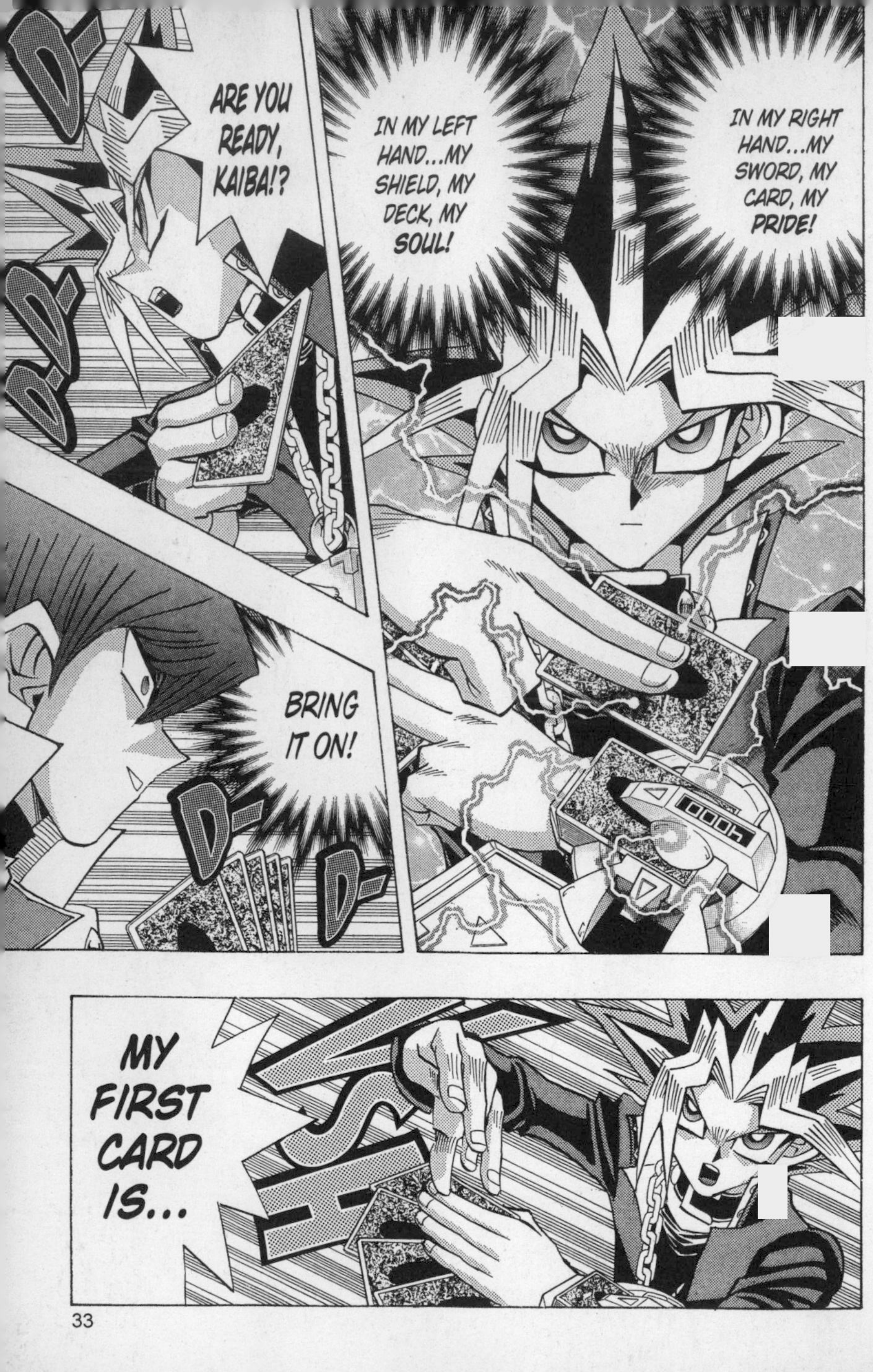
IN MY RIGHT HAND...MY SWORD, MY CARD, MY PRIDE!
IN MY LEFT HAND...MY SHIELD, MY DECK, MY SOUL!
ARE YOU READY, KAIBA!?
BRING IT ON!
MY FIRST CARD IS...

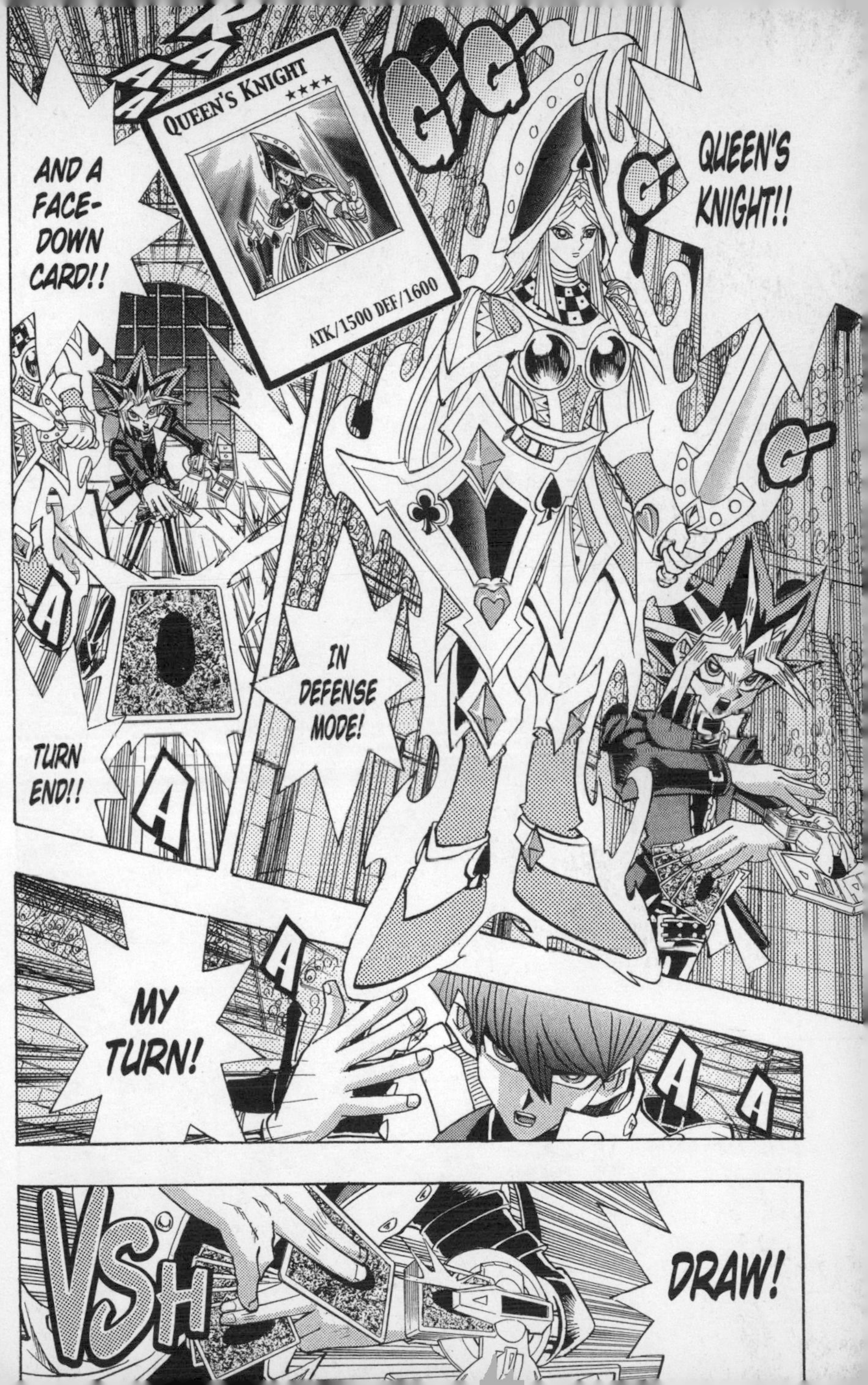
G G
G
QUEEN'S KNIGHT!!
G
QUEEN'S KNIGHT ★★★★
ATK/1500 DEF/1600
IN DEFENSE MODE!
KRAAA
AND A FACE-DOWN CARD!!
A
TURN END!!
A
A
MY TURN!
A
A
DRAW!
VSH

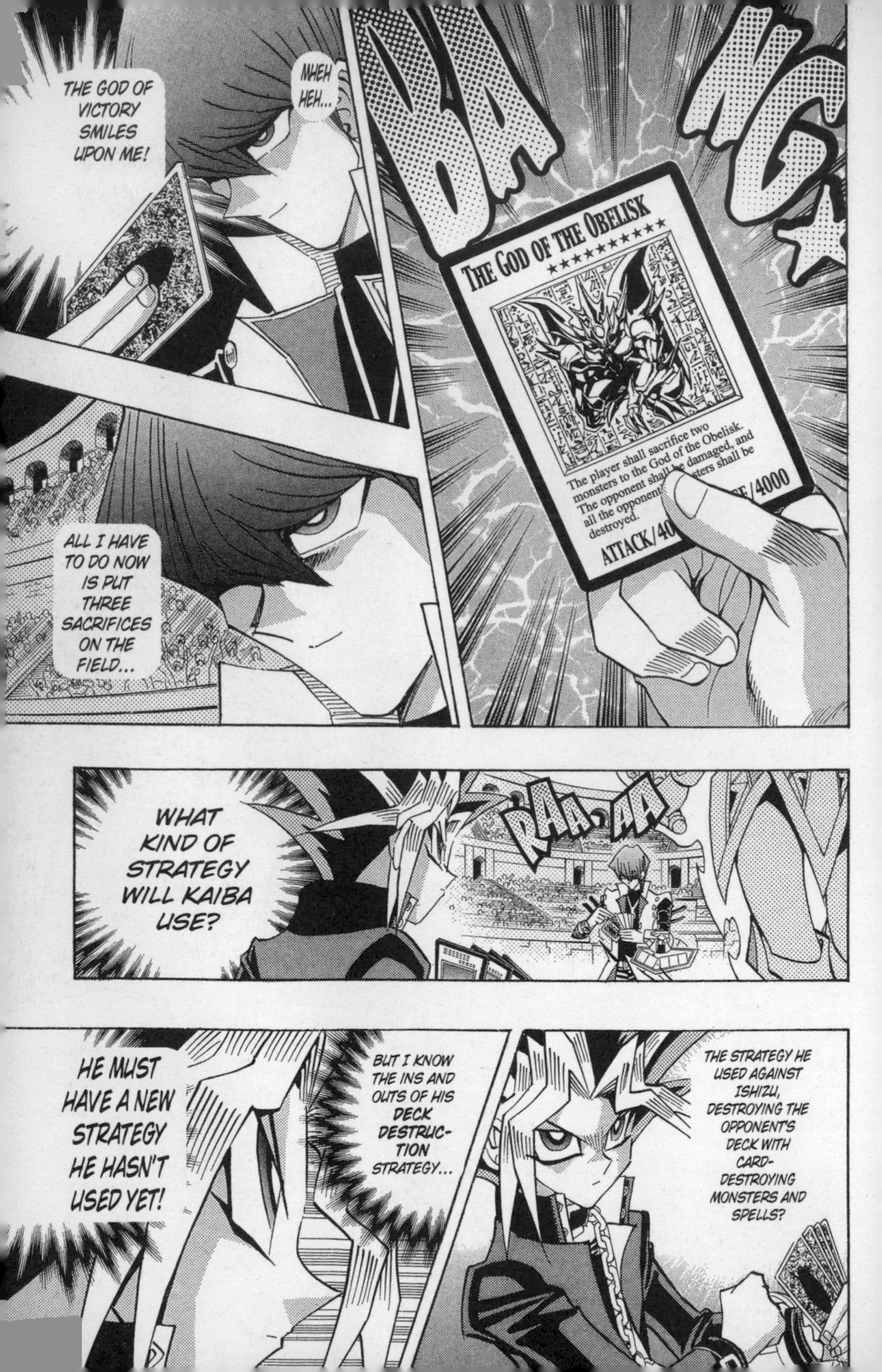
BA NG
THE GOD OF THE OBELISK
The player shall sacrifice two monsters to the God of the Obelisk. The opponent shall be damaged, and all the opponent
sters shall be destroyed.
ATTACK/40
SE/4000
MHEH HEH...
THE GOD OF VICTORY SMILES UPON ME!
ALL I HAVE TO DO NOW IS PUT THREE SACRIFICES ON THE FIELD...
RAA AA
WHAT KIND OF STRATEGY WILL KAIBA USE?
THE STRATEGY HE USED AGAINST ISHIZU, DESTROYING THE OPPONENT'S DECK WITH CARD-DESTROYING MONSTERS AND SPELLS?
BUT I KNOW THE INS AND OUTS OF HIS DECK DESTRUCTION STRATEGY...
HE MUST HAVE A NEW STRATEGY HE HASN'T USED YET!

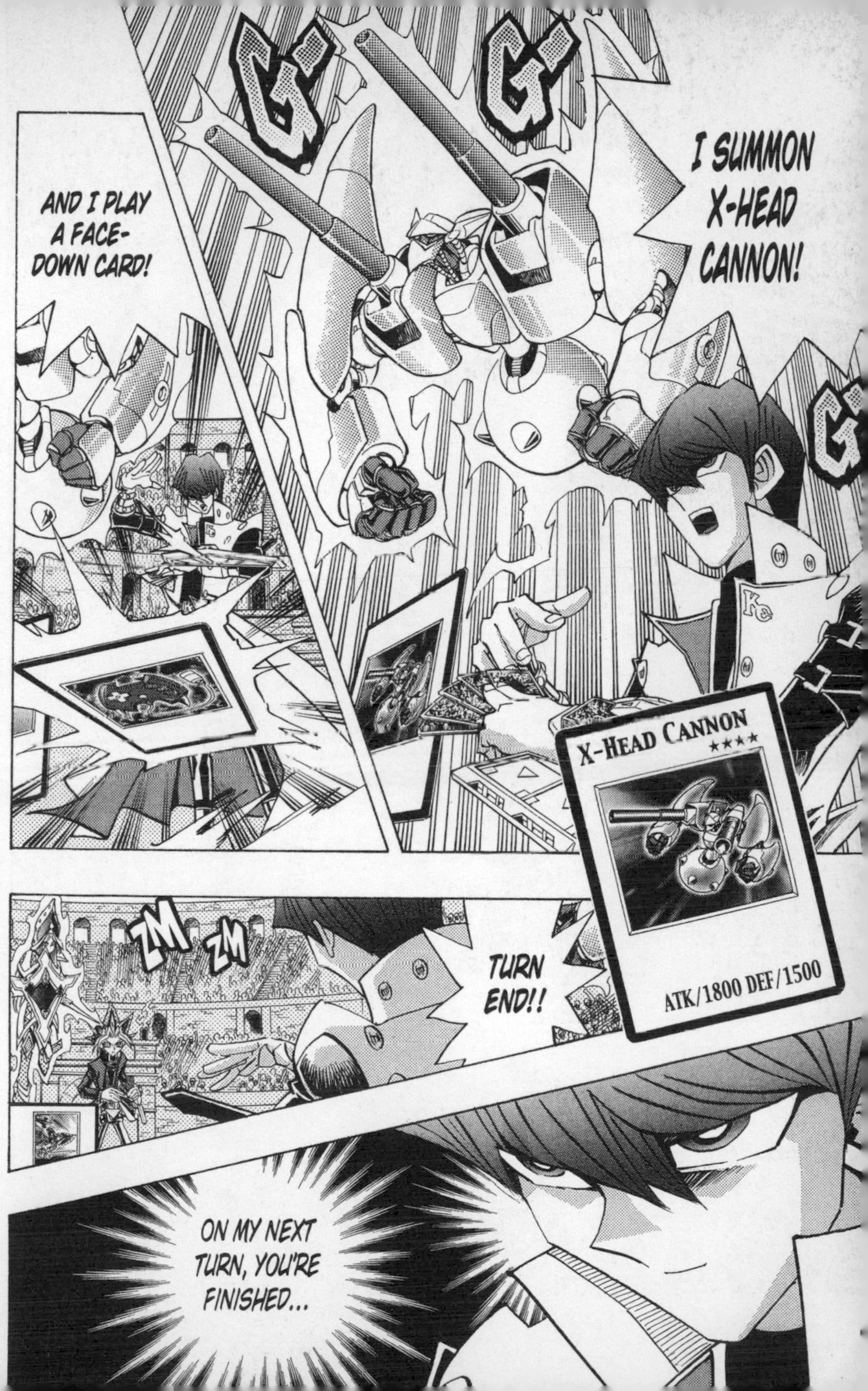
G
G
I SUMMON X-HEAD CANNON!
G
X-HEAD CANNON
★★★★
ATK/1800 DEF/1500
AND I PLAY A FACE-DOWN CARD!
TURN END!!
ZM
ZM
ON MY NEXT TURN, YOU'RE FINISHED...

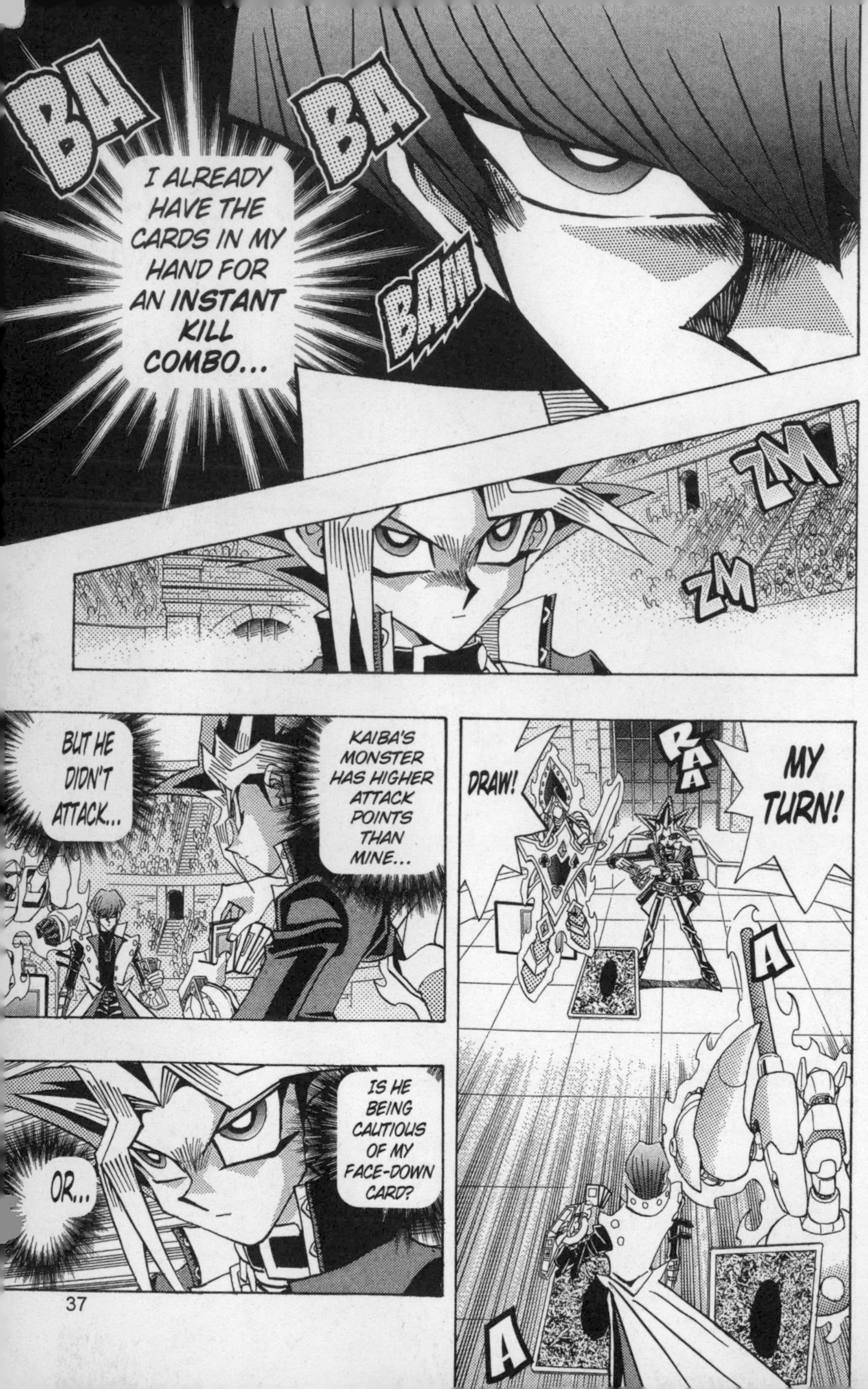
BA
BA
BAM
I ALREADY HAVE THE CARDS IN MY HAND FOR AN INSTANT KILL COMBO...
ZM
ZM
MY TURN!
RAA
DRAW!
A
A
KAIBA'S MONSTER HAS HIGHER ATTACK POINTS THAN MINE...
BUT HE DIDN'T ATTACK...
IS HE BEING CAUTIOUS OF MY FACE-DOWN CARD?
OR...

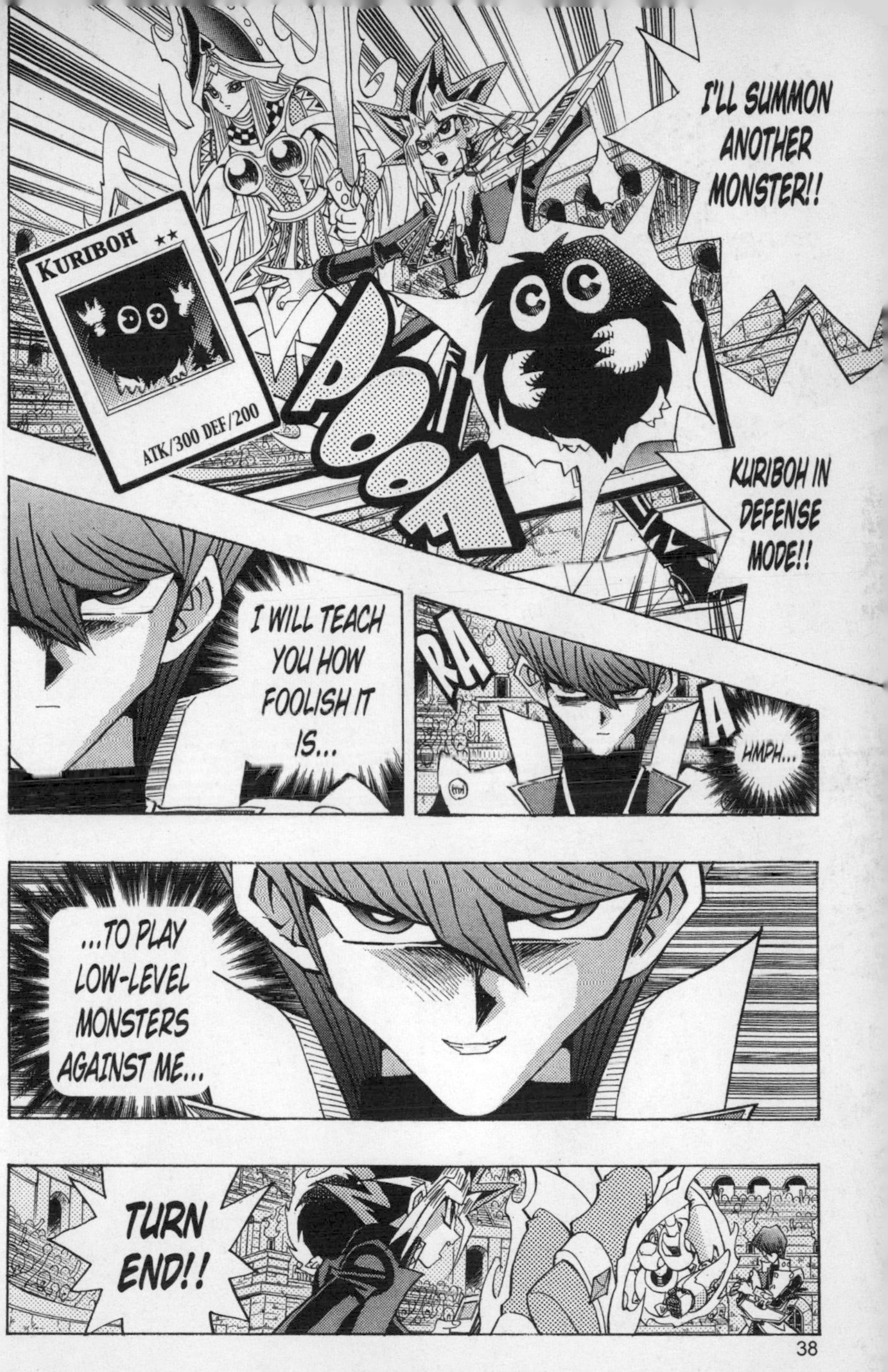
I'LL SUMMON ANOTHER MONSTER!!
KURIBOH
ATK/300 DEF/200
POOF
KURIBOH IN DEFENSE MODE!!
RA
A
HMPH...
I WILL TEACH YOU HOW FOOLISH IT IS...
...TO PLAY LOW-LEVEL MONSTERS AGAINST ME...
TURN END!!

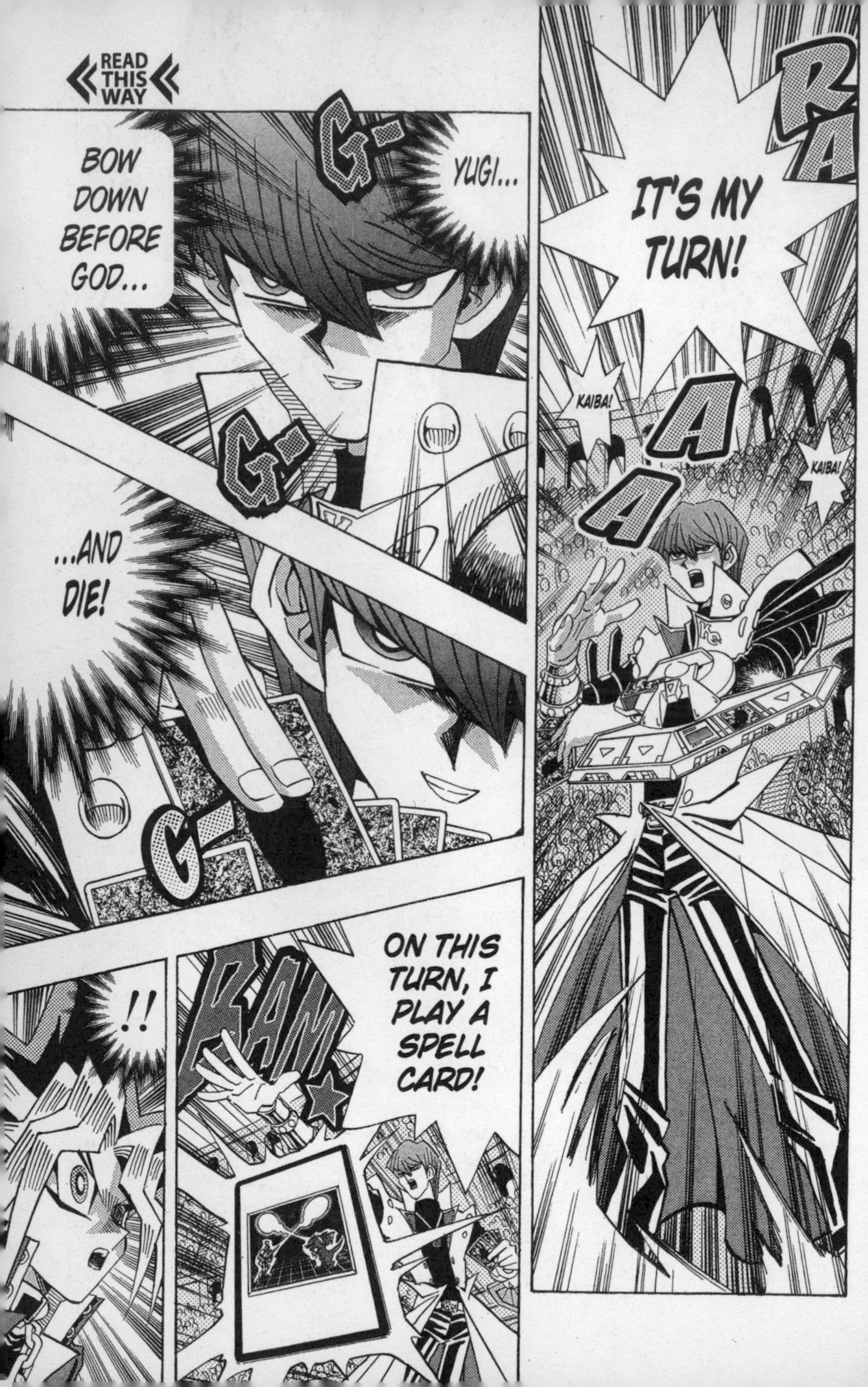
READ THIS WAY
RAAA
IT'S MY TURN!
KAIBA!
KAIBA!
G-
YUGI...
BOW DOWN BEFORE GOD...
G-
...AND DIE!
G-
BAM
ON THIS TURN, I PLAY A SPELL CARD!
!!

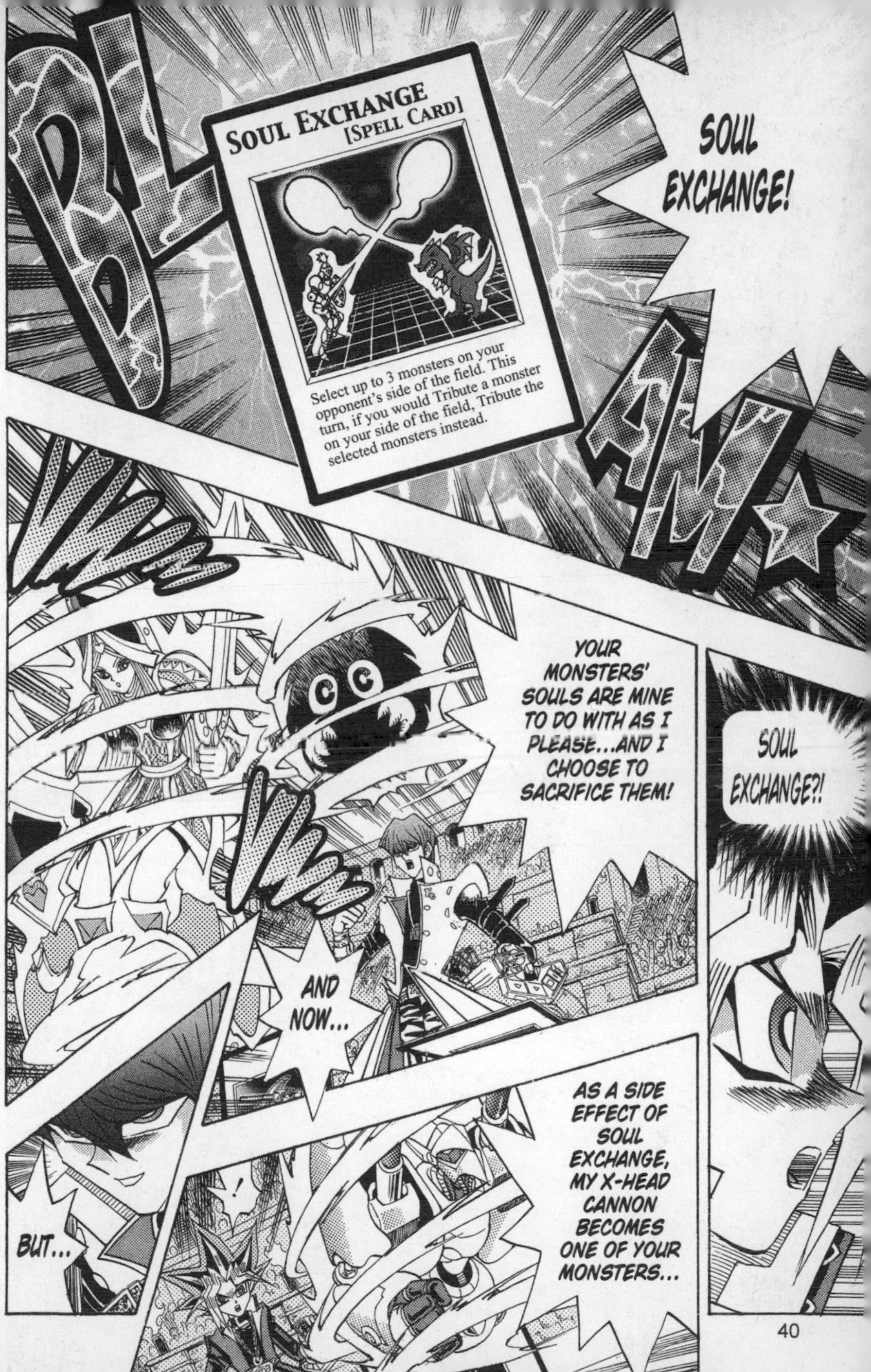
SOUL EXCHANGE!
SOUL EXCHANGE
[SPELL CARD]
Select up to 3 monsters on your opponent's side of the field. This turn, if you would Tribute a monster on your side of the field, Tribute the selected monsters instead.
SOUL EXCHANGE?!
YOUR MONSTERS' SOULS ARE MINE TO DO WITH AS I PLEASE...AND I CHOOSE TO SACRIFICE THEM!
AND NOW...
AS A SIDE EFFECT OF SOUL EXCHANGE, MY X-HEAD CANNON BECOMES ONE OF YOUR MONSTERS...
BUT...

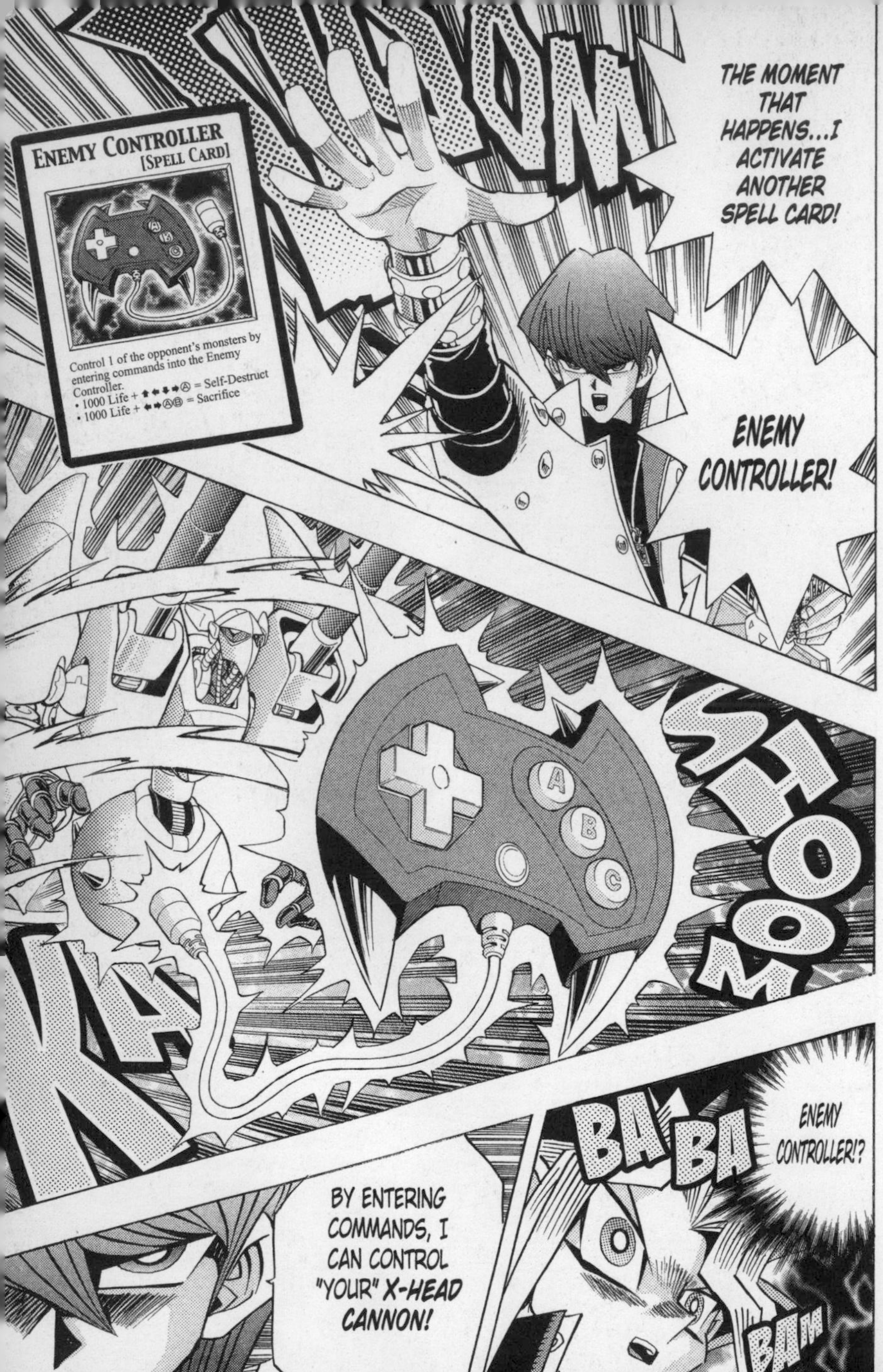
THE MOMENT THAT HAPPENS...I ACTIVATE ANOTHER SPELL CARD!
ENEMY CONTROLLER
[SPELL CARD]
Control 1 of the opponent's monsters by entering commands into the Enemy Controller.
• 1000 Life + ⬆⬅⬇➡Ⓐ = Self-Destruct
• 1000 Life + ⬅➡ⒶⒷ = Sacrifice
ENEMY CONTROLLER!
SHOOOM
ENEMY CONTROLLER!?
BA BA
BY ENTERING COMMANDS, I CAN CONTROL "YOUR" X-HEAD CANNON!
BAM

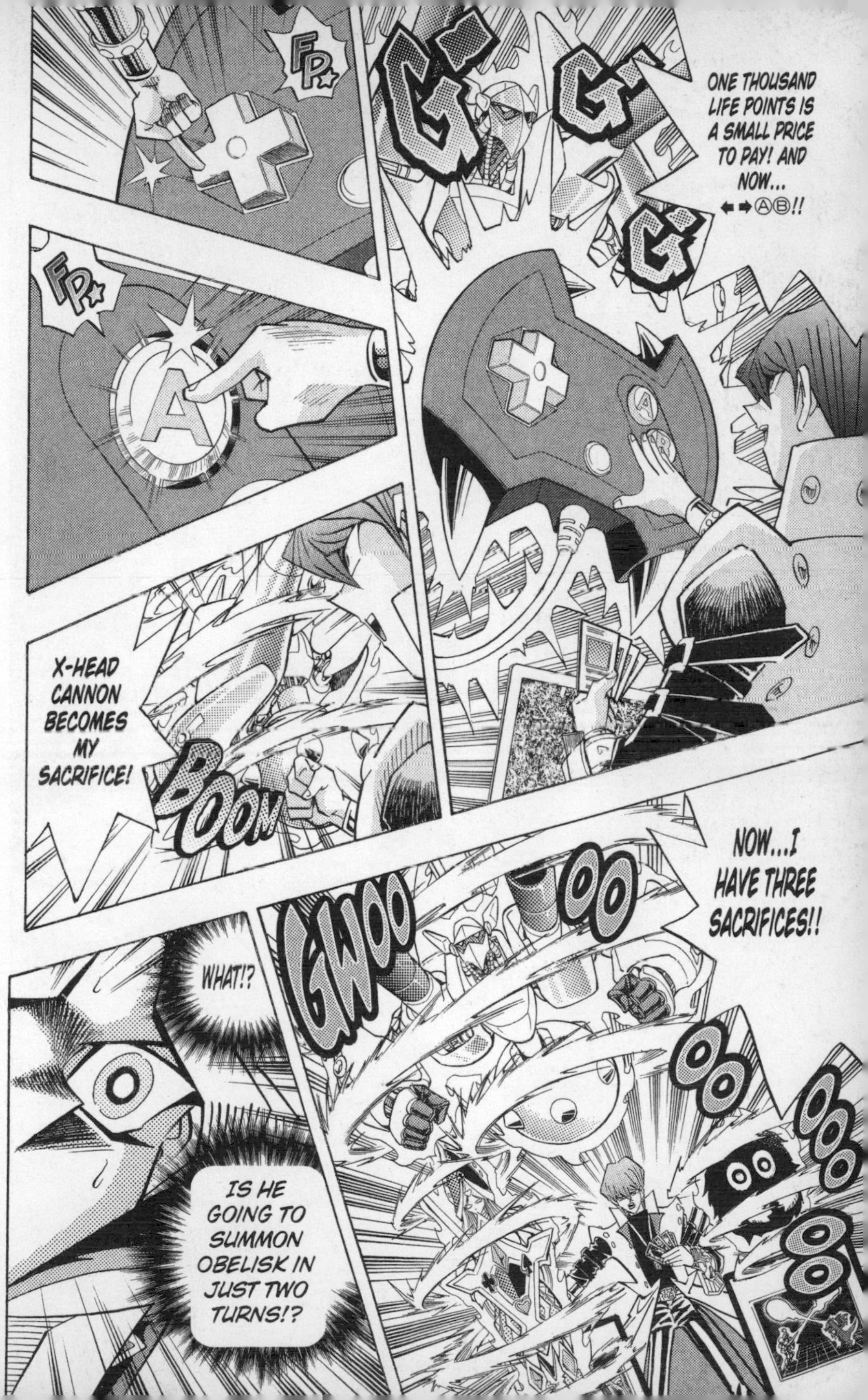

ONE THOUSAND LIFE POINTS IS A SMALL PRICE TO PAY! AND NOW...
←→ⒶⒷ!!
G G G
FP
FP
A
X-HEAD CANNON BECOMES MY SACRIFICE!
BOOM
NOW...I HAVE THREE SACRIFICES!!
GWOOOO
OOOOOOOO
WHAT!?
IS HE GOING TO SUMMON OBELISK IN JUST TWO TURNS!?

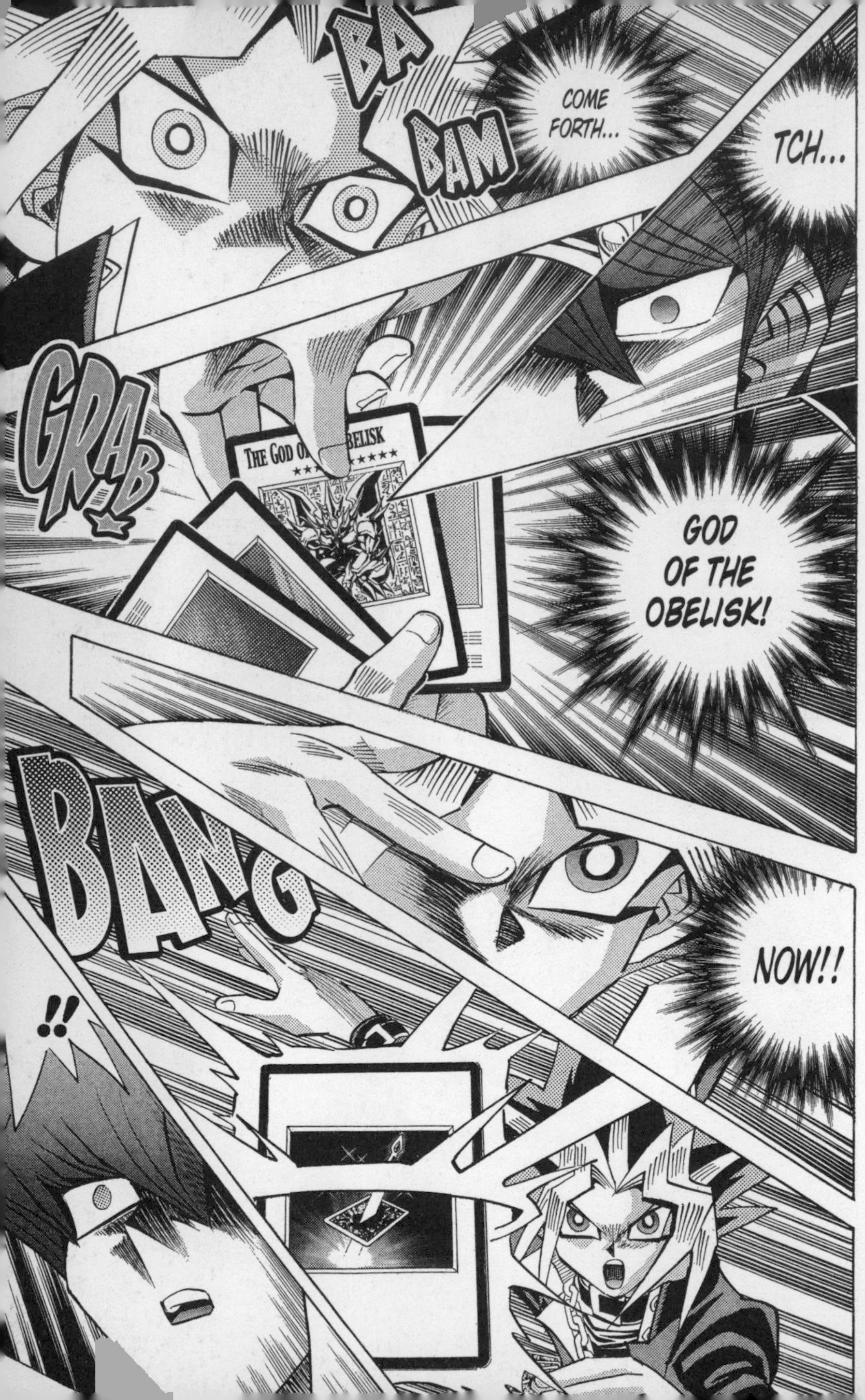
COME FORTH...
BA
BAM
TCH...
GOD OF THE OBELISK!
GRAB
NOW!!
BANG
!!

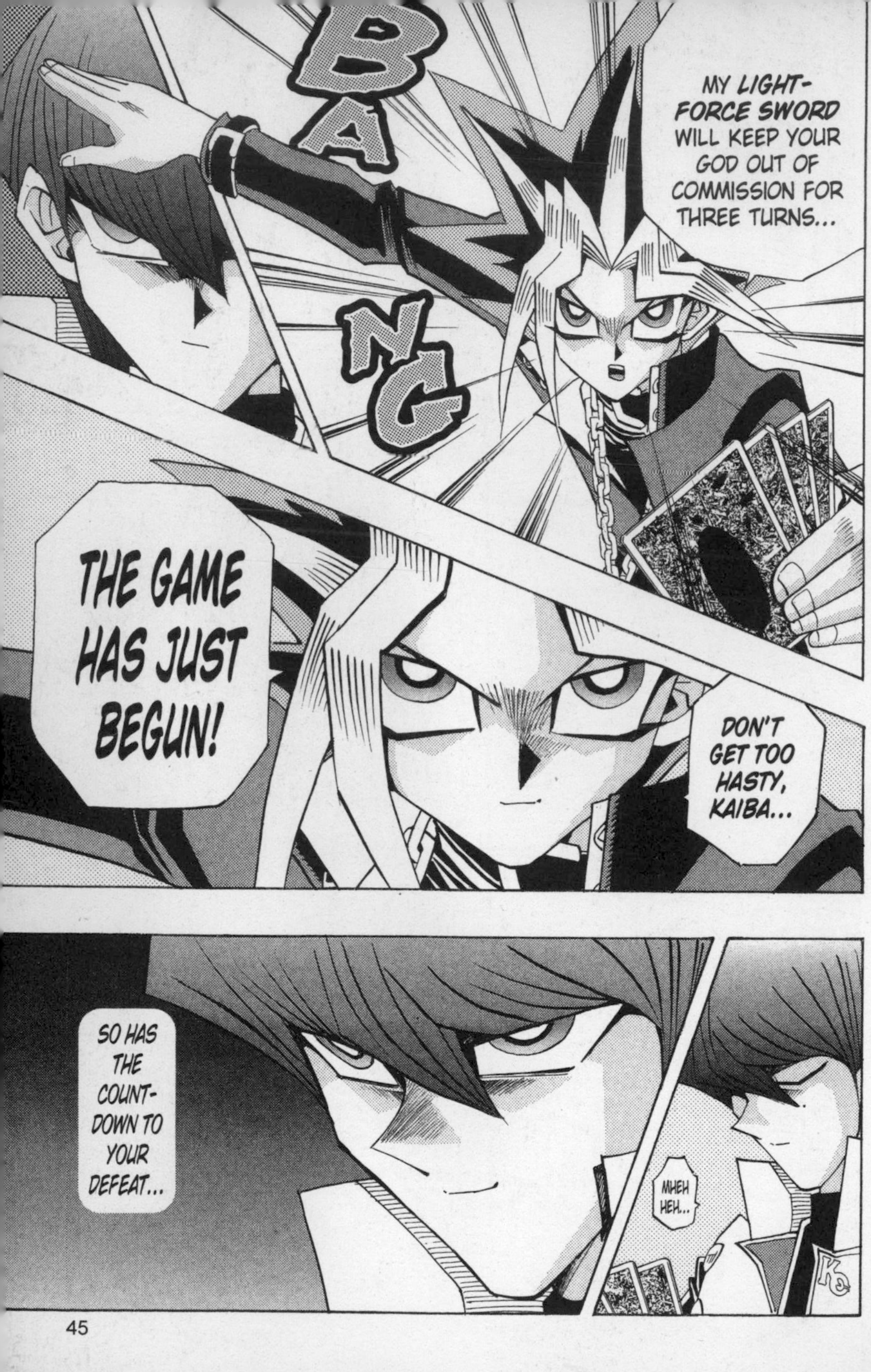
MY LIGHT-FORCE SWORD WILL KEEP YOUR GOD OUT OF COMMISSION FOR THREE TURNS...
BANG
DON'T GET TOO HASTY, KAIBA...
THE GAME HAS JUST BEGUN!
MHEH HEH...
SO HAS THE COUNT-DOWN TO YOUR DEFEAT...

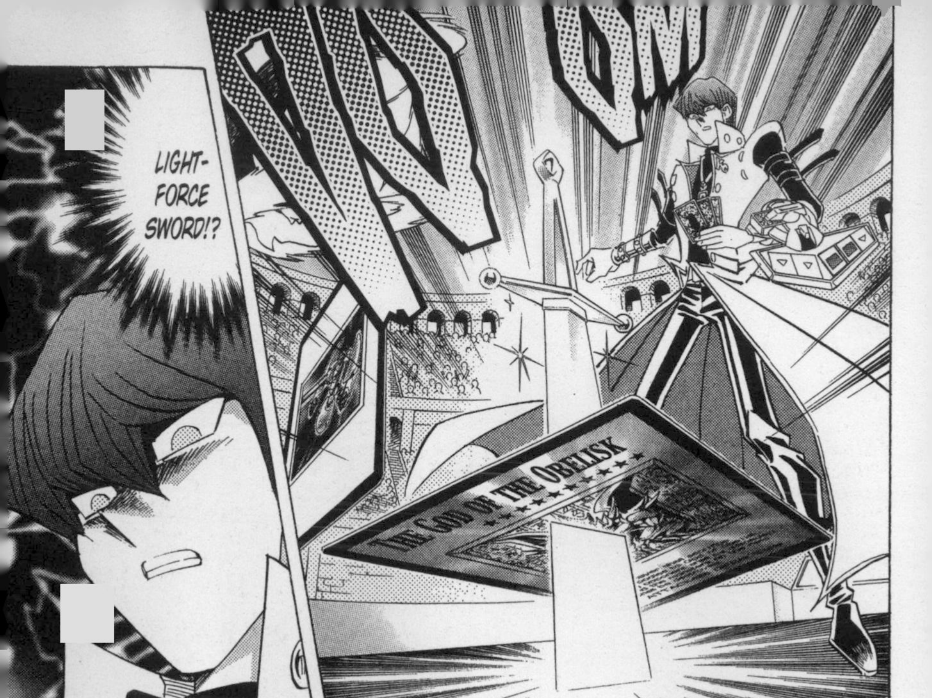
THE GOD OF THE OBELISK
LIGHT-FORCE SWORD!?
NICE TRY, KAIBA!
THAT SWORD WILL KEEP YOUR GOD CARD OUT OF PLAY FOR THREE TURNS!
LIGHTFORCE SWORD
[SPELL CARD]
Select 1 card at random from your opponent's hand. Keep it face-down and place it outside of the field. During your opponent's 4th turn, the card is returned to his/her hand in the Standby Phase.

Duel 194: God in Hand!!

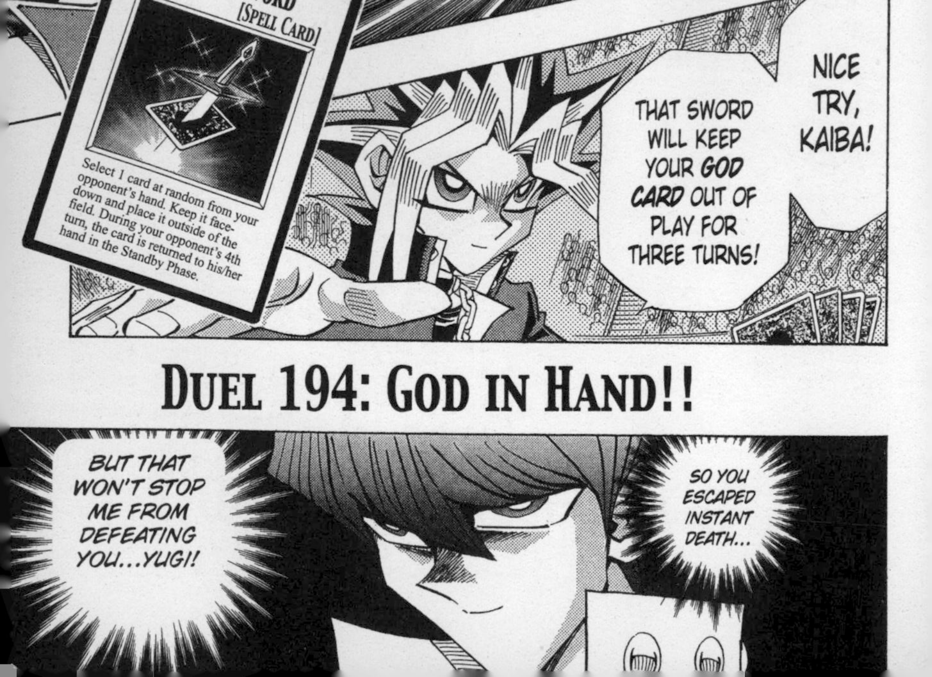
SO YOU ESCAPED INSTANT DEATH...
BUT THAT WON'T STOP ME FROM DEFEATING YOU...YUGI!

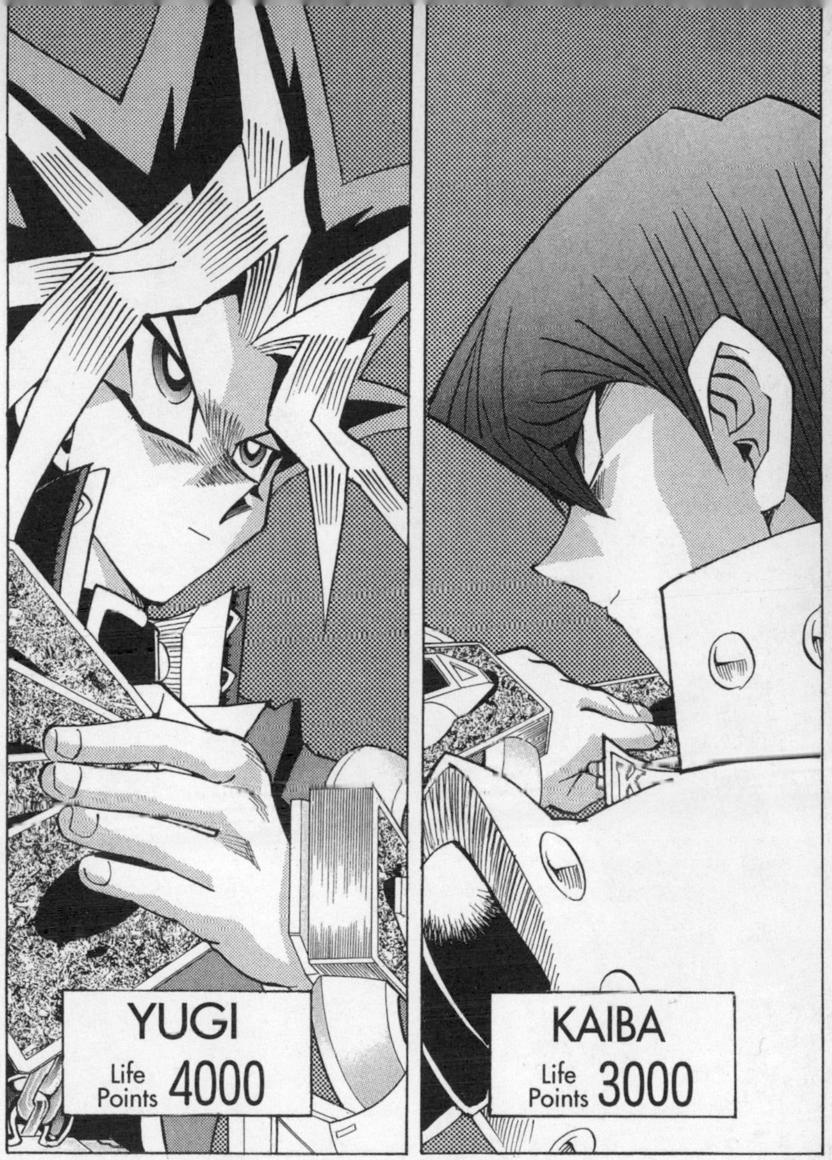
KAIBA
Life Points 3000
YUGI
Life Points 4000

DUEL 194: GOD IN HAND!!

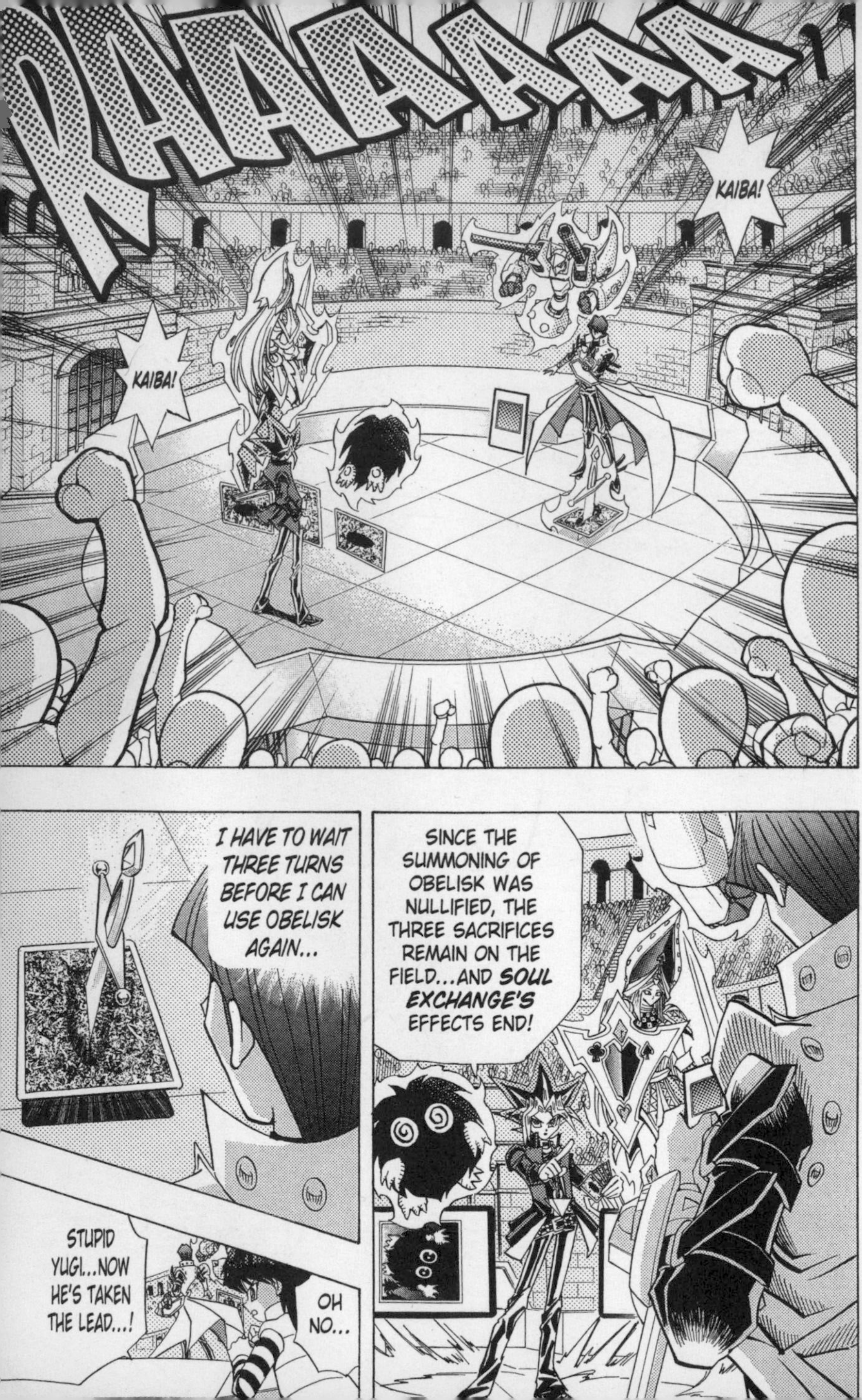
KAIBA!
KAIBA!
SINCE THE SUMMONING OF OBELISK WAS NULLIFIED, THE THREE SACRIFICES REMAIN ON THE FIELD...AND **SOUL EXCHANGE'S** EFFECTS END!
I HAVE TO WAIT THREE TURNS BEFORE I CAN USE OBELISK AGAIN...
OH NO...
STUPID YUGI...NOW HE'S TAKEN THE LEAD...!

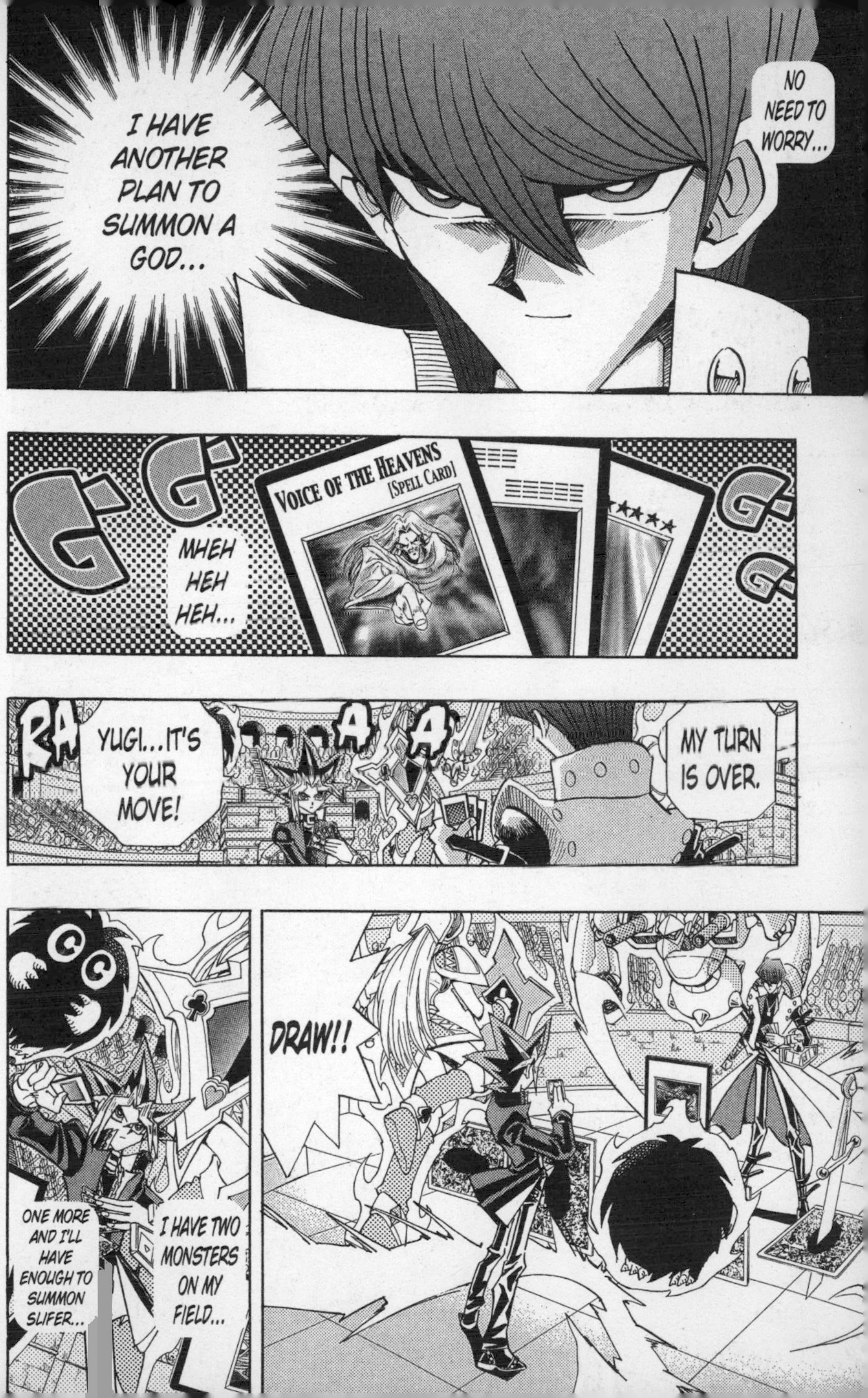
NO NEED TO WORRY...
I HAVE ANOTHER PLAN TO SUMMON A GOD...
G-G-
VOICE OF THE HEAVENS [SPELL CARD]
G G
MHEH HEH HEH...
MY TURN IS OVER.
A A
YUGI...IT'S YOUR MOVE!
RA
DRAW!!
I HAVE TWO MONSTERS ON MY FIELD...
ONE MORE AND I'LL HAVE ENOUGH TO SUMMON SLIFER...

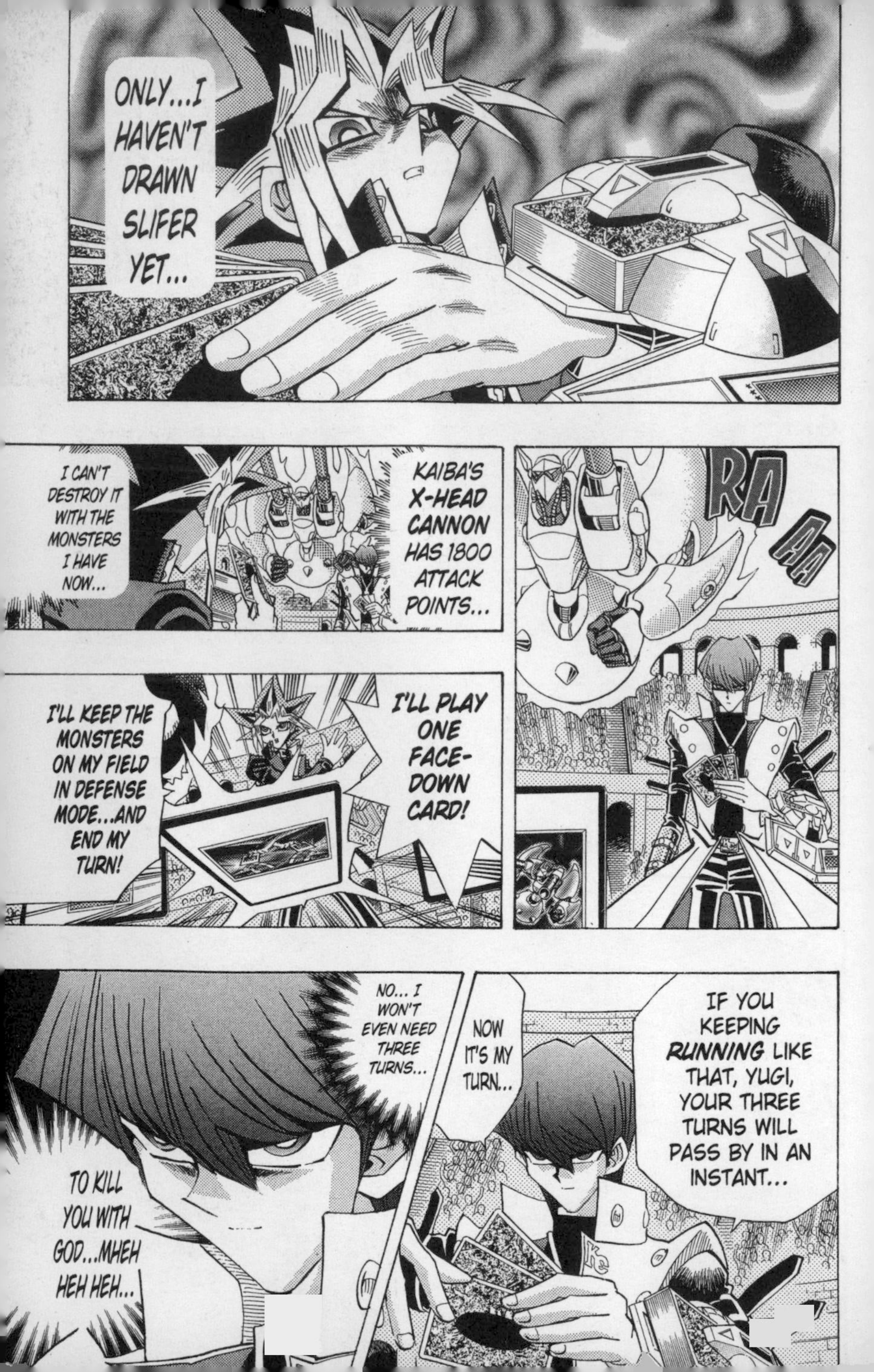
ONLY...I HAVEN'T DRAWN SLIFER YET...
RA AA
KAIBA'S X-HEAD CANNON HAS 1800 ATTACK POINTS...
I CAN'T DESTROY IT WITH THE MONSTERS I HAVE NOW...
I'LL PLAY ONE FACE-DOWN CARD!
I'LL KEEP THE MONSTERS ON MY FIELD IN DEFENSE MODE...AND END MY TURN!
IF YOU KEEPING RUNNING LIKE THAT, YUGI, YOUR THREE TURNS WILL PASS BY IN AN INSTANT...
NOW IT'S MY TURN...
NO... I WON'T EVEN NEED THREE TURNS...
TO KILL YOU WITH GOD...MHEH HEH HEH...

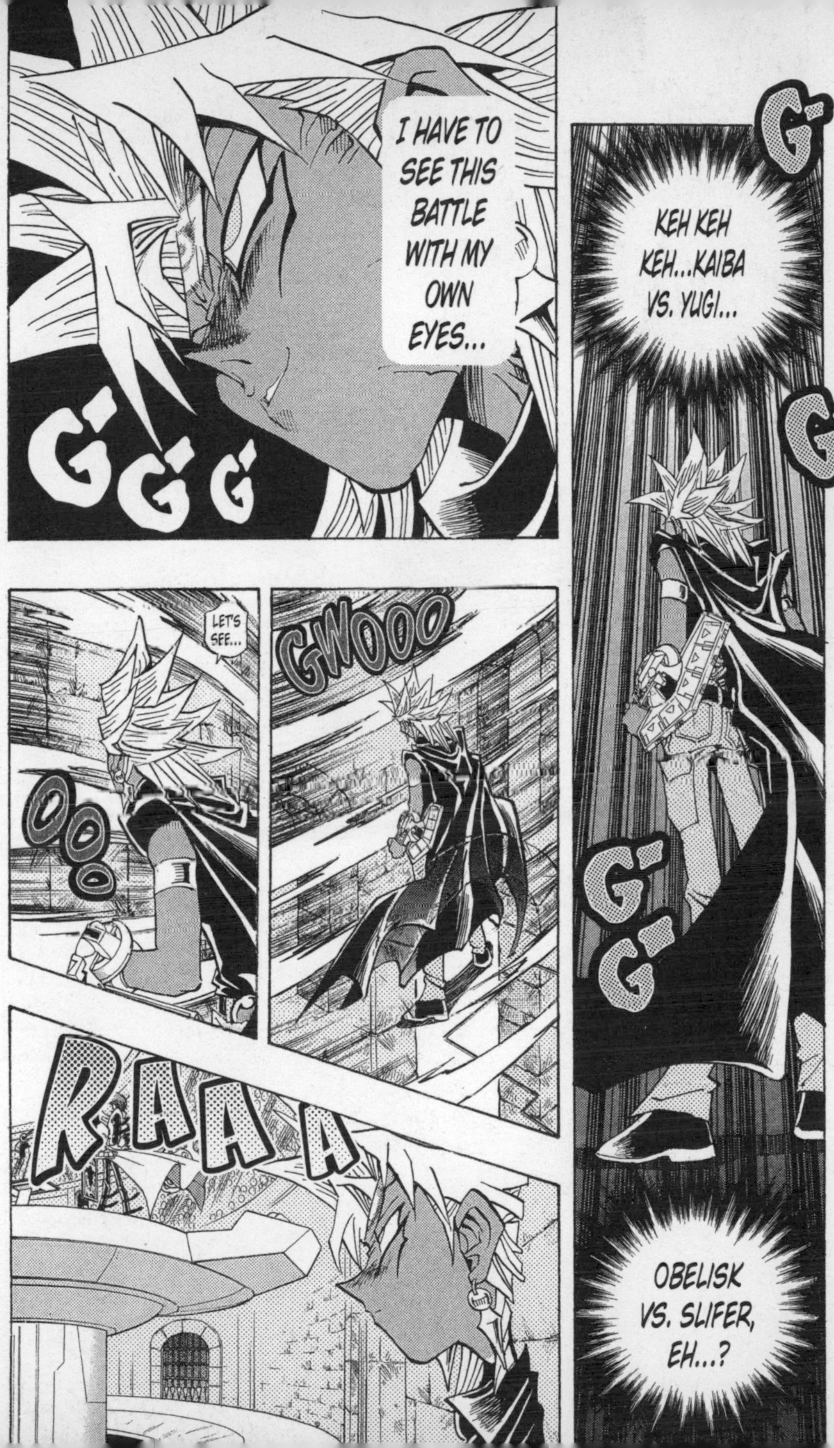
G
KEH KEH KEH...KAIBA VS. YUGI...
G
G
G
OBELISK VS. SLIFER, EH...?
I HAVE TO SEE THIS BATTLE WITH MY OWN EYES...
GGG
GWOOO
LET'S SEE...
OOOO
RAAA

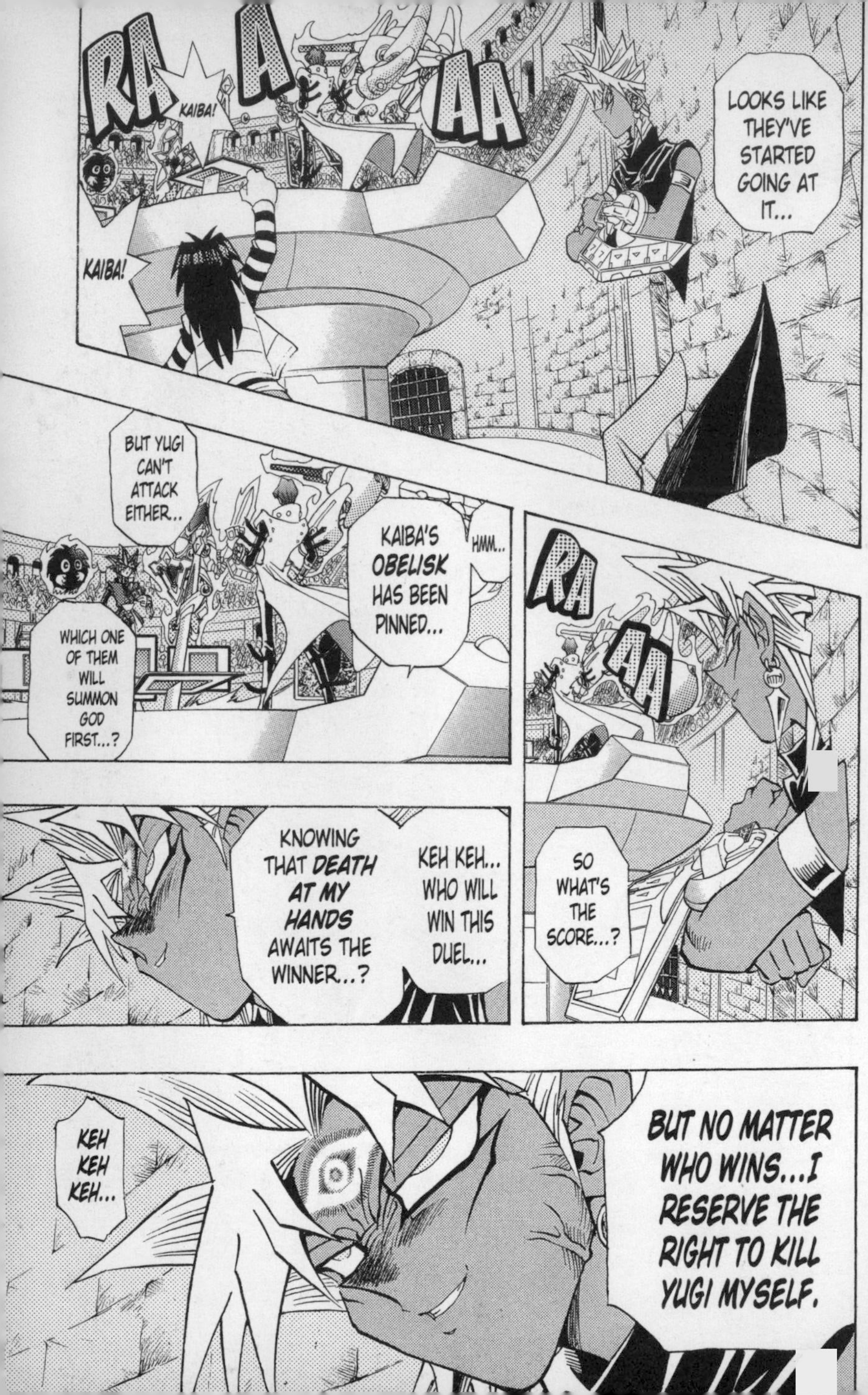
LOOKS LIKE THEY'VE STARTED GOING AT IT...
RA A AA
KAIBA!
KAIBA!
RA AA
SO WHAT'S THE SCORE...?
HMM...
KAIBA'S OBELISK HAS BEEN PINNED...
BUT YUGI CAN'T ATTACK EITHER...
WHICH ONE OF THEM WILL SUMMON GOD FIRST...?
KEH KEH... WHO WILL WIN THIS DUEL...
KNOWING THAT DEATH AT MY HANDS AWAITS THE WINNER...?
BUT NO MATTER WHO WINS...I RESERVE THE RIGHT TO KILL YUGI MYSELF.
KEH KEH KEH...

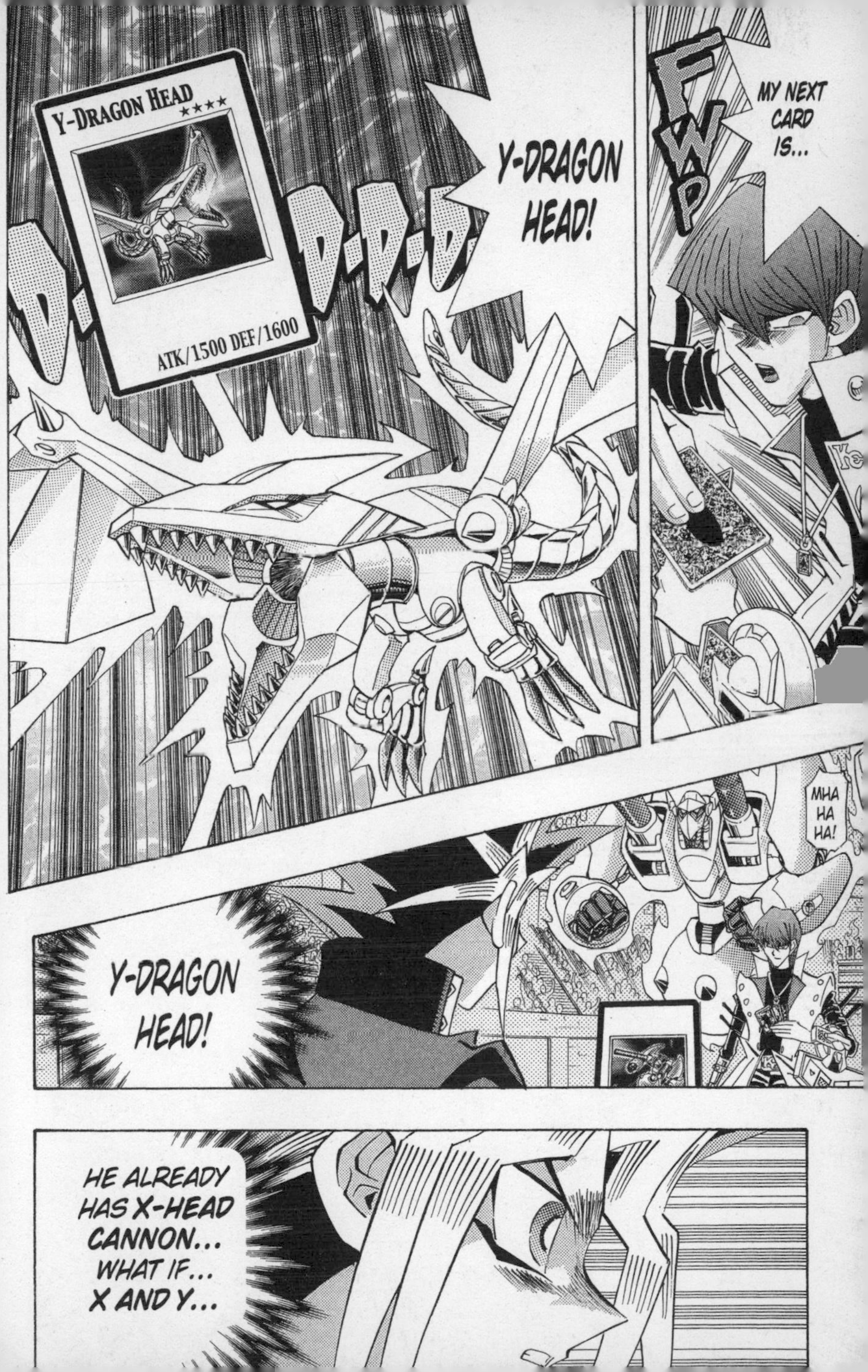
FWP
MY NEXT CARD IS...
Y-DRAGON HEAD ★★★★
ATK/1500 DEF/1600
D-D-D
Y-DRAGON HEAD!
MHA HA HA!
Y-DRAGON HEAD!
HE ALREADY HAS X-HEAD CANNON... WHAT IF... X AND Y...

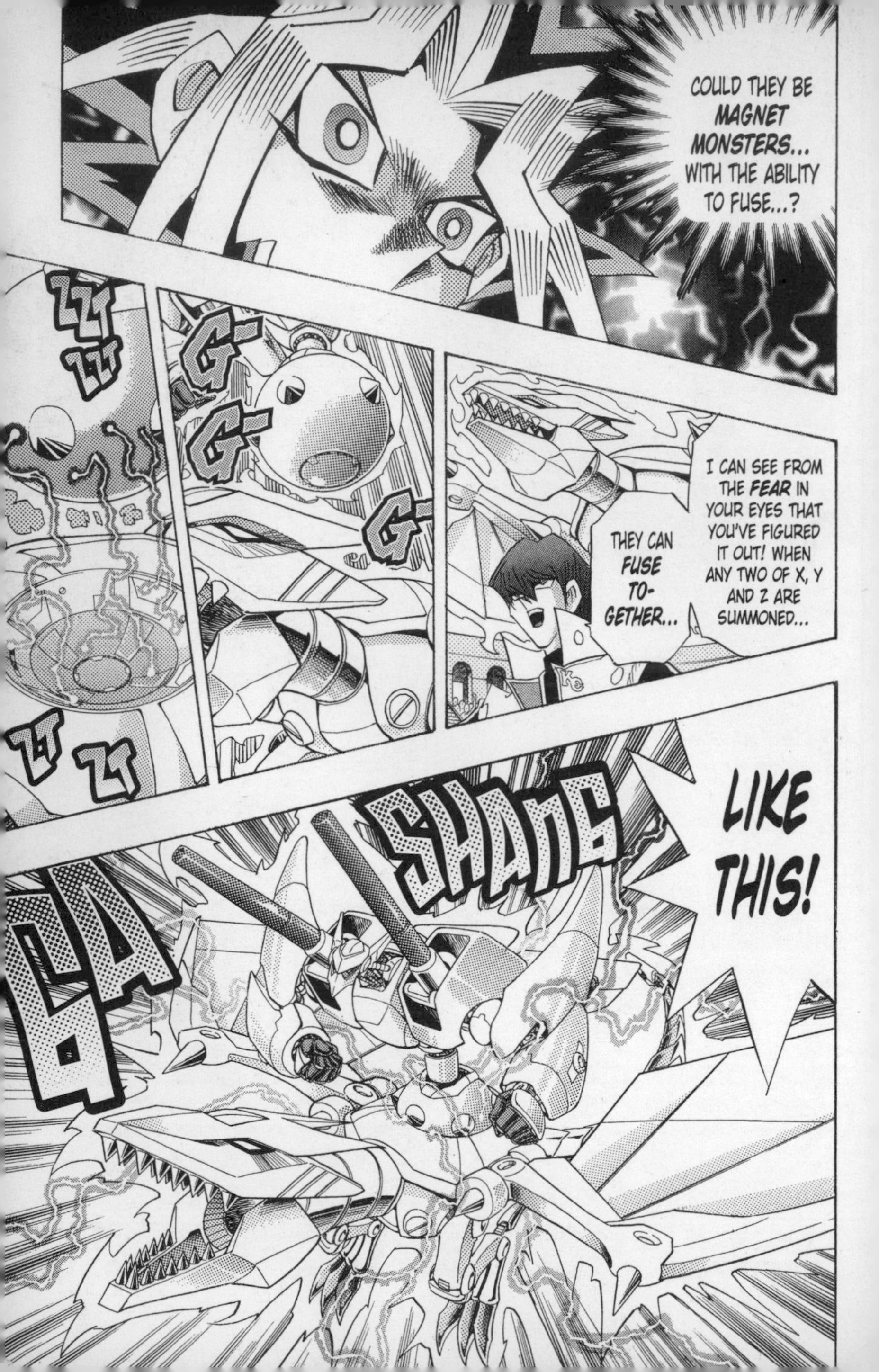
COULD THEY BE MAGNET MONSTERS... WITH THE ABILITY TO FUSE...?
I CAN SEE FROM THE FEAR IN YOUR EYES THAT YOU'VE FIGURED IT OUT! WHEN ANY TWO OF X, Y AND Z ARE SUMMONED...
THEY CAN FUSE TO-GETHER...
G- G- G-
LIKE THIS!
SHANG

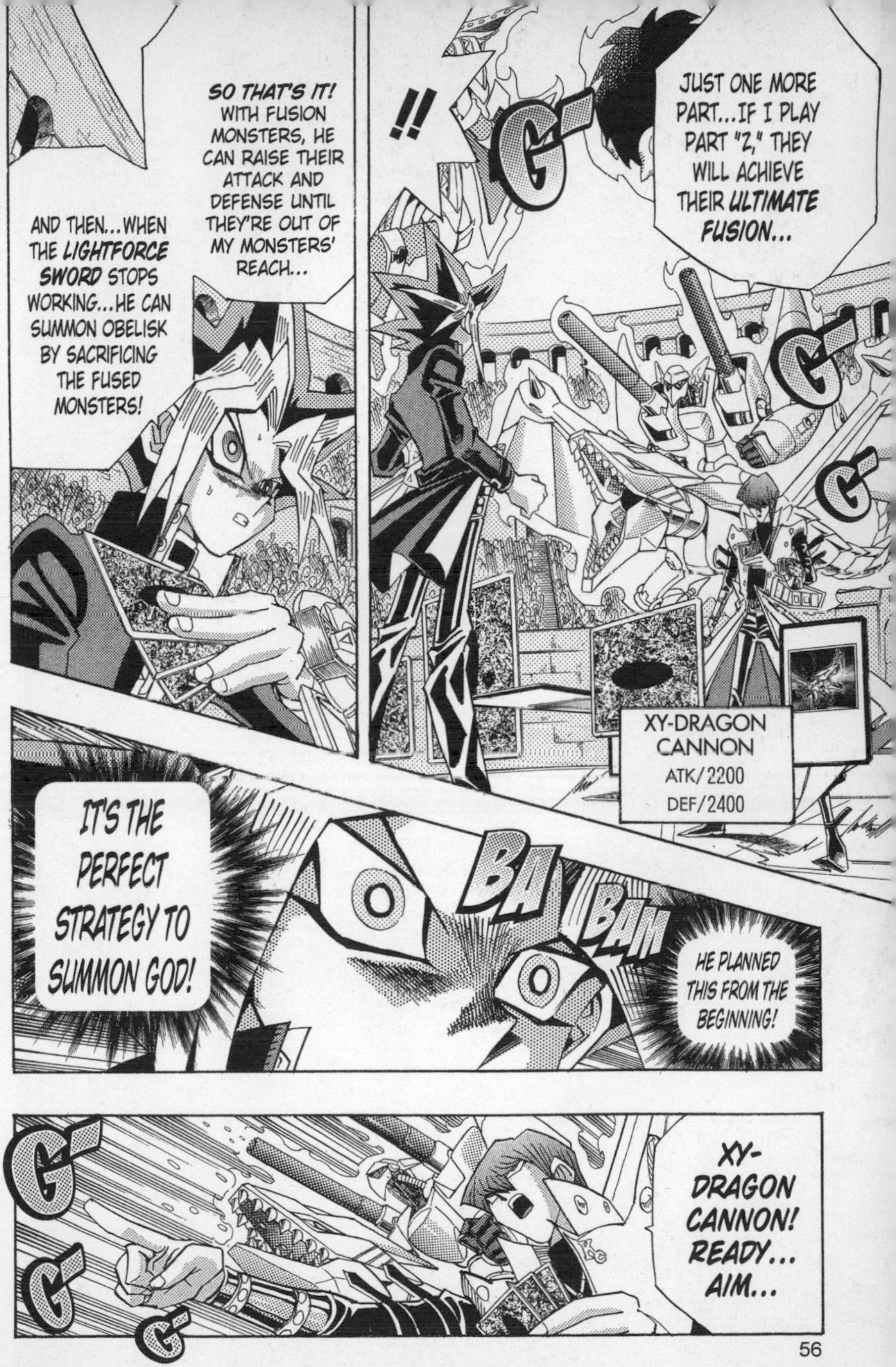
JUST ONE MORE PART...IF I PLAY PART "Z," THEY WILL ACHIEVE THEIR ULTIMATE FUSION...
G
!!
G
G
XY-DRAGON CANNON
ATK/2200
DEF/2400
SO THAT'S IT! WITH FUSION MONSTERS, HE CAN RAISE THEIR ATTACK AND DEFENSE UNTIL THEY'RE OUT OF MY MONSTERS' REACH...
AND THEN...WHEN THE LIGHTFORCE SWORD STOPS WORKING...HE CAN SUMMON OBELISK BY SACRIFICING THE FUSED MONSTERS!
HE PLANNED THIS FROM THE BEGINNING!
BA BAM
IT'S THE PERFECT STRATEGY TO SUMMON GOD!
XY-DRAGON CANNON! READY... AIM...
G
G
G

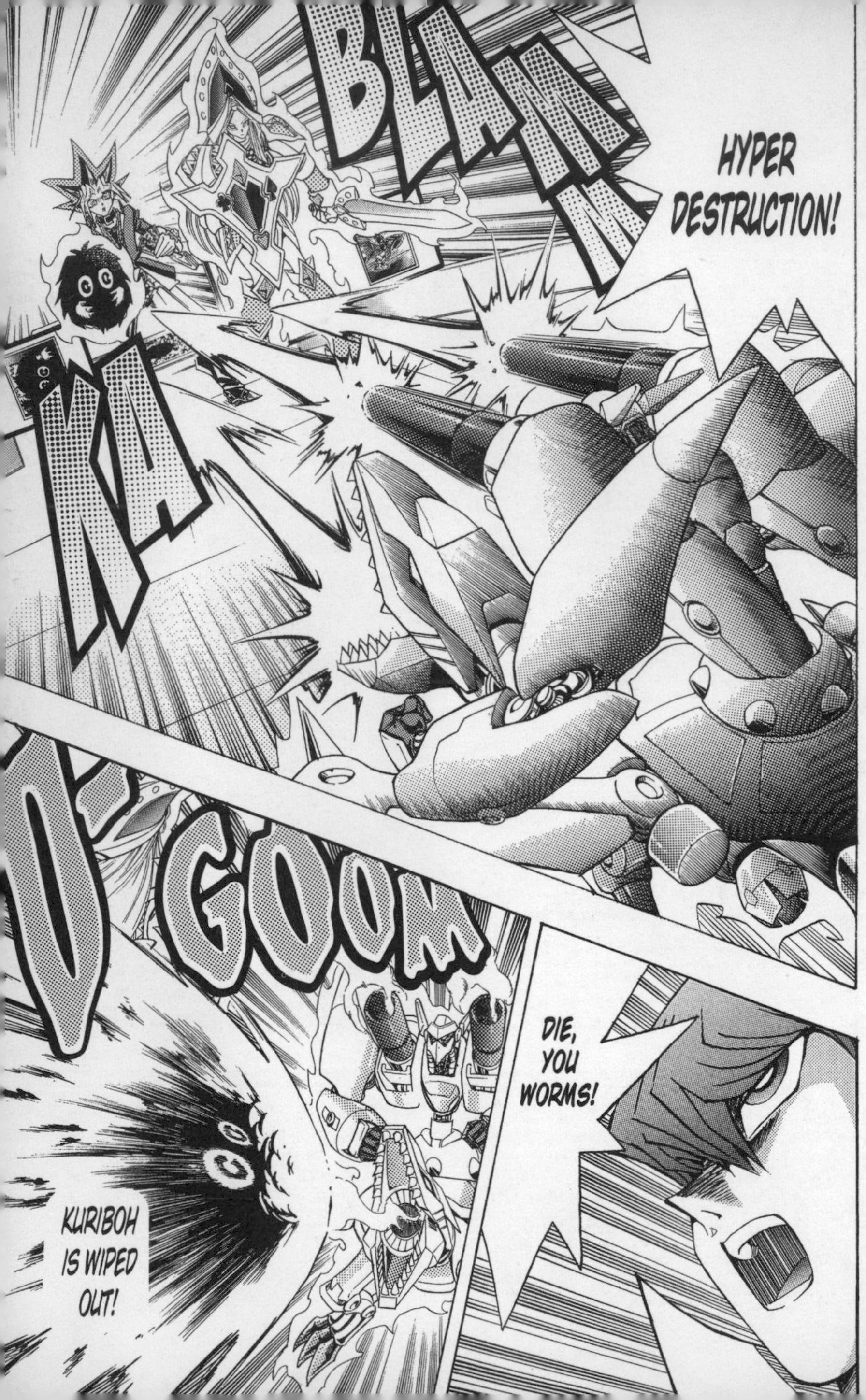
HYPER DESTRUCTION!
BLAM
KA
DIE, YOU WORMS!
GOOM
KURIBOH IS WIPED OUT!

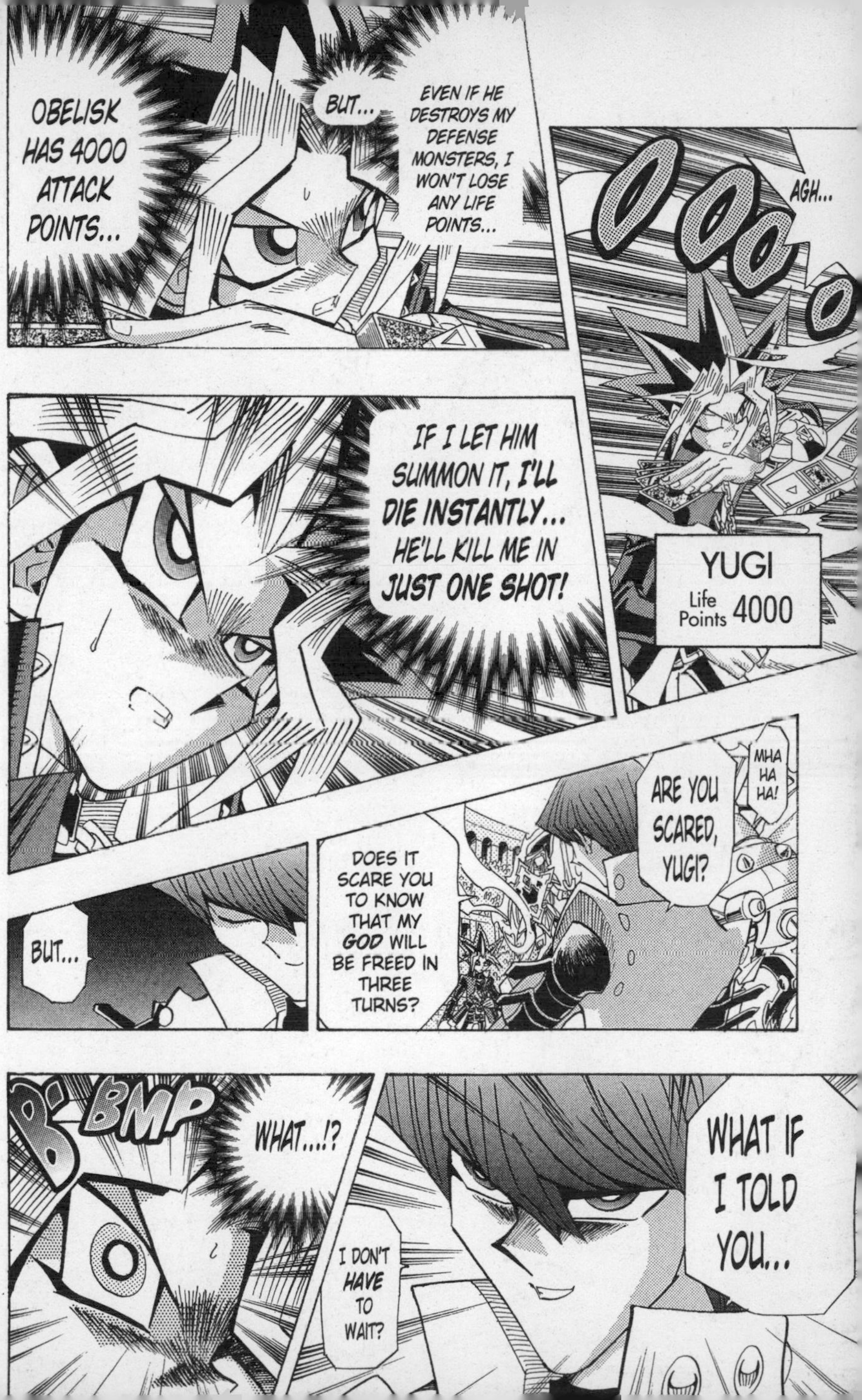
AGH...
YUGI
Life Points 4000
EVEN IF HE DESTROYS MY DEFENSE MONSTERS, I WON'T LOSE ANY LIFE POINTS...
BUT...
OBELISK HAS 4000 ATTACK POINTS...
IF I LET HIM SUMMON IT, I'LL DIE INSTANTLY... HE'LL KILL ME IN JUST ONE SHOT!
MHA HA HA!
ARE YOU SCARED, YUGI?
DOES IT SCARE YOU TO KNOW THAT MY GOD WILL BE FREED IN THREE TURNS?
BUT...
WHAT IF I TOLD YOU...
I DON'T HAVE TO WAIT?
WHAT...!?
BMP

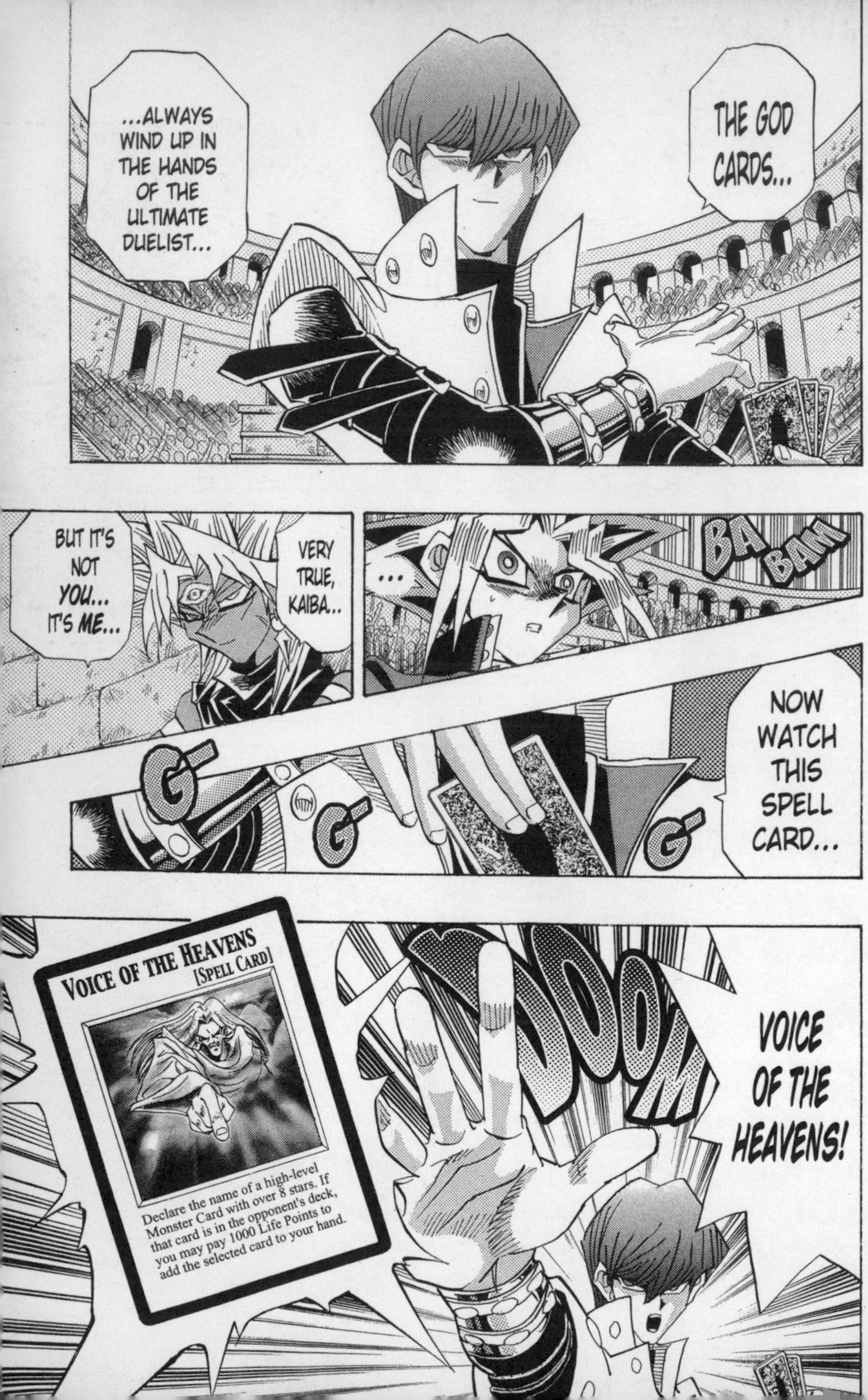
THE GOD CARDS...
...ALWAYS WIND UP IN THE HANDS OF THE ULTIMATE DUELIST...
BA BAM
...
VERY TRUE, KAIBA...
BUT IT'S NOT YOU... IT'S ME...
NOW WATCH THIS SPELL CARD...
G
G
G
VOICE OF THE HEAVENS!
DOOOM
VOICE OF THE HEAVENS
[SPELL CARD]
Declare the name of a high-level Monster Card with over 8 stars. If that card is in the opponent's deck, you may pay 1000 Life Points to add the selected card to your hand.

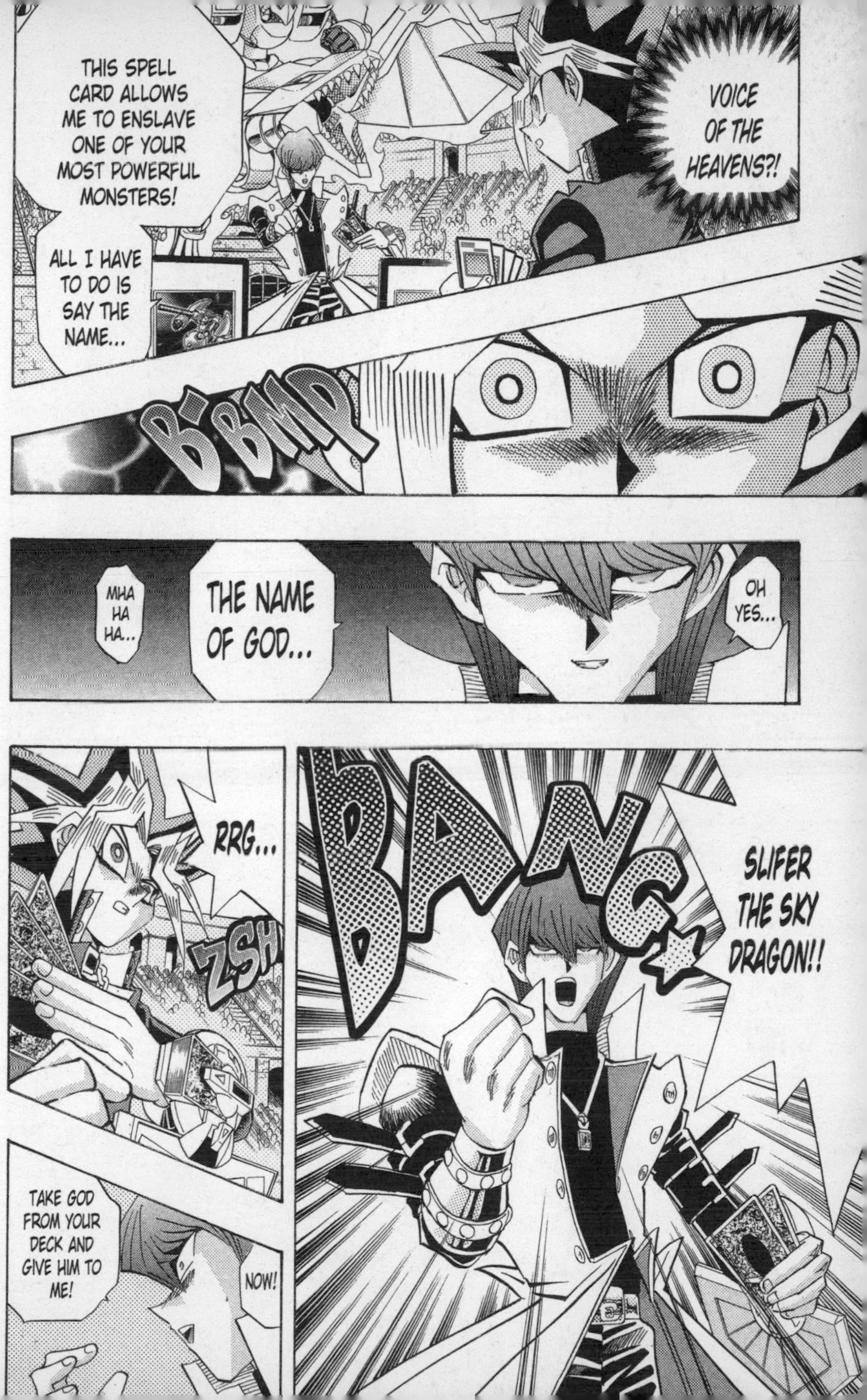
VOICE OF THE HEAVENS?!
THIS SPELL CARD ALLOWS ME TO ENSLAVE ONE OF YOUR MOST POWERFUL MONSTERS!
ALL I HAVE TO DO IS SAY THE NAME...
B'BMP
OH YES...
THE NAME OF GOD...
MHA HA HA...
BANG
SLIFER THE SKY DRAGON!!
RRG...
ZSH
TAKE GOD FROM YOUR DECK AND GIVE HIM TO ME!
NOW!

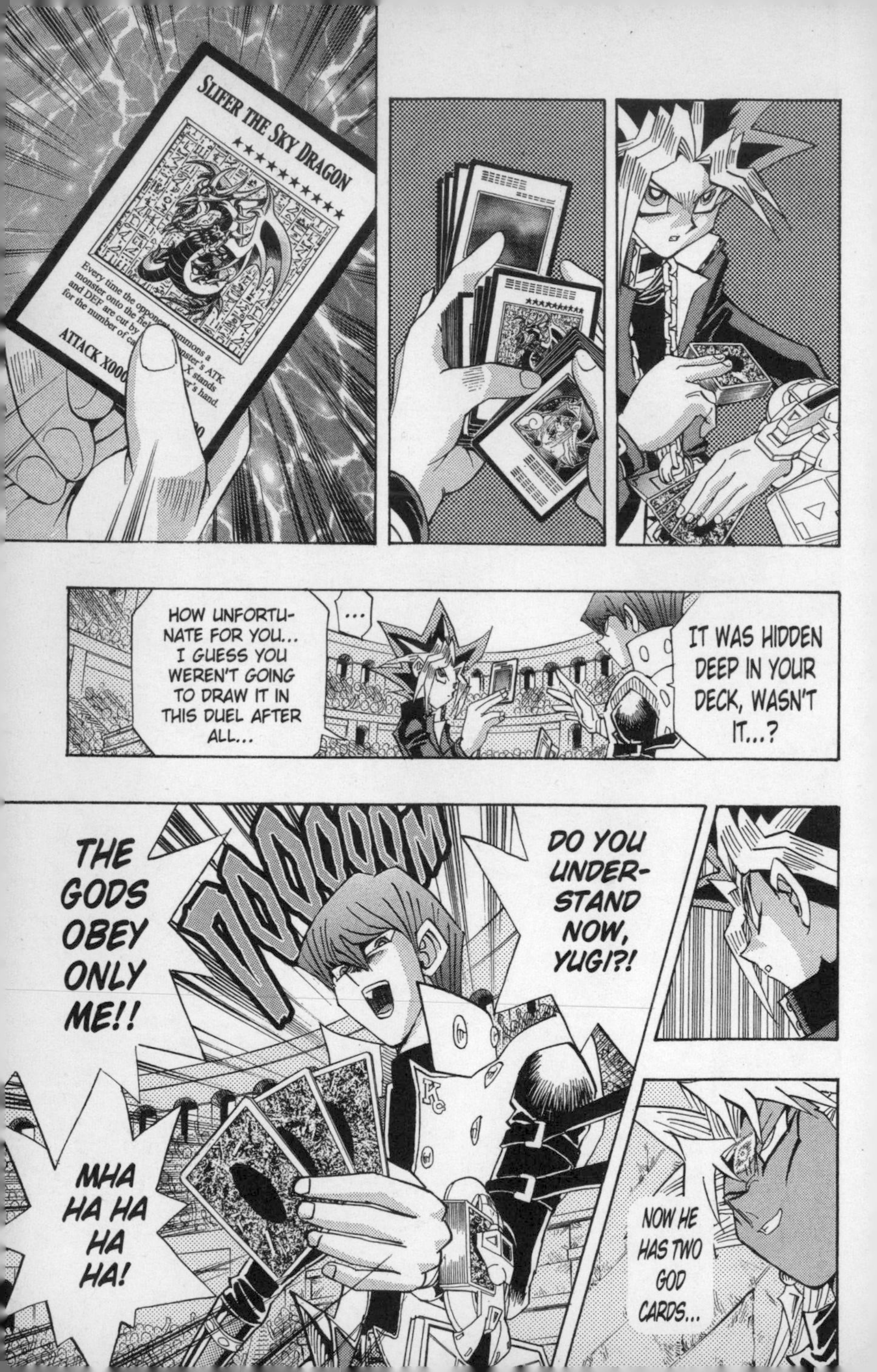
SLIFER THE SKY DRAGON
IT WAS HIDDEN DEEP IN YOUR DECK, WASN'T IT...?
...
HOW UNFORTUNATE FOR YOU... I GUESS YOU WEREN'T GOING TO DRAW IT IN THIS DUEL AFTER ALL...
NOW HE HAS TWO GOD CARDS...
DO YOU UNDERSTAND NOW, YUGI?!
THE GODS OBEY ONLY ME!!
MHA HA HA HA HA!

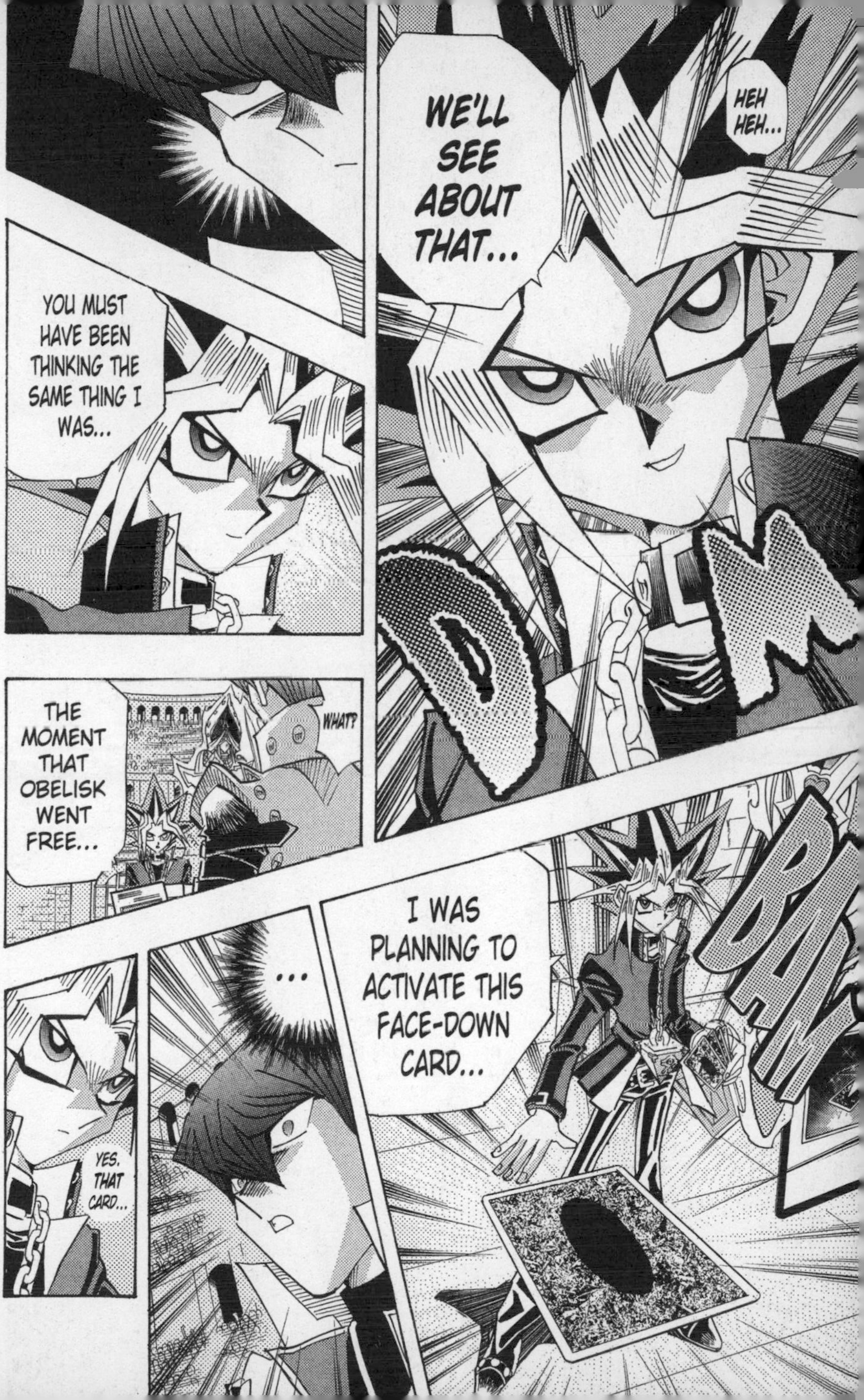
HEH HEH...
WE'LL SEE ABOUT THAT...
YOU MUST HAVE BEEN THINKING THE SAME THING I WAS...
WHAT?
THE MOMENT THAT OBELISK WENT FREE...
I WAS PLANNING TO ACTIVATE THIS FACE-DOWN CARD...
...
YES. THAT CARD...

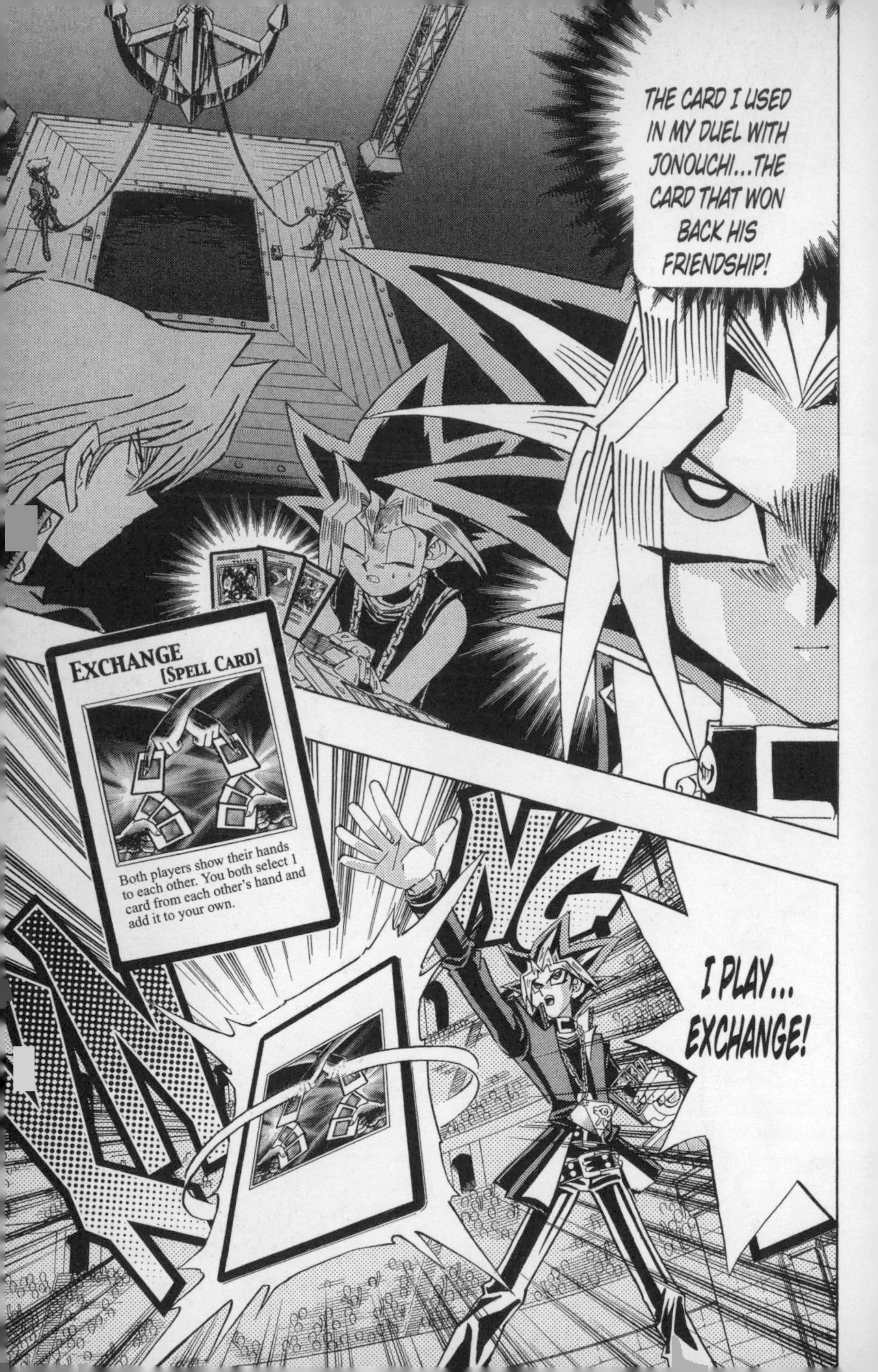
THE CARD I USED IN MY DUEL WITH JONOUCHI...THE CARD THAT WON BACK HIS FRIENDSHIP!
EXCHANGE
[SPELL CARD]
Both players show their hands to each other. You both select 1 card from each other's hand and add it to your own.
I PLAY... EXCHANGE!

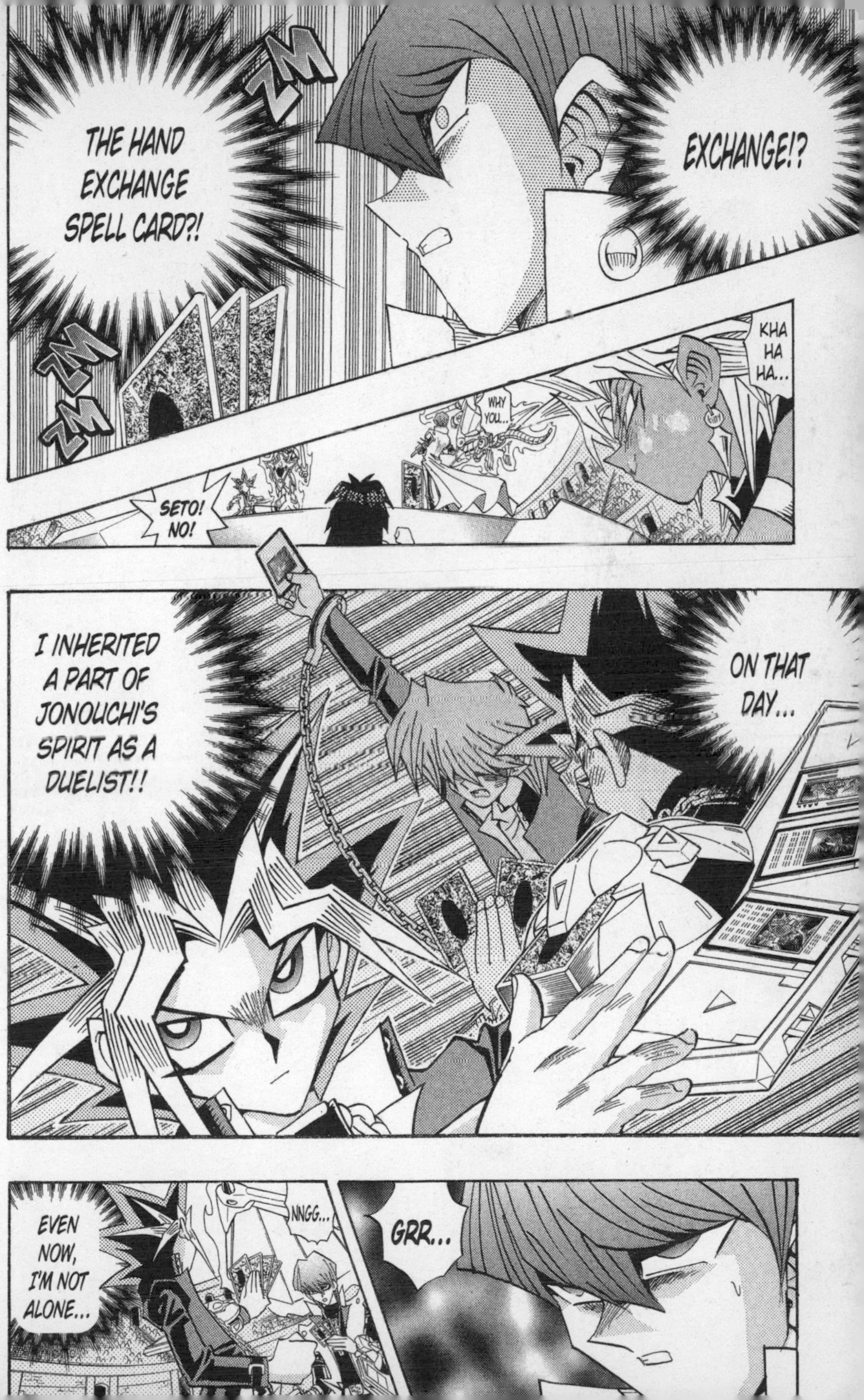

ZM
EXCHANGE!?
THE HAND EXCHANGE SPELL CARD?!
ZM ZM
KHA HA HA...
WHY YOU...
SETO! NO!
ON THAT DAY...
I INHERITED A PART OF JONOUCHI'S SPIRIT AS A DUELIST!!
GRR...
NNGG...
EVEN NOW, I'M NOT ALONE...

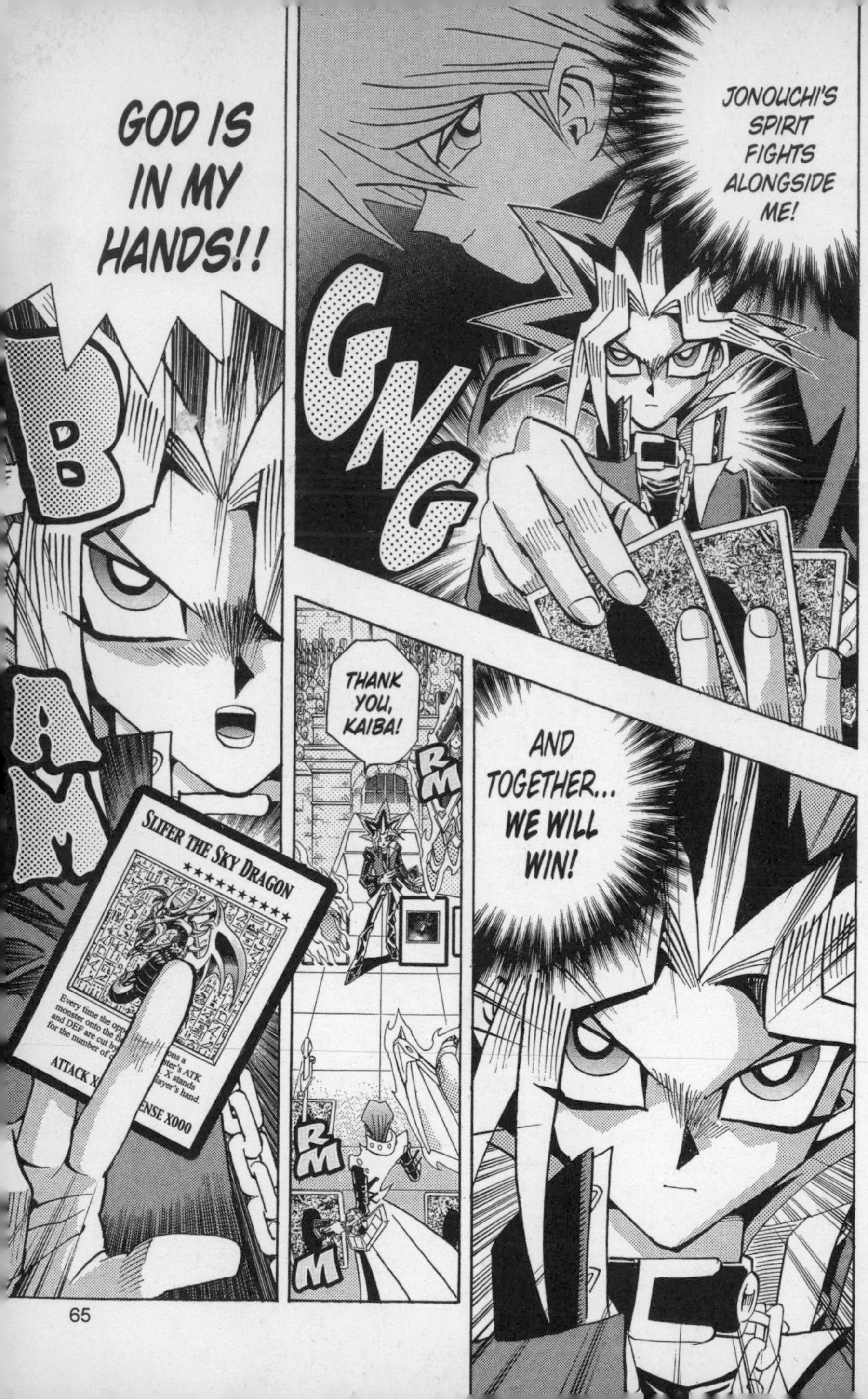

JONOUCHI'S SPIRIT FIGHTS ALONGSIDE ME!
GNG
AND TOGETHER... WE WILL WIN!
THANK YOU, KAIBA!
RM
RM
M
GOD IS IN MY HANDS!!
BAM
SLIFER THE SKY DRAGON

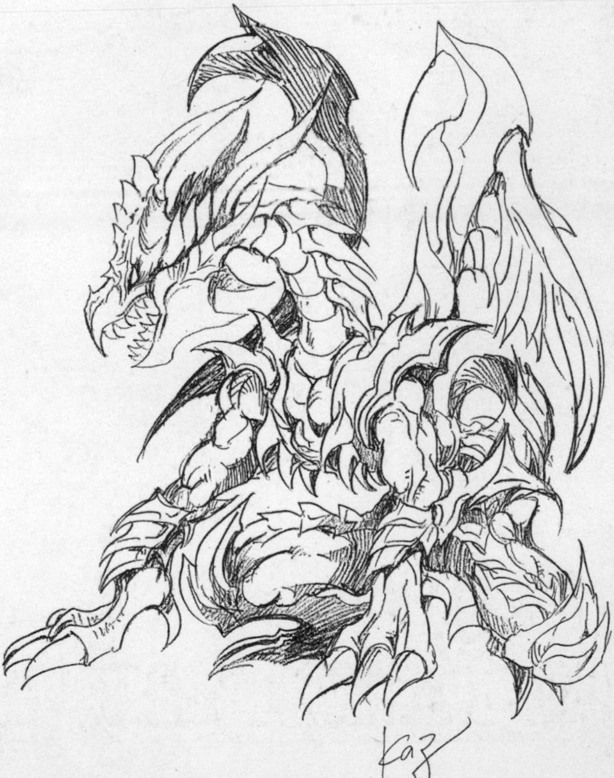
Kaz

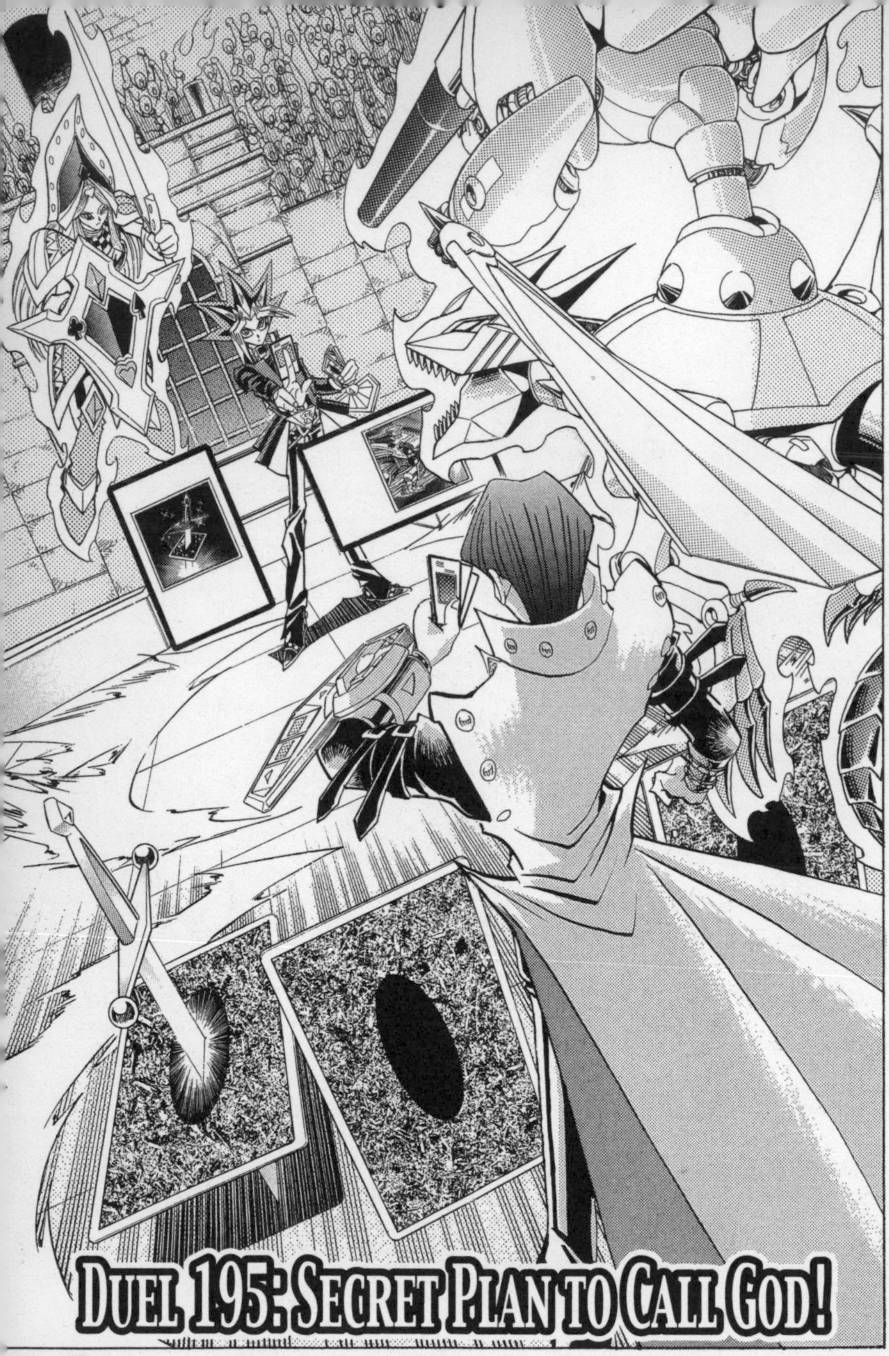
Duel 195: Secret Plan to Call God!

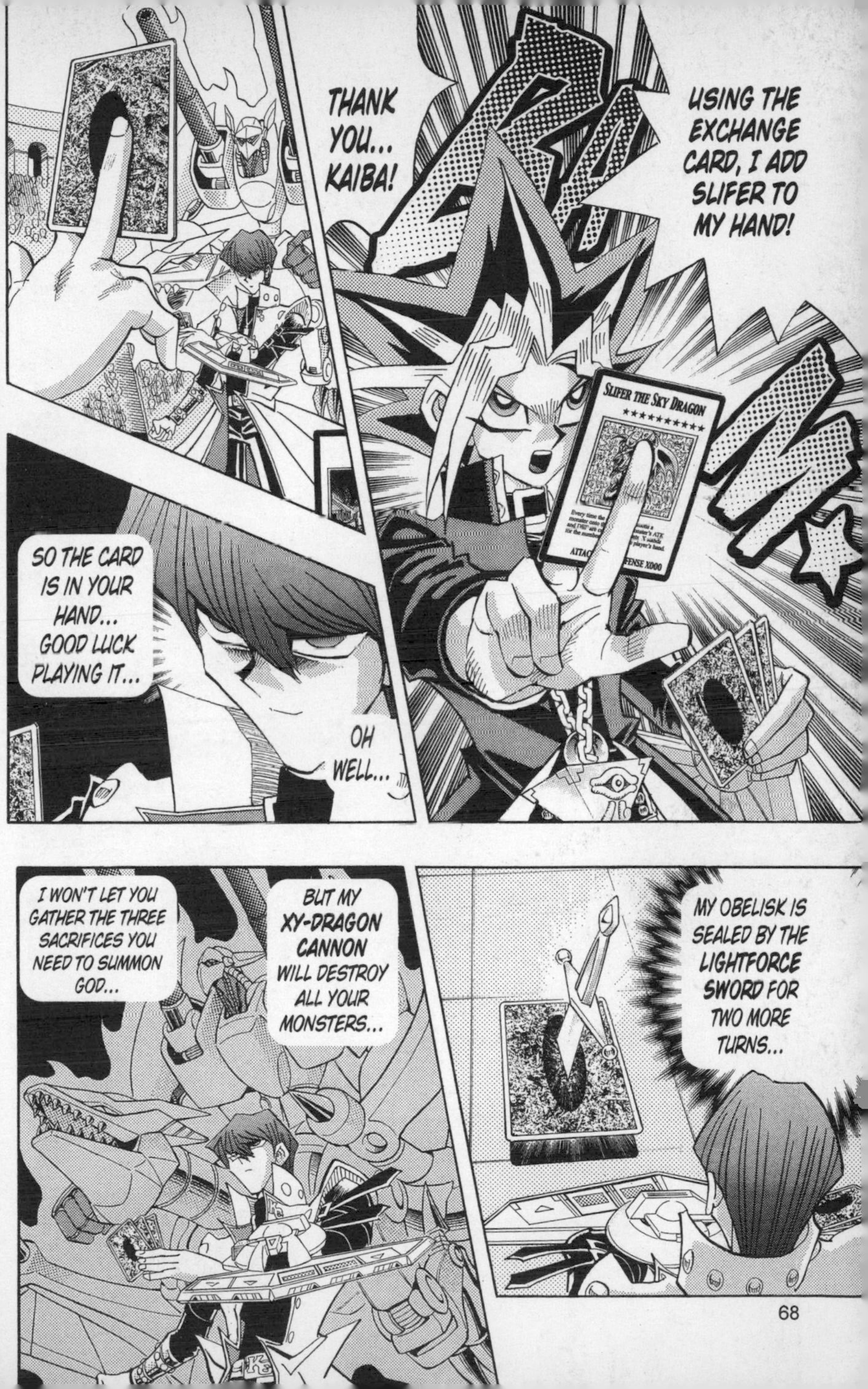
USING THE EXCHANGE CARD, I ADD SLIFER TO MY HAND!
THANK YOU... KAIBA!
SLIFER THE SKY DRAGON
SO THE CARD IS IN YOUR HAND... GOOD LUCK PLAYING IT...
OH WELL...
MY OBELISK IS SEALED BY THE LIGHTFORCE SWORD FOR TWO MORE TURNS...
I WON'T LET YOU GATHER THE THREE SACRIFICES YOU NEED TO SUMMON GOD...
BUT MY XY-DRAGON CANNON WILL DESTROY ALL YOUR MONSTERS...

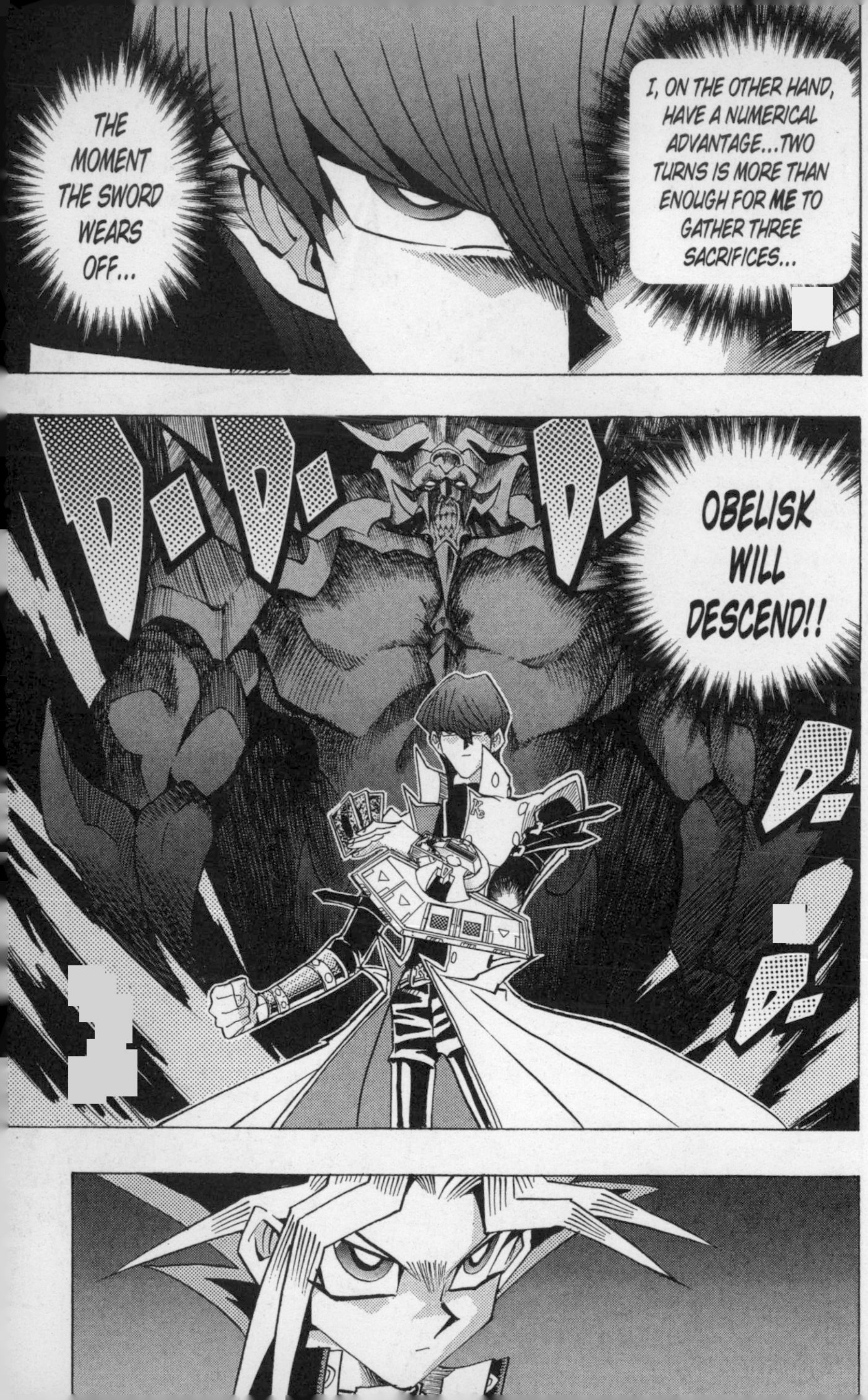

I, ON THE OTHER HAND, HAVE A NUMERICAL ADVANTAGE...TWO TURNS IS MORE THAN ENOUGH FOR ME TO GATHER THREE SACRIFICES...
THE MOMENT THE SWORD WEARS OFF...
OBELISK WILL DESCEND!!
D.. D..
D.. D.. D..

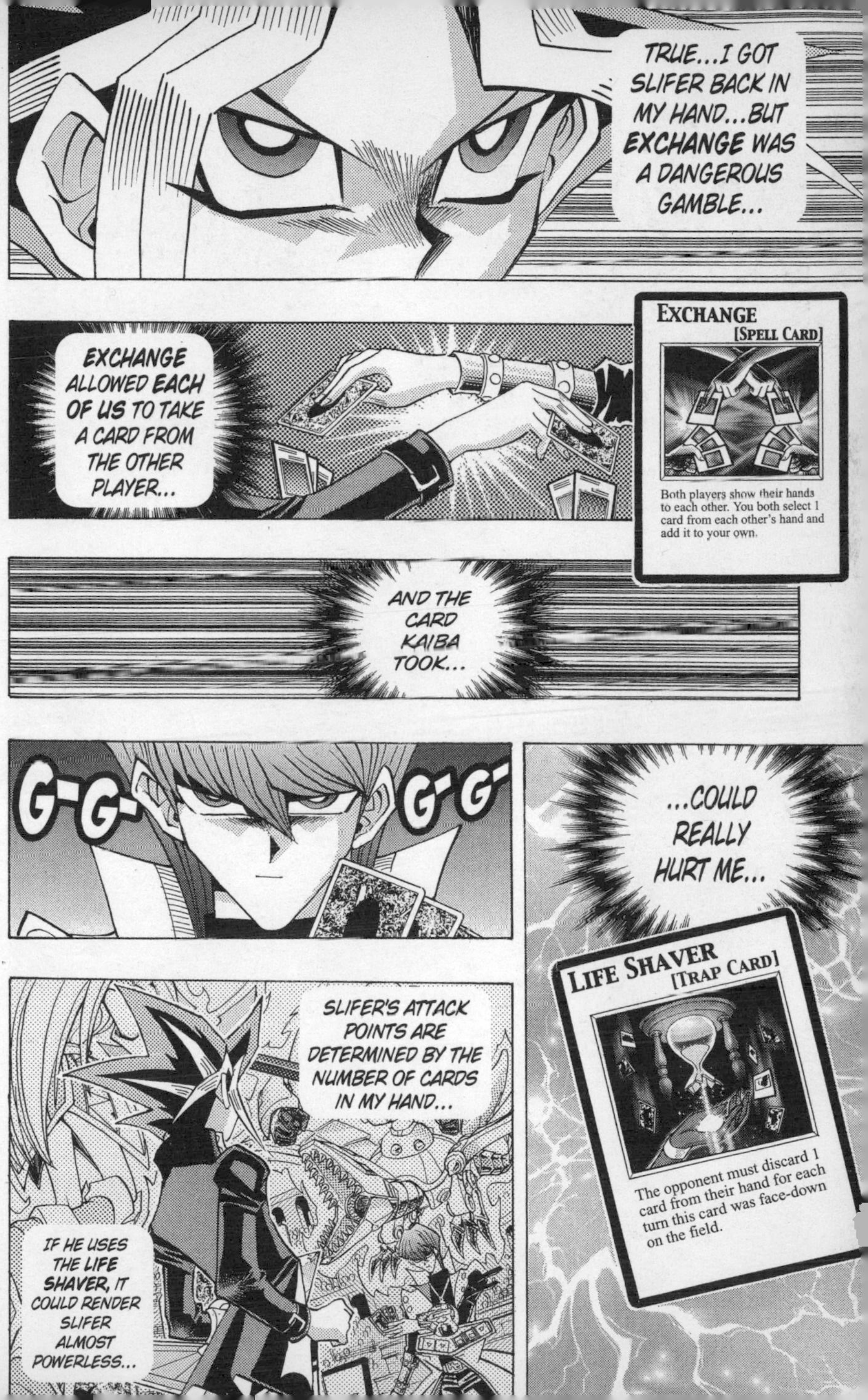
TRUE...I GOT SLIFER BACK IN MY HAND...BUT EXCHANGE WAS A DANGEROUS GAMBLE...
EXCHANGE
[SPELL CARD]
Both players show their hands to each other. You both select 1 card from each other's hand and add it to your own.
EXCHANGE ALLOWED EACH OF US TO TAKE A CARD FROM THE OTHER PLAYER...
AND THE CARD KAIBA TOOK...
...COULD REALLY HURT ME...
LIFE SHAVER
[TRAP CARD]
The opponent must discard 1 card from their hand for each turn this card was face-down on the field.
G-G- G-G-
SLIFER'S ATTACK POINTS ARE DETERMINED BY THE NUMBER OF CARDS IN MY HAND...
IF HE USES THE LIFE SHAVER, IT COULD RENDER SLIFER ALMOST POWERLESS...

READ THIS WAY

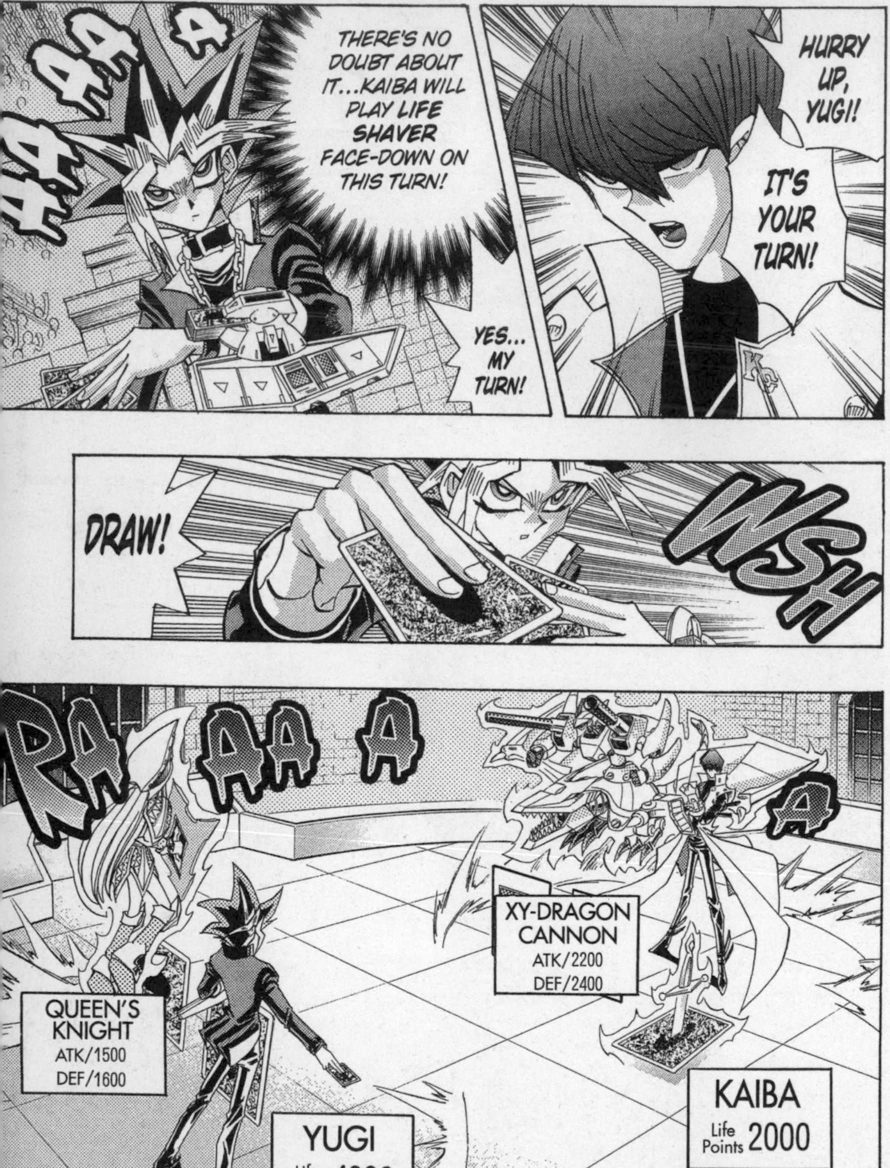

HURRY UP, YUGI!
IT'S YOUR TURN!
THERE'S NO DOUBT ABOUT IT...KAIBA WILL PLAY LIFE SHAVER FACE-DOWN ON THIS TURN!
YES... MY TURN!
DRAW!
RA AA A A
XY-DRAGON CANNON ATK/2200 DEF/2400
KAIBA Life Points 2000
QUEEN'S KNIGHT ATK/1500 DEF/1600
YUGI Life Points 4000

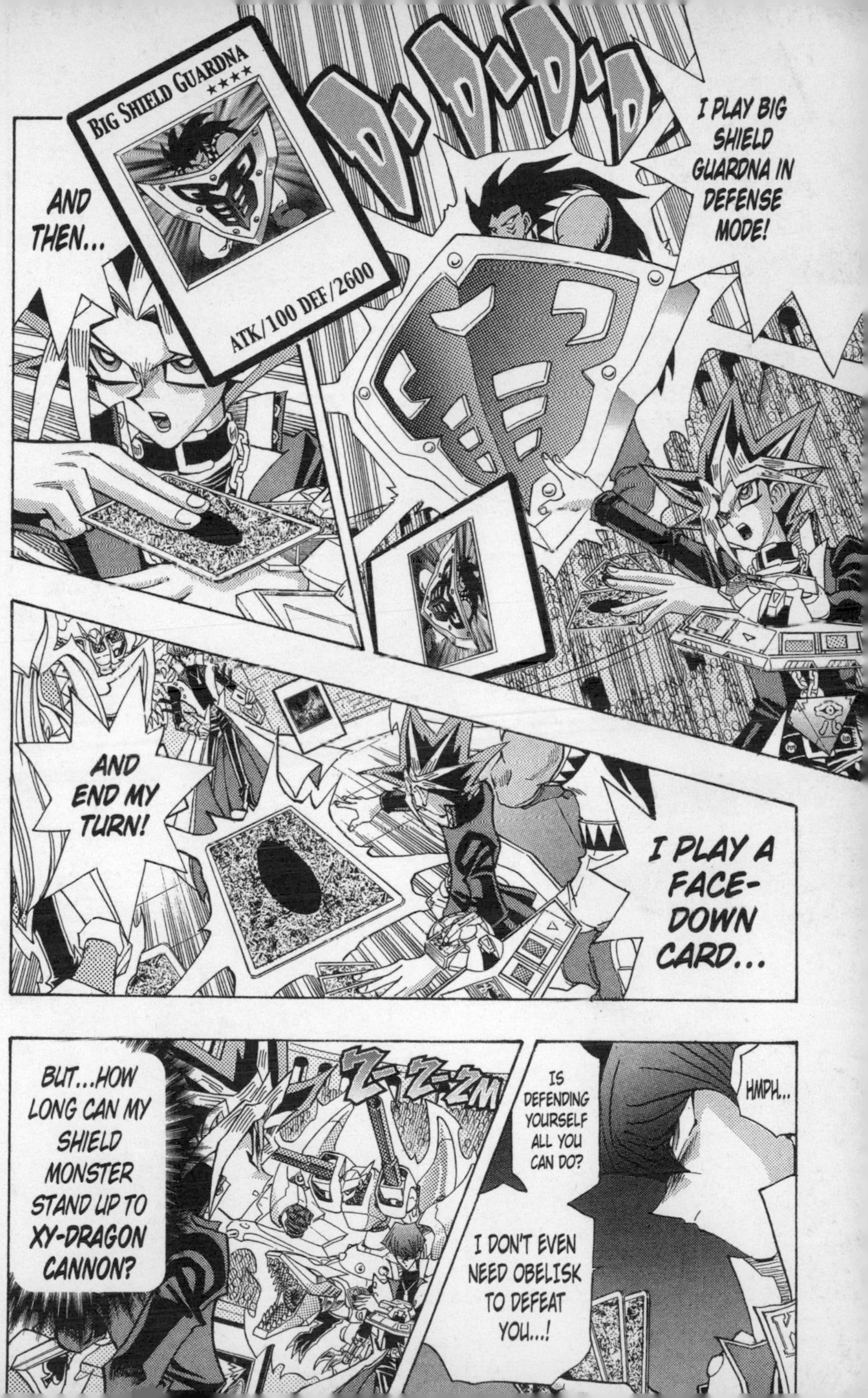
D-D-D-D
I PLAY BIG SHIELD GUARDNA IN DEFENSE MODE!
BIG SHIELD GUARDNA ★★★★
ATK/100 DEF/2600
AND THEN...
I PLAY A FACE-DOWN CARD...
AND END MY TURN!
HMPH...
IS DEFENDING YOURSELF ALL YOU CAN DO?
I DON'T EVEN NEED OBELISK TO DEFEAT YOU...!
Z-Z-ZM
BUT...HOW LONG CAN MY SHIELD MONSTER STAND UP TO XY-DRAGON CANNON?

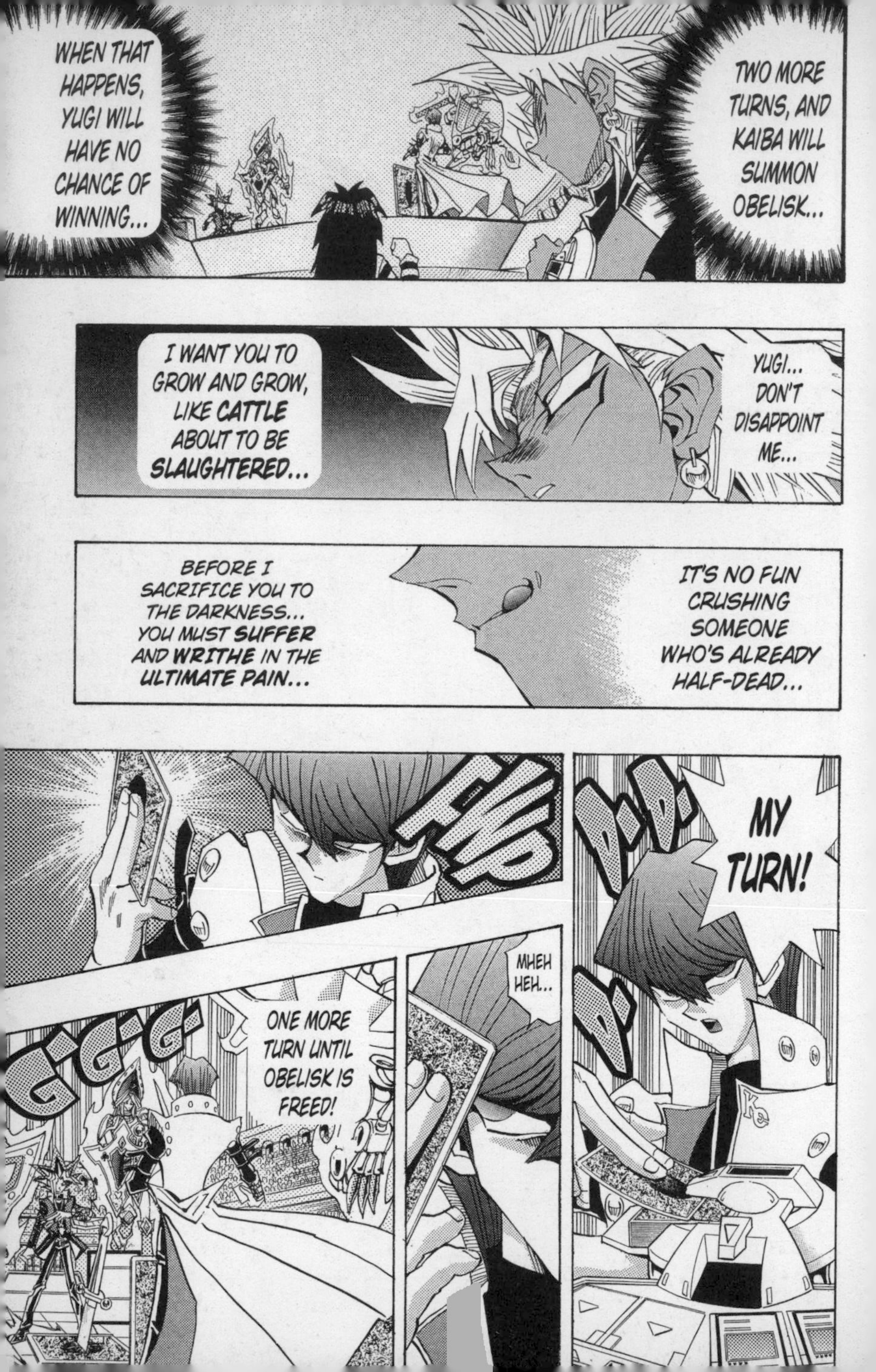
TWO MORE TURNS, AND KAIBA WILL SUMMON OBELISK...
WHEN THAT HAPPENS, YUGI WILL HAVE NO CHANCE OF WINNING...
YUGI... DON'T DISAPPOINT ME...
I WANT YOU TO GROW AND GROW, LIKE **CATTLE** ABOUT TO BE **SLAUGHTERED...**
IT'S NO FUN CRUSHING SOMEONE WHO'S ALREADY HALF-DEAD...
BEFORE I SACRIFICE YOU TO THE DARKNESS... YOU MUST **SUFFER** AND **WRITHE** IN THE **ULTIMATE PAIN...**
MY TURN!
D-D-
D-
FWIP
MHEH HEH...
G-G-G
ONE MORE TURN UNTIL OBELISK IS FREED!

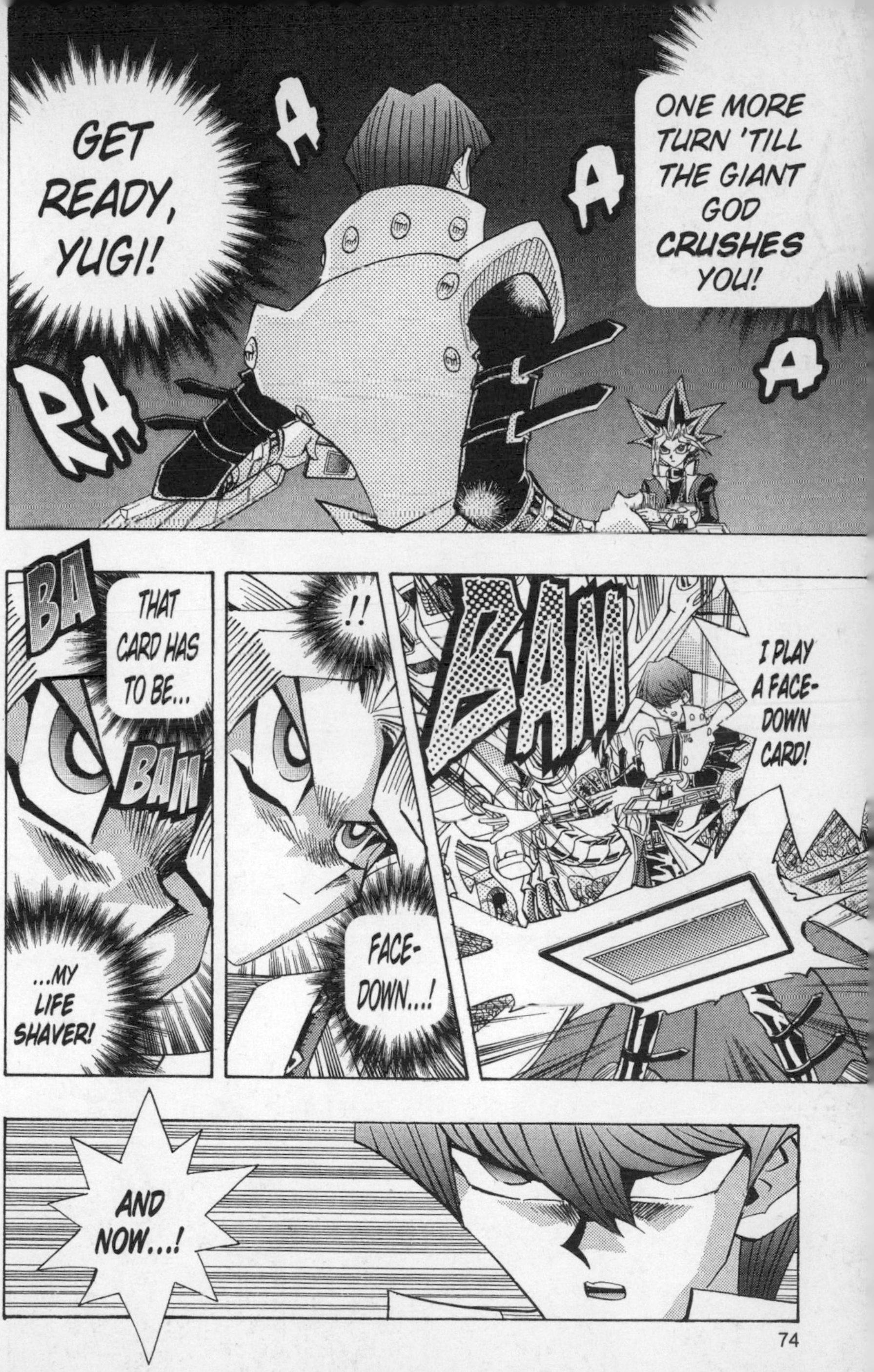
ONE MORE TURN 'TILL THE GIANT GOD CRUSHES YOU!
A
A
A
GET READY, YUGI!
RA
I PLAY A FACE-DOWN CARD!
BAM
!!
FACE-DOWN...!
THAT CARD HAS TO BE...
BA
BAM
...MY LIFE SHAVER!
AND NOW...!

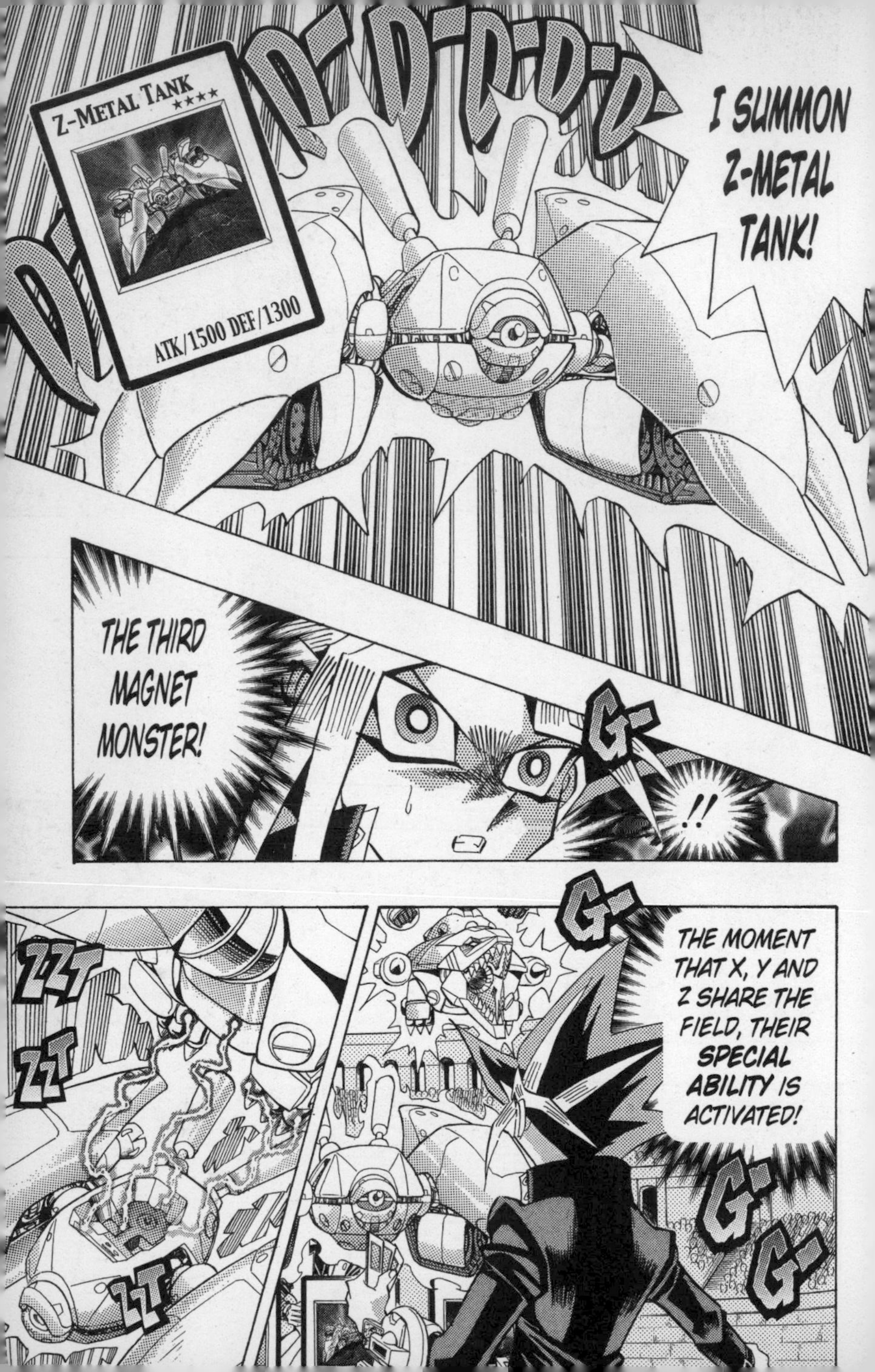
I SUMMON Z-METAL TANK!
Z-METAL TANK ★★★★
ATK/1500 DEF/1300
THE THIRD MAGNET MONSTER!
G-
!!
G-
THE MOMENT THAT X, Y AND Z SHARE THE FIELD, THEIR SPECIAL ABILITY IS ACTIVATED!
G-
G-
ZZT
ZZT
ZZT

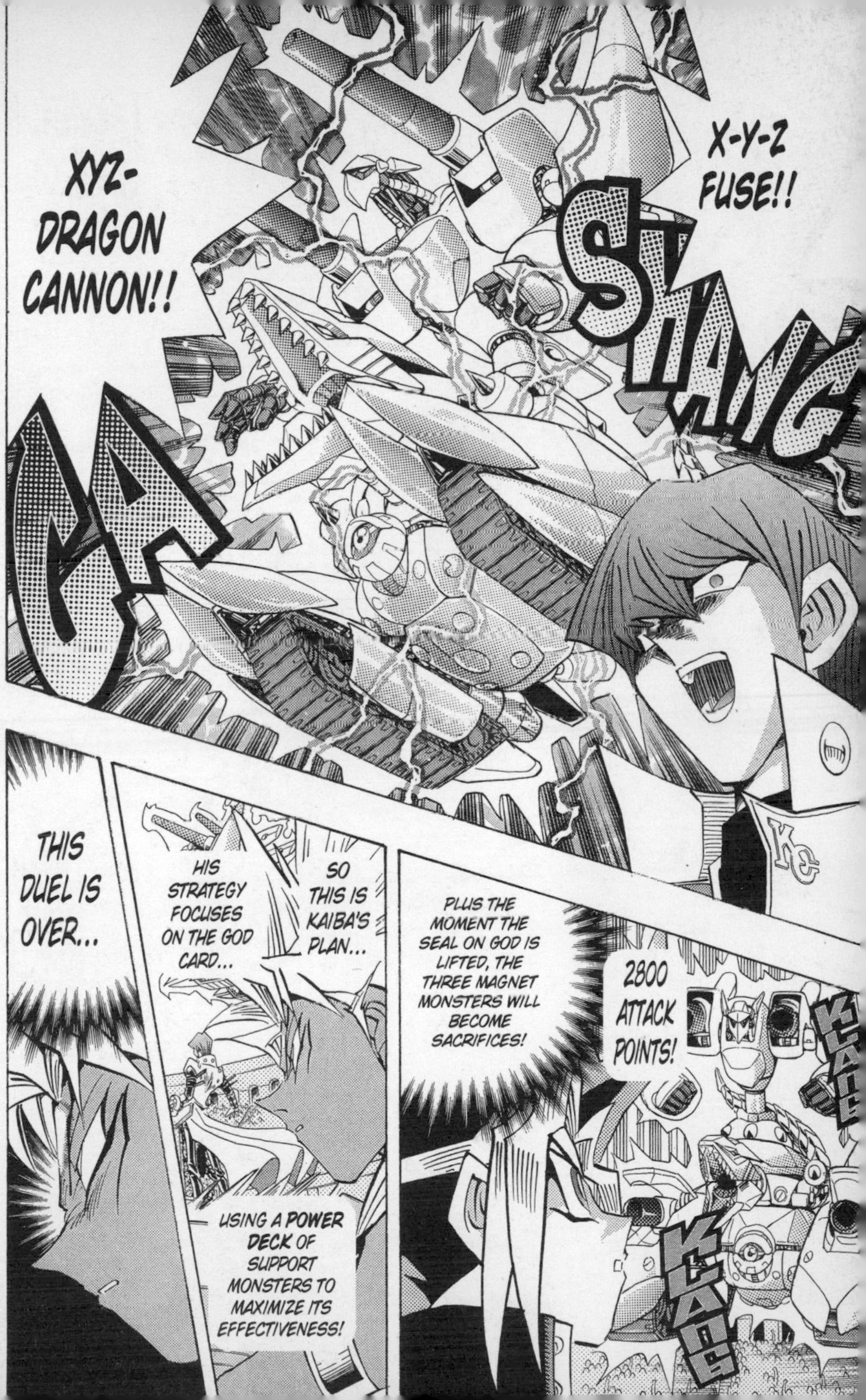

X-Y-Z FUSE!!
SHANG
XYZ-DRAGON CANNON!!
CA
2800 ATTACK POINTS!
PLUS THE MOMENT THE SEAL ON GOD IS LIFTED, THE THREE MAGNET MONSTERS WILL BECOME SACRIFICES!
SO THIS IS KAIBA'S PLAN...
HIS STRATEGY FOCUSES ON THE GOD CARD...
USING A POWER DECK OF SUPPORT MONSTERS TO MAXIMIZE ITS EFFECTIVENESS!
THIS DUEL IS OVER...

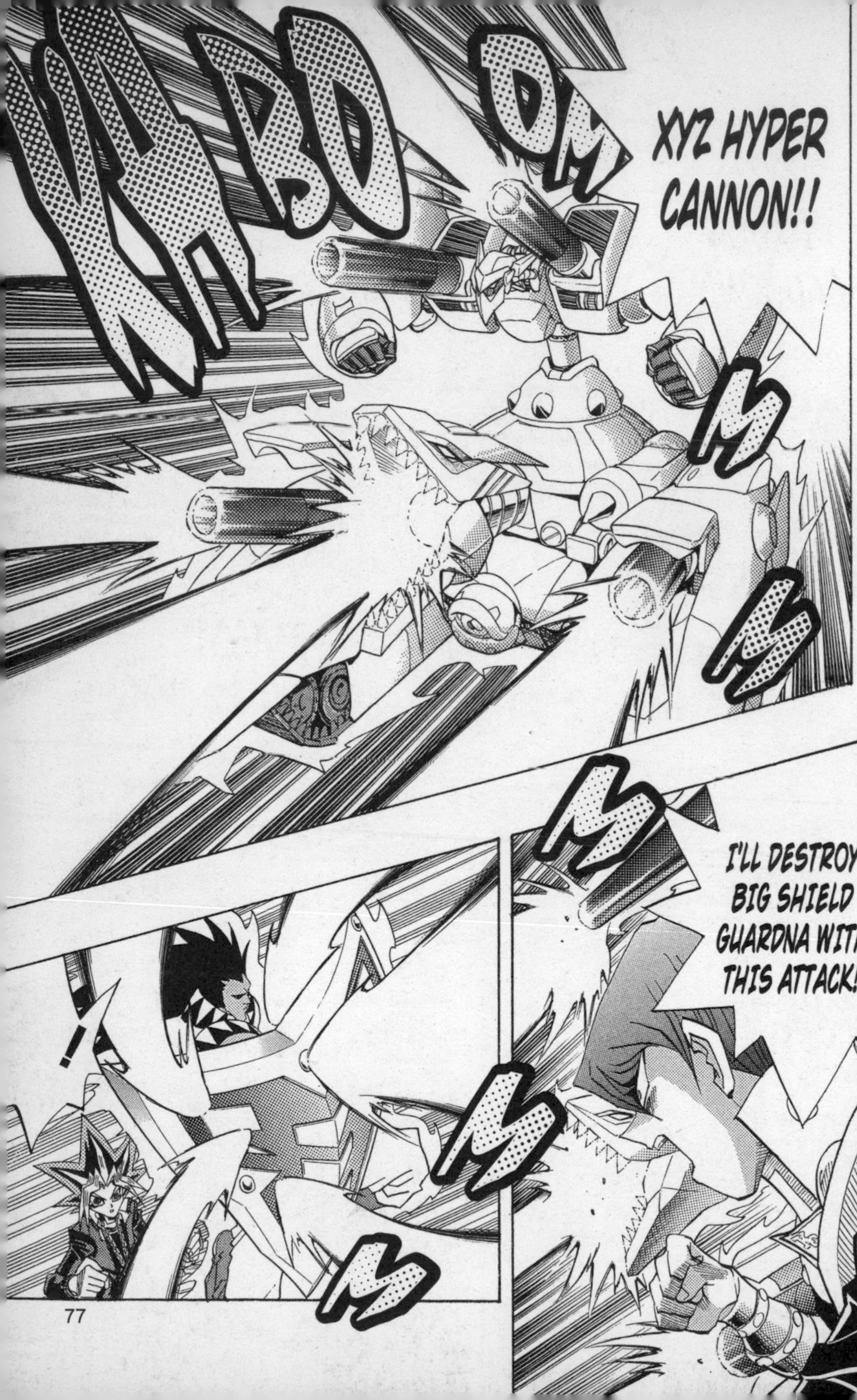
XYZ HYPER CANNON!!
I'LL DESTROY BIG SHIELD GUARDNA WITH THIS ATTACK!
!

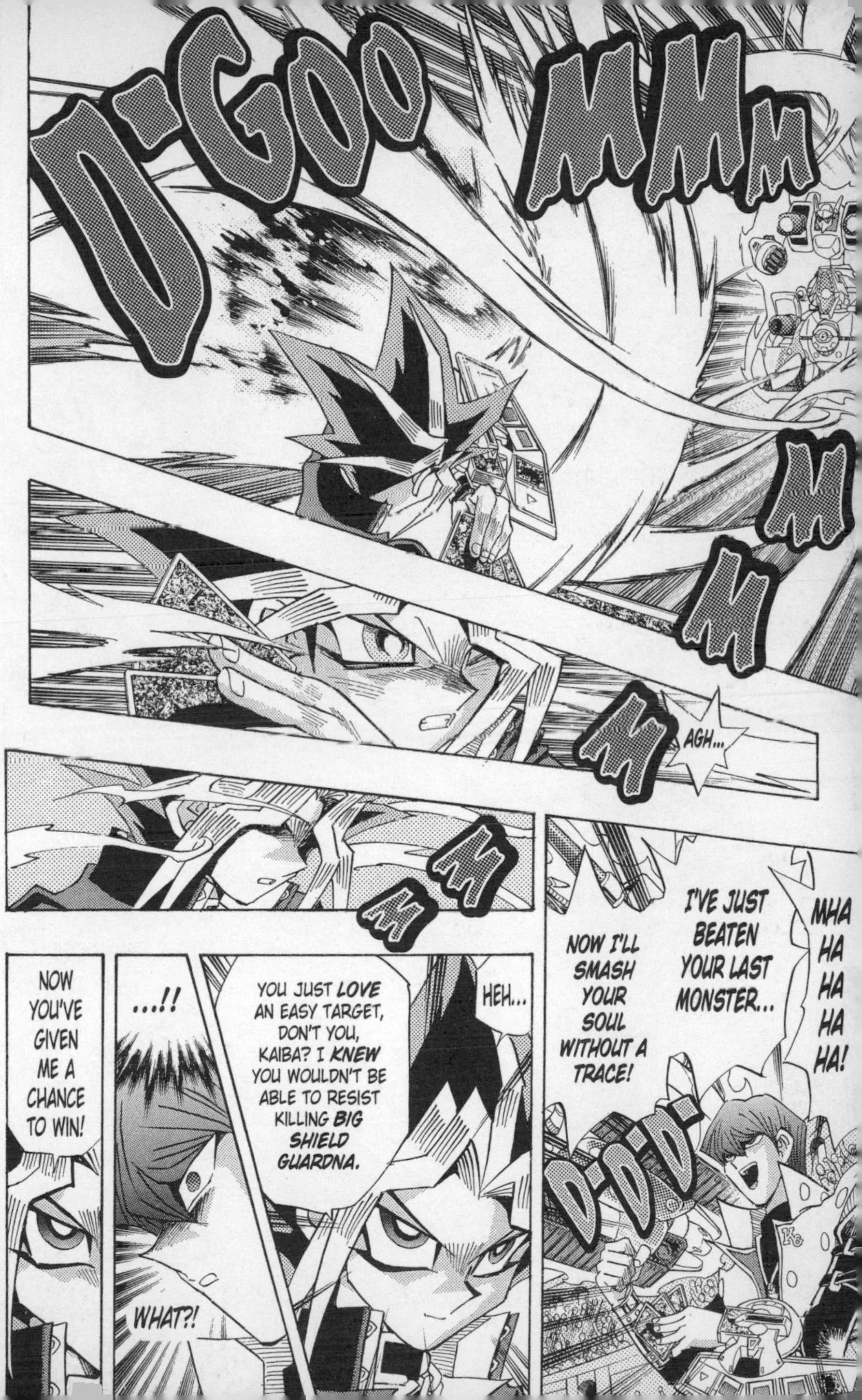
D-GOO MMMM
MMMMMM
AGH...
MHA HA HA HA HA!
I'VE JUST BEATEN YOUR LAST MONSTER...
NOW I'LL SMASH YOUR SOUL WITHOUT A TRACE!
D-D-D
HEH...
YOU JUST *LOVE* AN EASY TARGET, DON'T YOU, KAIBA? I *KNEW* YOU WOULDN'T BE ABLE TO RESIST KILLING *BIG SHIELD GUARDNA.*
...!!
NOW YOU'VE GIVEN ME A CHANCE TO WIN!
WHAT?!

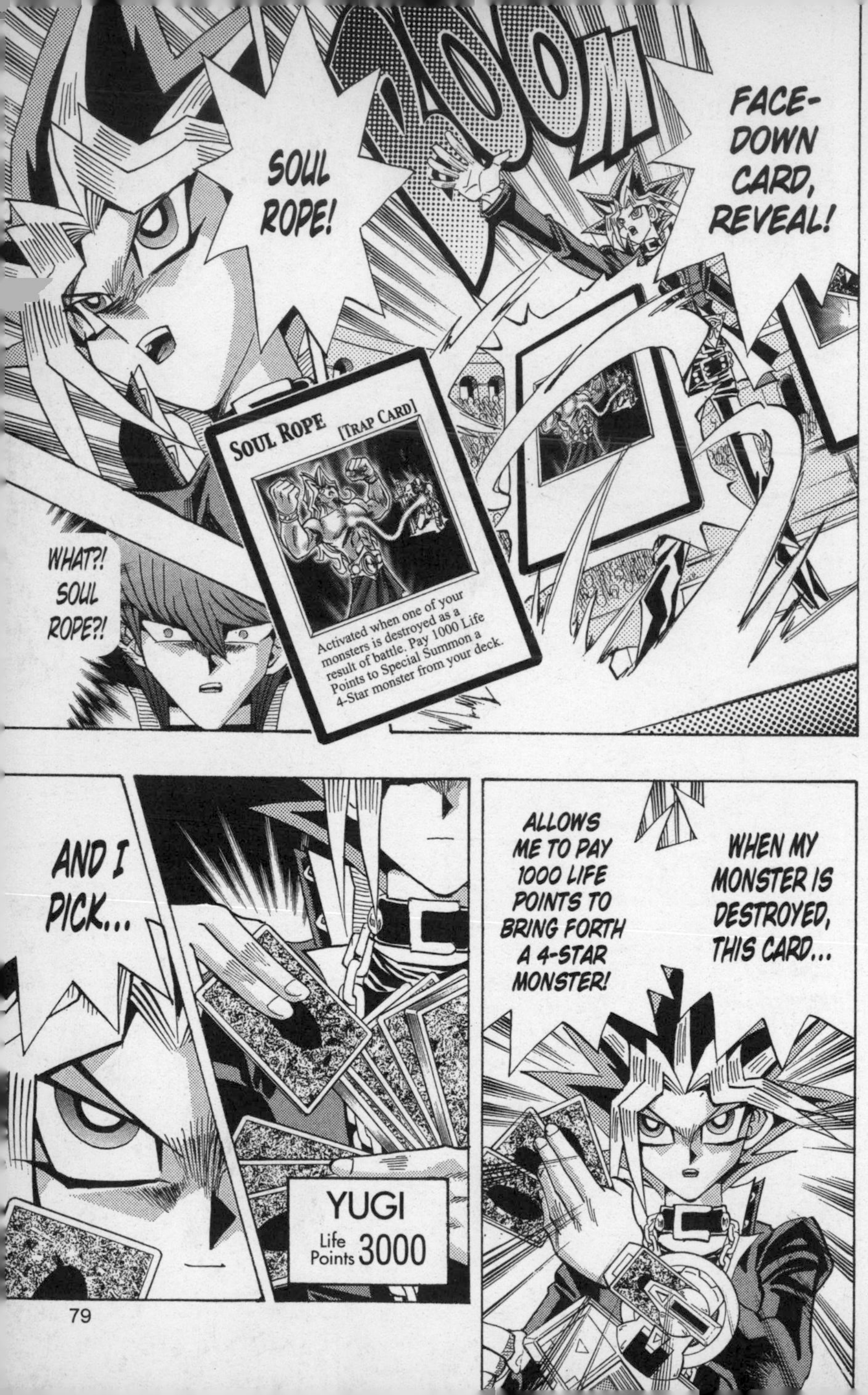
FACE-DOWN CARD, REVEAL!
DOOM
SOUL ROPE!
SOUL ROPE [TRAP CARD]
Activated when one of your monsters is destroyed as a result of battle. Pay 1000 Life Points to Special Summon a 4-Star monster from your deck.
WHAT?! SOUL ROPE?!
WHEN MY MONSTER IS DESTROYED, THIS CARD...
ALLOWS ME TO PAY 1000 LIFE POINTS TO BRING FORTH A 4-STAR MONSTER!
AND I PICK...
YUGI
Life Points 3000

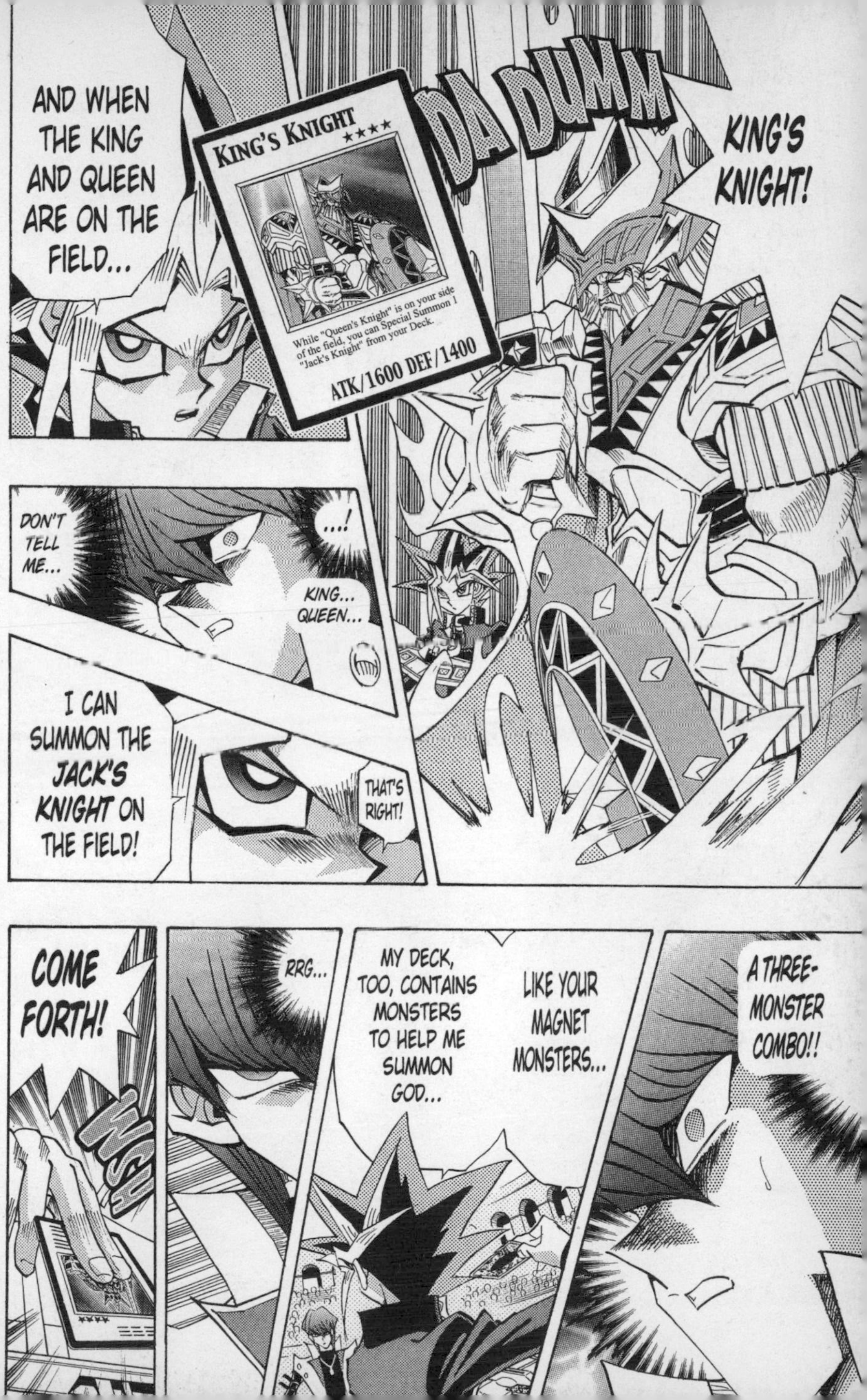
DA DUMM
KING'S KNIGHT!
AND WHEN THE KING AND QUEEN ARE ON THE FIELD...
KING'S KNIGHT ★★★★
While "Queen's Knight" is on your side of the field, you can Special Summon 1 "Jack's Knight" from your Deck.
ATK/1600 DEF/1400
...!
DON'T TELL ME...
KING... QUEEN...
I CAN SUMMON THE JACK'S KNIGHT ON THE FIELD!
THAT'S RIGHT!
A THREE-MONSTER COMBO!!
MY DECK, TOO, CONTAINS MONSTERS TO HELP ME SUMMON GOD...
LIKE YOUR MAGNET MONSTERS...
RRG...
COME FORTH!
WSH

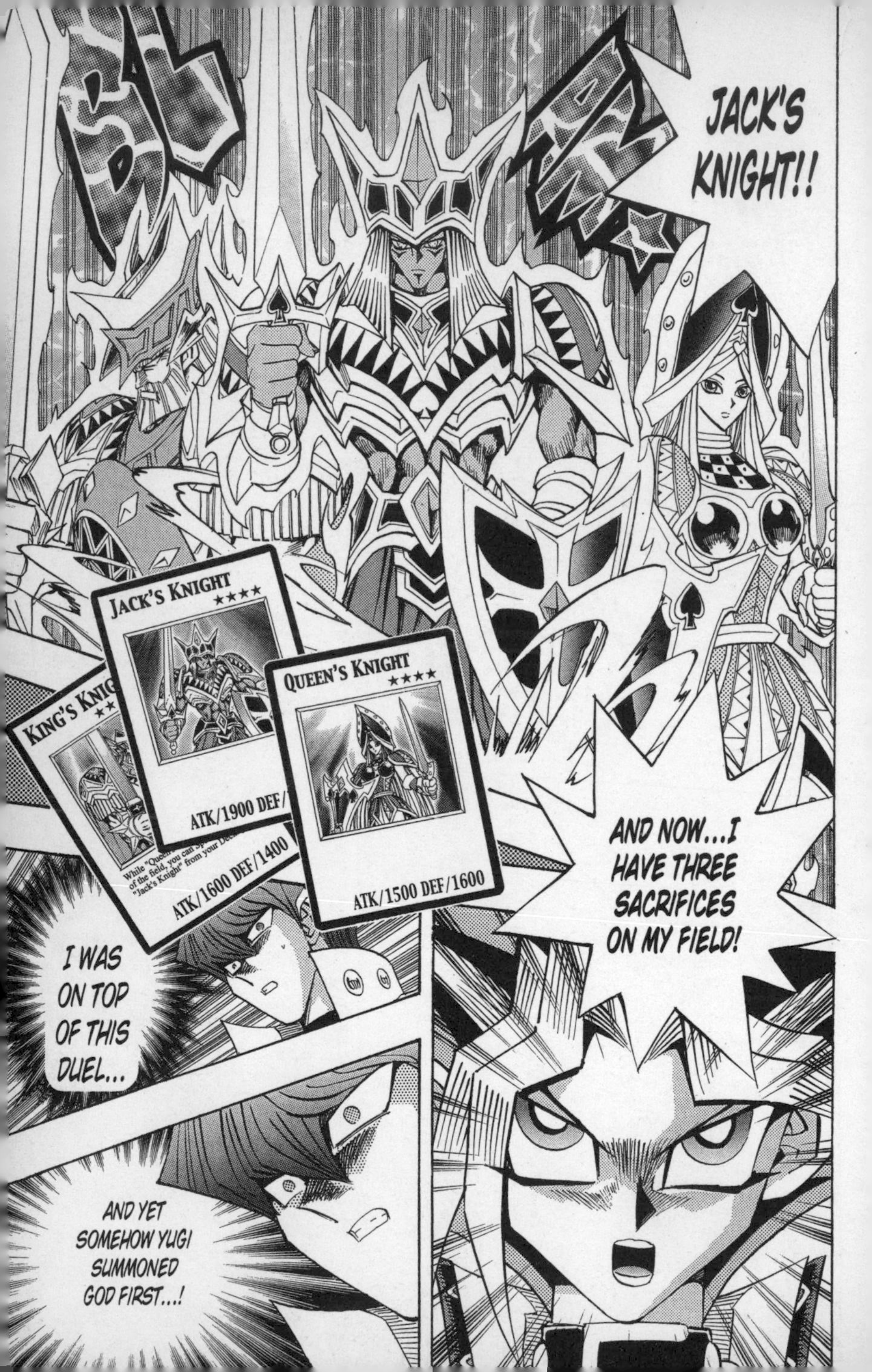
JACK'S KNIGHT!!
JACK'S KNIGHT
QUEEN'S KNIGHT
ATK/1500 DEF/1600
ATK/1600 DEF/1400
AND NOW...I HAVE THREE SACRIFICES ON MY FIELD!
I WAS ON TOP OF THIS DUEL...
AND YET SOMEHOW YUGI SUMMONED GOD FIRST...!

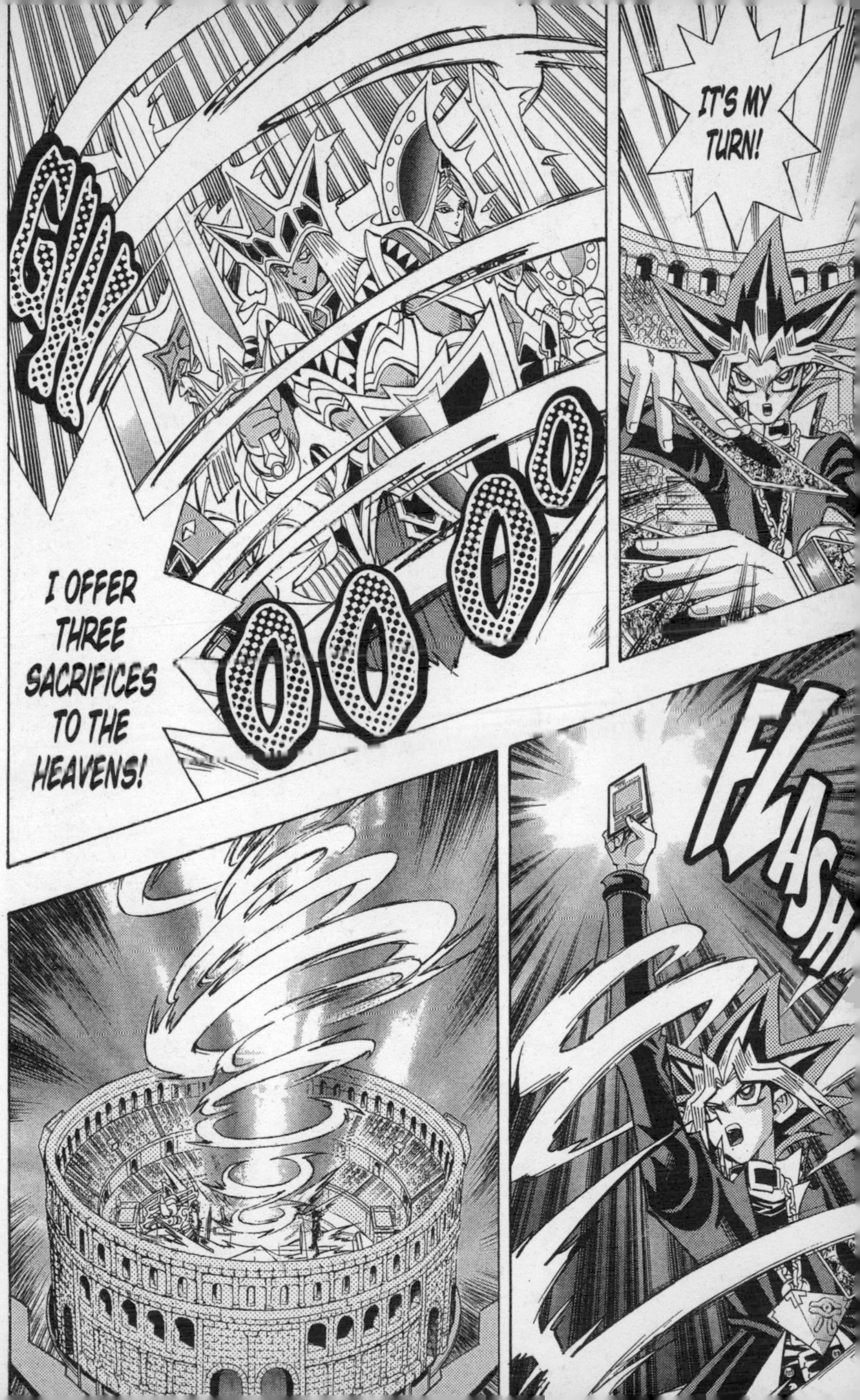
IT'S MY TURN!
I OFFER THREE SACRIFICES TO THE HEAVENS!
FLASH

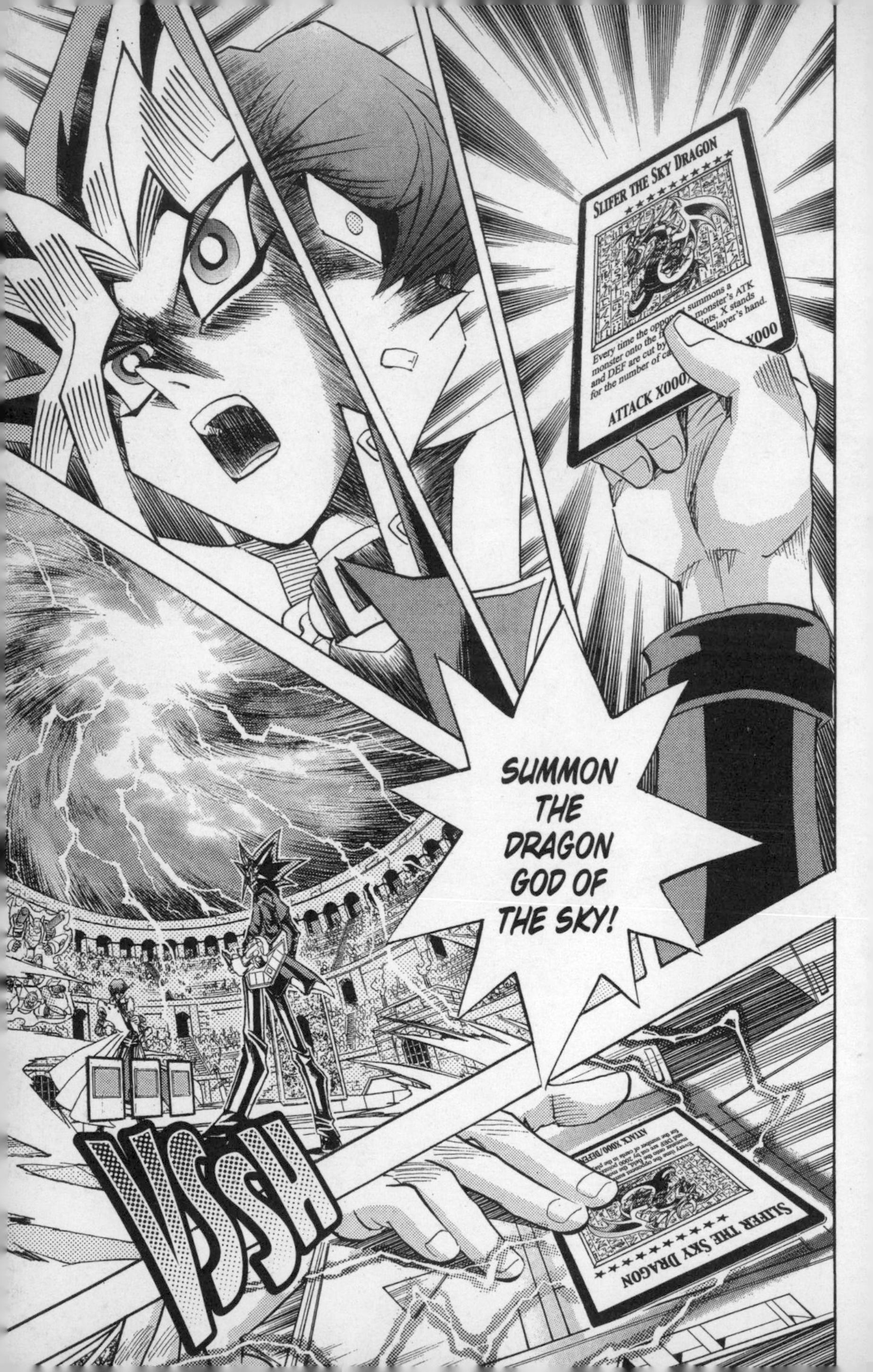
SLIFER THE SKY DRAGON
SUMMON THE DRAGON GOD OF THE SKY!
VSSH
SLIFER THE SKY DRAGON

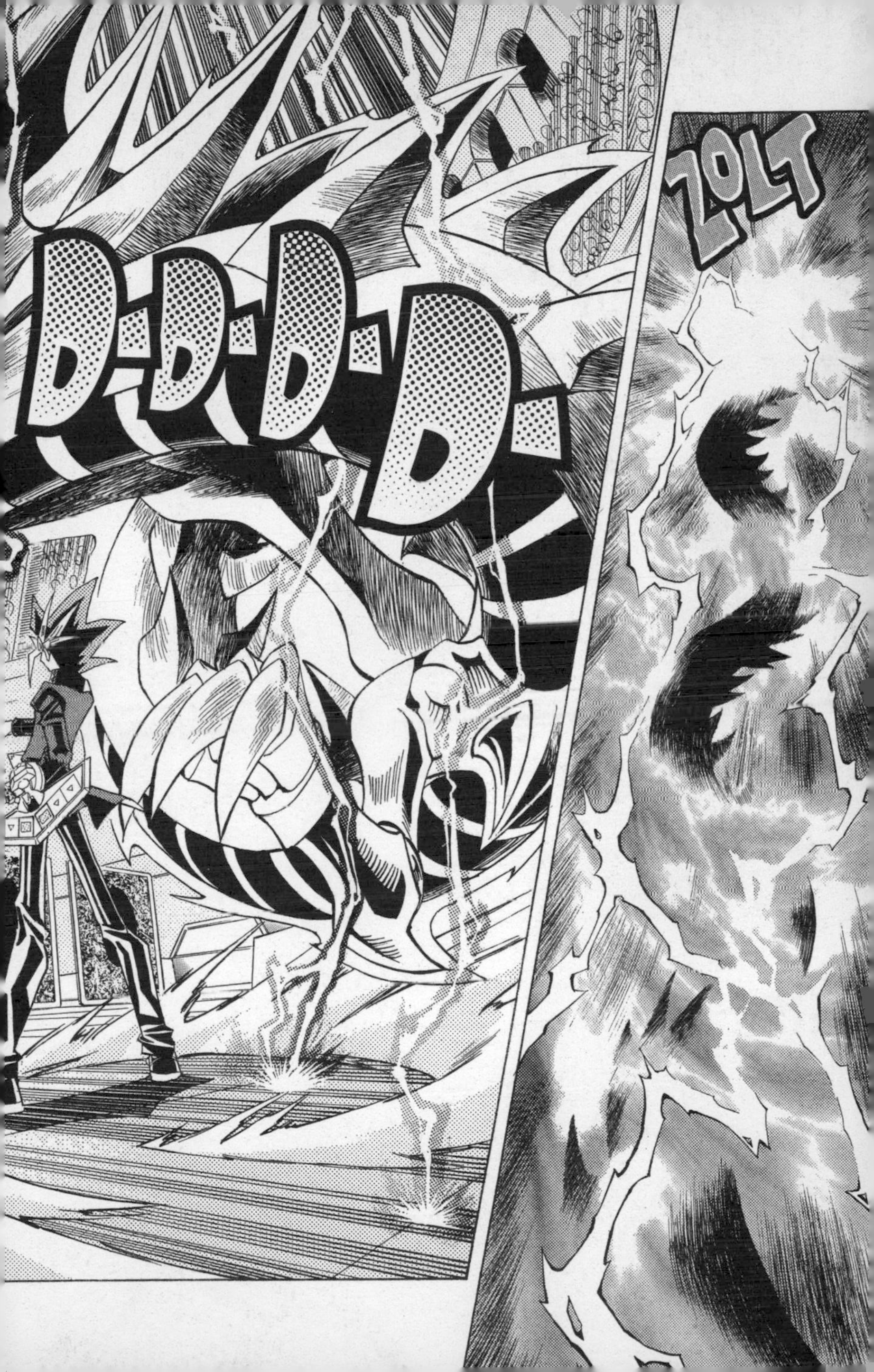
ZOLT
D-D-D-D-

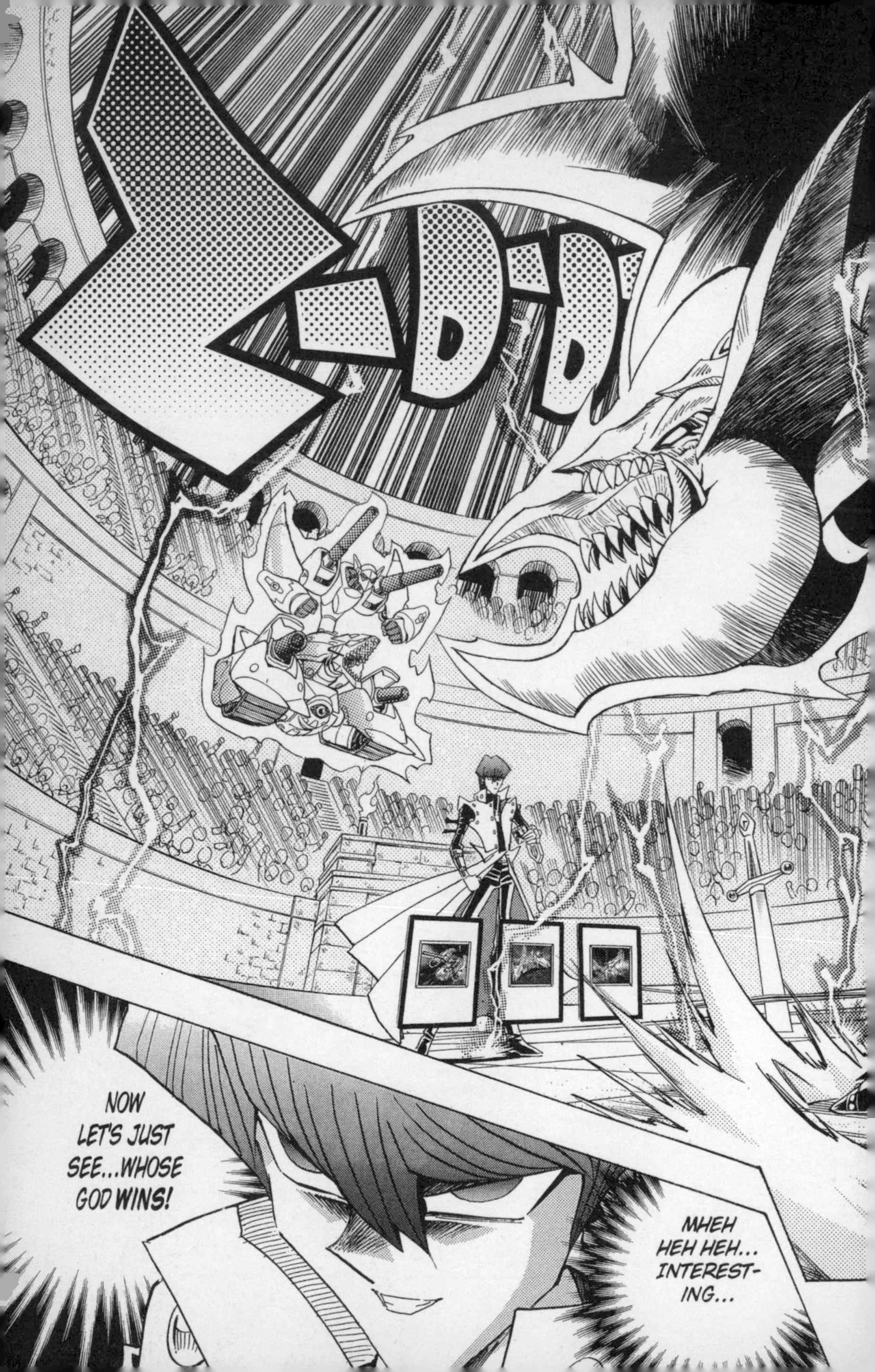
MHEH HEH HEH... INTERESTING...
NOW LET'S JUST SEE...WHOSE GOD WINS!

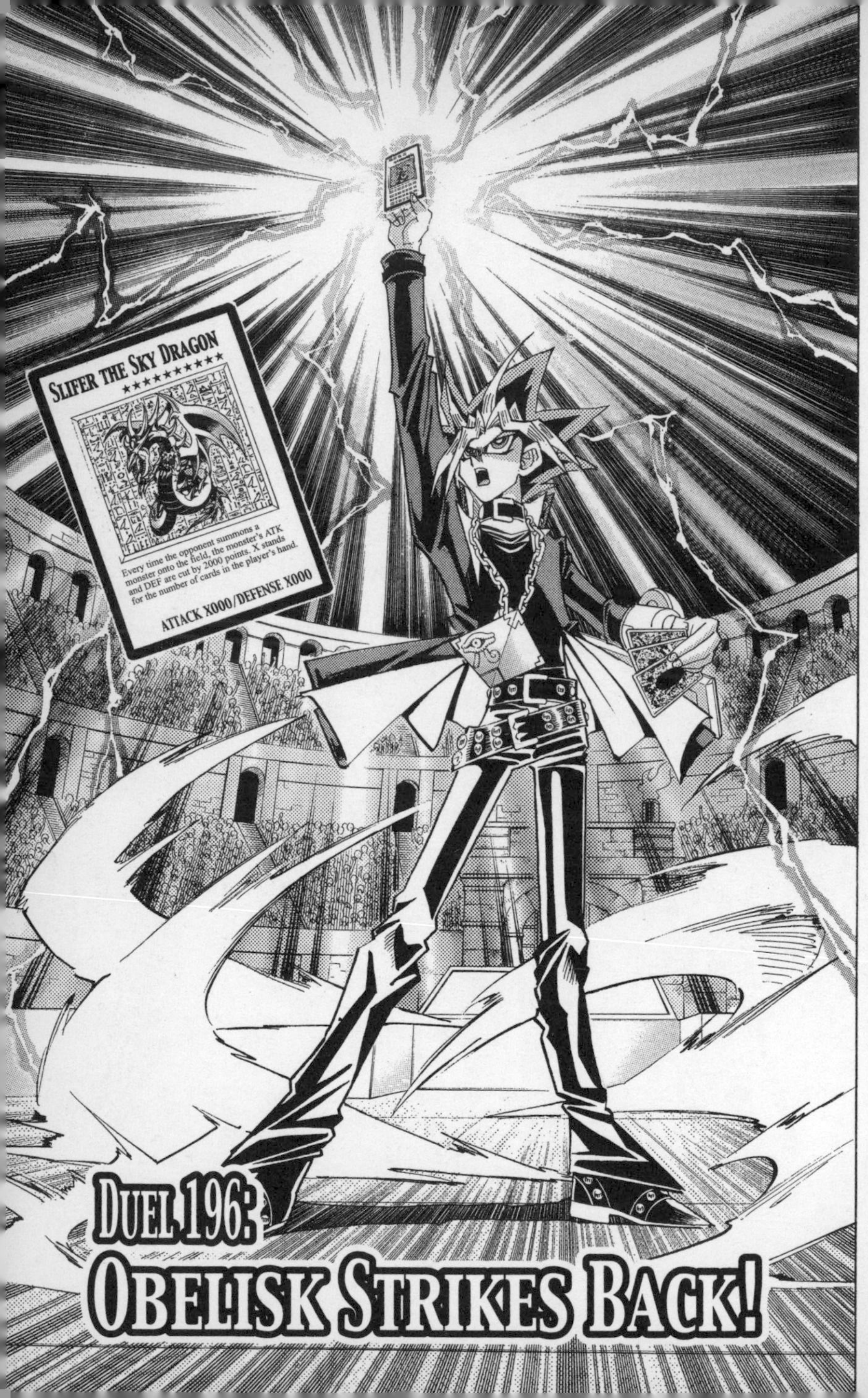
SLIFER THE SKY DRAGON
★★★★★★★★★★
Every time the opponent summons a monster onto the field, the monster's ATK and DEF are cut by 2000 points. X stands for the number of cards in the player's hand.
ATTACK X000/DEFENSE X000
DUEL 196:
OBELISK STRIKES BACK!

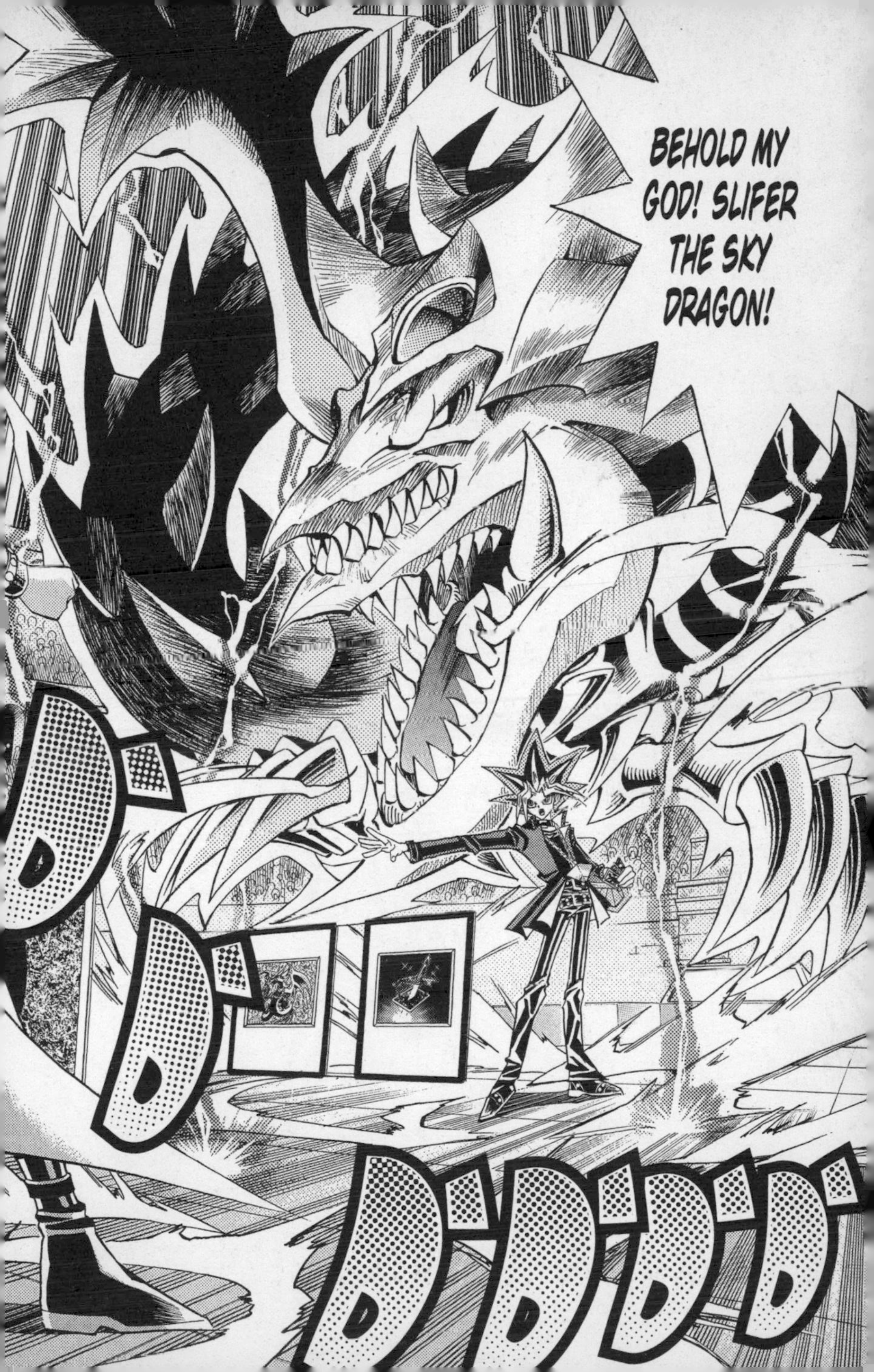
BEHOLD MY GOD! SLIFER THE SKY DRAGON!

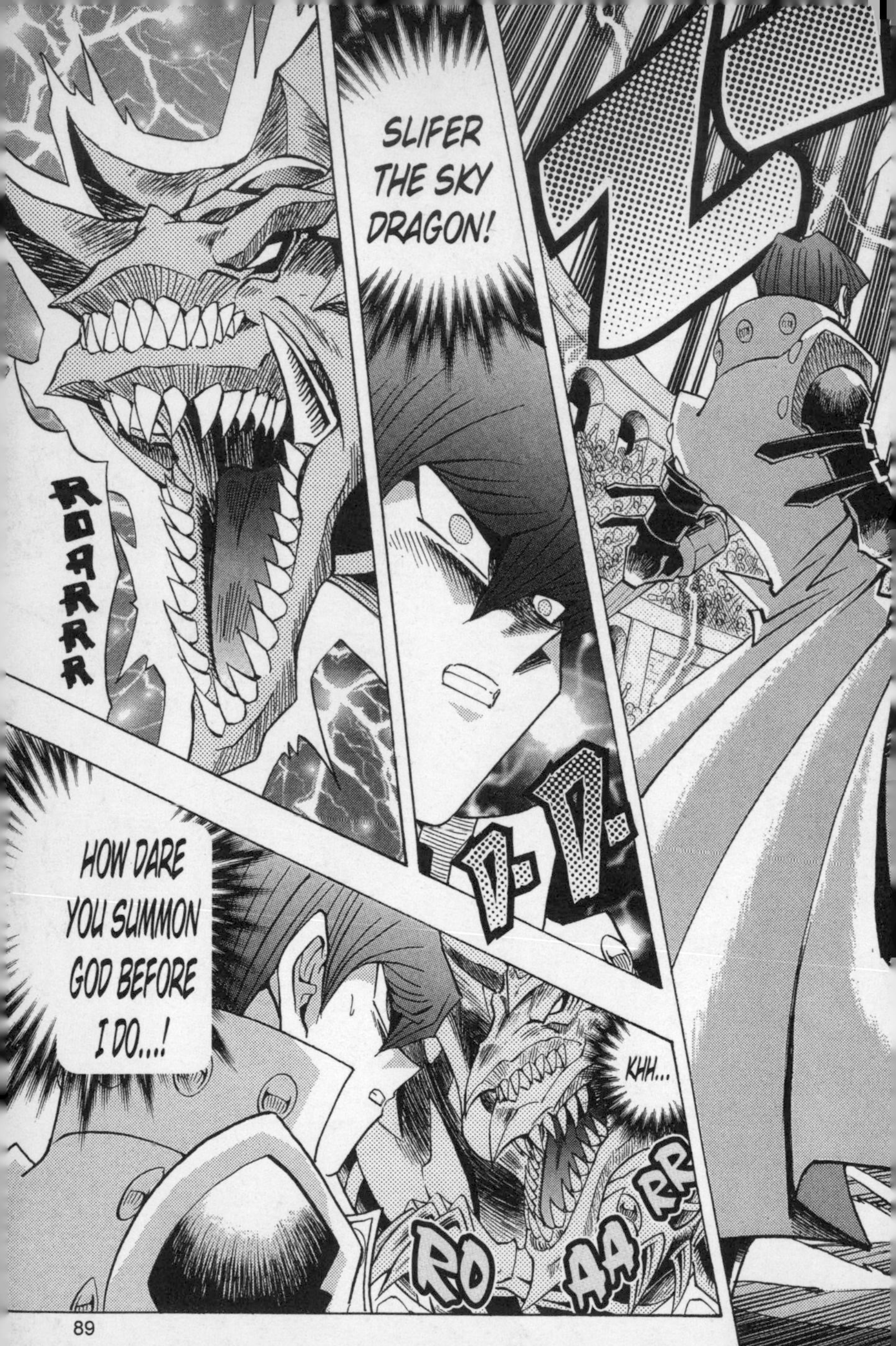
SLIFER THE SKY DRAGON!
D-D-
ROARRRR
KHH...
HOW DARE YOU SUMMON GOD BEFORE I DO...!
ROAARR

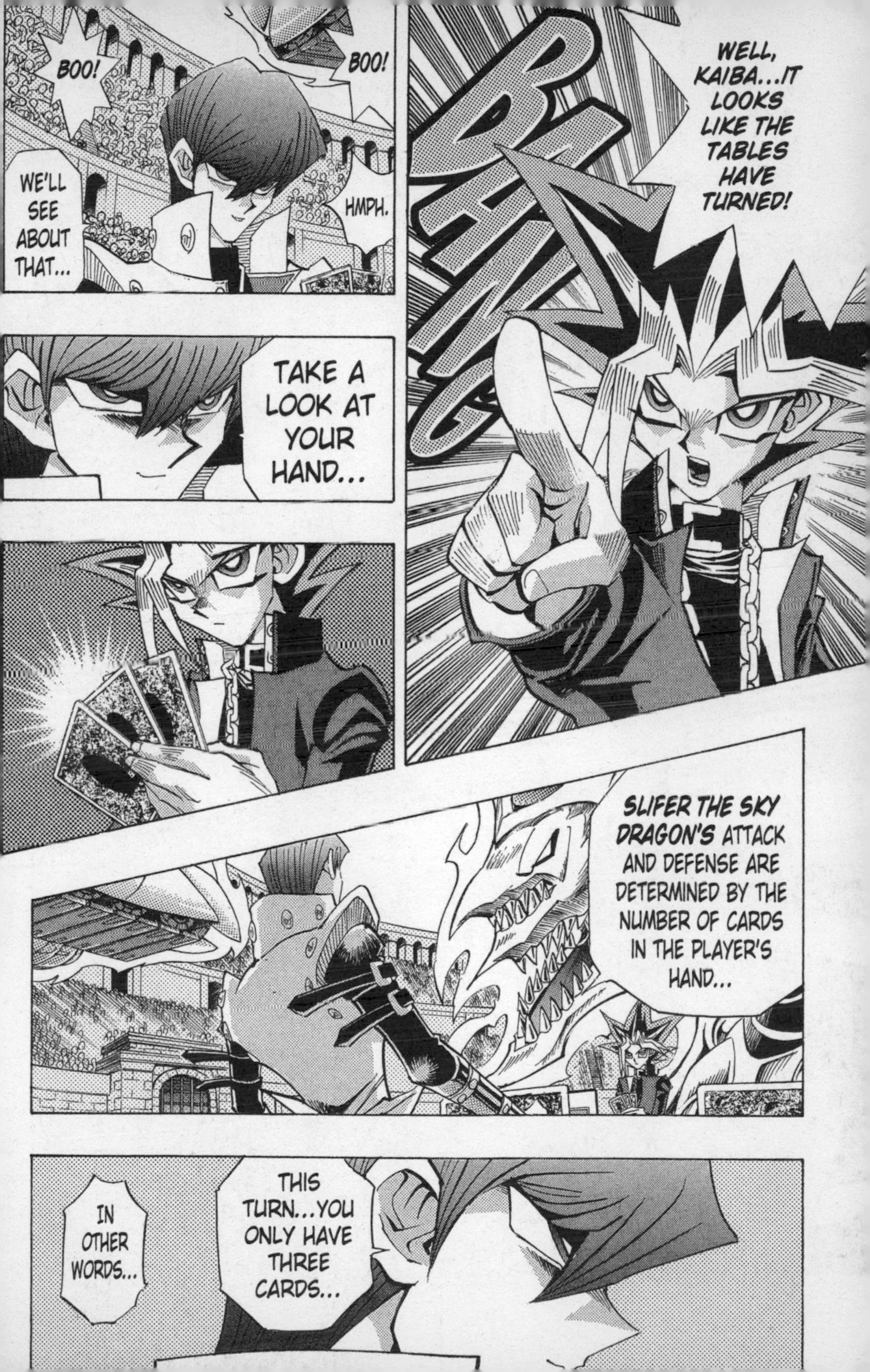
WELL, KAIBA...IT LOOKS LIKE THE TABLES HAVE TURNED!
BOO!
BOO!
HMPH.
WE'LL SEE ABOUT THAT...
TAKE A LOOK AT YOUR HAND...
SLIFER THE SKY DRAGON'S ATTACK AND DEFENSE ARE DETERMINED BY THE NUMBER OF CARDS IN THE PLAYER'S HAND...
THIS TURN...YOU ONLY HAVE THREE CARDS...
IN OTHER WORDS...

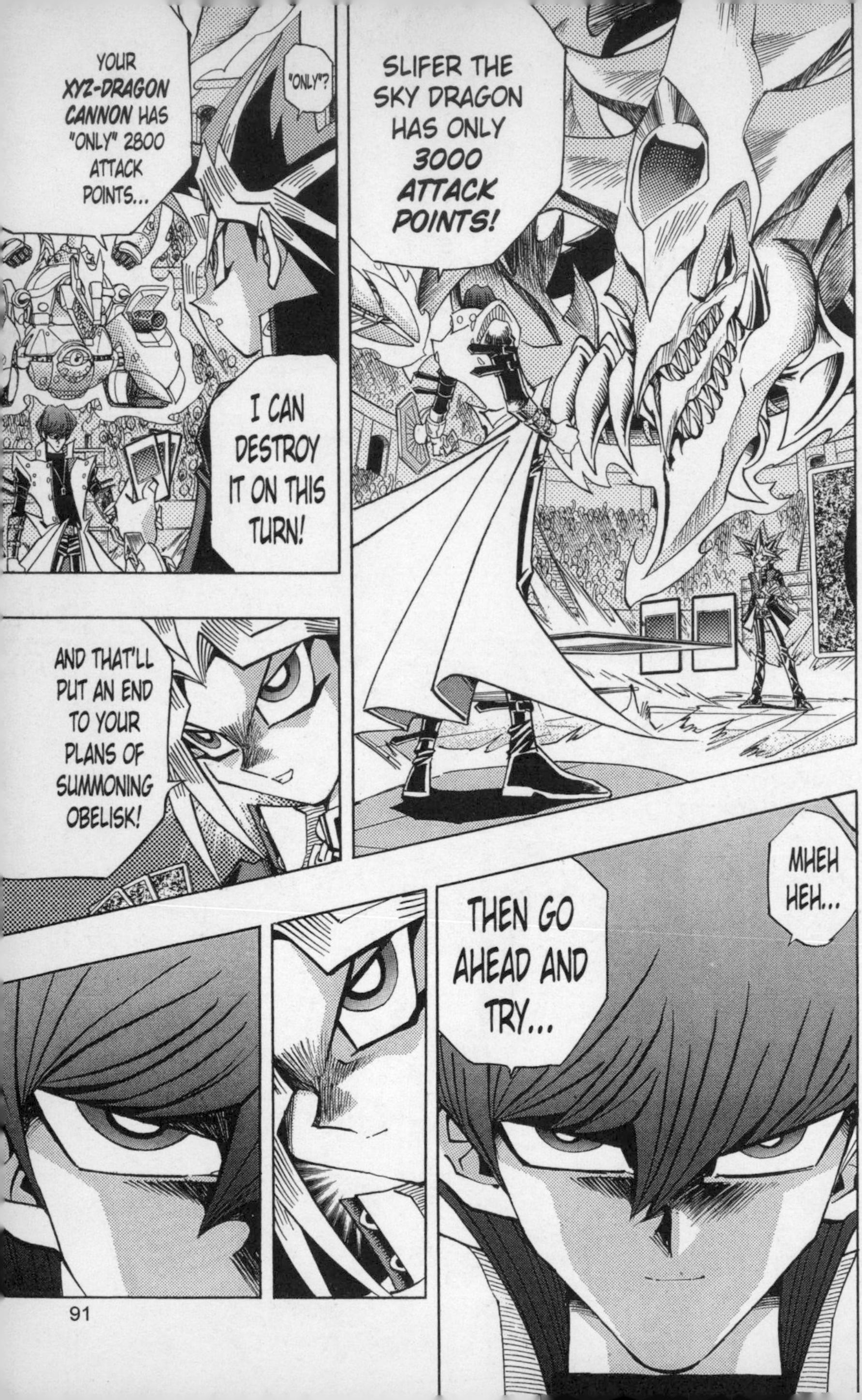
SLIFER THE SKY DRAGON HAS ONLY 3000 ATTACK POINTS!
"ONLY"?
YOUR XYZ-DRAGON CANNON HAS "ONLY" 2800 ATTACK POINTS...
I CAN DESTROY IT ON THIS TURN!
AND THAT'LL PUT AN END TO YOUR PLANS OF SUMMONING OBELISK!
MHEH HEH...
THEN GO AHEAD AND TRY...

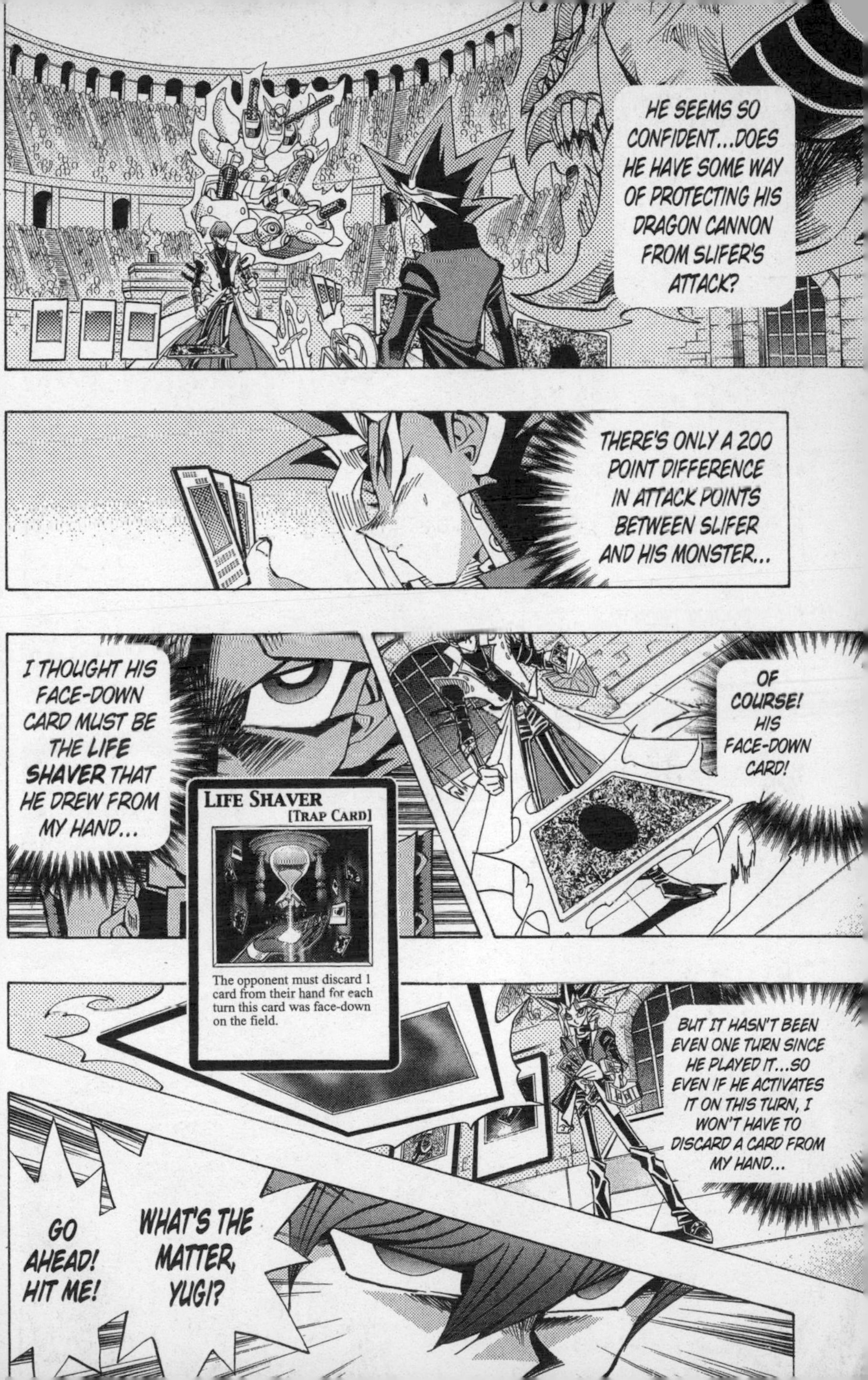
HE SEEMS SO CONFIDENT...DOES HE HAVE SOME WAY OF PROTECTING HIS DRAGON CANNON FROM SLIFER'S ATTACK?
THERE'S ONLY A 200 POINT DIFFERENCE IN ATTACK POINTS BETWEEN SLIFER AND HIS MONSTER...
OF COURSE! HIS FACE-DOWN CARD!
I THOUGHT HIS FACE-DOWN CARD MUST BE THE LIFE SHAVER THAT HE DREW FROM MY HAND...
LIFE SHAVER
[TRAP CARD]
The opponent must discard 1 card from their hand for each turn this card was face-down on the field.
BUT IT HASN'T BEEN EVEN ONE TURN SINCE HE PLAYED IT...SO EVEN IF HE ACTIVATES IT ON THIS TURN, I WON'T HAVE TO DISCARD A CARD FROM MY HAND...
WHAT'S THE MATTER, YUGI?
GO AHEAD! HIT ME!

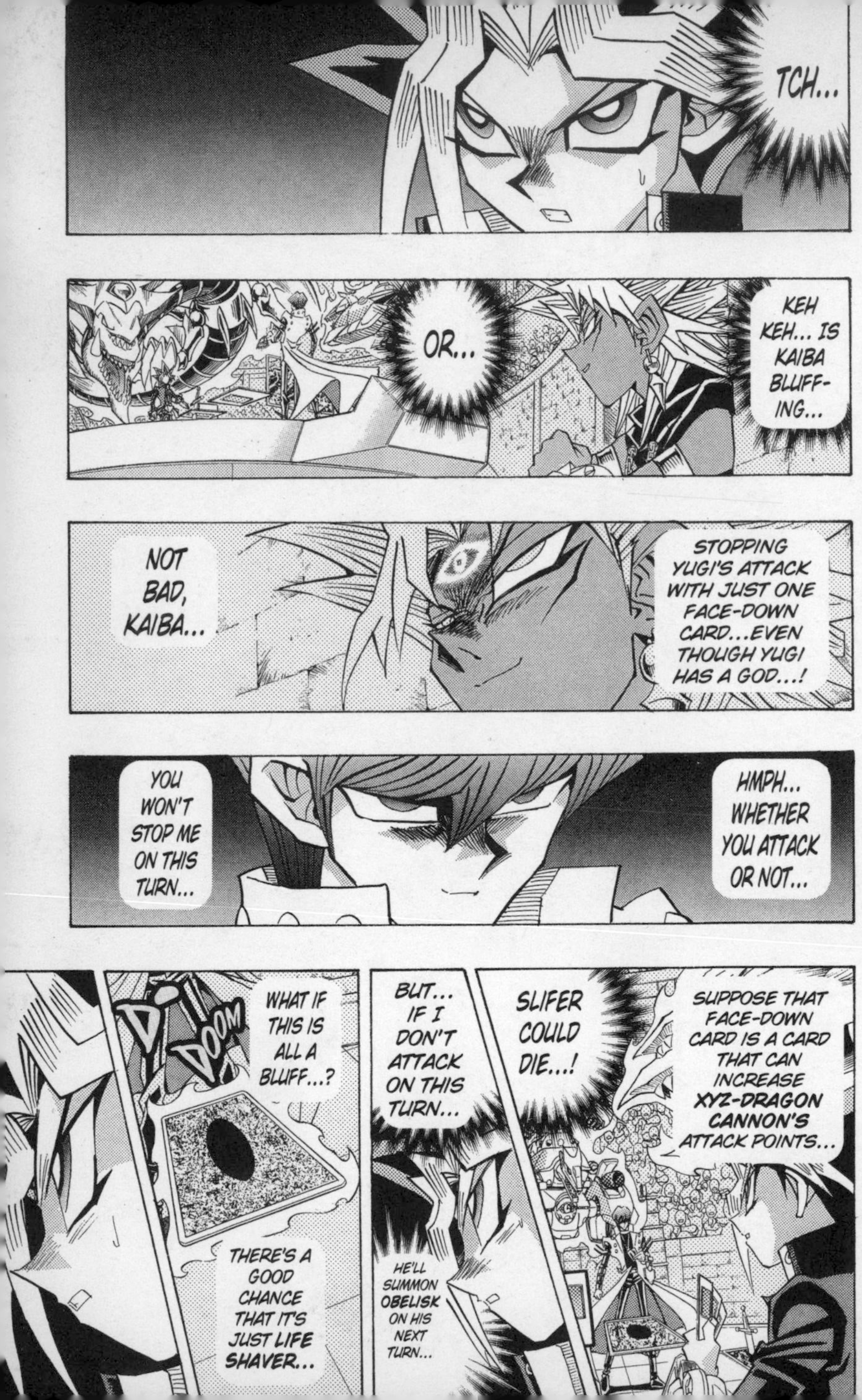
TCH...
KEH KEH... IS KAIBA BLUFFING...
OR...
STOPPING YUGI'S ATTACK WITH JUST ONE FACE-DOWN CARD...EVEN THOUGH YUGI HAS A GOD...!
NOT BAD, KAIBA...
HMPH... WHETHER YOU ATTACK OR NOT...
YOU WON'T STOP ME ON THIS TURN...
SUPPOSE THAT FACE-DOWN CARD IS A CARD THAT CAN INCREASE **XYZ-DRAGON CANNON'S** ATTACK POINTS...
SLIFER COULD DIE...!
BUT... IF I DON'T ATTACK ON THIS TURN...
HE'LL SUMMON OBELISK ON HIS NEXT TURN...
D DOOM
WHAT IF THIS IS ALL A BLUFF...?
THERE'S A GOOD CHANCE THAT IT'S JUST **LIFE SHAVER**...

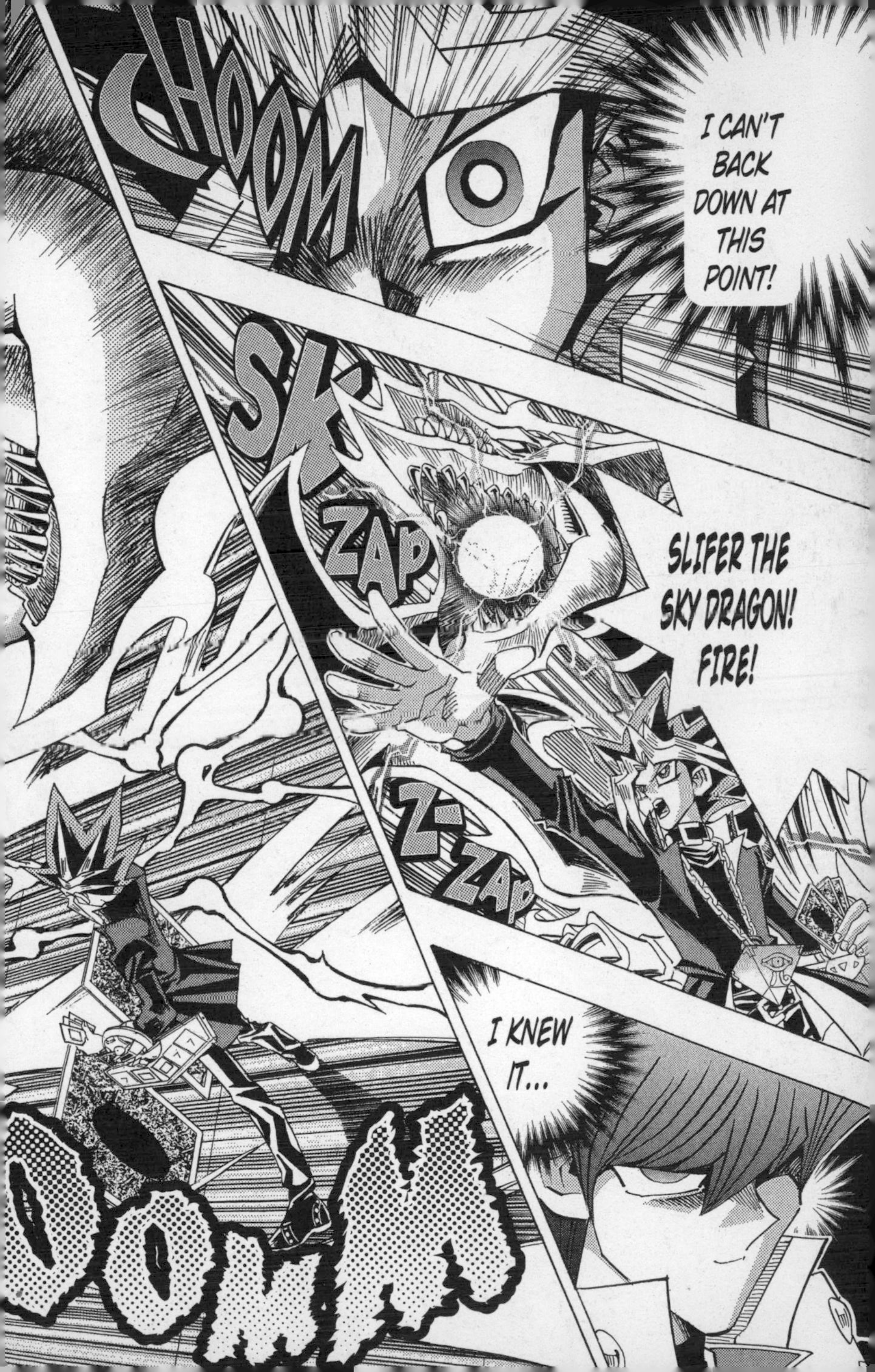
CHOOM
I CAN'T BACK DOWN AT THIS POINT!
SK
ZAP
SLIFER THE SKY DRAGON! FIRE!
Z-ZAP
I KNEW IT...
DOOM

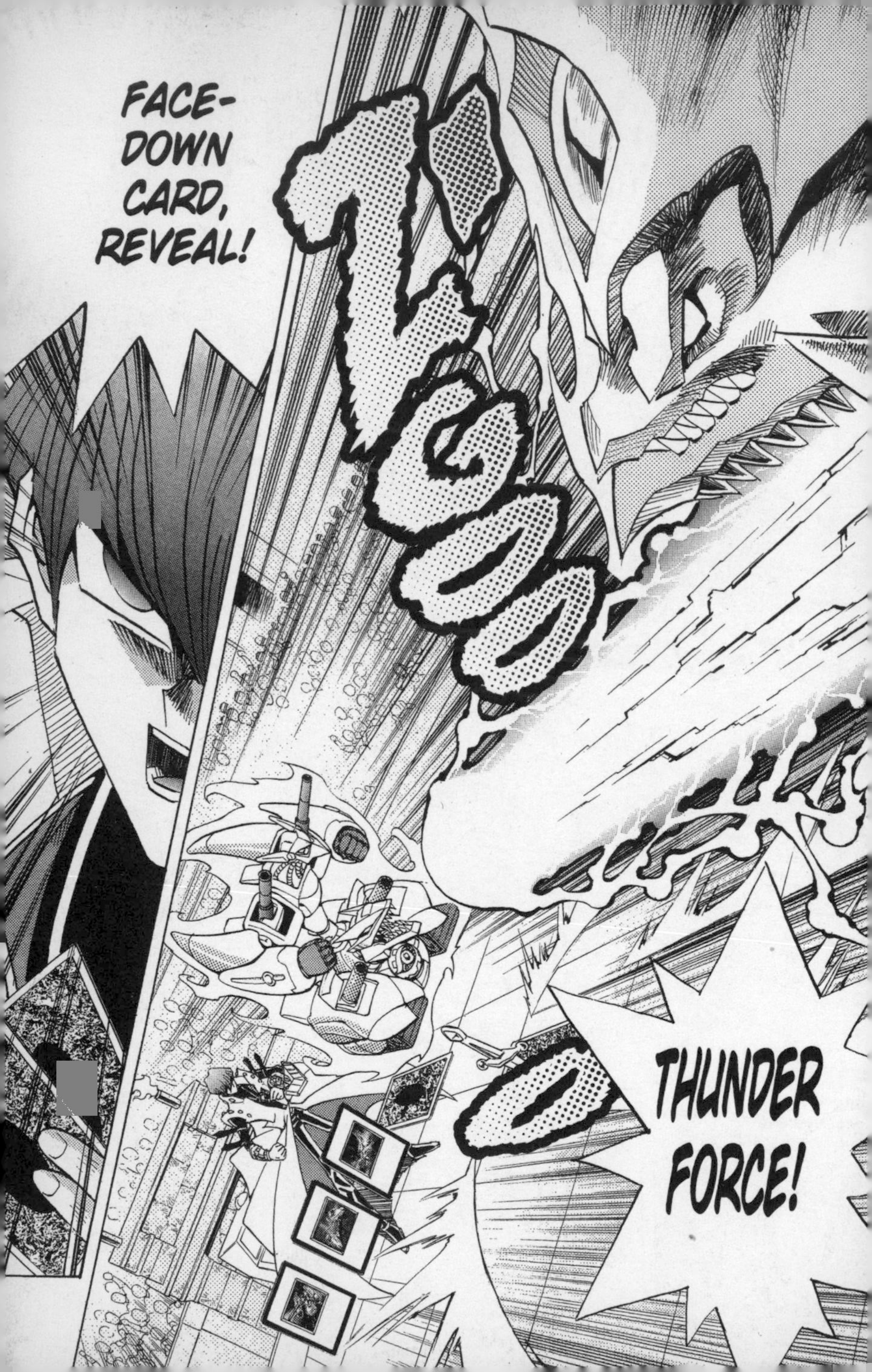
THUNDER FORCE!
FACE-DOWN CARD, REVEAL!

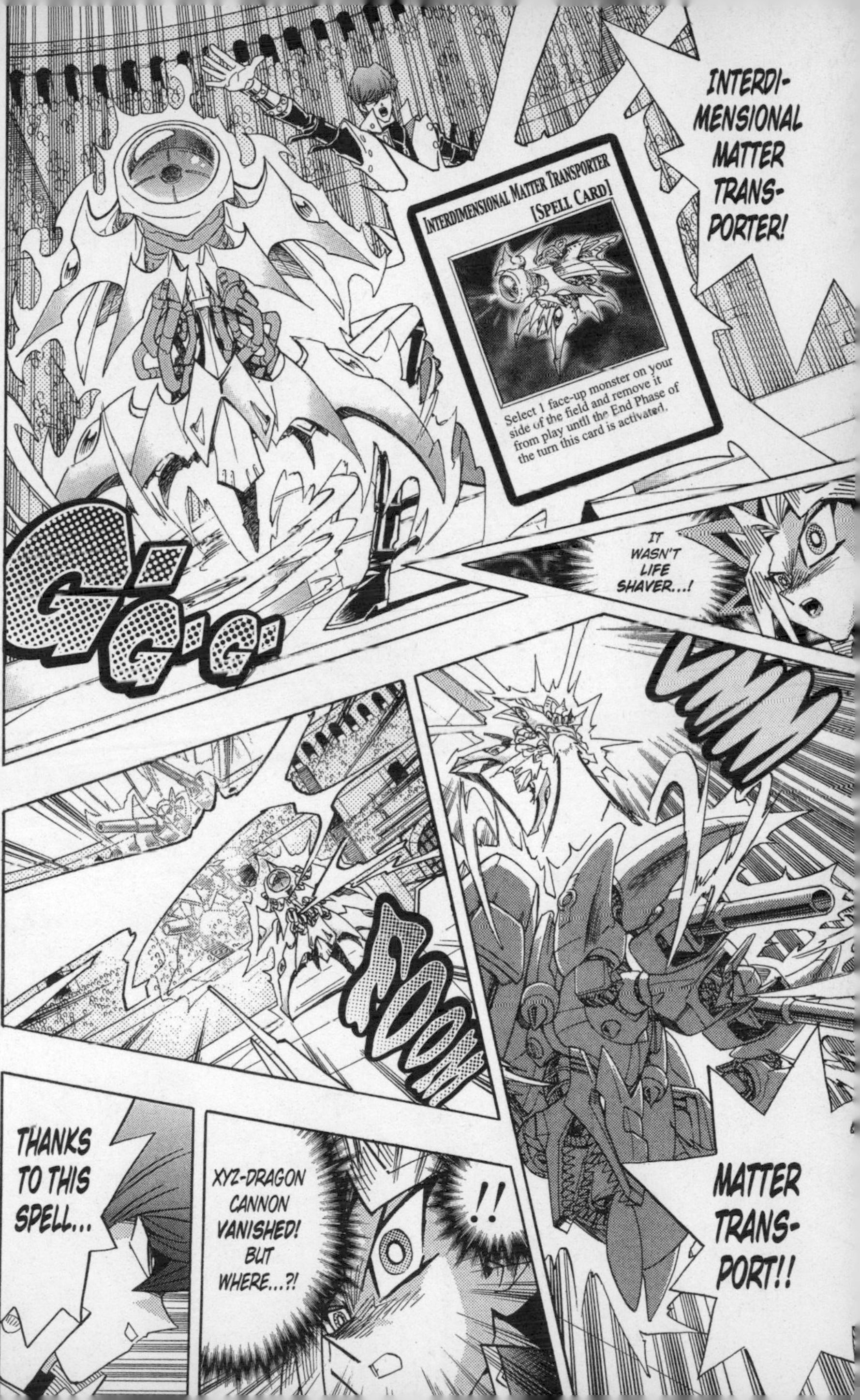
INTERDIMENSIONAL MATTER TRANSPORTER!
INTERDIMENSIONAL MATTER TRANSPORTER
[SPELL CARD]
Select 1 face-up monster on your side of the field and remove it from play until the End Phase of the turn this card is activated.
G'G'G'
IT WASN'T LIFE SHAVER...!
MATTER TRANS-PORT!!
!!
XYZ-DRAGON CANNON VANISHED! BUT WHERE...?!
THANKS TO THIS SPELL...

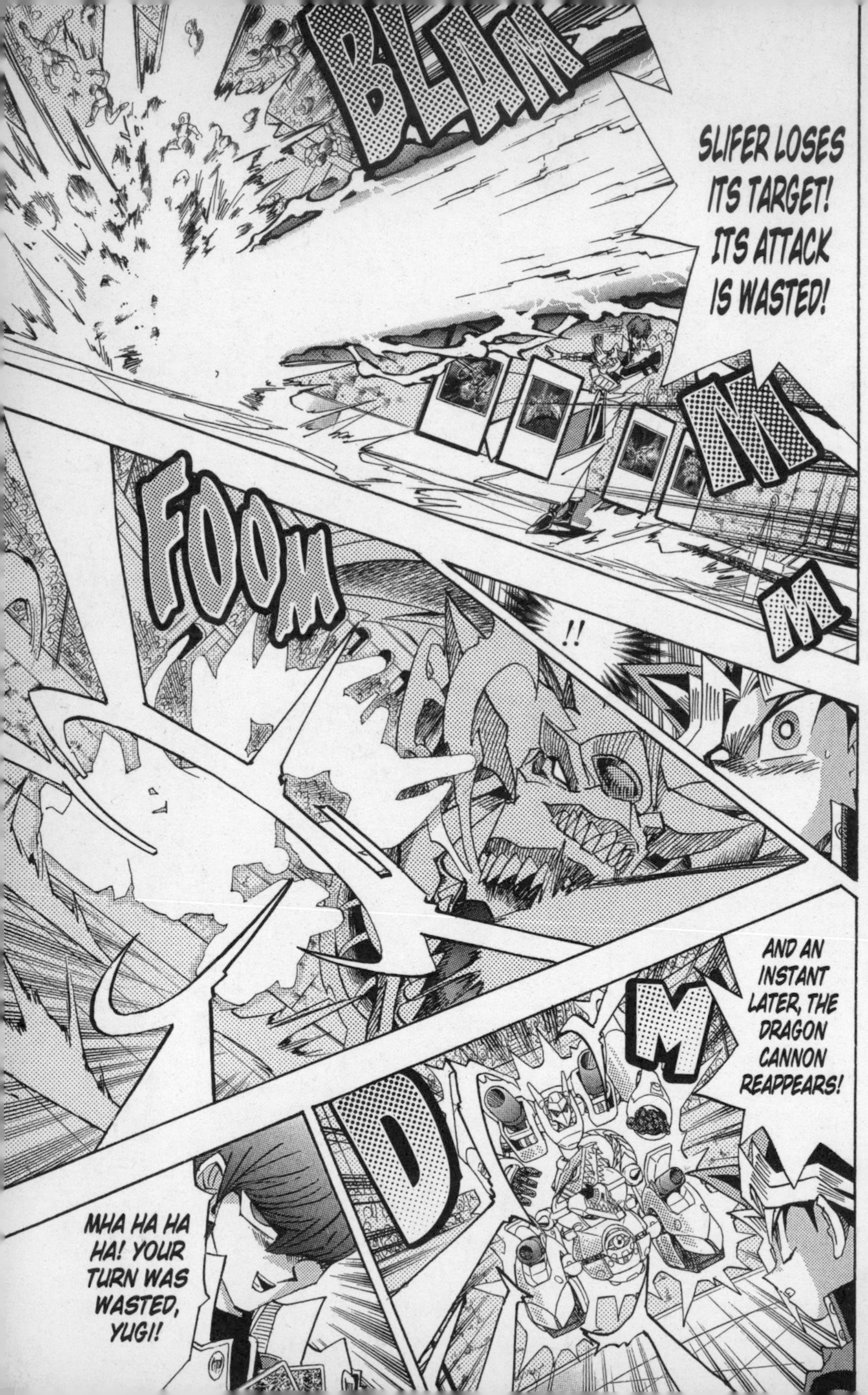
BLAM
SLIFER LOSES ITS TARGET! ITS ATTACK IS WASTED!
M
M
M
FOOM
!!
AND AN INSTANT LATER, THE DRAGON CANNON REAPPEARS!
M
D
MHA HA HA HA! YOUR TURN WAS WASTED, YUGI!

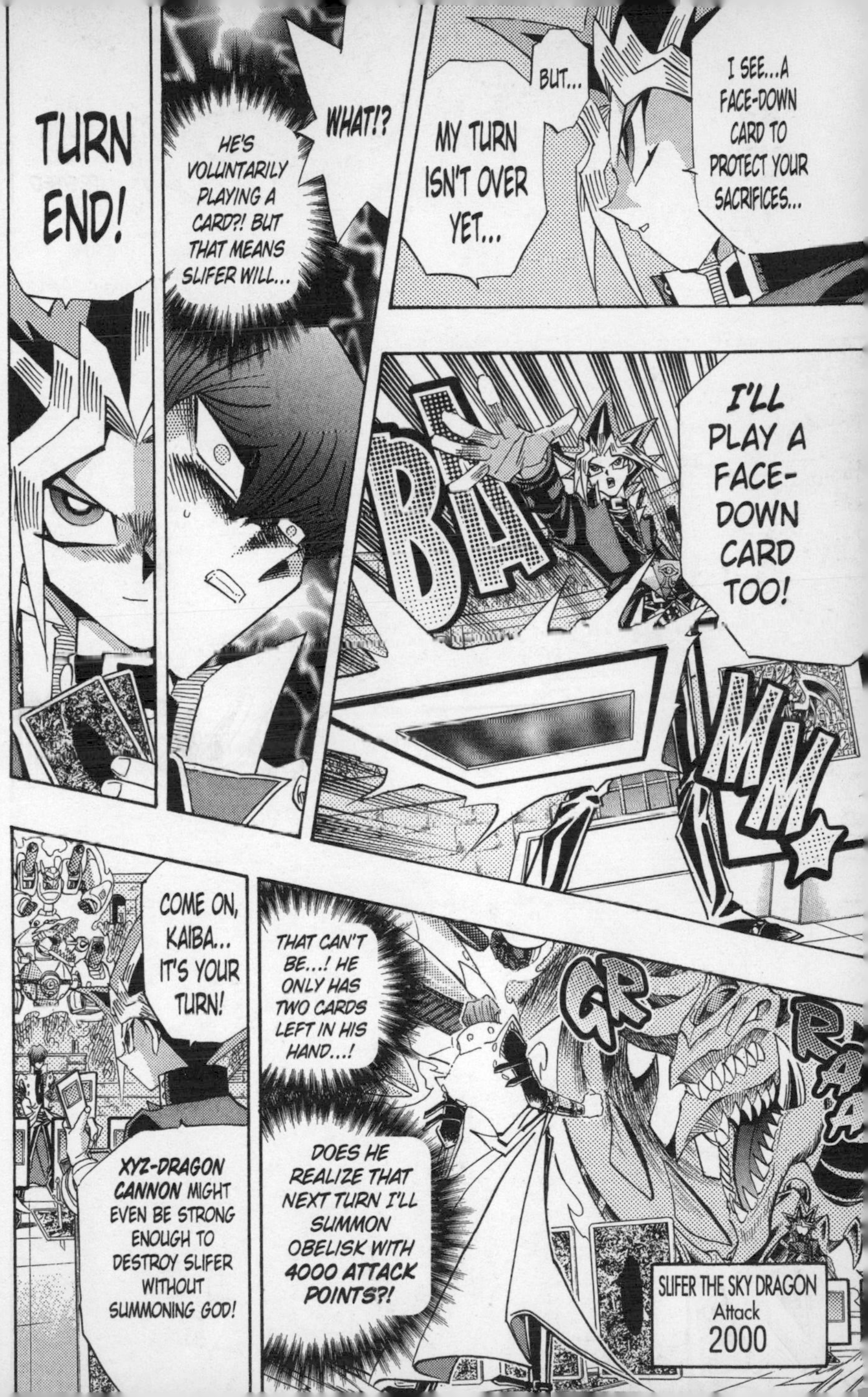
I SEE...A FACE-DOWN CARD TO PROTECT YOUR SACRIFICES...
BUT...
MY TURN ISN'T OVER YET...
I'LL PLAY A FACE-DOWN CARD TOO!
BAM
WHAT!?
HE'S VOLUNTARILY PLAYING A CARD?! BUT THAT MEANS SLIFER WILL...
TURN END!
GRRAA
SLIFER THE SKY DRAGON Attack 2000
DOES HE REALIZE THAT NEXT TURN I'LL SUMMON OBELISK WITH 4000 ATTACK POINTS?!
THAT CAN'T BE...! HE ONLY HAS TWO CARDS LEFT IN HIS HAND...!
COME ON, KAIBA... IT'S YOUR TURN!
XYZ-DRAGON CANNON MIGHT EVEN BE STRONG ENOUGH TO DESTROY SLIFER WITHOUT SUMMONING GOD!

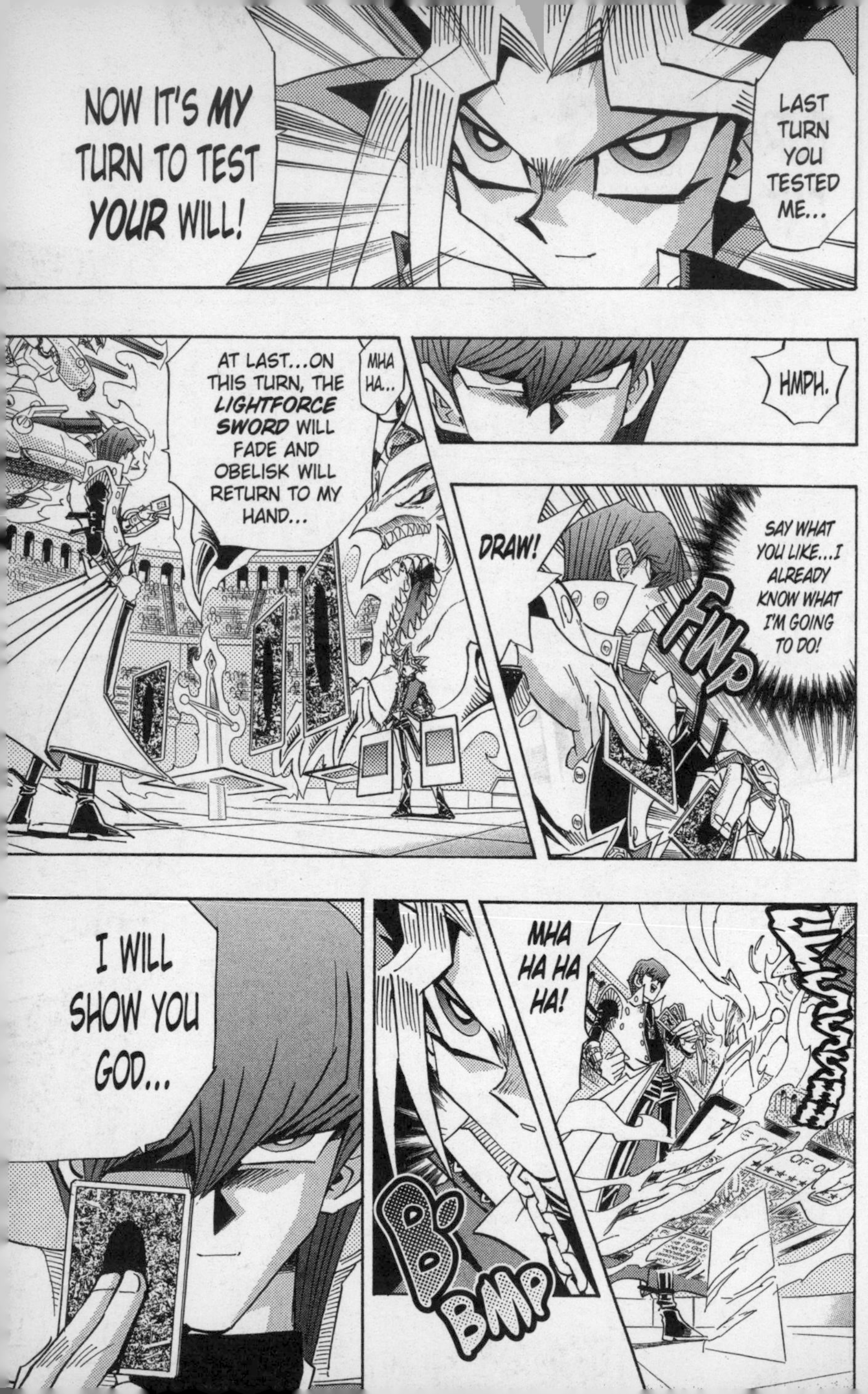
LAST TURN YOU TESTED ME...
NOW IT'S *MY* TURN TO TEST *YOUR* WILL!
HMPH.
SAY WHAT YOU LIKE...I ALREADY KNOW WHAT I'M GOING TO DO!
DRAW!
FWP
MHA HA...
AT LAST...ON THIS TURN, THE ***LIGHTFORCE SWORD*** WILL FADE AND OBELISK WILL RETURN TO MY HAND...
MHA HA HA HA!
B BMP
I WILL SHOW YOU GOD...

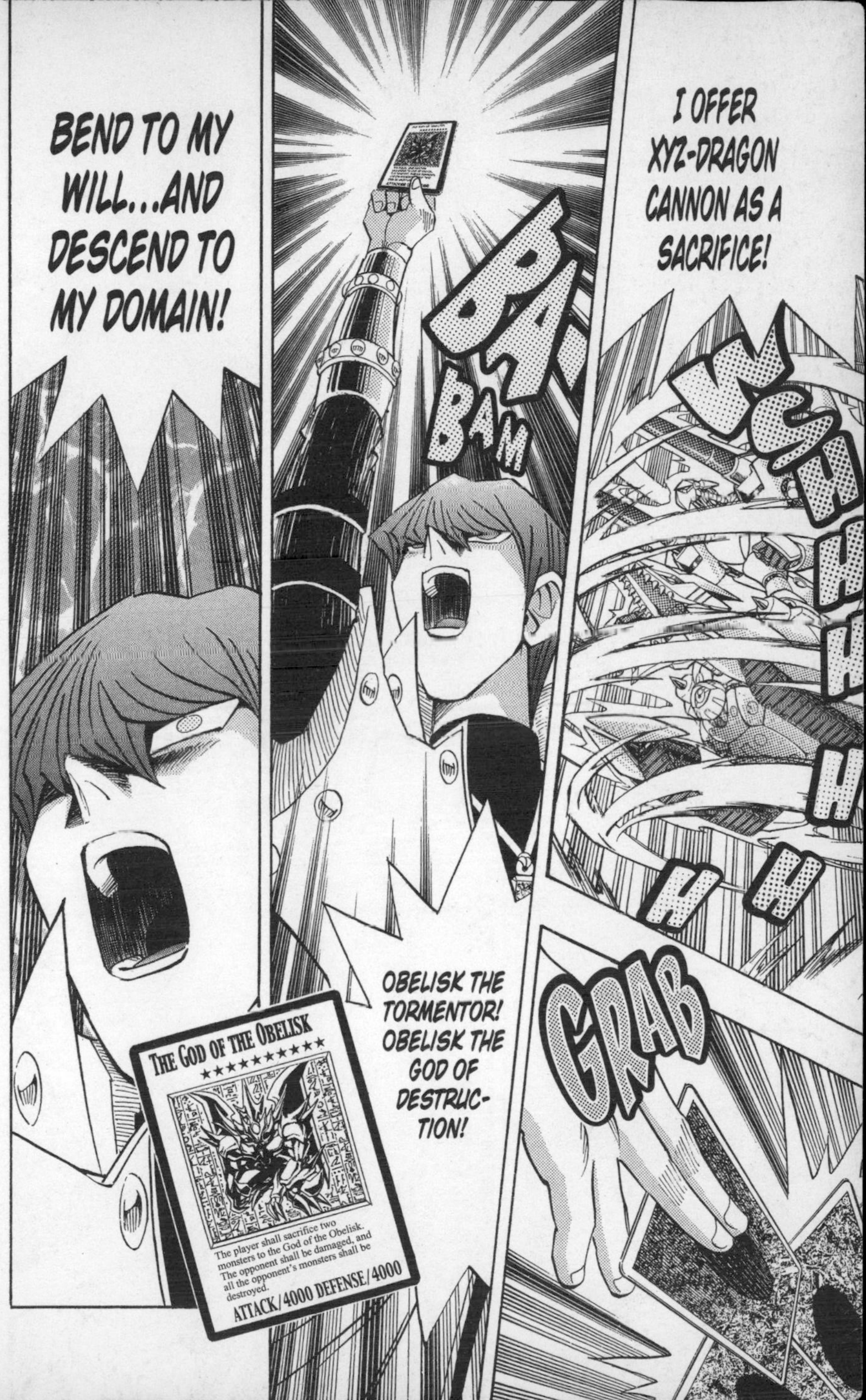
I OFFER XYZ-DRAGON CANNON AS A SACRIFICE!
WSHHHHHH
GRAB
BA-BAM
OBELISK THE TORMENTOR! OBELISK THE GOD OF DESTRUC-TION!
BEND TO MY WILL...AND DESCEND TO MY DOMAIN!
THE GOD OF THE OBELISK
The player shall sacrifice two monsters to the God of the Obelisk. The opponent shall be damaged, and all the opponent's monsters shall be destroyed.
ATTACK/4000 DEFENSE/4000

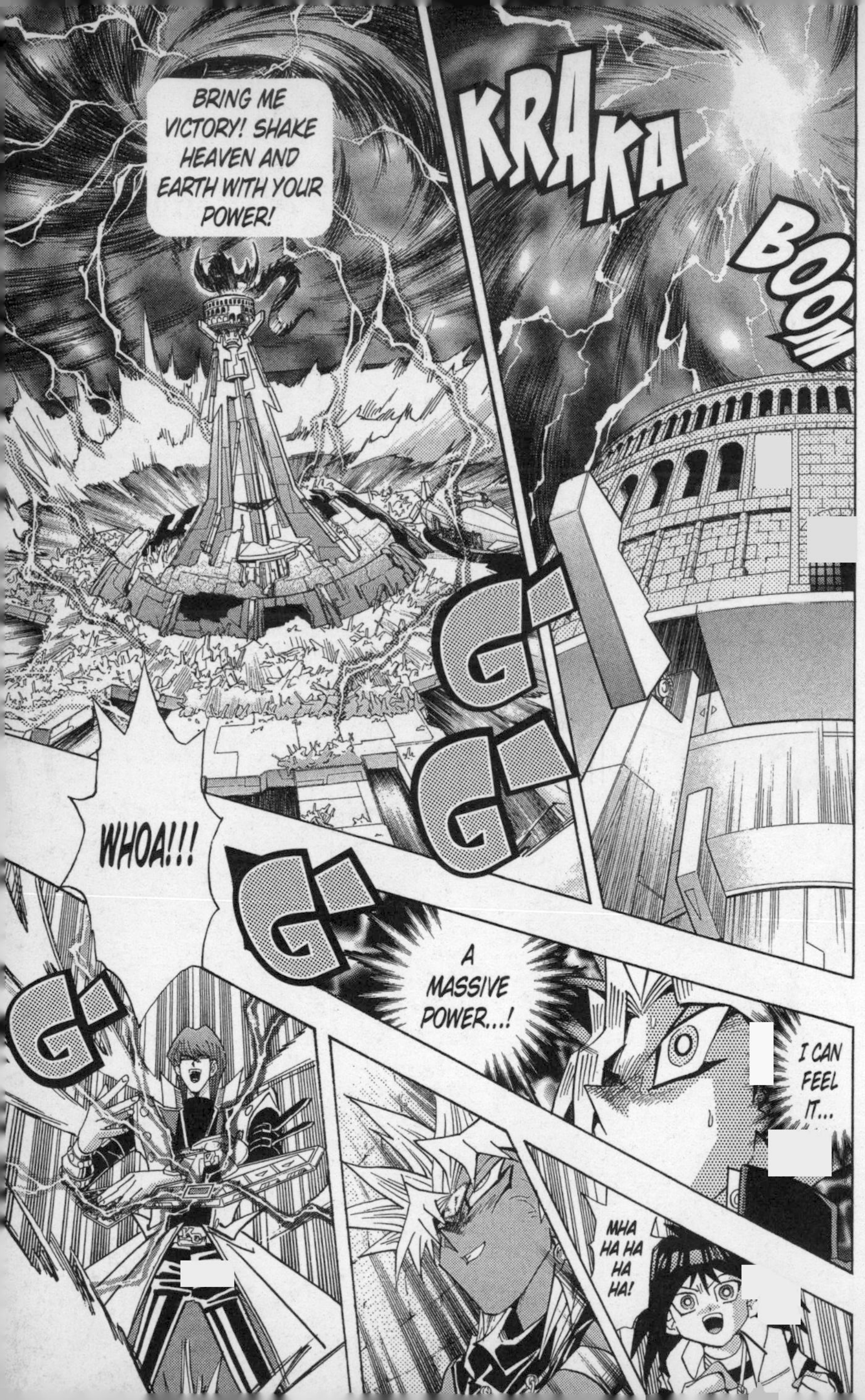
KRAKA
BOOM
BRING ME VICTORY! SHAKE HEAVEN AND EARTH WITH YOUR POWER!
G G G
WHOA!!!
G G
I CAN FEEL IT...
A MASSIVE POWER...!
MHA HA HA HA HA HA!

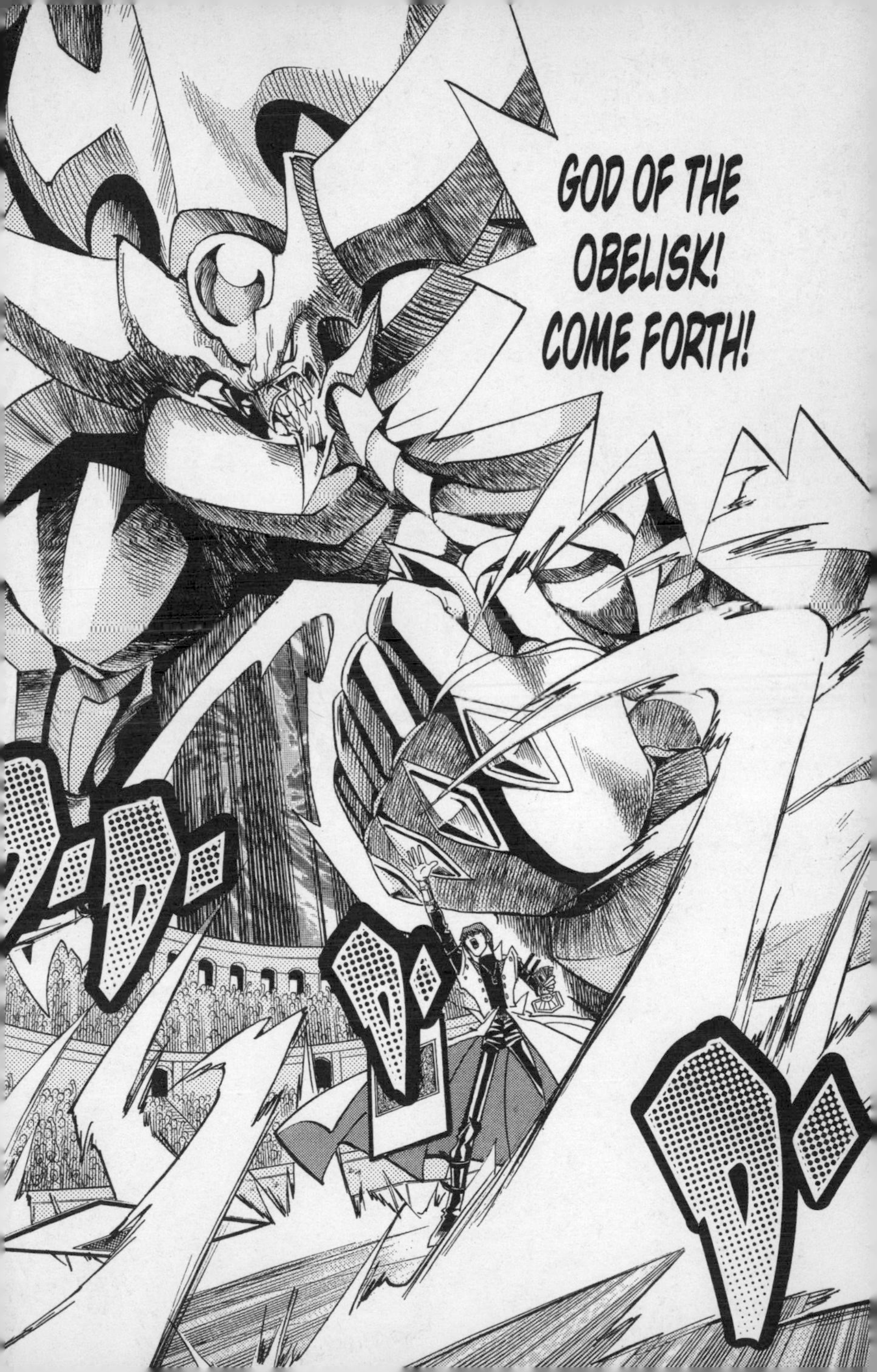
GOD OF THE OBELISK! COME FORTH!

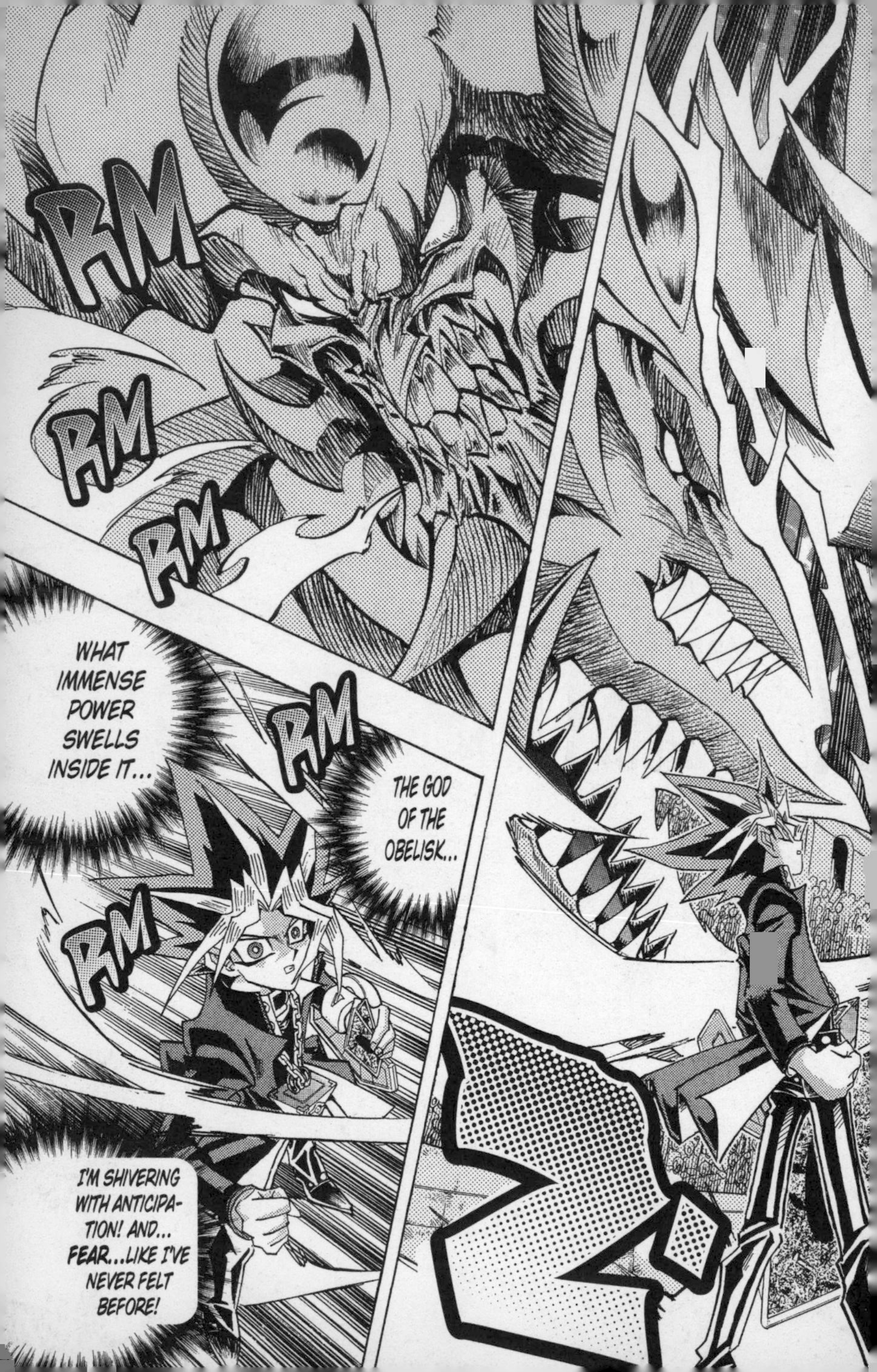
RM
RM
RM
RM
THE GOD OF THE OBELISK...
WHAT IMMENSE POWER SWELLS INSIDE IT...
RM
I'M SHIVERING WITH ANTICIPA-TION! AND... FEAR...LIKE I'VE NEVER FELT BEFORE!

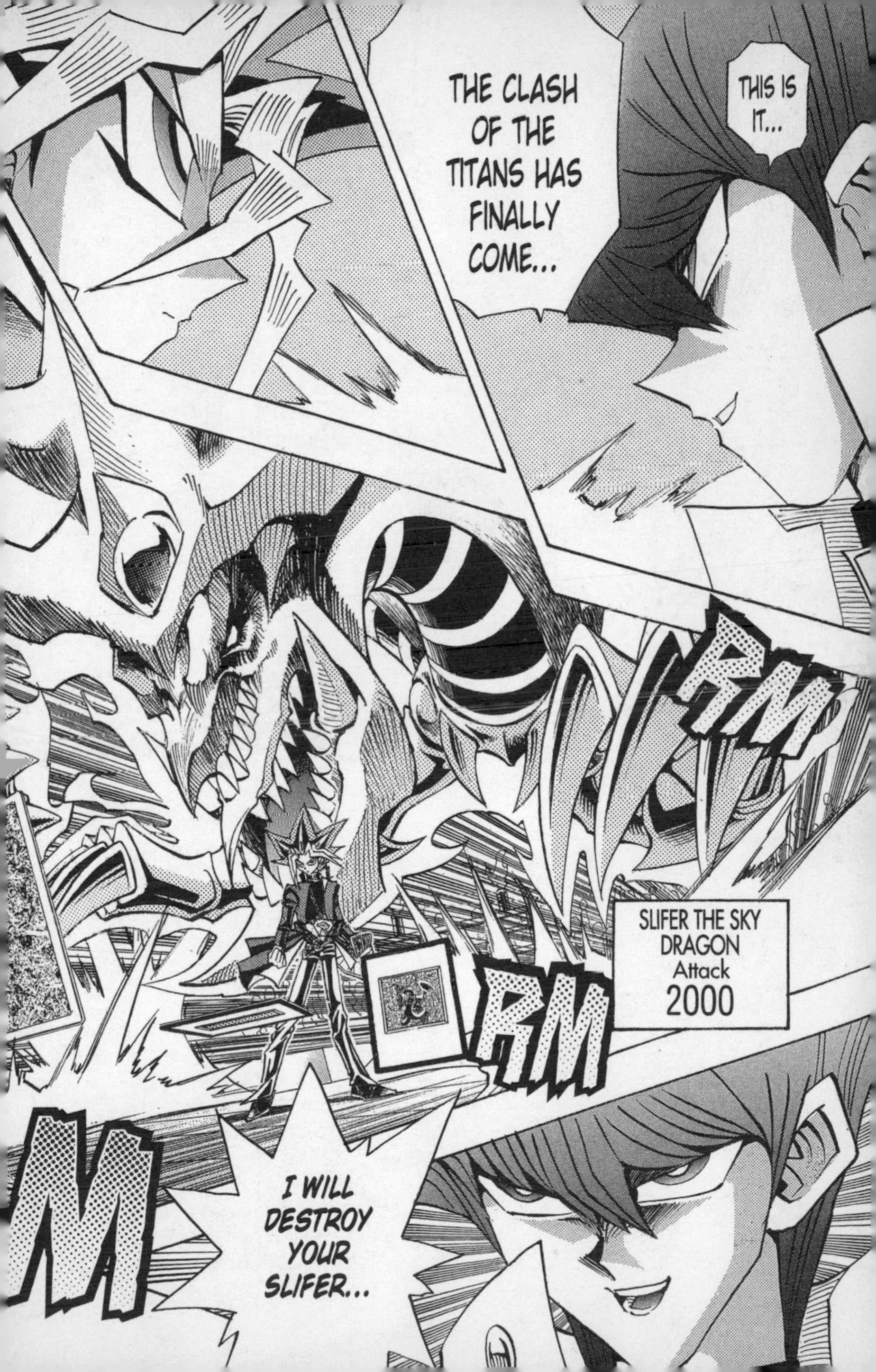
THIS IS IT...
THE CLASH OF THE TITANS HAS FINALLY COME...
RM
SLIFER THE SKY DRAGON Attack 2000
RM
M
I WILL DESTROY YOUR SLIFER...

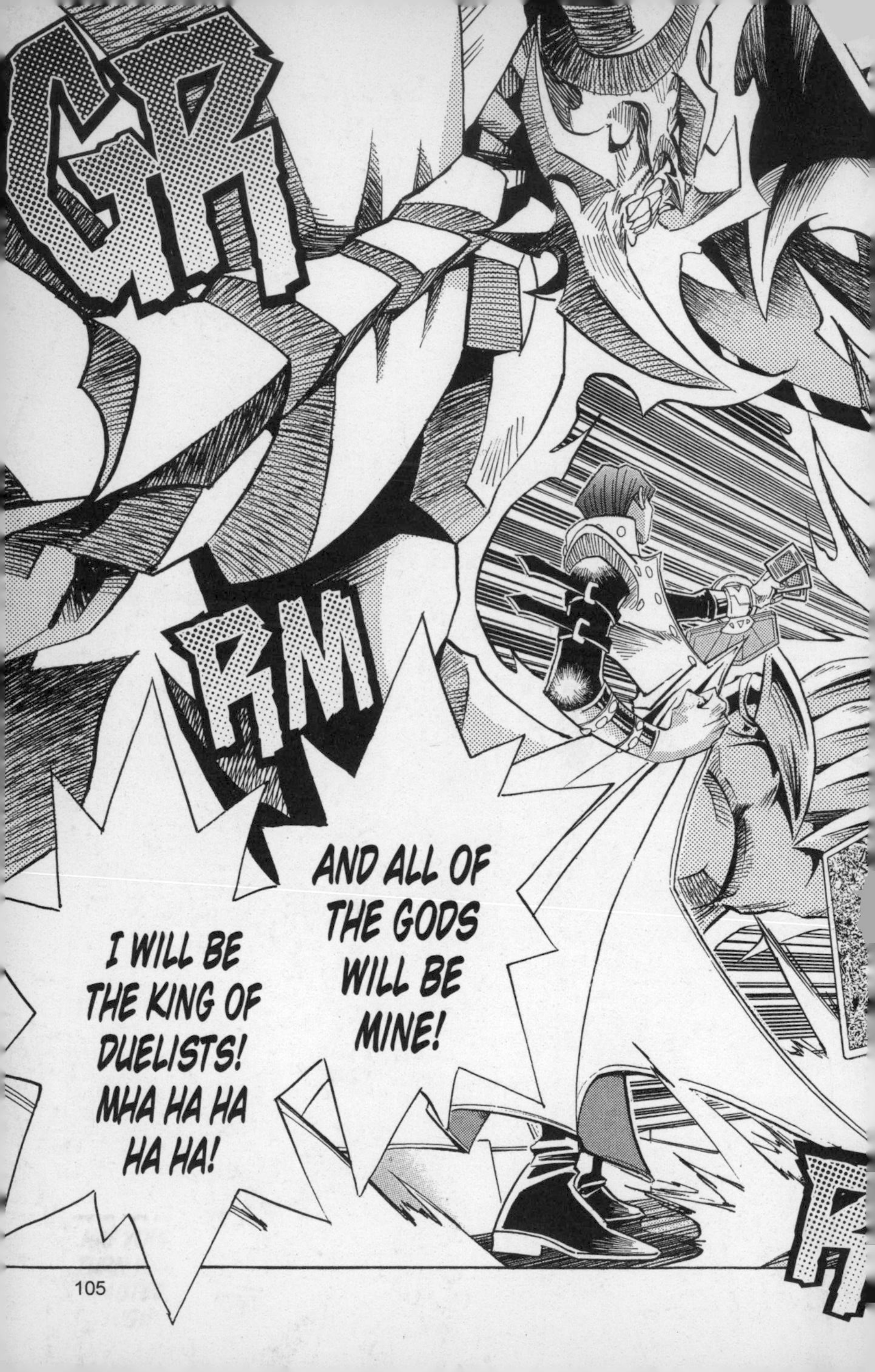
GR
RM
AND ALL OF THE GODS WILL BE MINE!
I WILL BE THE KING OF DUELISTS! MHA HA HA HA HA!

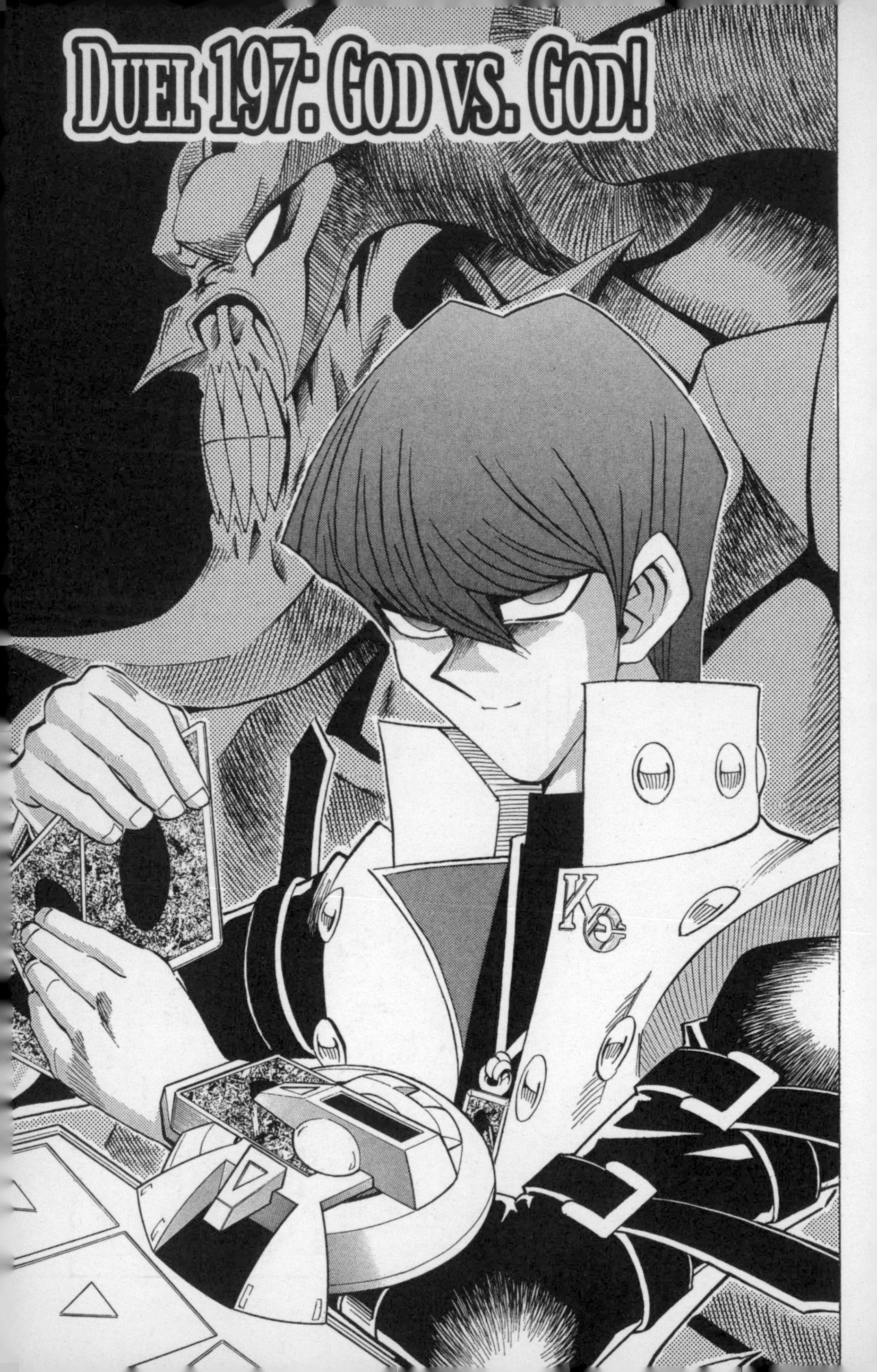
DUEL 197: GOD VS. GOD!
KC

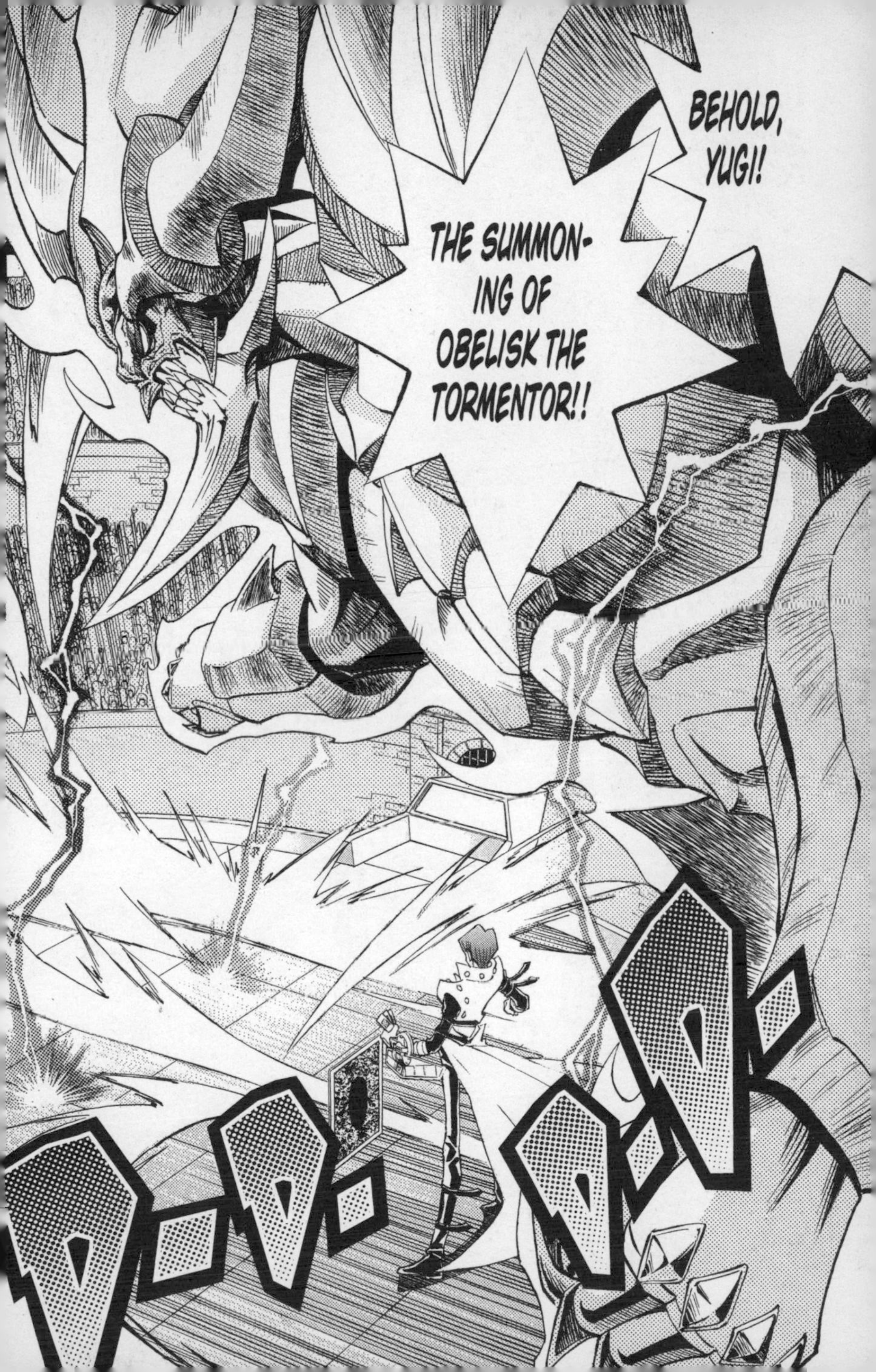
BEHOLD, YUGI!
THE SUMMON-ING OF OBELISK THE TORMENTOR!!

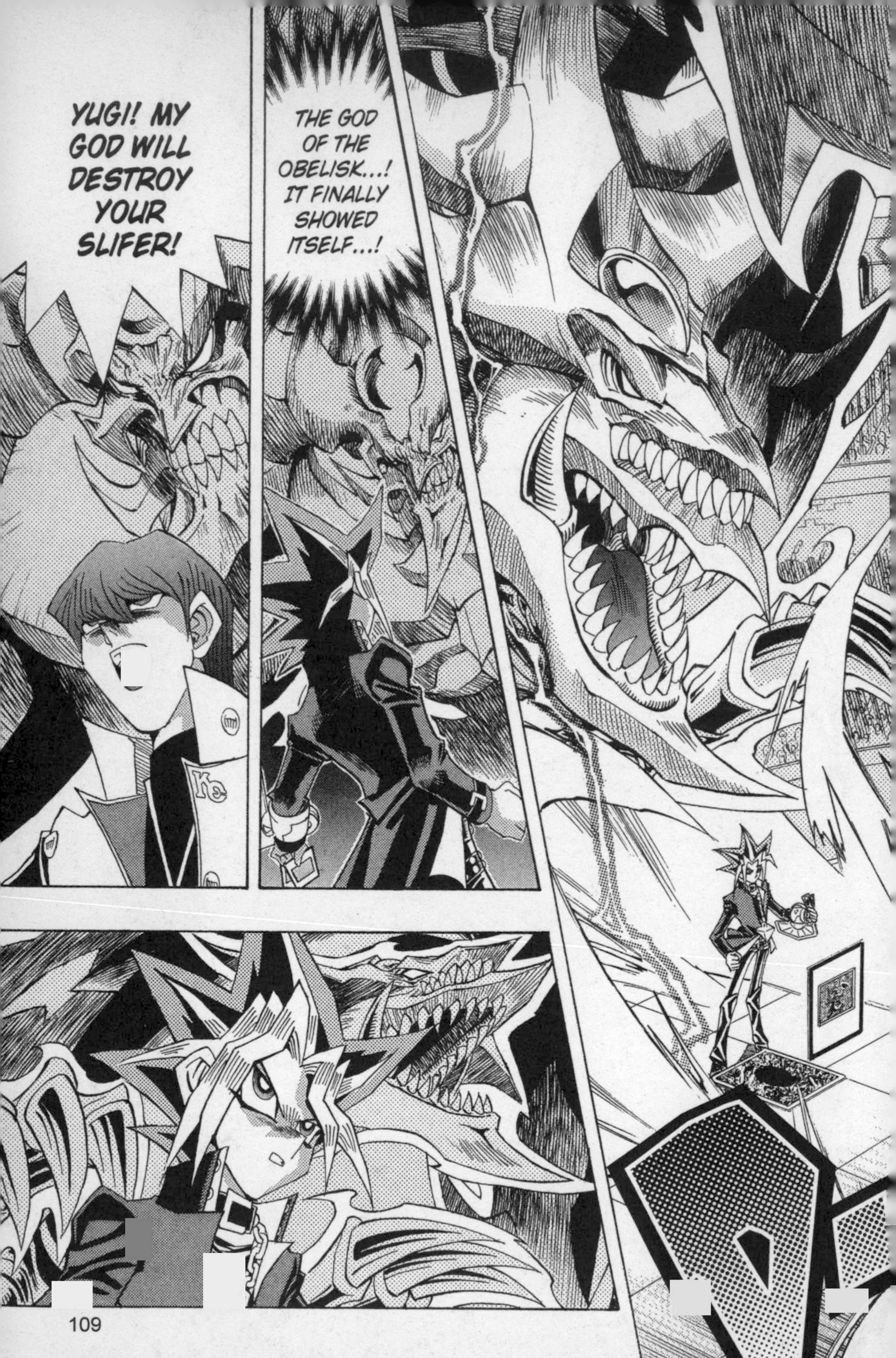
THE GOD OF THE OBELISK...! IT FINALLY SHOWED ITSELF...!
YUGI! MY GOD WILL DESTROY YOUR SLIFER!

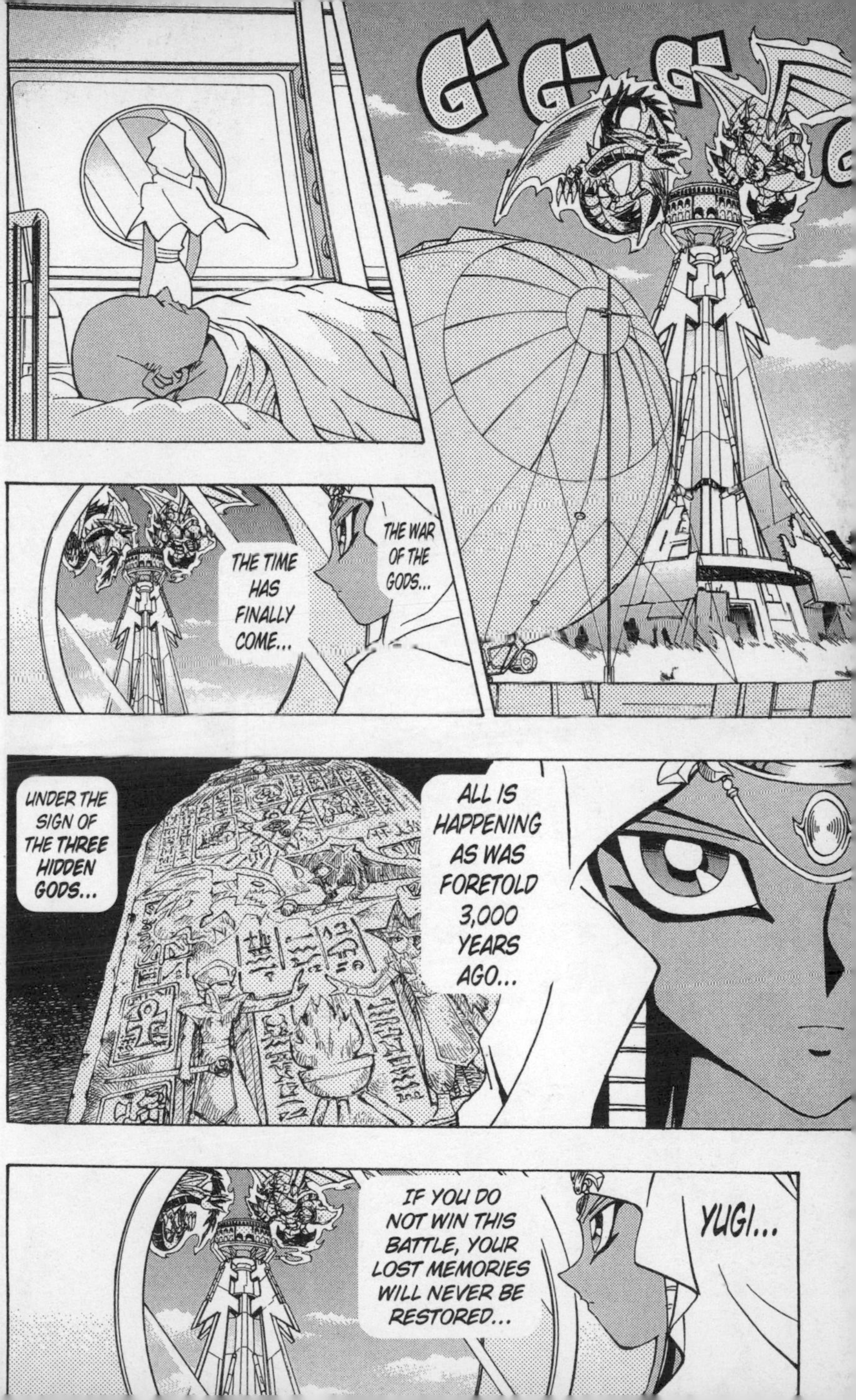
G G G G
THE WAR OF THE GODS...
THE TIME HAS FINALLY COME...
ALL IS HAPPENING AS WAS FORETOLD 3,000 YEARS AGO...
UNDER THE SIGN OF THE THREE HIDDEN GODS...
YUGI...
IF YOU DO NOT WIN THIS BATTLE, YOUR LOST MEMORIES WILL NEVER BE RESTORED...

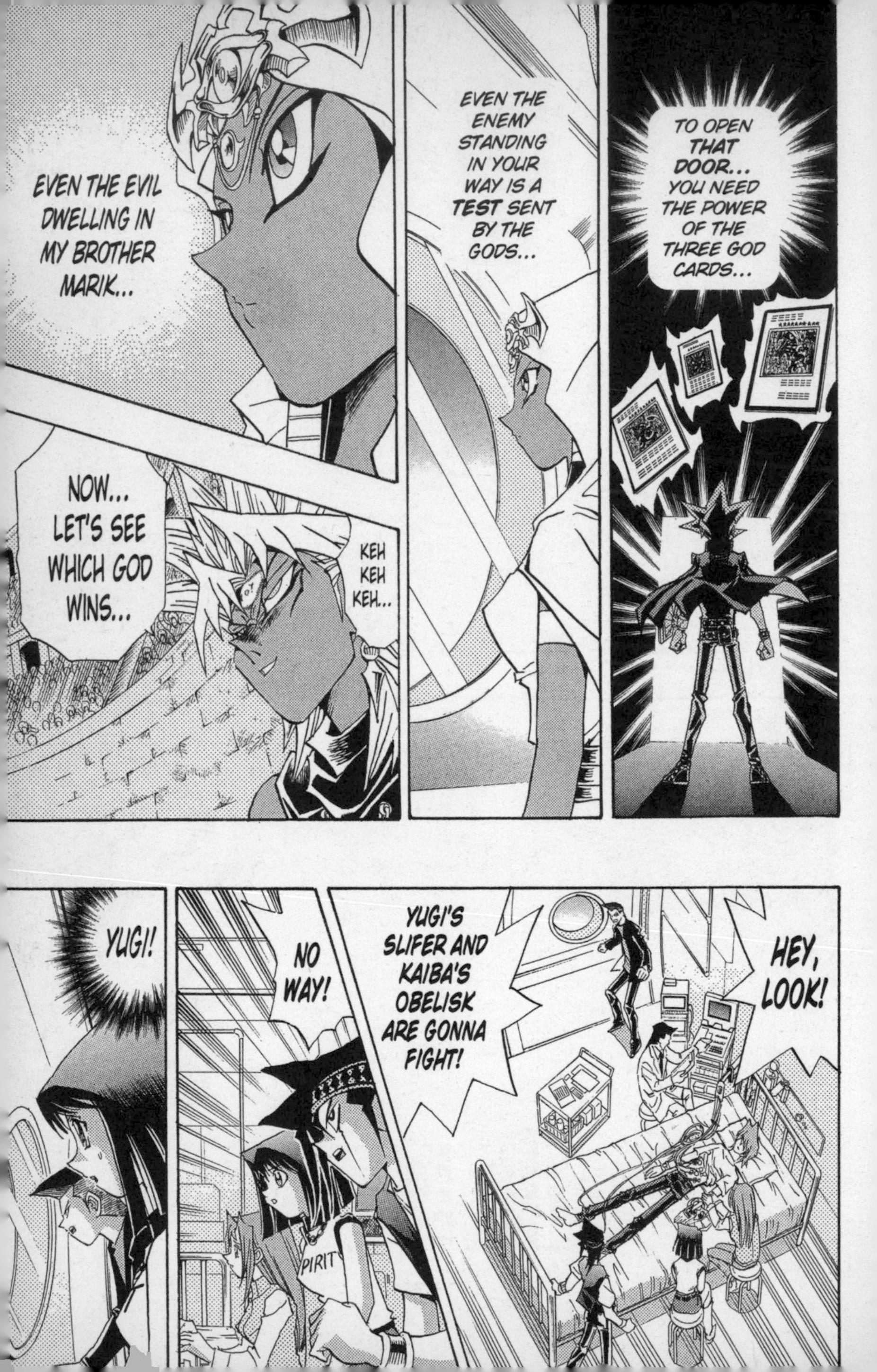
TO OPEN THAT DOOR... YOU NEED THE POWER OF THE THREE GOD CARDS...
EVEN THE ENEMY STANDING IN YOUR WAY IS A TEST SENT BY THE GODS...
EVEN THE EVIL DWELLING IN MY BROTHER MARIK...
NOW... LET'S SEE WHICH GOD WINS...
KEH KEH KEH...
HEY, LOOK!
YUGI'S SLIFER AND KAIBA'S OBELISK ARE GONNA FIGHT!
NO WAY!
YUGI!
PIRIT

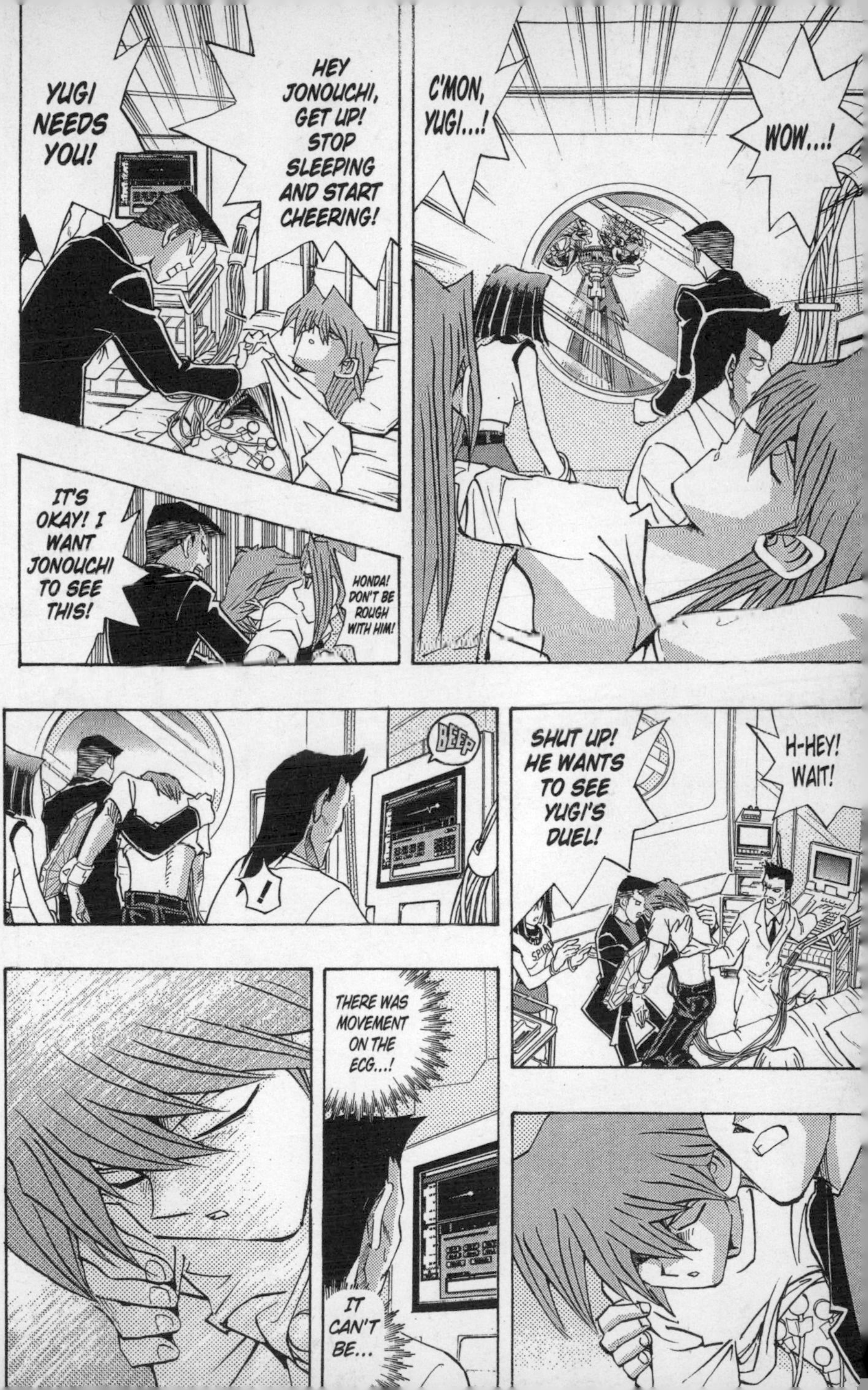
WOW...!
C'MON, YUGI...!
HEY JONOUCHI, GET UP! STOP SLEEPING AND START CHEERING!
YUGI NEEDS YOU!
HONDA! DON'T BE ROUGH WITH HIM!
IT'S OKAY! I WANT JONOUCHI TO SEE THIS!
H-HEY! WAIT!
SHUT UP! HE WANTS TO SEE YUGI'S DUEL!
BEEP
!
THERE WAS MOVEMENT ON THE ECG...!
IT CAN'T BE...

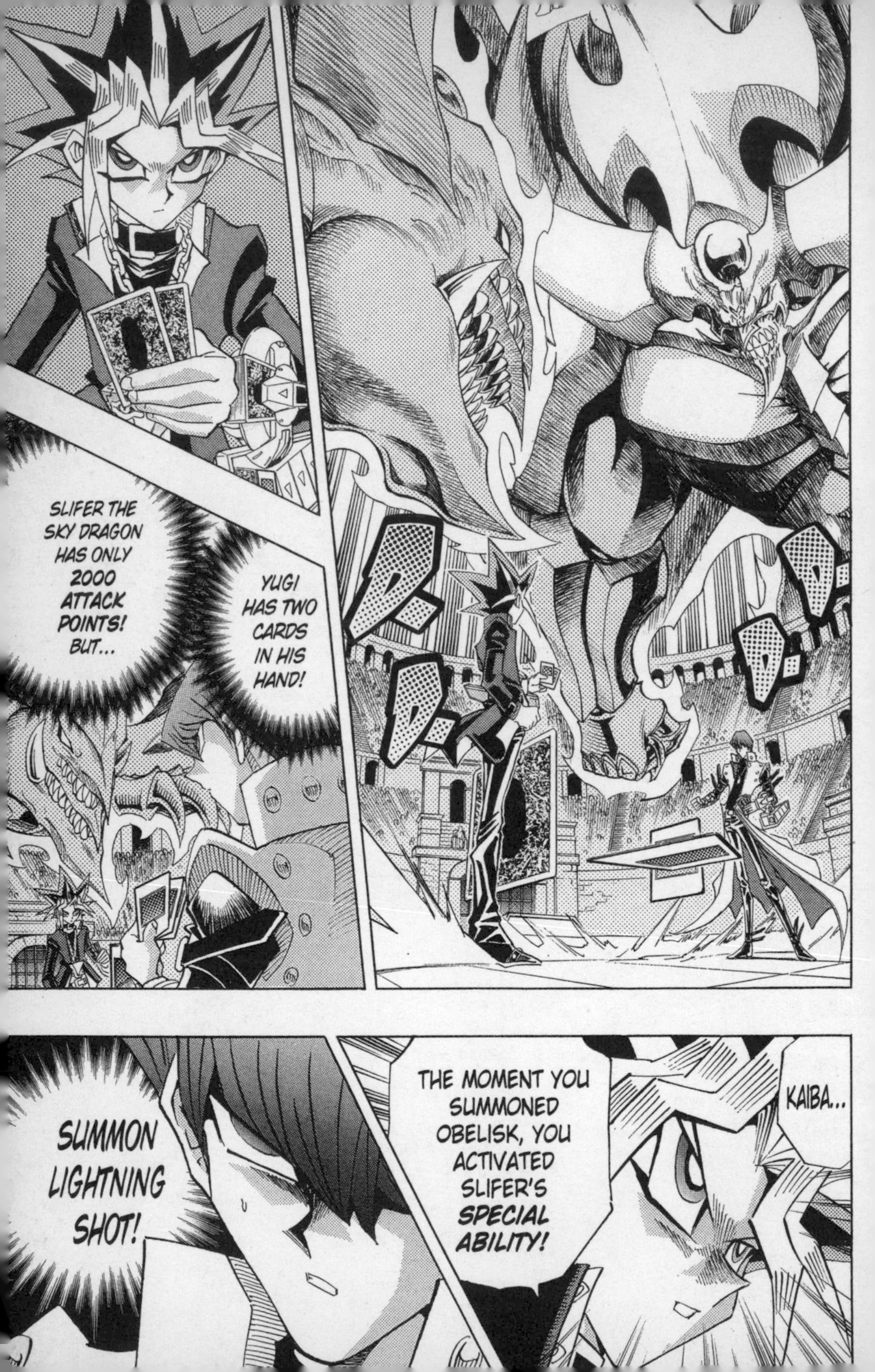
SLIFER THE SKY DRAGON HAS ONLY 2000 ATTACK POINTS! BUT...
YUGI HAS TWO CARDS IN HIS HAND!
KAIBA...
THE MOMENT YOU SUMMONED OBELISK, YOU ACTIVATED SLIFER'S SPECIAL ABILITY!
SUMMON LIGHTNING SHOT!

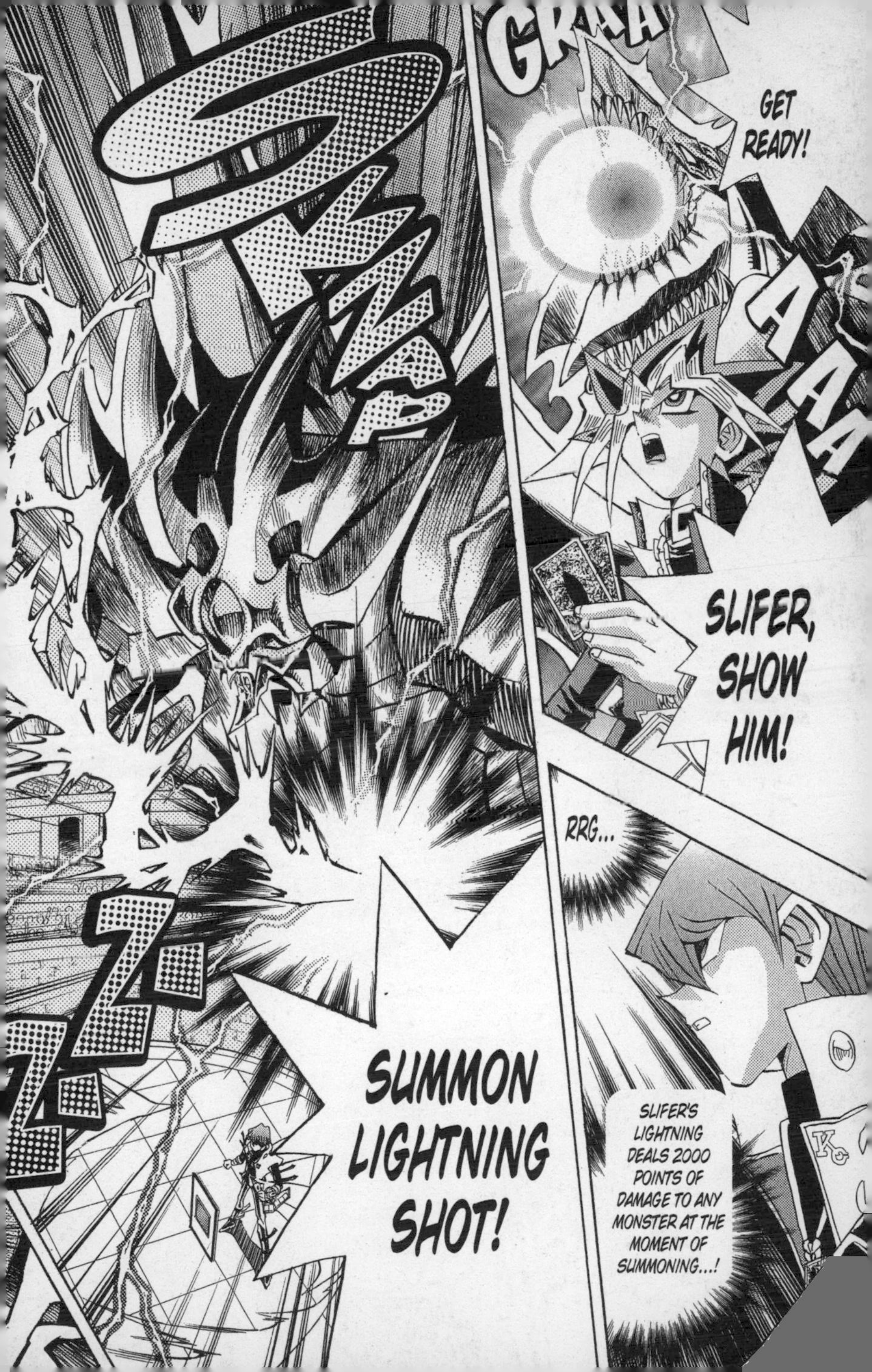
GET READY!
SLIFER, SHOW HIM!
RRG...
SLIFER'S LIGHTNING DEALS 2000 POINTS OF DAMAGE TO ANY MONSTER AT THE MOMENT OF SUMMONING...!
SUMMON LIGHTNING SHOT!

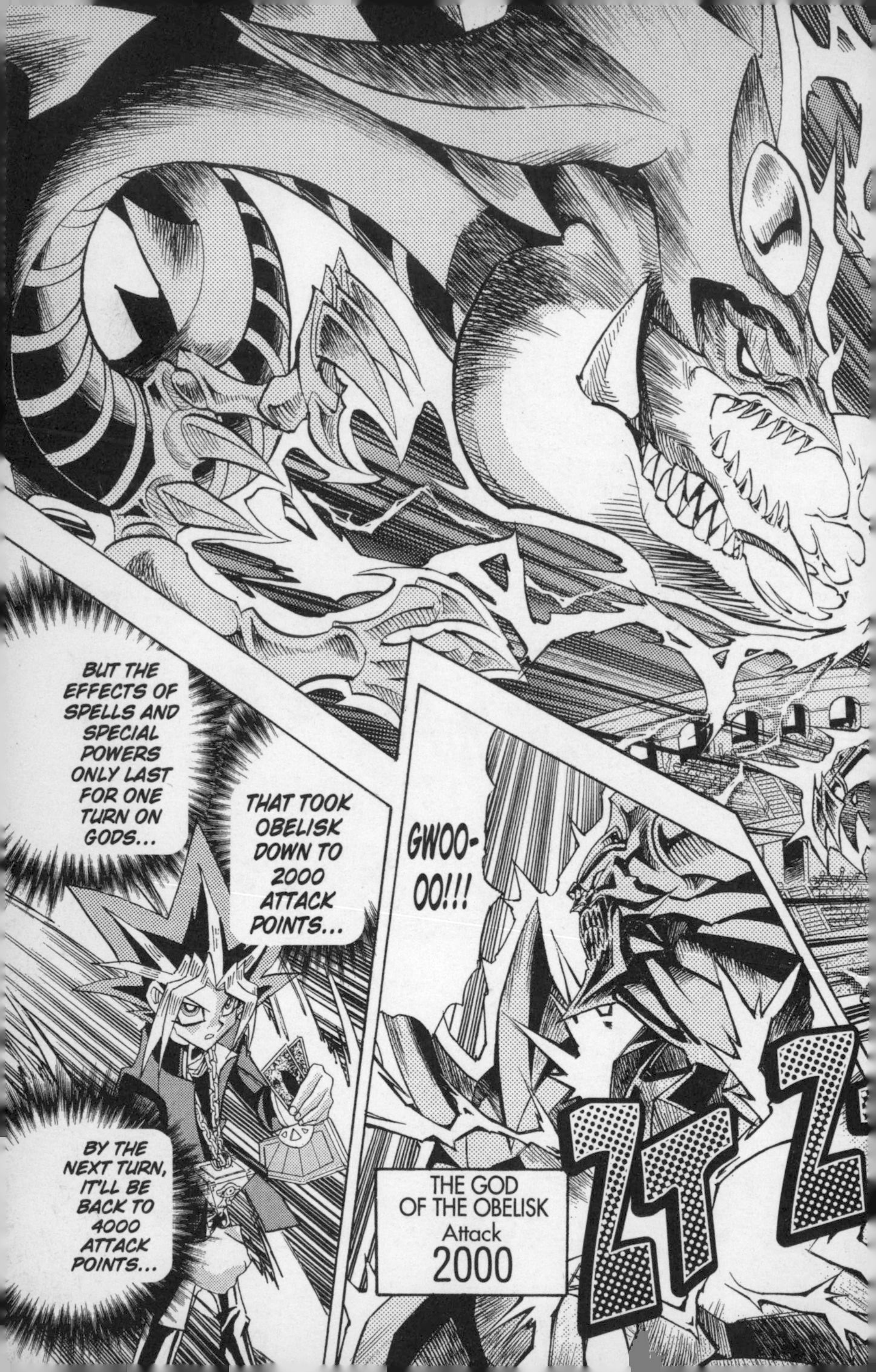
GWOO-OO!!!
THE GOD OF THE OBELISK Attack 2000
THAT TOOK OBELISK DOWN TO 2000 ATTACK POINTS...
BUT THE EFFECTS OF SPELLS AND SPECIAL POWERS ONLY LAST FOR ONE TURN ON GODS...
BY THE NEXT TURN, IT'LL BE BACK TO 4000 ATTACK POINTS...

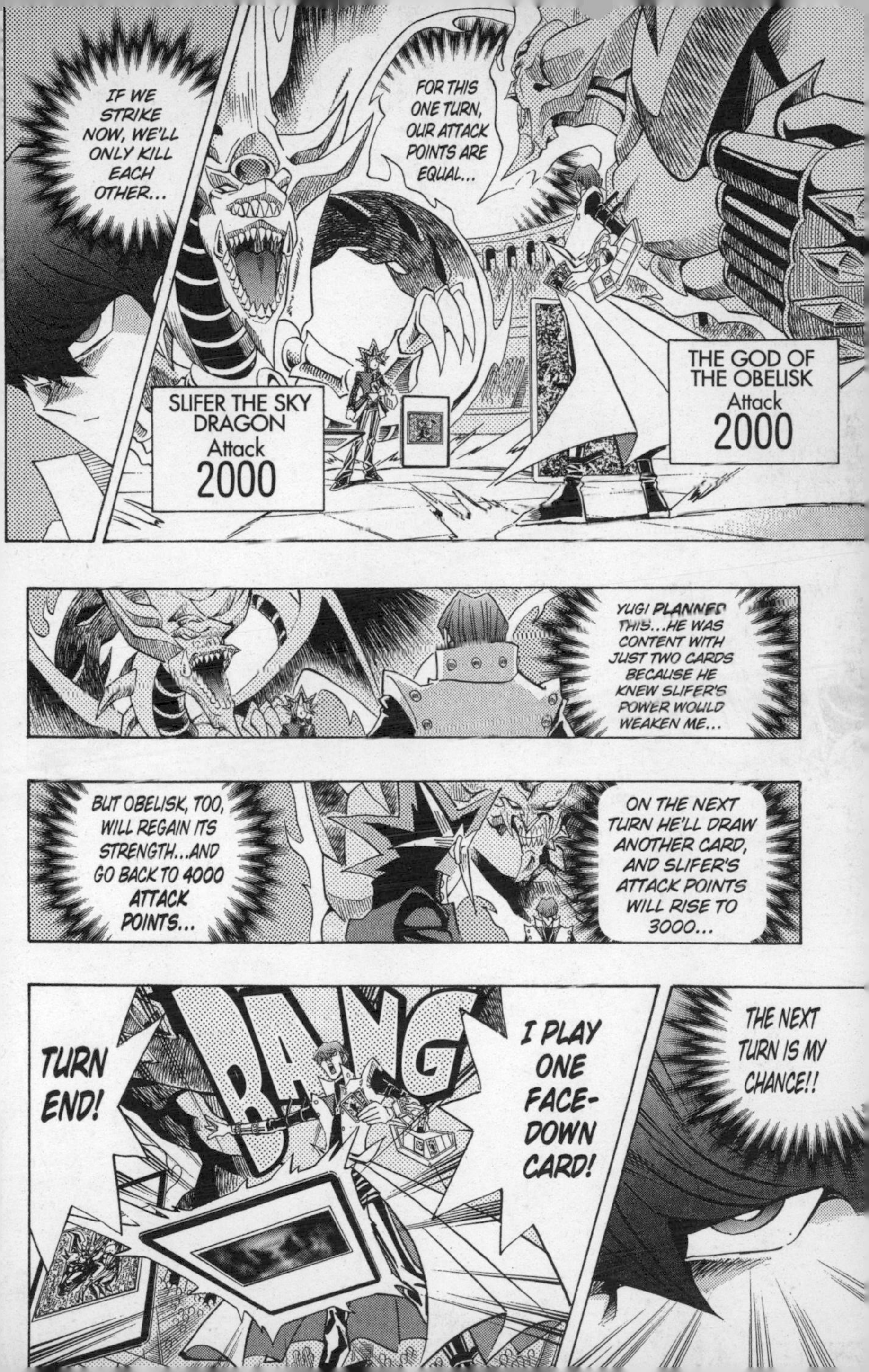
FOR THIS ONE TURN, OUR ATTACK POINTS ARE EQUAL...
IF WE STRIKE NOW, WE'LL ONLY KILL EACH OTHER...
THE GOD OF THE OBELISK Attack 2000
SLIFER THE SKY DRAGON Attack 2000
YUGI PLANNED THIS...HE WAS CONTENT WITH JUST TWO CARDS BECAUSE HE KNEW SLIFER'S POWER WOULD WEAKEN ME...
ON THE NEXT TURN HE'LL DRAW ANOTHER CARD, AND SLIFER'S ATTACK POINTS WILL RISE TO 3000...
BUT OBELISK, TOO, WILL REGAIN ITS STRENGTH...AND GO BACK TO 4000 ATTACK POINTS...
THE NEXT TURN IS MY CHANCE!!
I PLAY ONE FACE-DOWN CARD!
BANG
TURN END!

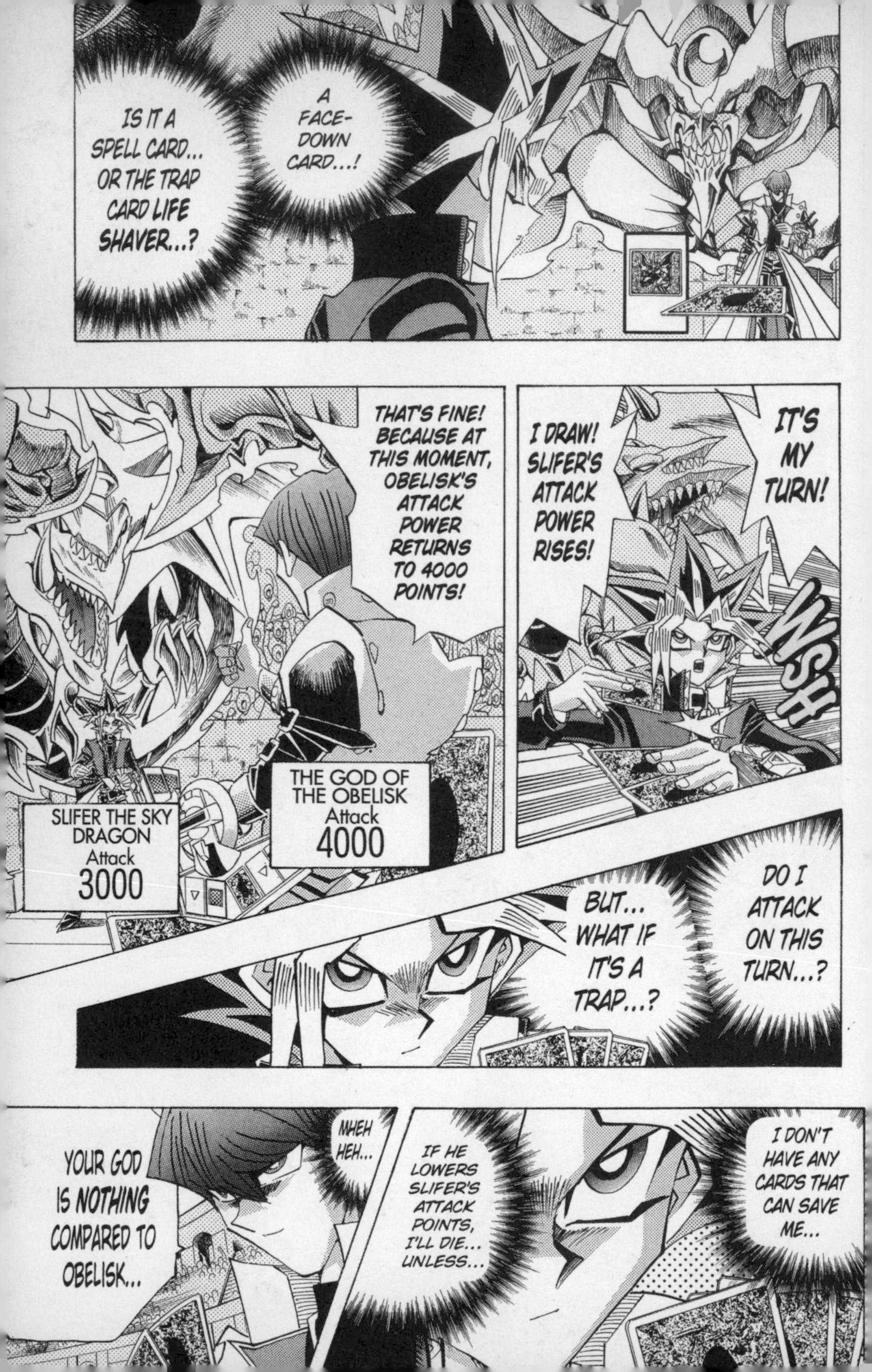
A FACE-DOWN CARD...!
IS IT A SPELL CARD... OR THE TRAP CARD LIFE SHAVER...?
IT'S MY TURN!
I DRAW! SLIFER'S ATTACK POWER RISES!
WSH
THAT'S FINE! BECAUSE AT THIS MOMENT, OBELISK'S ATTACK POWER RETURNS TO 4000 POINTS!
THE GOD OF THE OBELISK Attack 4000
SLIFER THE SKY DRAGON Attack 3000
DO I ATTACK ON THIS TURN...?
BUT... WHAT IF IT'S A TRAP...?
I DON'T HAVE ANY CARDS THAT CAN SAVE ME...
IF HE LOWERS SLIFER'S ATTACK POINTS, I'LL DIE... UNLESS...
MHEH HEH...
YOUR GOD IS NOTHING COMPARED TO OBELISK...

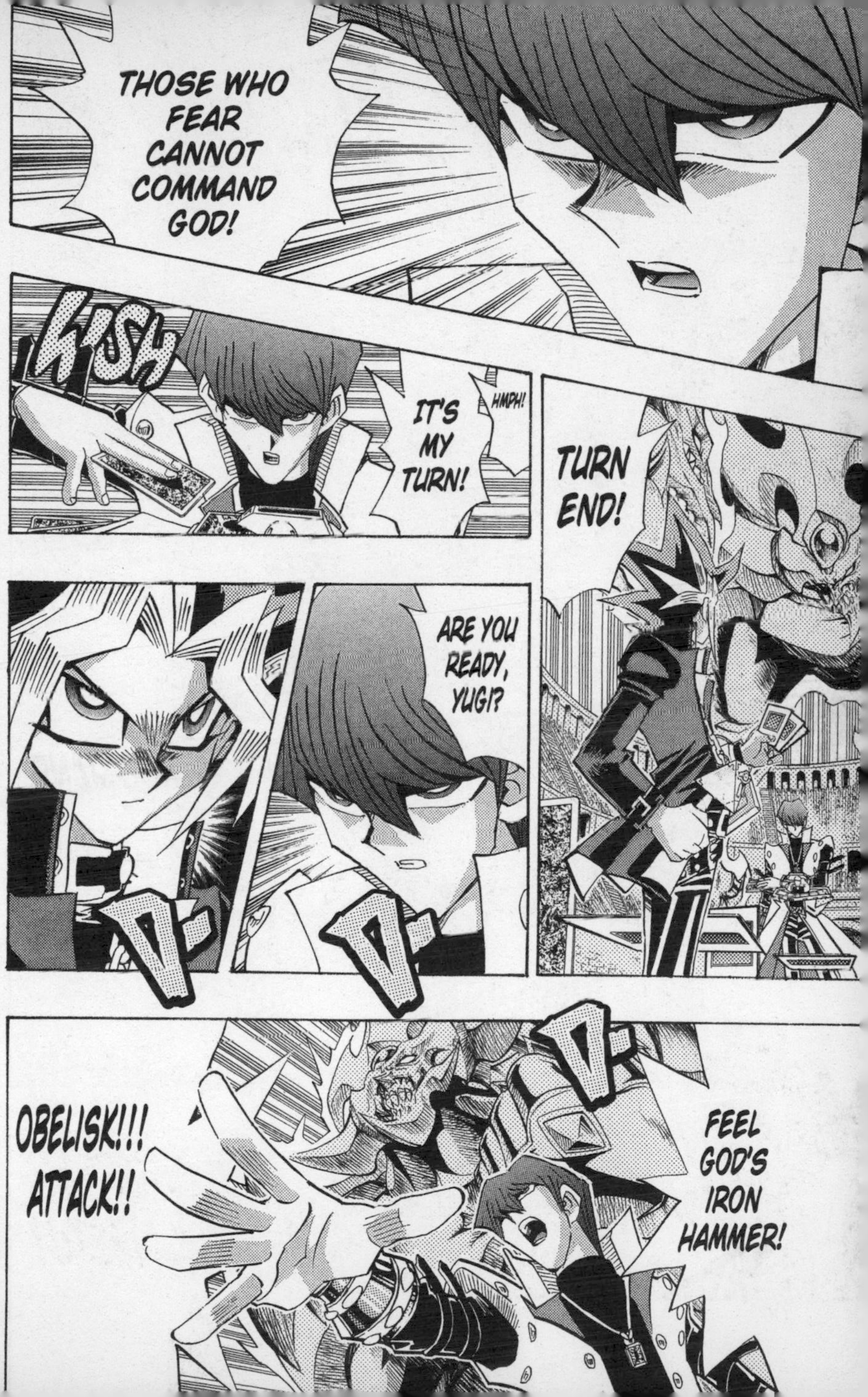
THOSE WHO FEAR CANNOT COMMAND GOD!
TURN END!
HMPH!
IT'S MY TURN!
WISH
ARE YOU READY, YUGI?
FEEL GOD'S IRON HAMMER!
OBELISK!!! ATTACK!!

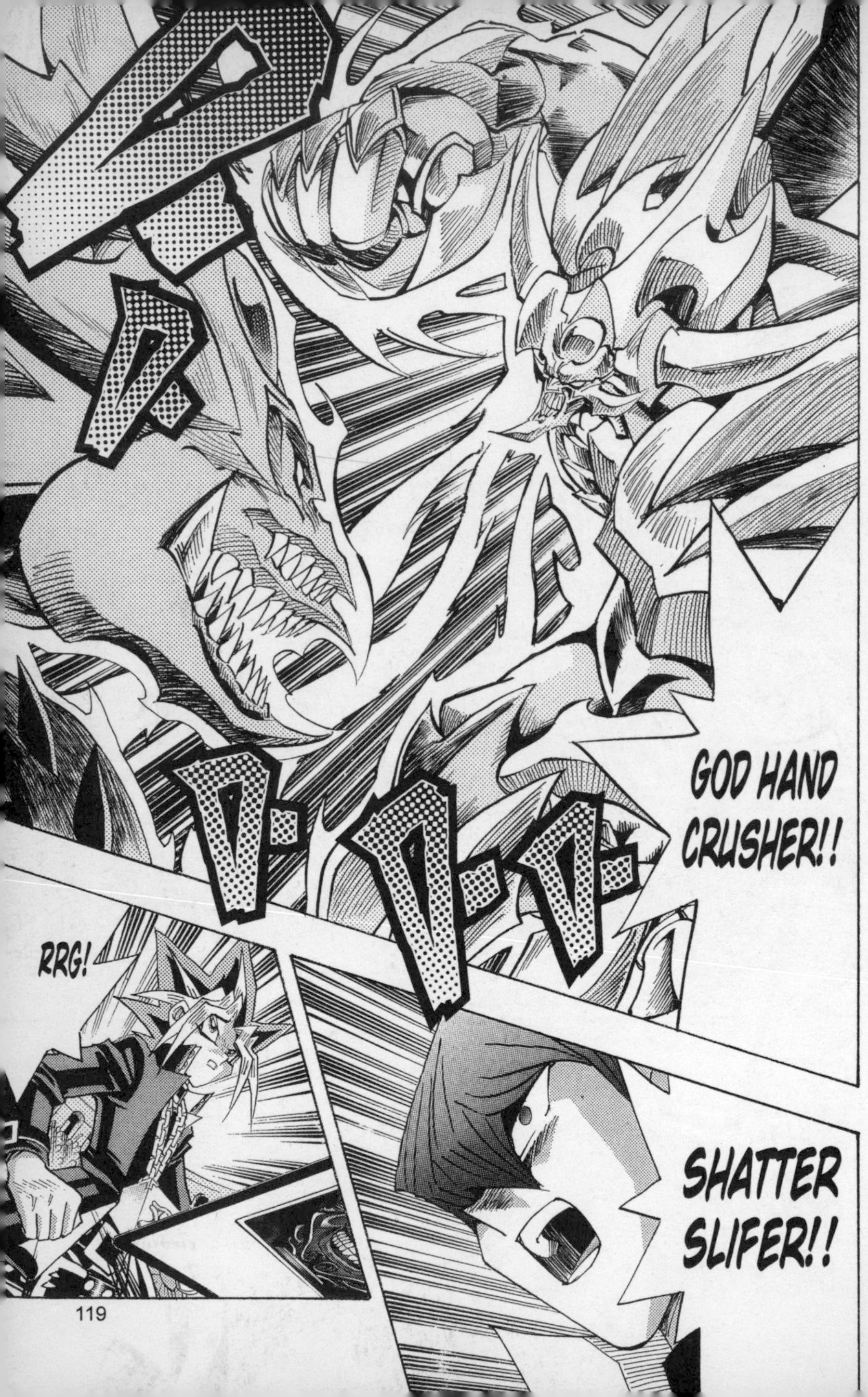
GOD HAND CRUSHER!!
SHATTER SLIFER!!
RRG!

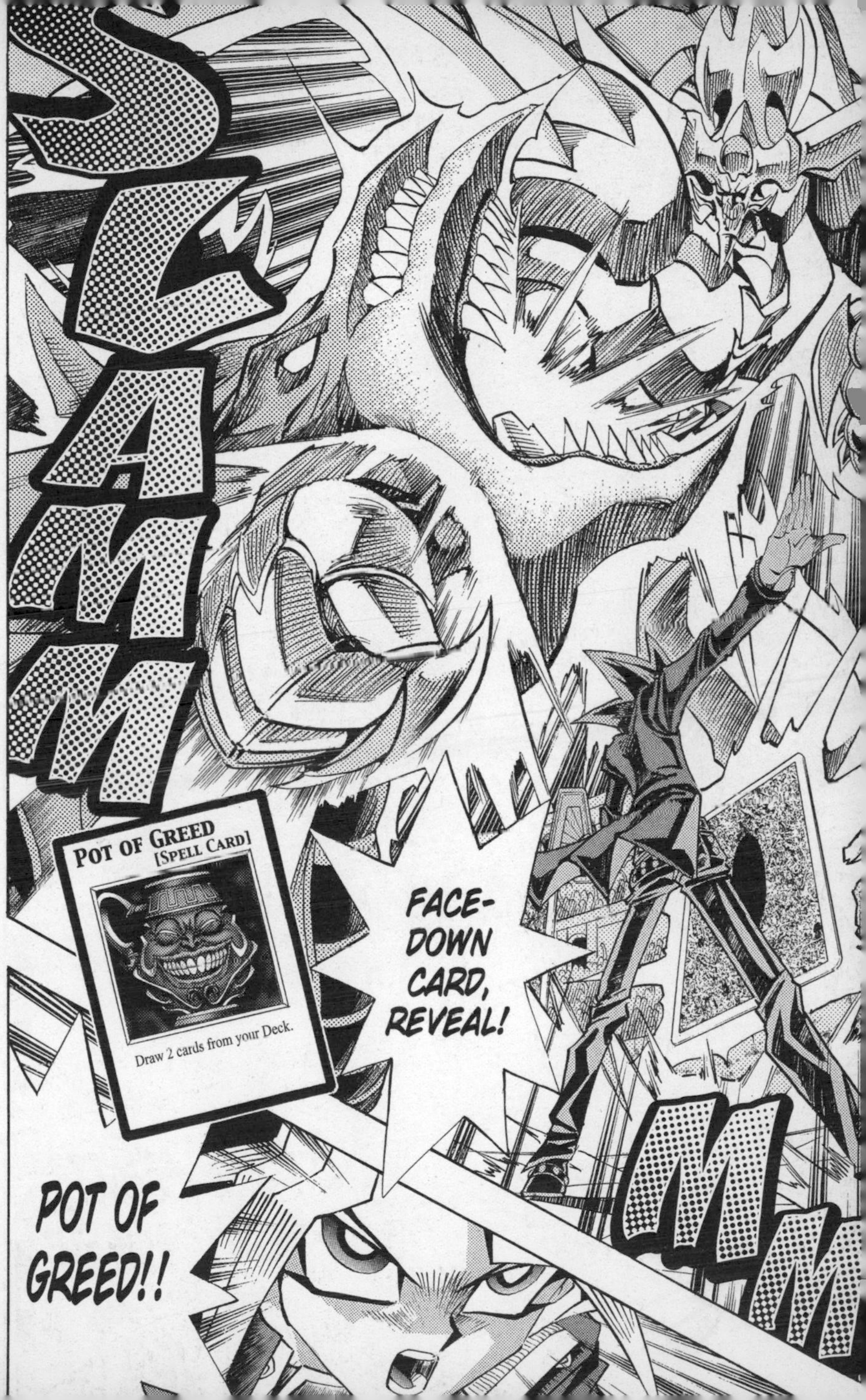
SLAMM
FACE-DOWN CARD, REVEAL!
POT OF GREED [SPELL CARD]
Draw 2 cards from your Deck.
MMM
POT OF GREED!!

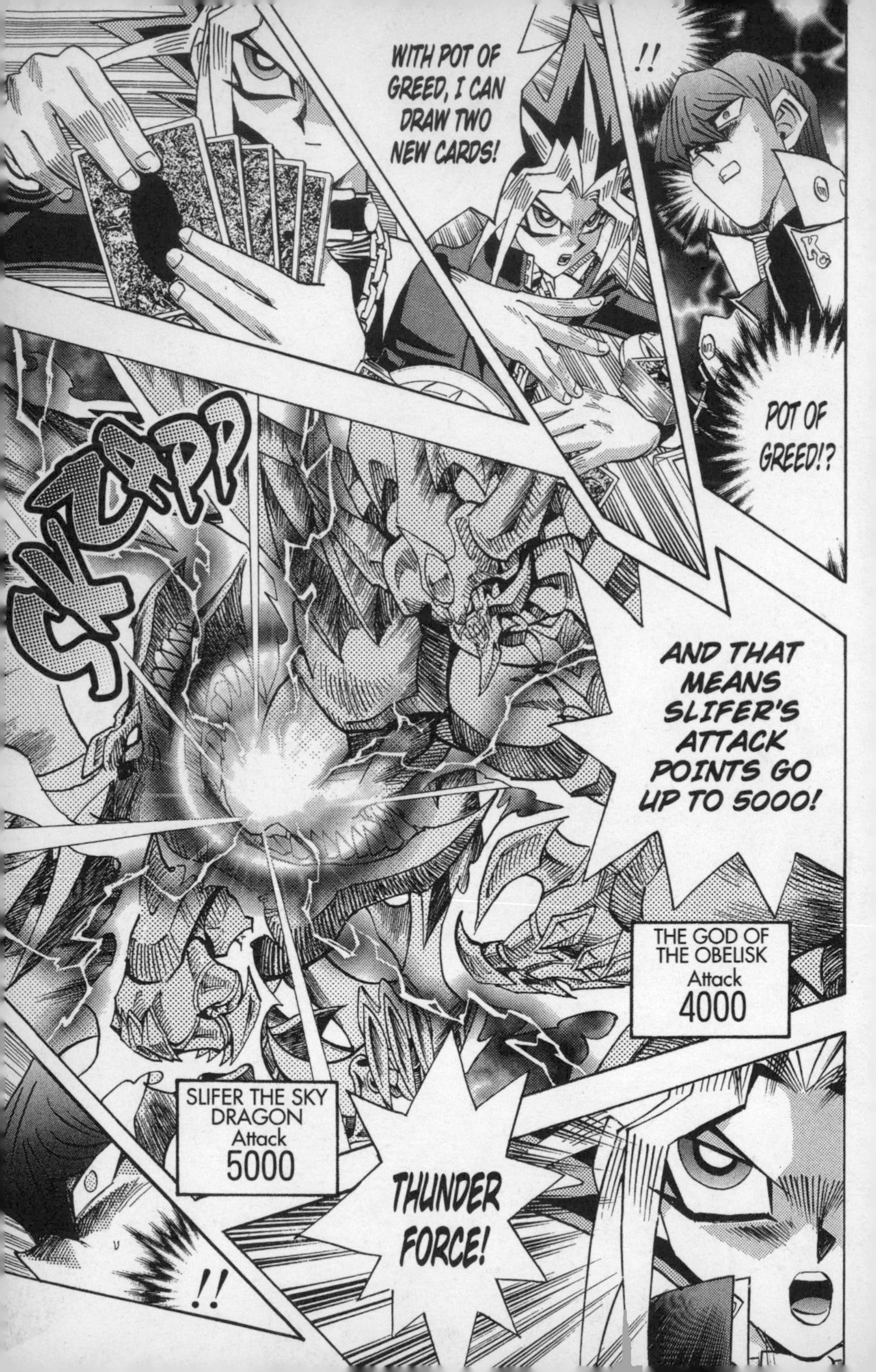
!!
POT OF GREED!?
WITH POT OF GREED, I CAN DRAW TWO NEW CARDS!
AND THAT MEANS SLIFER'S ATTACK POINTS GO UP TO 5000!
THE GOD OF THE OBELISK
Attack
4000
SLIFER THE SKY DRAGON
Attack
5000
THUNDER FORCE!
!!

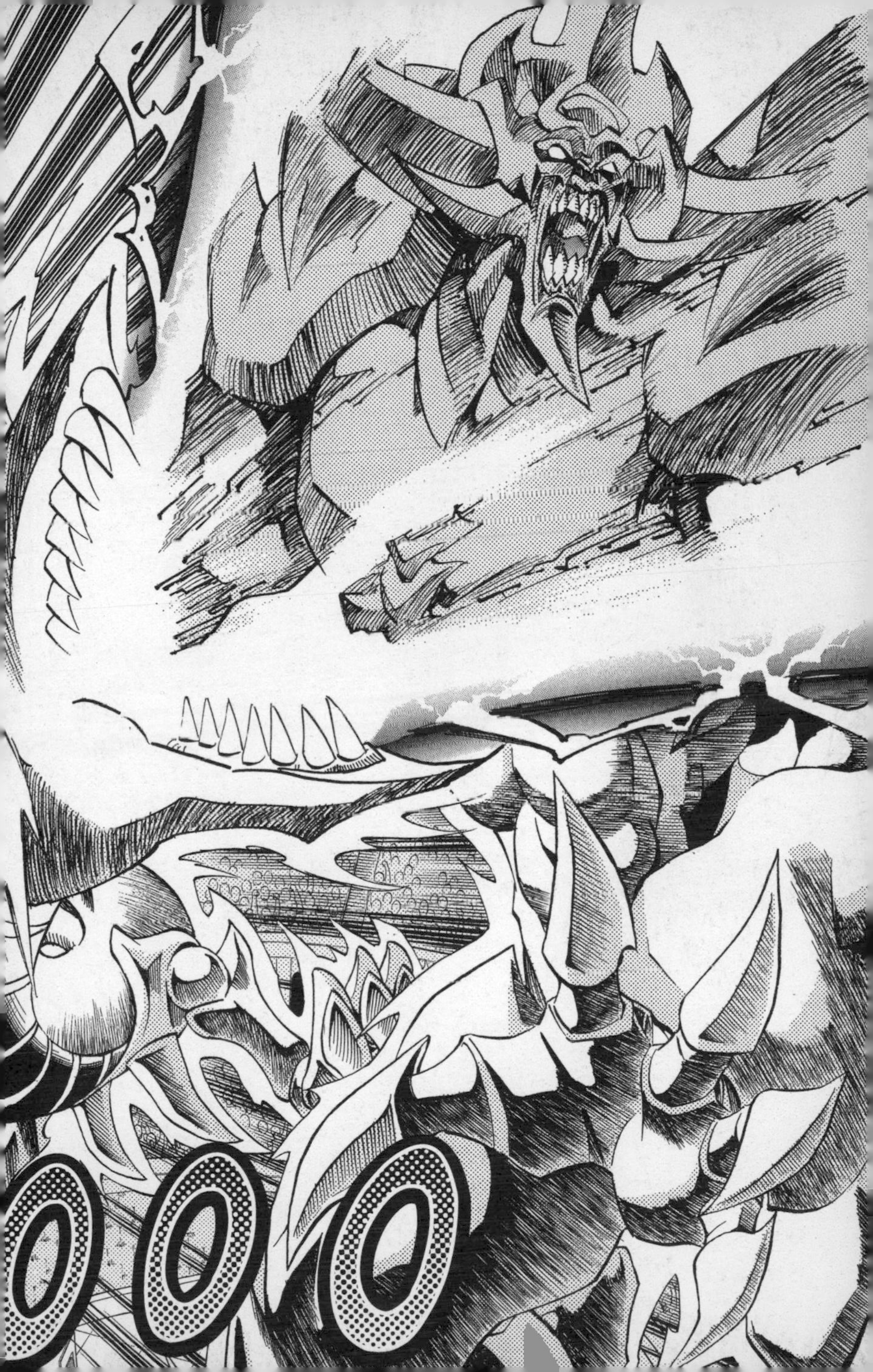

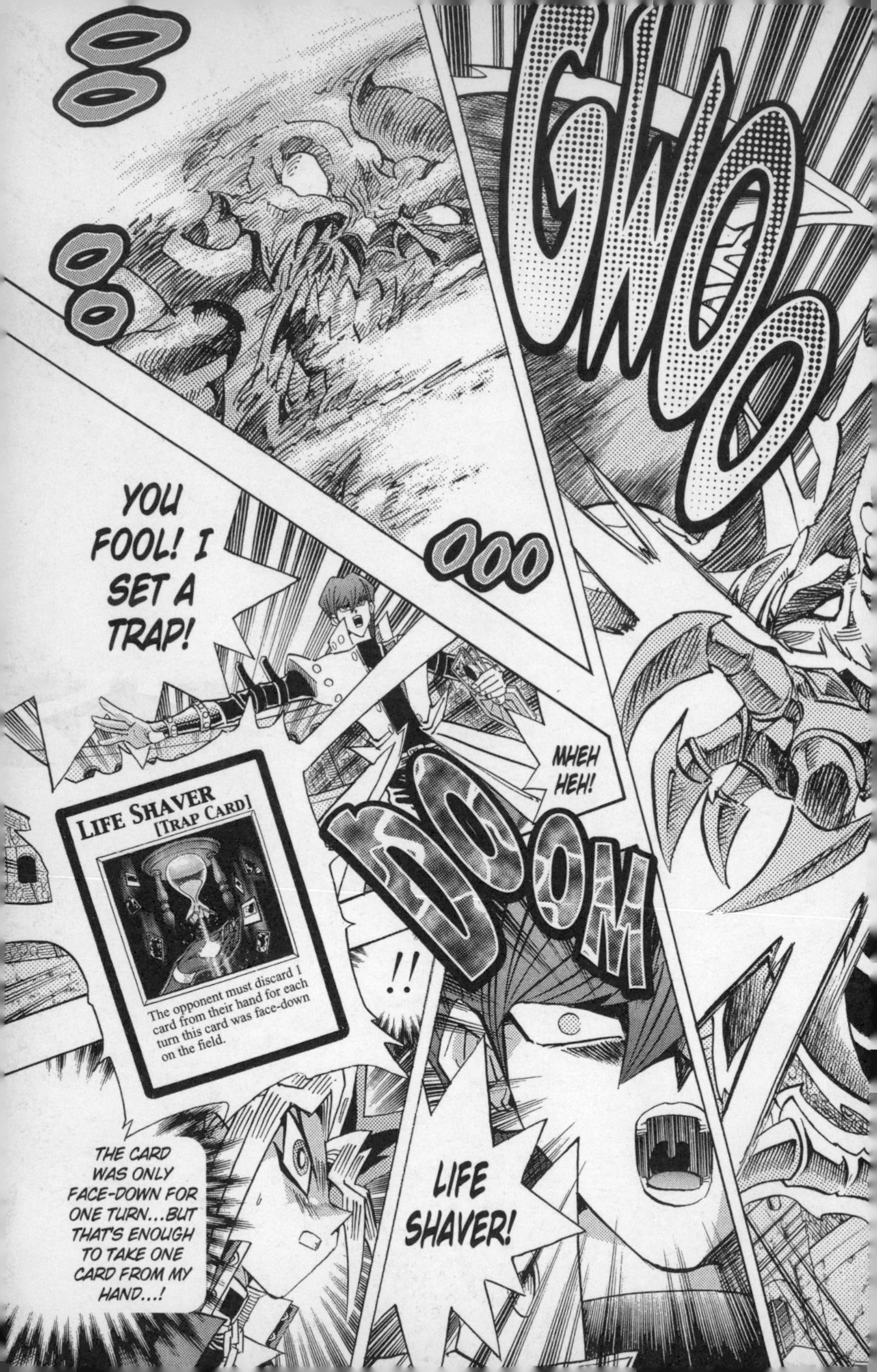
GWOO
OO
OO
OOO
YOU FOOL! I SET A TRAP!
MHEH HEH!
DOOOM
!!
LIFE SHAVER!
LIFE SHAVER
[TRAP CARD]
The opponent must discard 1 card from their hand for each turn this card was face-down on the field.
THE CARD WAS ONLY FACE-DOWN FOR ONE TURN...BUT THAT'S ENOUGH TO TAKE ONE CARD FROM MY HAND...!

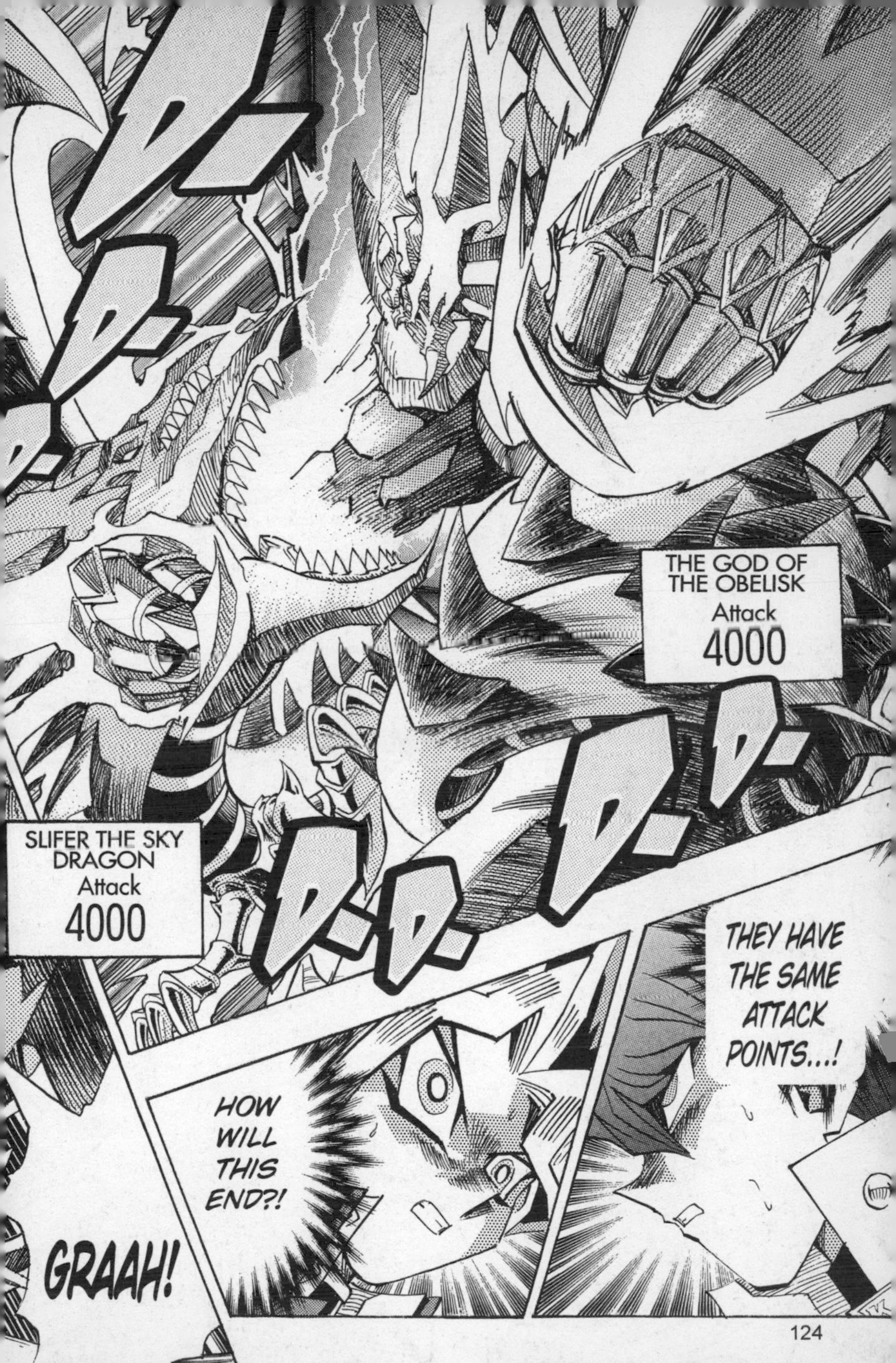
THE GOD OF THE OBELISK
Attack
4000
D- D- D-
SLIFER THE SKY DRAGON
Attack
4000
D- D- D- D-
THEY HAVE THE SAME ATTACK POINTS...!
HOW WILL THIS END?!
GRAAH!

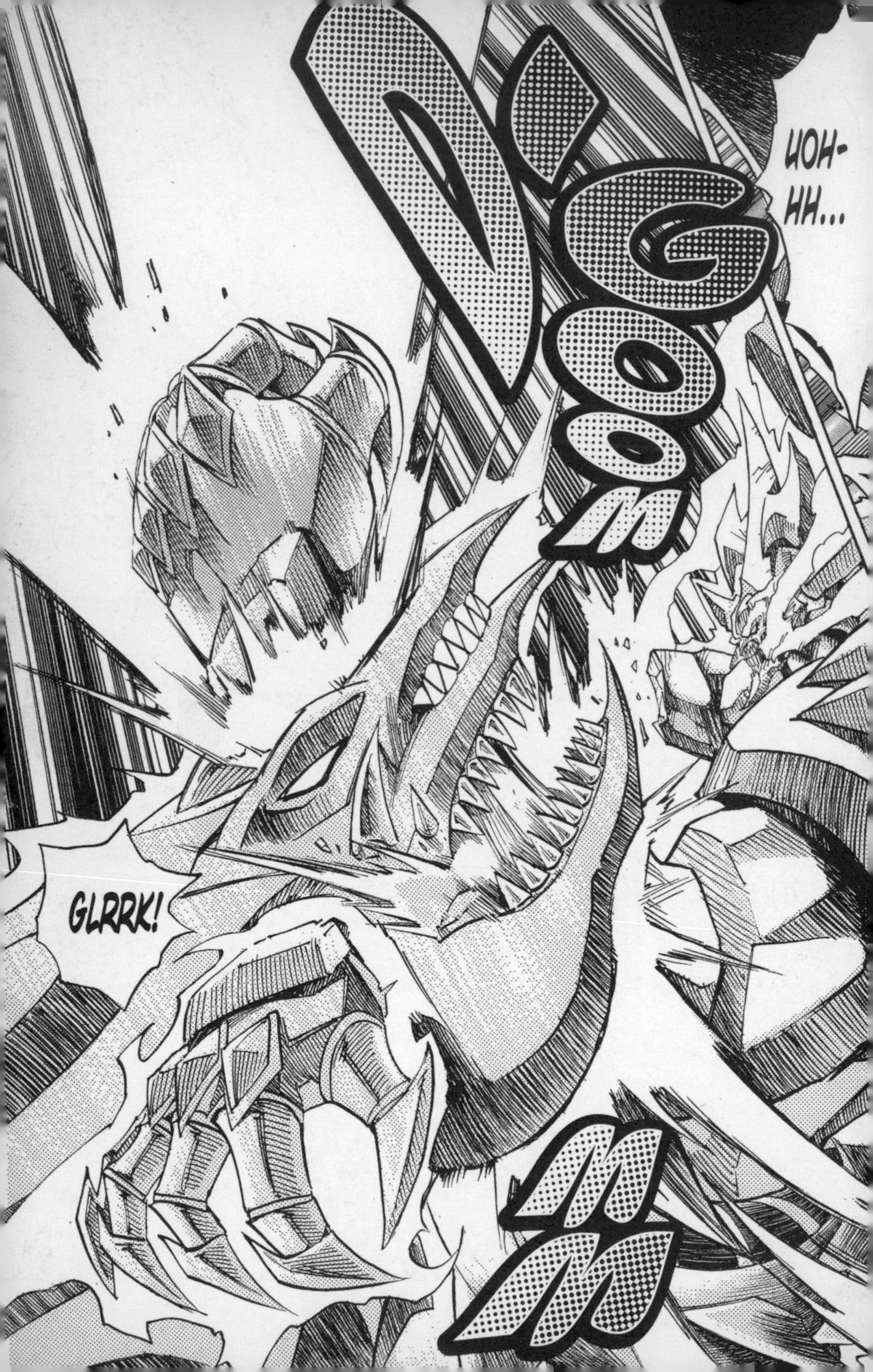
UOH-HH...
GLRRK!

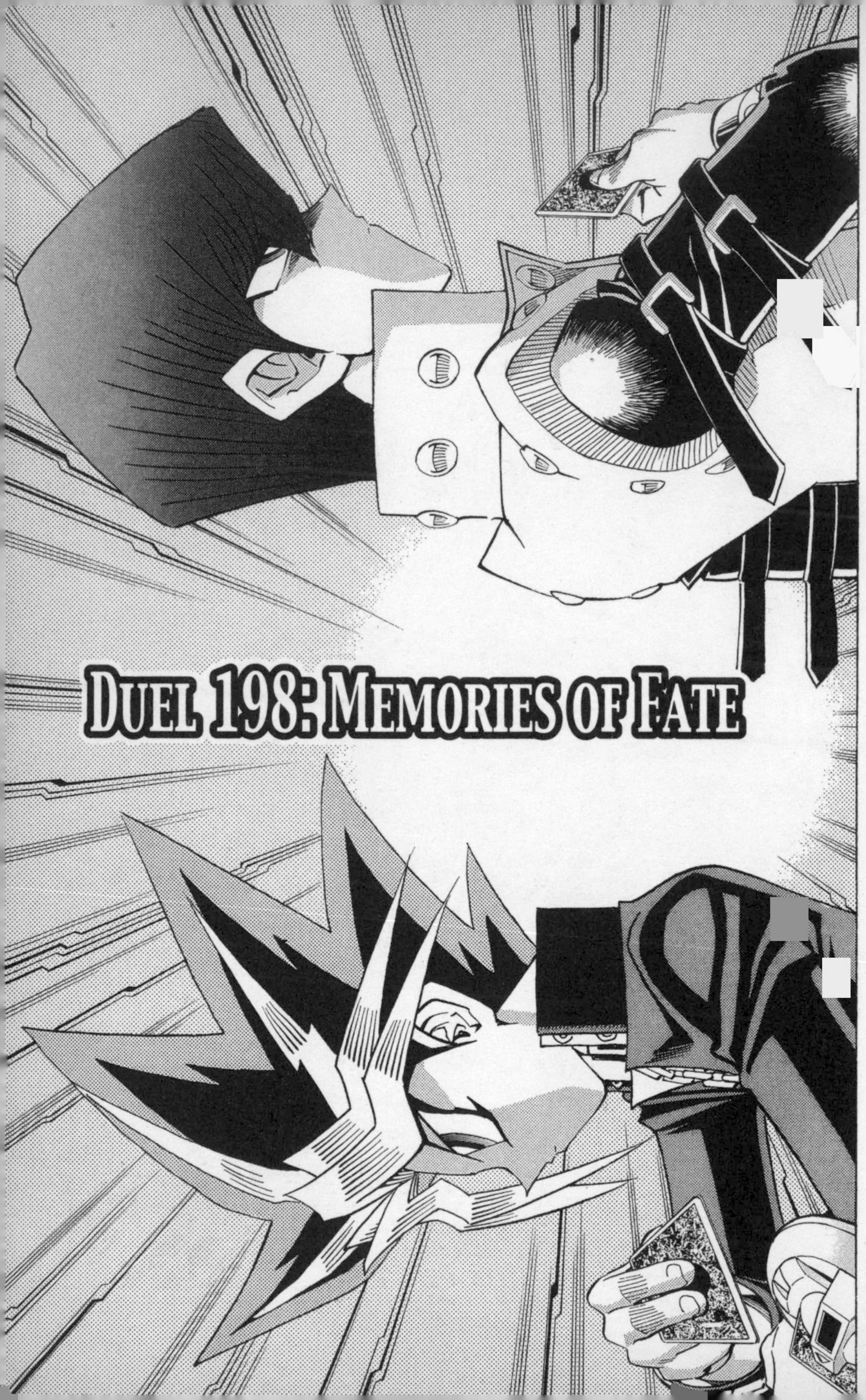
DUEL 198: MEMORIES OF FATE

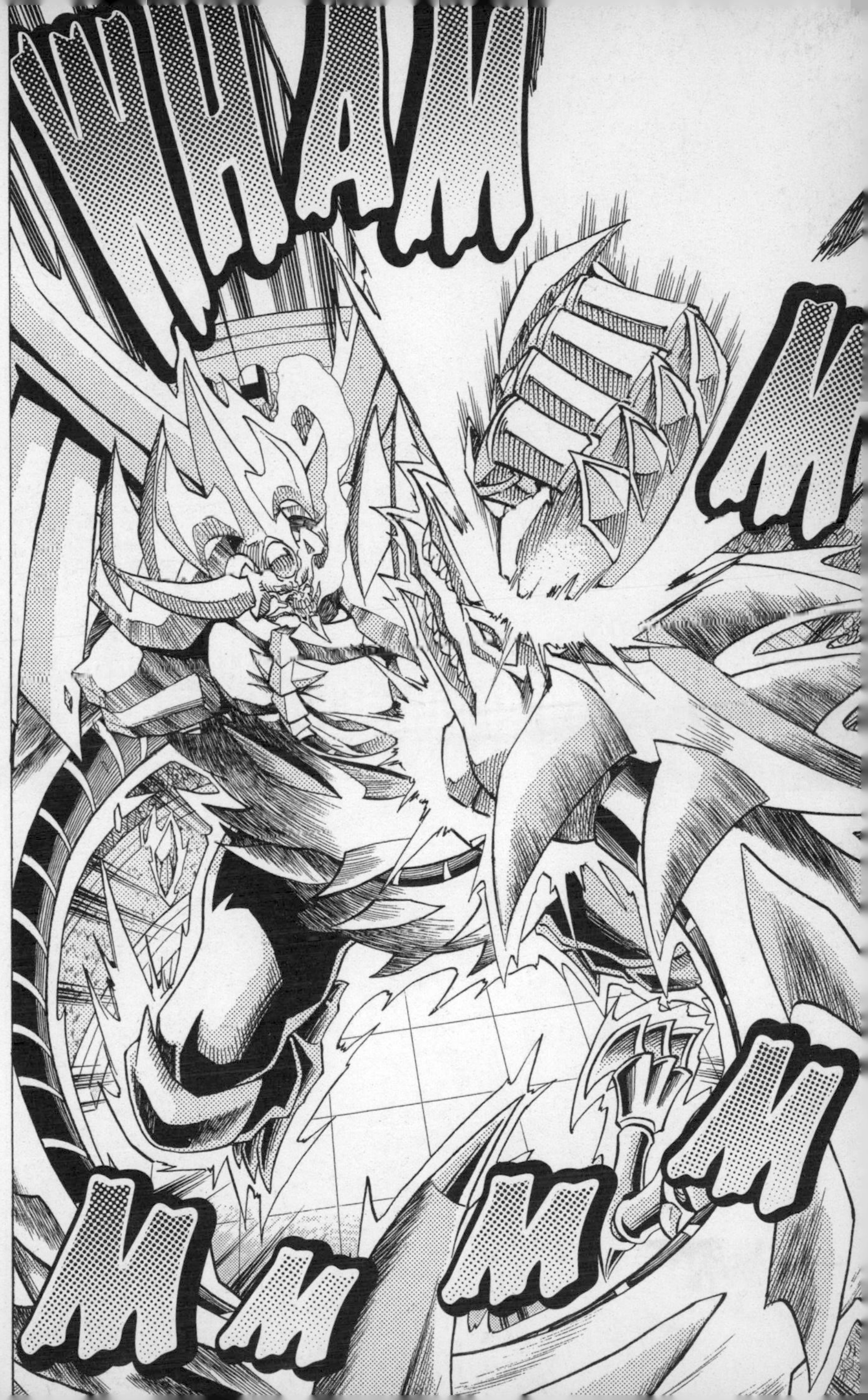
WHAMMMMMM

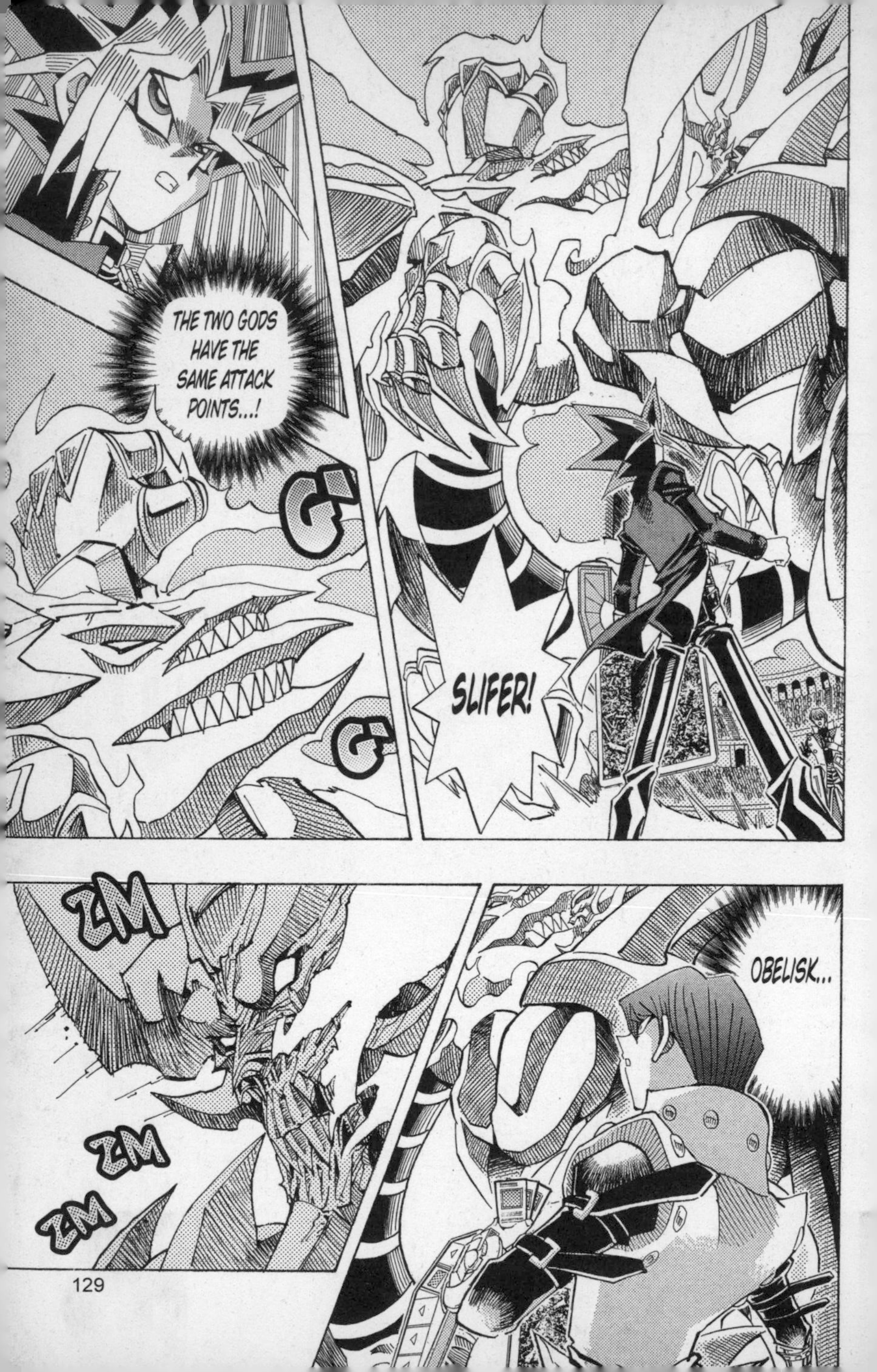
SLIFER!
THE TWO GODS HAVE THE SAME ATTACK POINTS...!
G
G
OBELISK...
Z-M
Z-M
Z-M

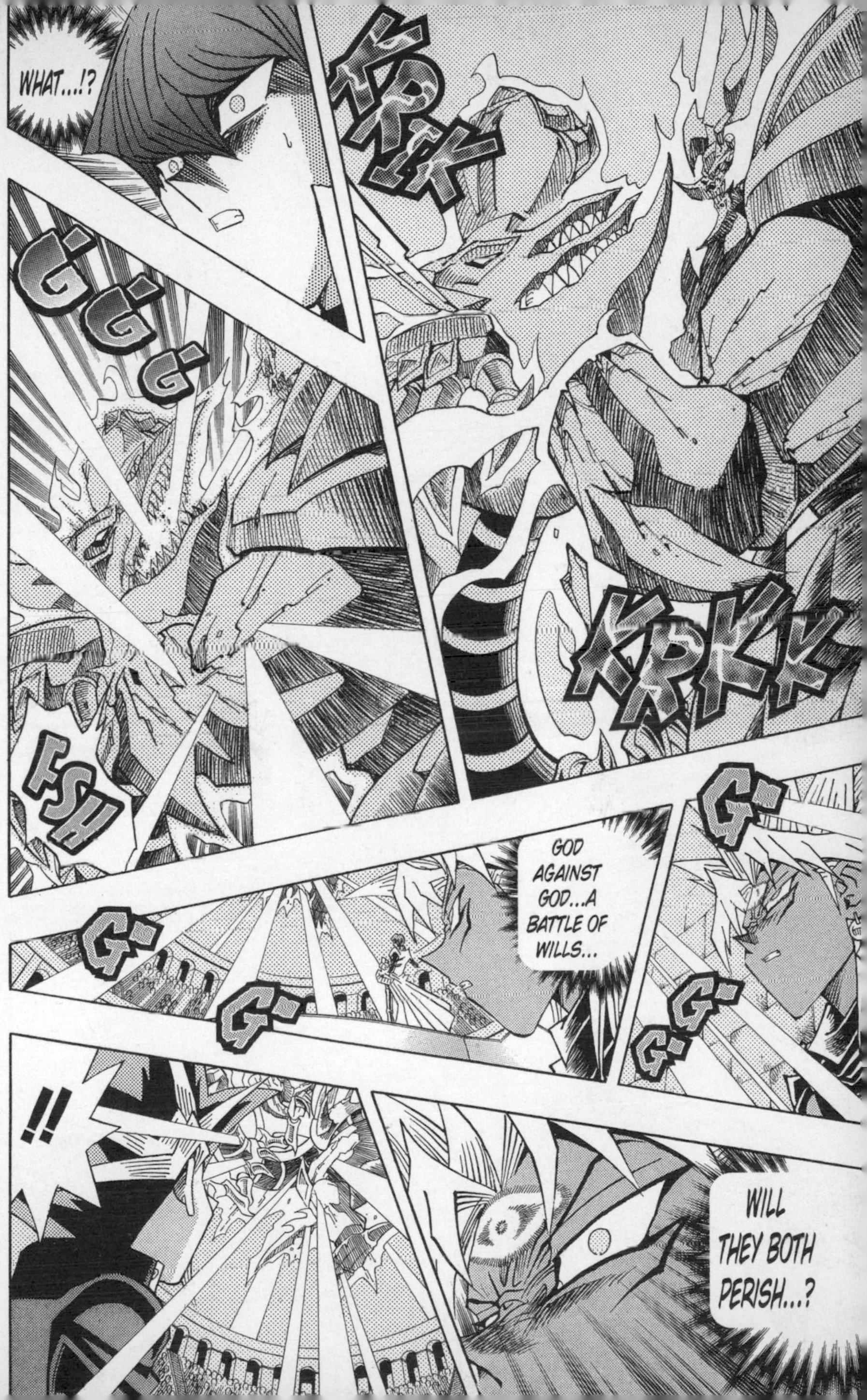
KRKK
KRKK
WHAT...!?
G G G
FSH
G
GOD AGAINST GOD...A BATTLE OF WILLS...
G G
G
G
WILL THEY BOTH PERISH...?
!!

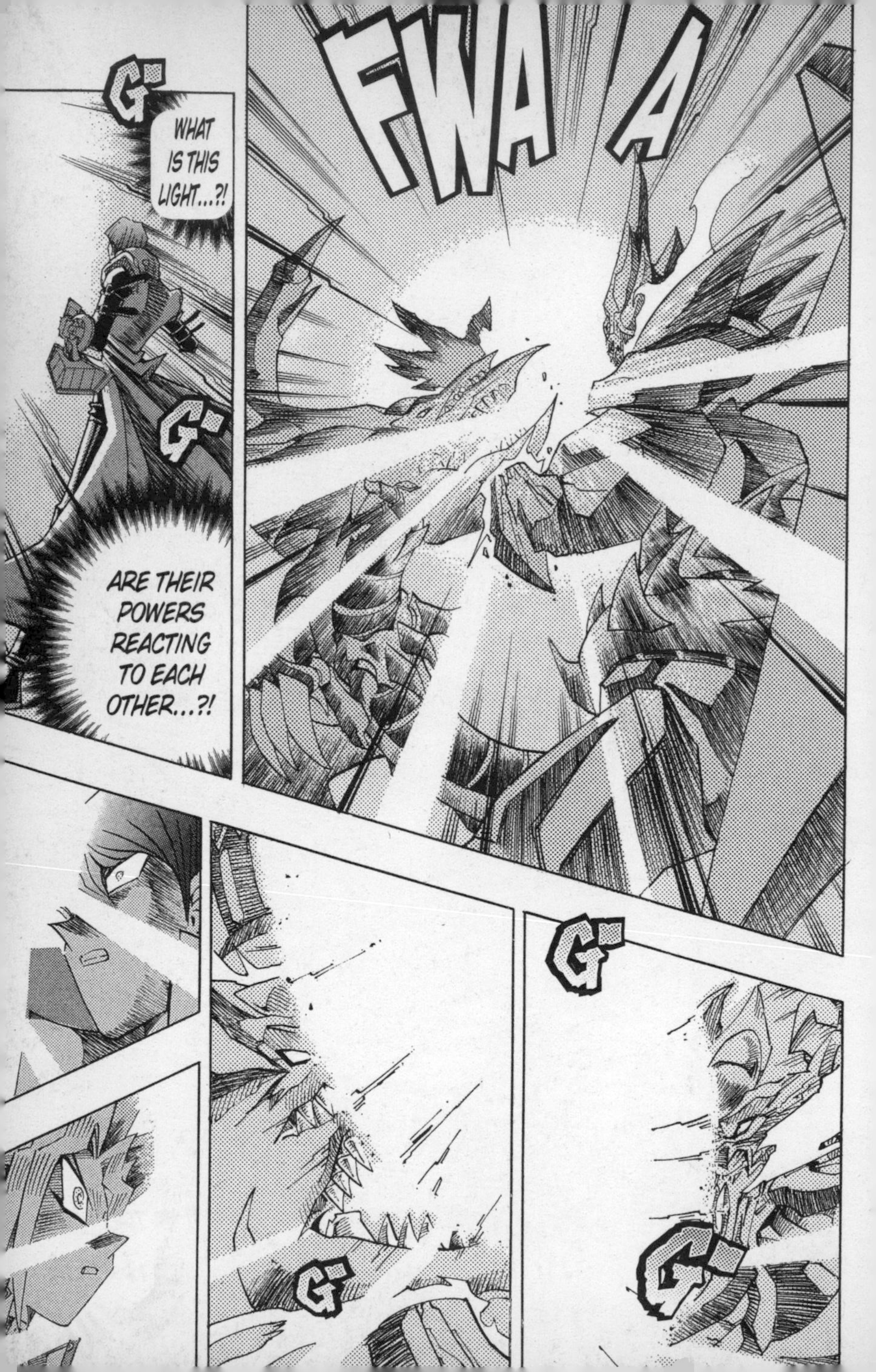
FWA A
G
WHAT IS THIS LIGHT...?!
G
ARE THEIR POWERS REACTING TO EACH OTHER...?!
G
G
G

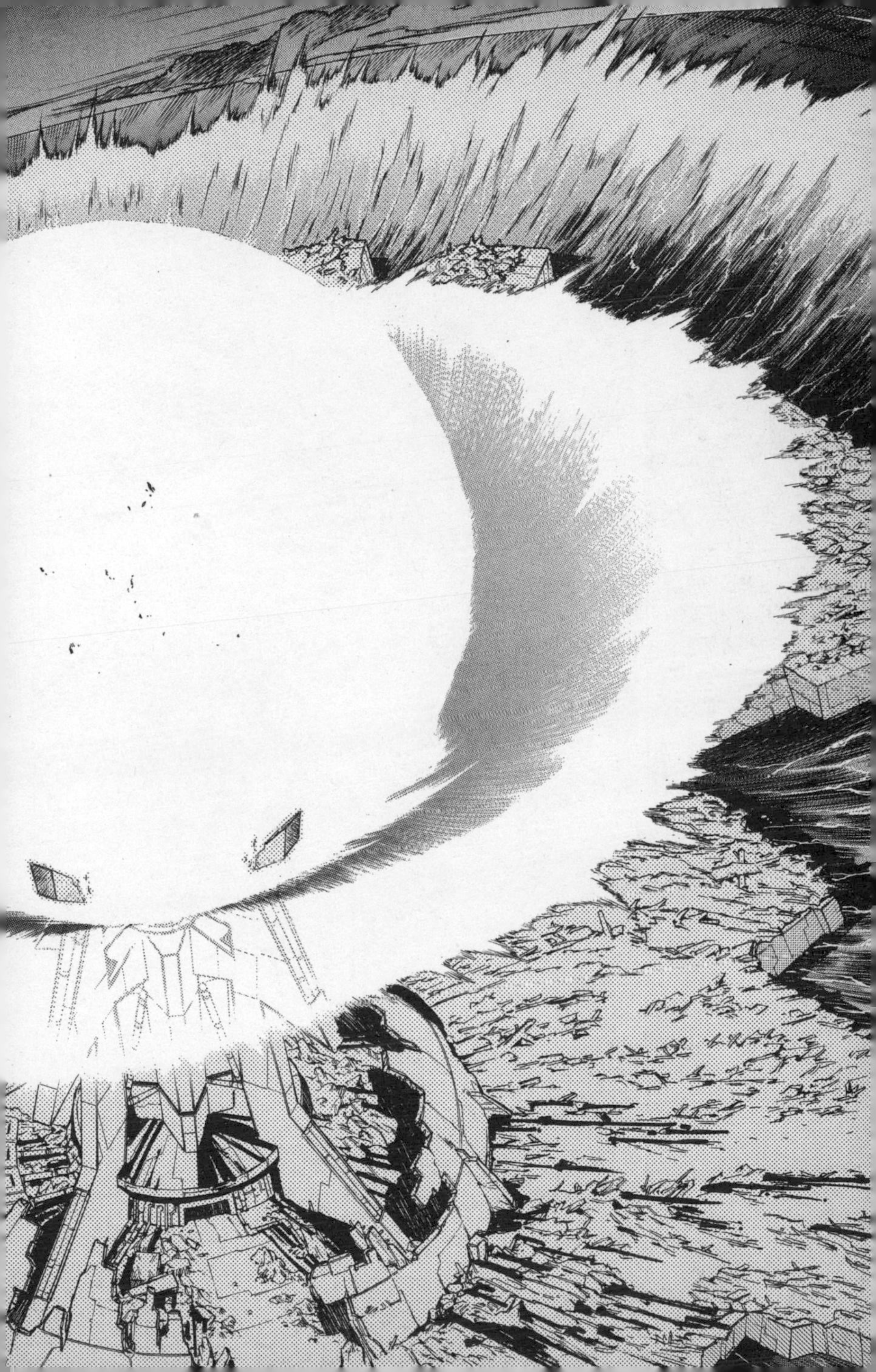

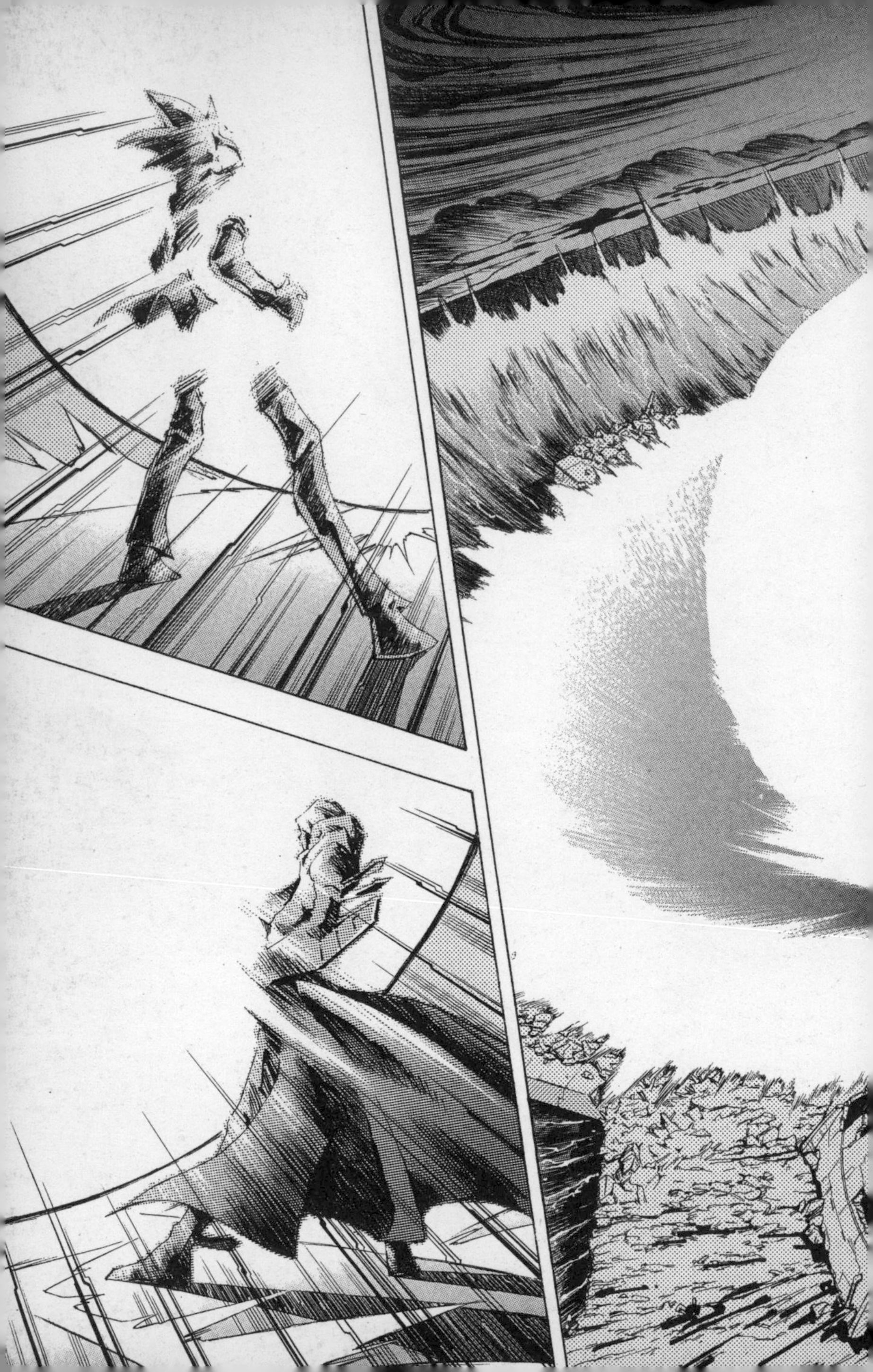

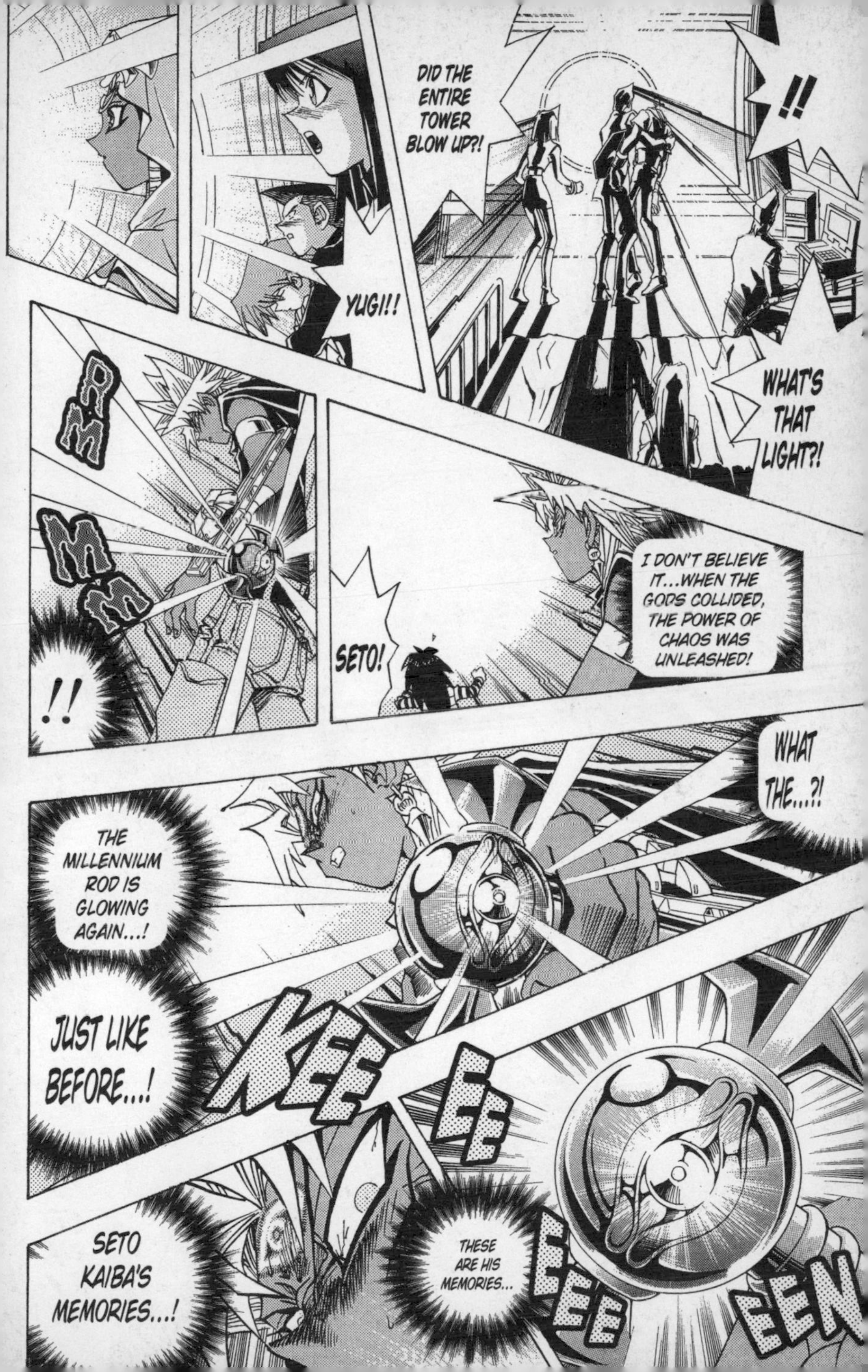
!!
DID THE ENTIRE TOWER BLOW UP?!
WHAT'S THAT LIGHT?!
YUGI!!
I DON'T BELIEVE IT...WHEN THE GODS COLLIDED, THE POWER OF CHAOS WAS UNLEASHED!
SETO!
RM
MMM
!!
WHAT THE...?!
THE MILLENNIUM ROD IS GLOWING AGAIN...!
JUST LIKE BEFORE...!
KEE
EE
EEE
EEN
THESE ARE HIS MEMORIES...
SETO KAIBA'S MEMORIES...!

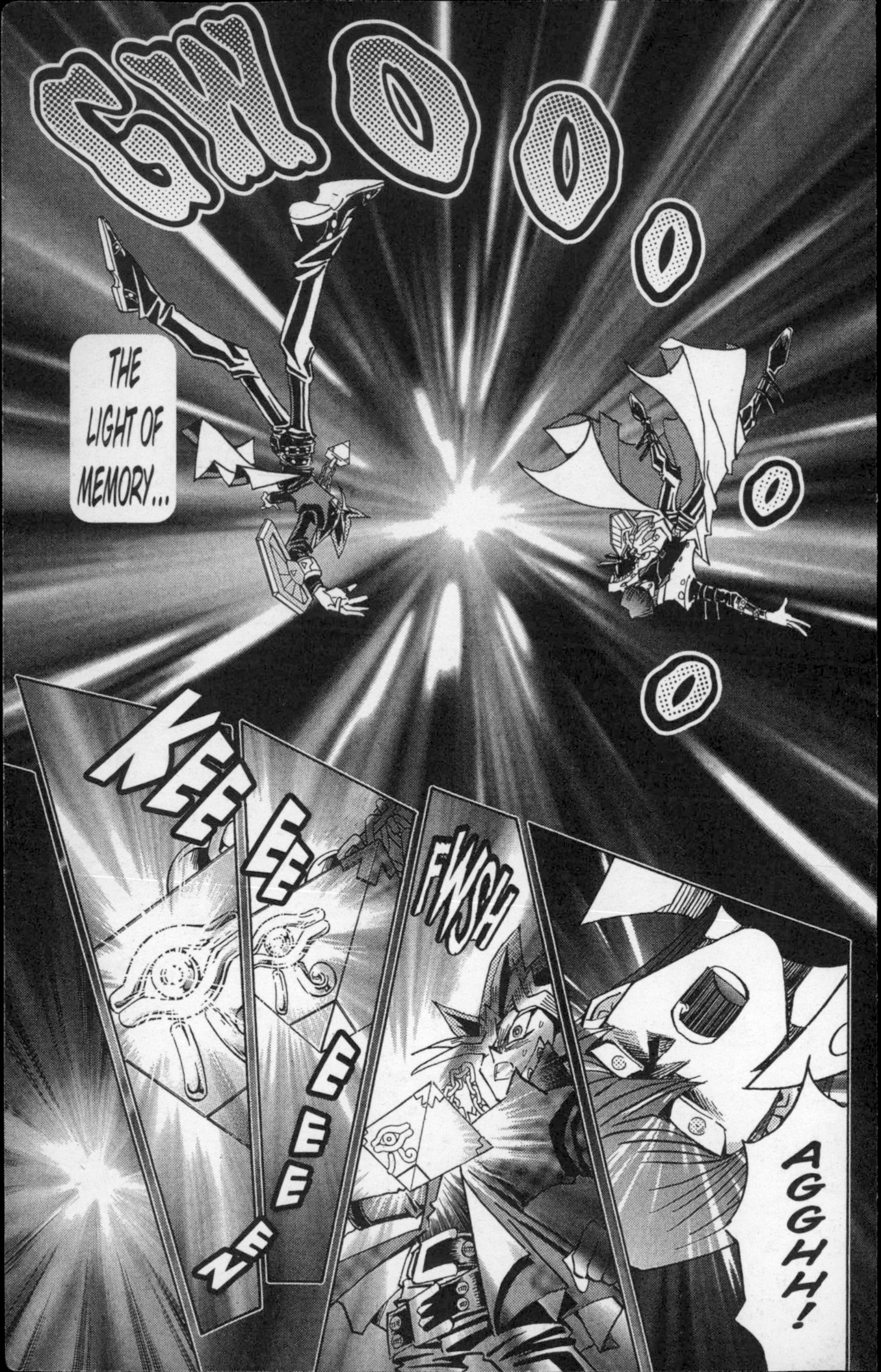
GWOOOOOO
THE LIGHT OF MEMORY...
AGGHH!
FWSH
KEEEEEEEEN

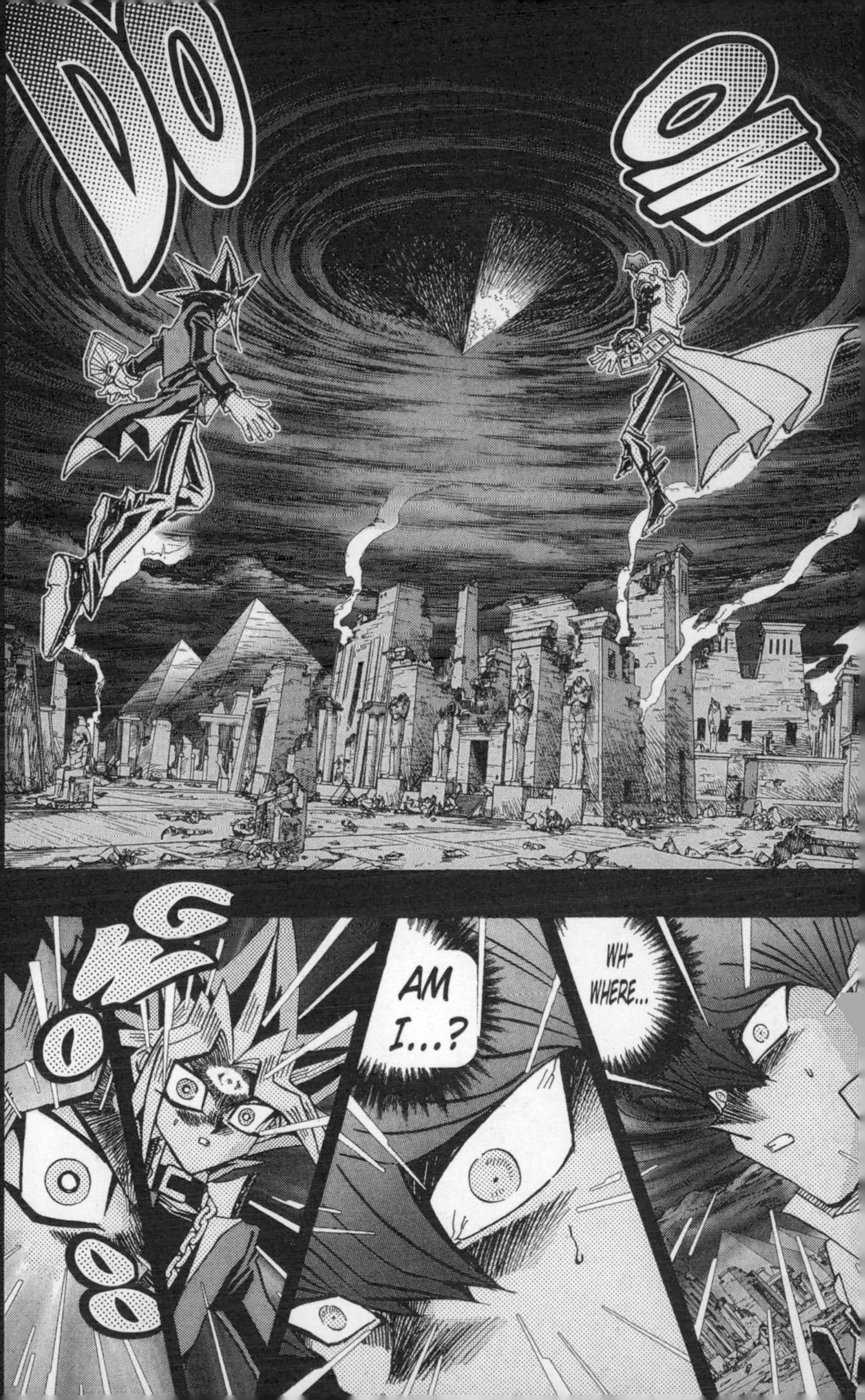
DOOM
WH- WHERE...
AM I...?
GWOOOO

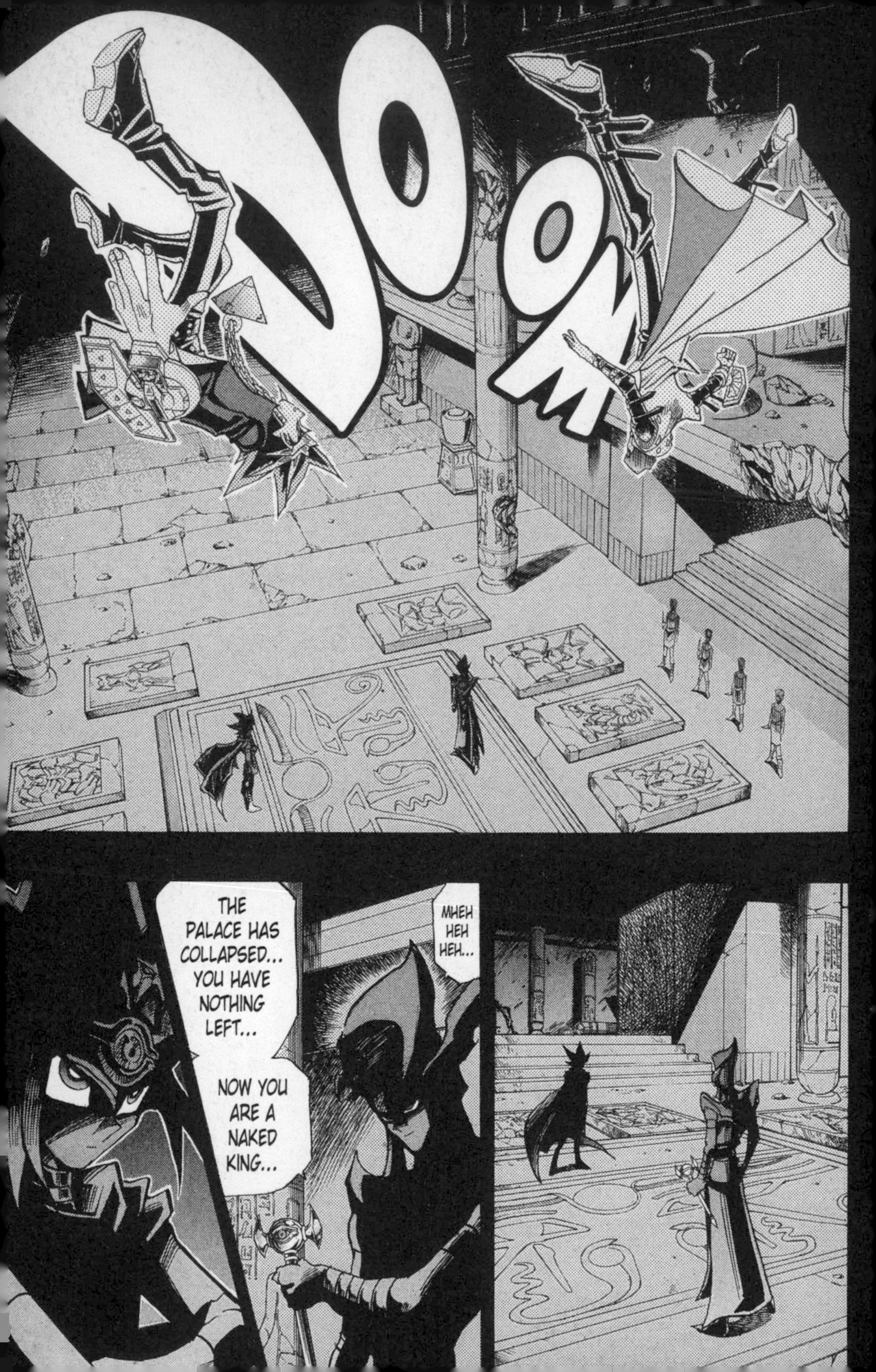
DOOM
MHEH HEH HEH...
THE PALACE HAS COLLAPSED... YOU HAVE NOTHING LEFT...
NOW YOU ARE A NAKED KING...

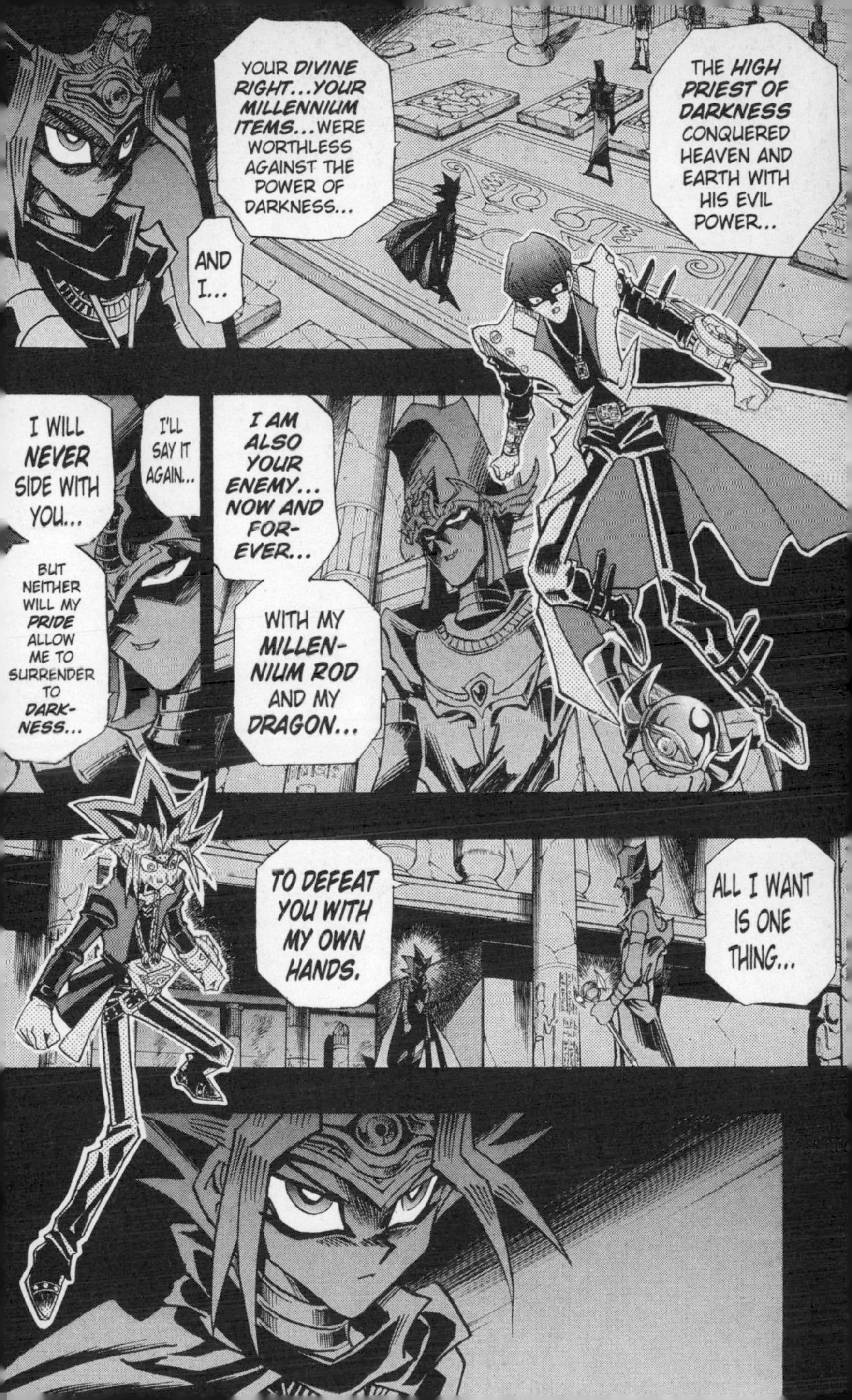
THE HIGH PRIEST OF DARKNESS CONQUERED HEAVEN AND EARTH WITH HIS EVIL POWER...
YOUR DIVINE RIGHT...YOUR MILLENNIUM ITEMS...WERE WORTHLESS AGAINST THE POWER OF DARKNESS...
AND I...
I AM ALSO YOUR ENEMY... NOW AND FOR-EVER...
WITH MY MILLEN-NIUM ROD AND MY DRAGON...
I'LL SAY IT AGAIN...
I WILL NEVER SIDE WITH YOU...
BUT NEITHER WILL MY PRIDE ALLOW ME TO SURRENDER TO DARK-NESS...
ALL I WANT IS ONE THING...
TO DEFEAT YOU WITH MY OWN HANDS.

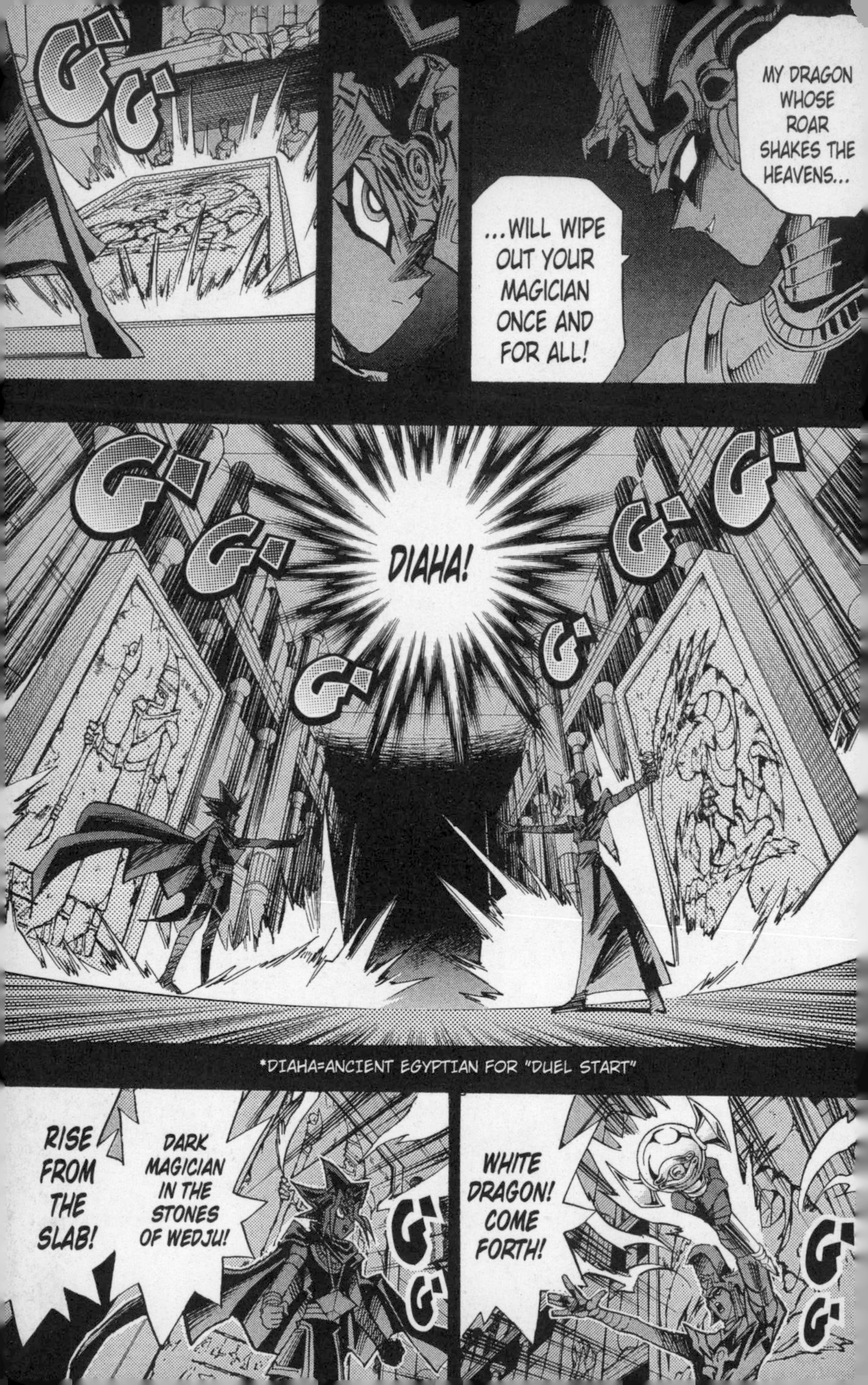
MY DRAGON WHOSE ROAR SHAKES THE HEAVENS...
...WILL WIPE OUT YOUR MAGICIAN ONCE AND FOR ALL!
G G
G G G G
DIAHA!
G G G G
*DIAHA=ANCIENT EGYPTIAN FOR "DUEL START"
WHITE DRAGON! COME FORTH!
G G
DARK MAGICIAN IN THE STONES OF WEDJU!
RISE FROM THE SLAB!
G G

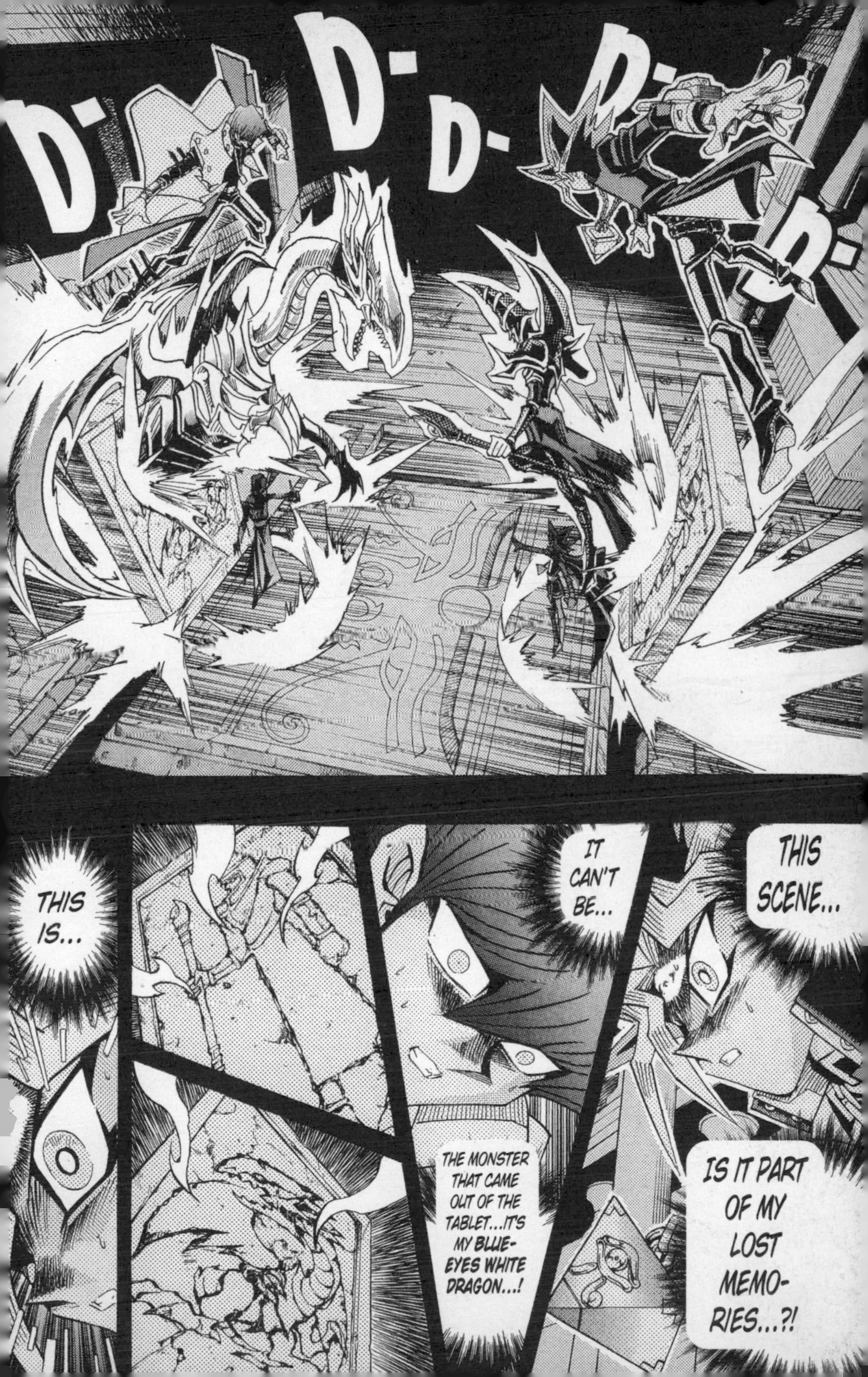
D- D- D- D- D- D-
THIS SCENE...
IS IT PART OF MY LOST MEMORIES...?!
IT CAN'T BE...
THE MONSTER THAT CAME OUT OF THE TABLET...IT'S MY BLUE-EYES WHITE DRAGON...!
THIS IS...

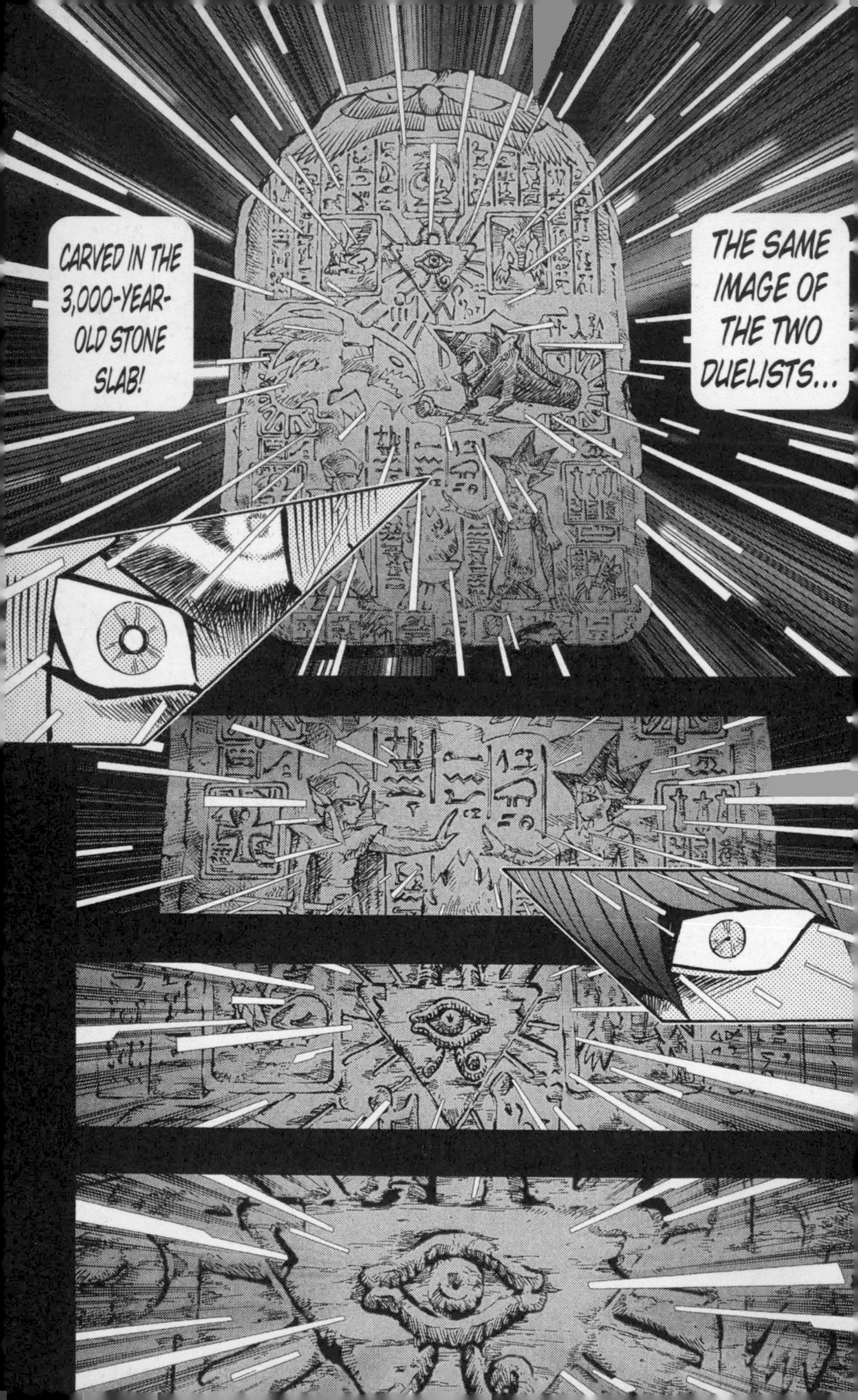
THE SAME IMAGE OF THE TWO DUELISTS...
CARVED IN THE 3,000-YEAR-OLD STONE SLAB!

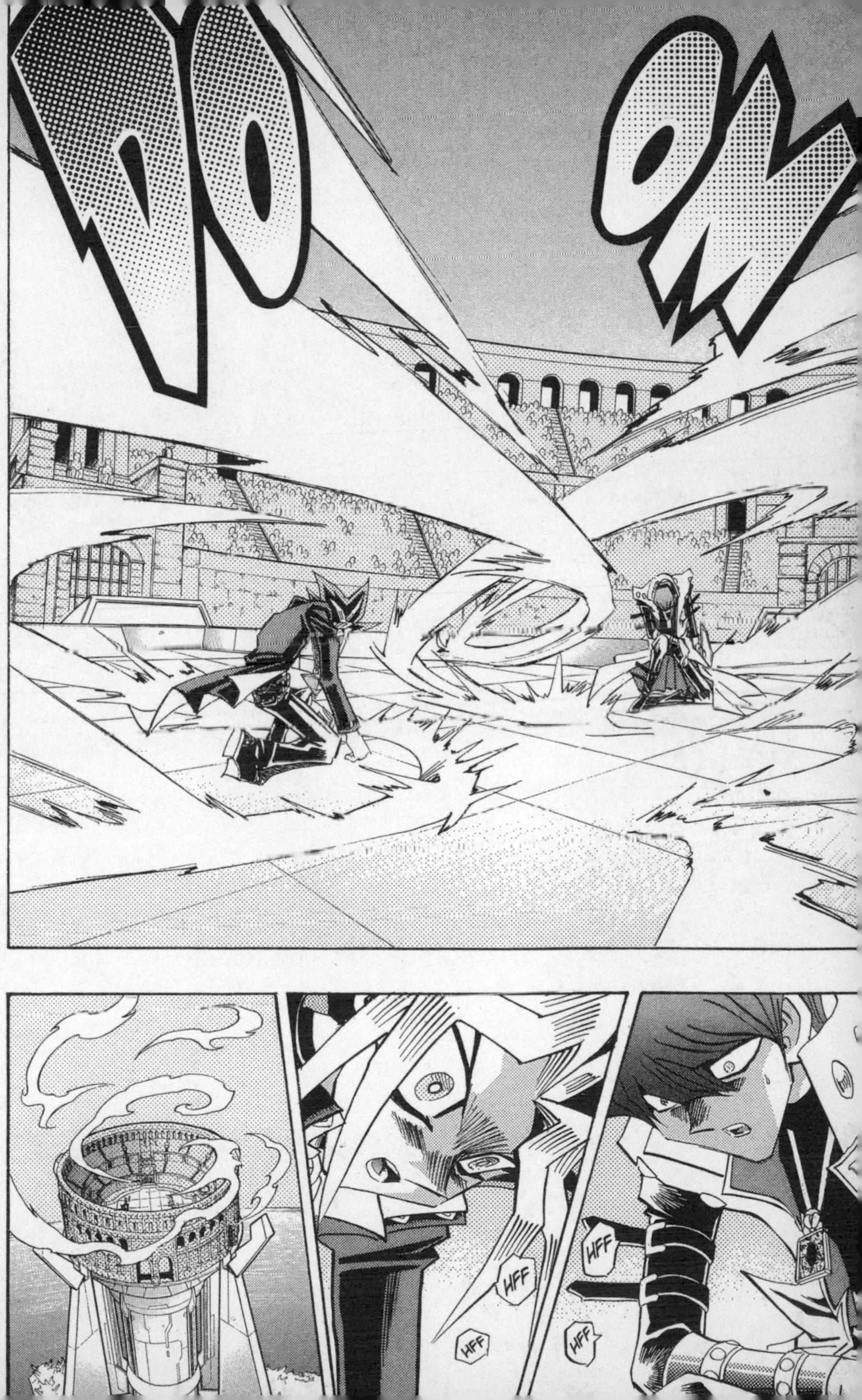
DOOM
HFF
HFF
HFF
HFF

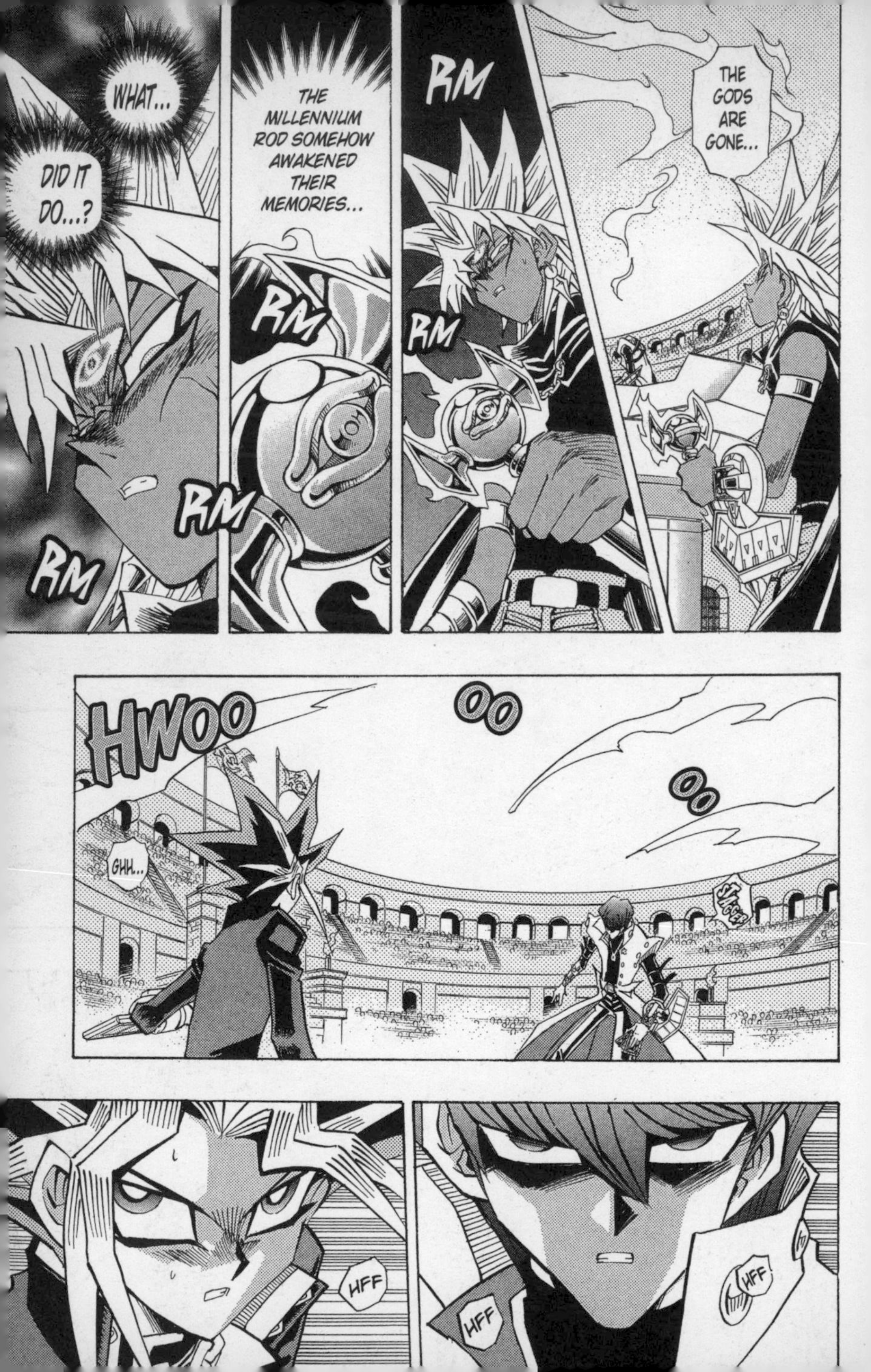
THE GODS ARE GONE...
RM
RM
THE MILLENNIUM ROD SOMEHOW AWAKENED THEIR MEMORIES...
RM
WHAT...
DID IT DO...?
RM
RM
OO
OO
HWOO
GHH...
HFF
HFF
HFF

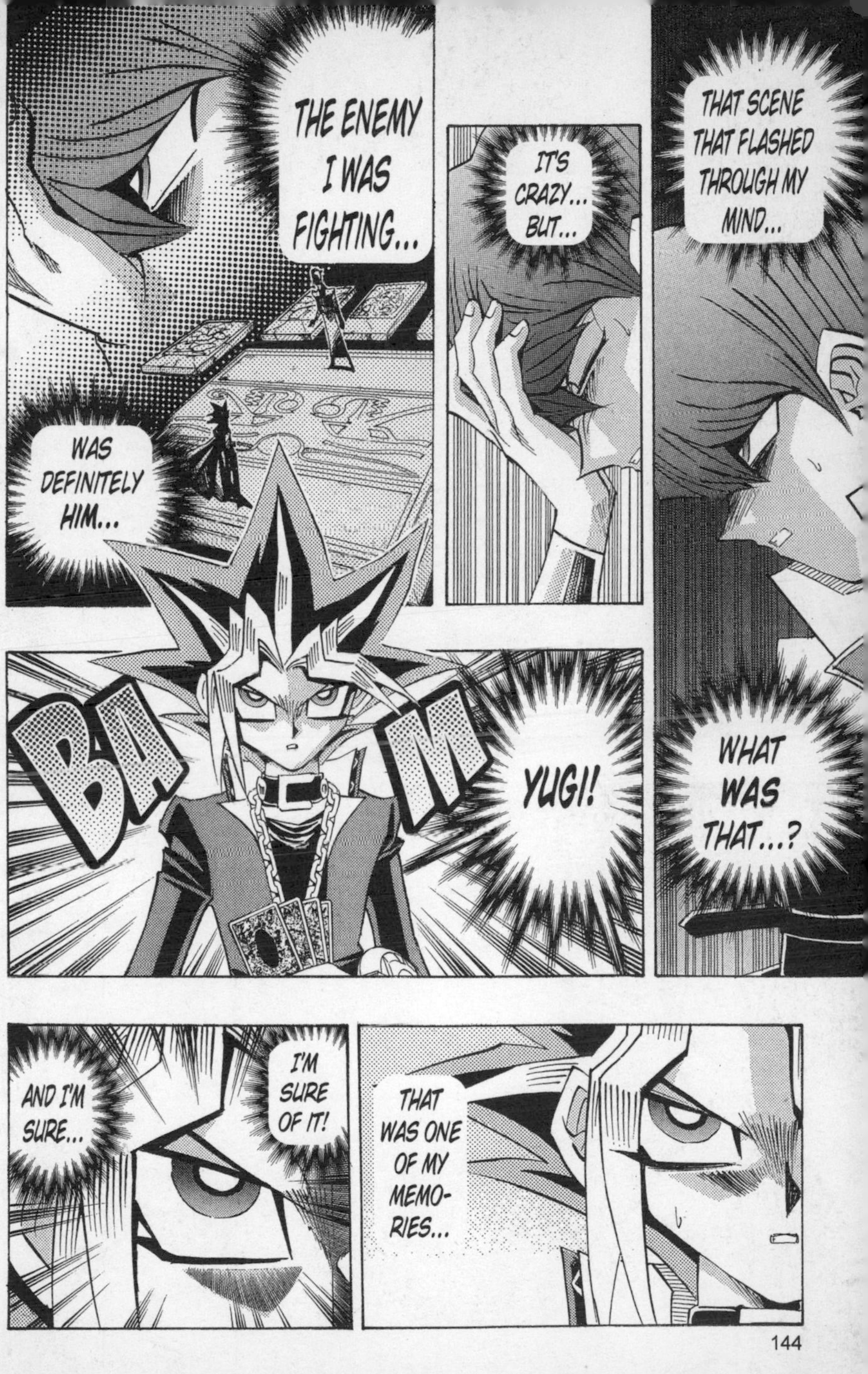
THAT SCENE THAT FLASHED THROUGH MY MIND...
WHAT WAS THAT...?
IT'S CRAZY... BUT...
THE ENEMY I WAS FIGHTING...
WAS DEFINITELY HIM...
BAM
YUGI!
THAT WAS ONE OF MY MEMO-RIES...
I'M SURE OF IT!
AND I'M SURE...

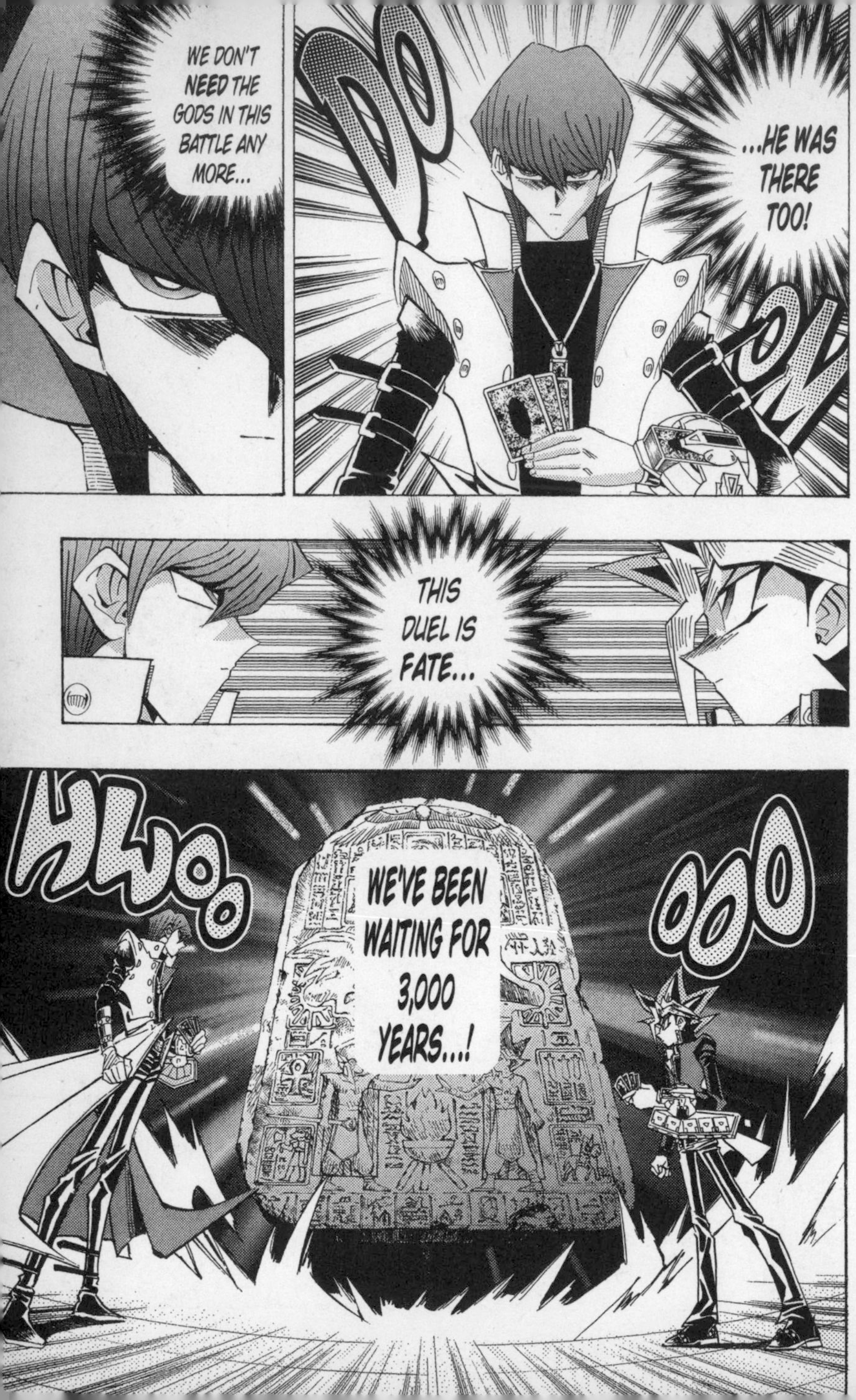
...HE WAS THERE TOO!
WE DON'T NEED THE GODS IN THIS BATTLE ANY MORE...
THIS DUEL IS FATE...
WE'VE BEEN WAITING FOR 3,000 YEARS...!

READ THIS WAY

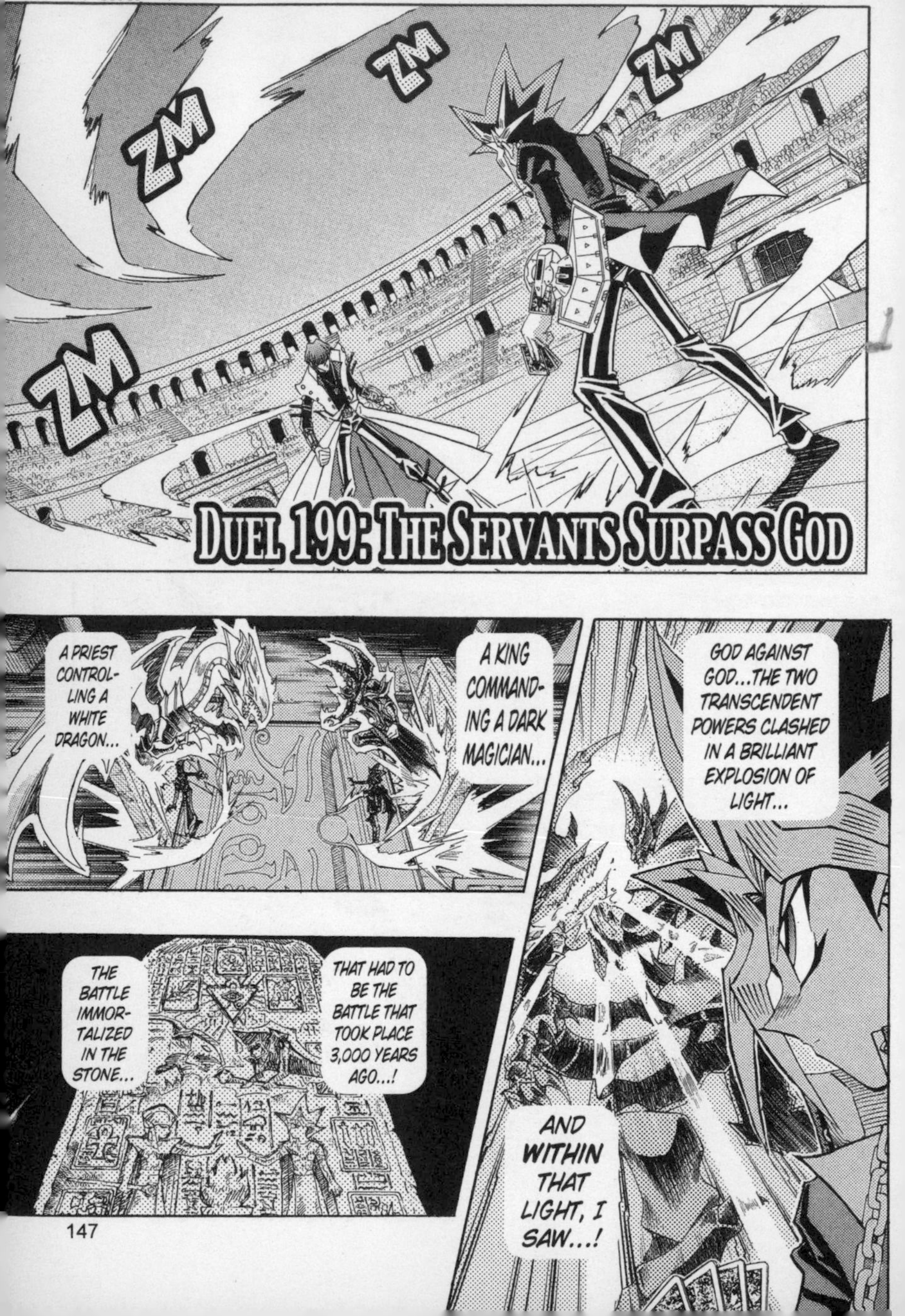
ZM
ZM
ZM
ZM
Duel 199: The Servants Surpass God
GOD AGAINST GOD...THE TWO TRANSCENDENT POWERS CLASHED IN A BRILLIANT EXPLOSION OF LIGHT...
AND WITHIN THAT LIGHT, I SAW...!
A KING COMMAND-ING A DARK MAGICIAN...
A PRIEST CONTROL-LING A WHITE DRAGON...
THAT HAD TO BE THE BATTLE THAT TOOK PLACE 3,000 YEARS AGO...!
THE BATTLE IMMOR-TALIZED IN THE STONE...

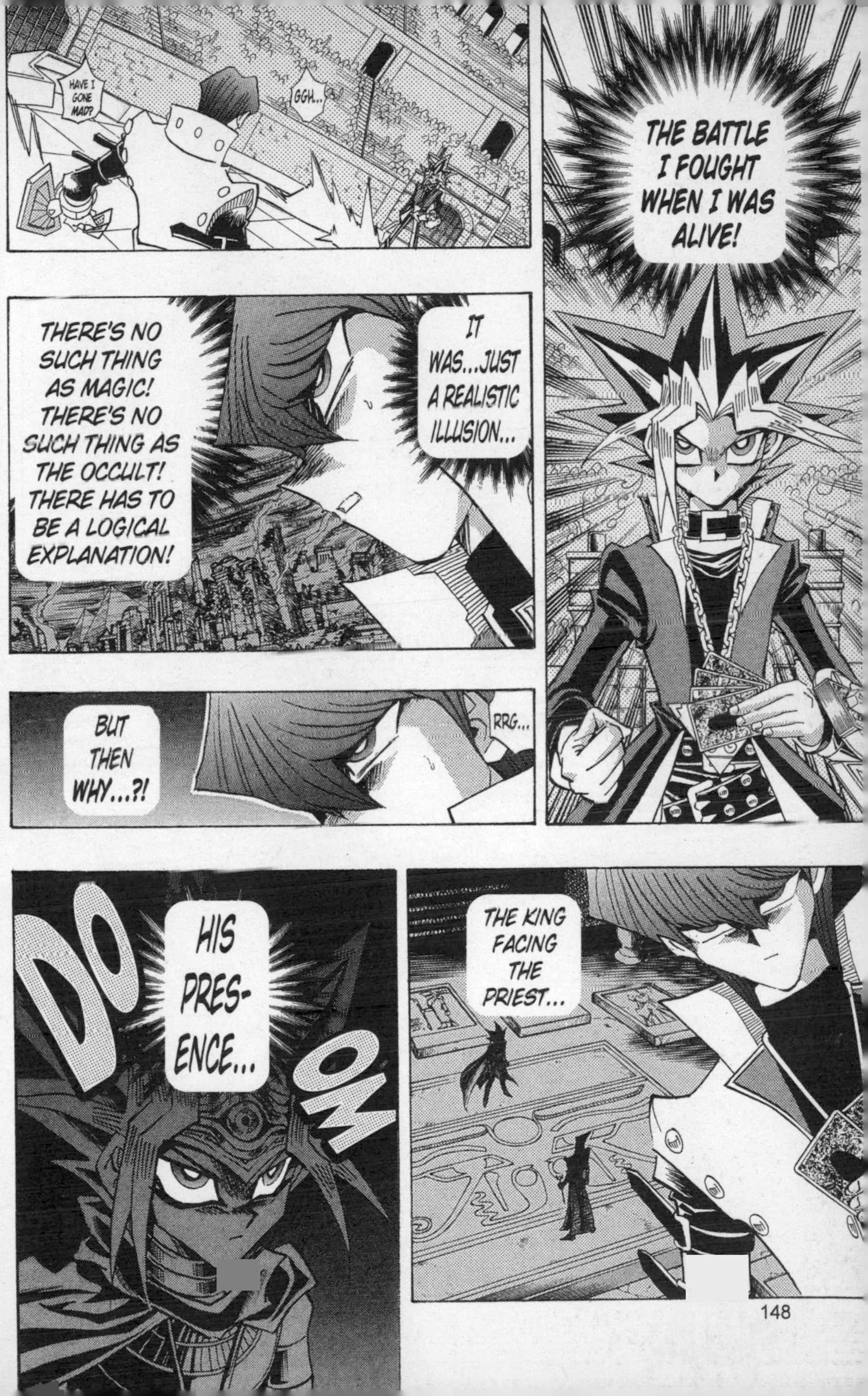
THE BATTLE I FOUGHT WHEN I WAS ALIVE!
GGH...
HAVE I GONE MAD?
IT WAS...JUST A REALISTIC ILLUSION...
THERE'S NO SUCH THING AS MAGIC! THERE'S NO SUCH THING AS THE OCCULT! THERE HAS TO BE A LOGICAL EXPLANATION!
RRG...
BUT THEN WHY...?!
THE KING FACING THE PRIEST...
HIS PRES-ENCE...
DOOM

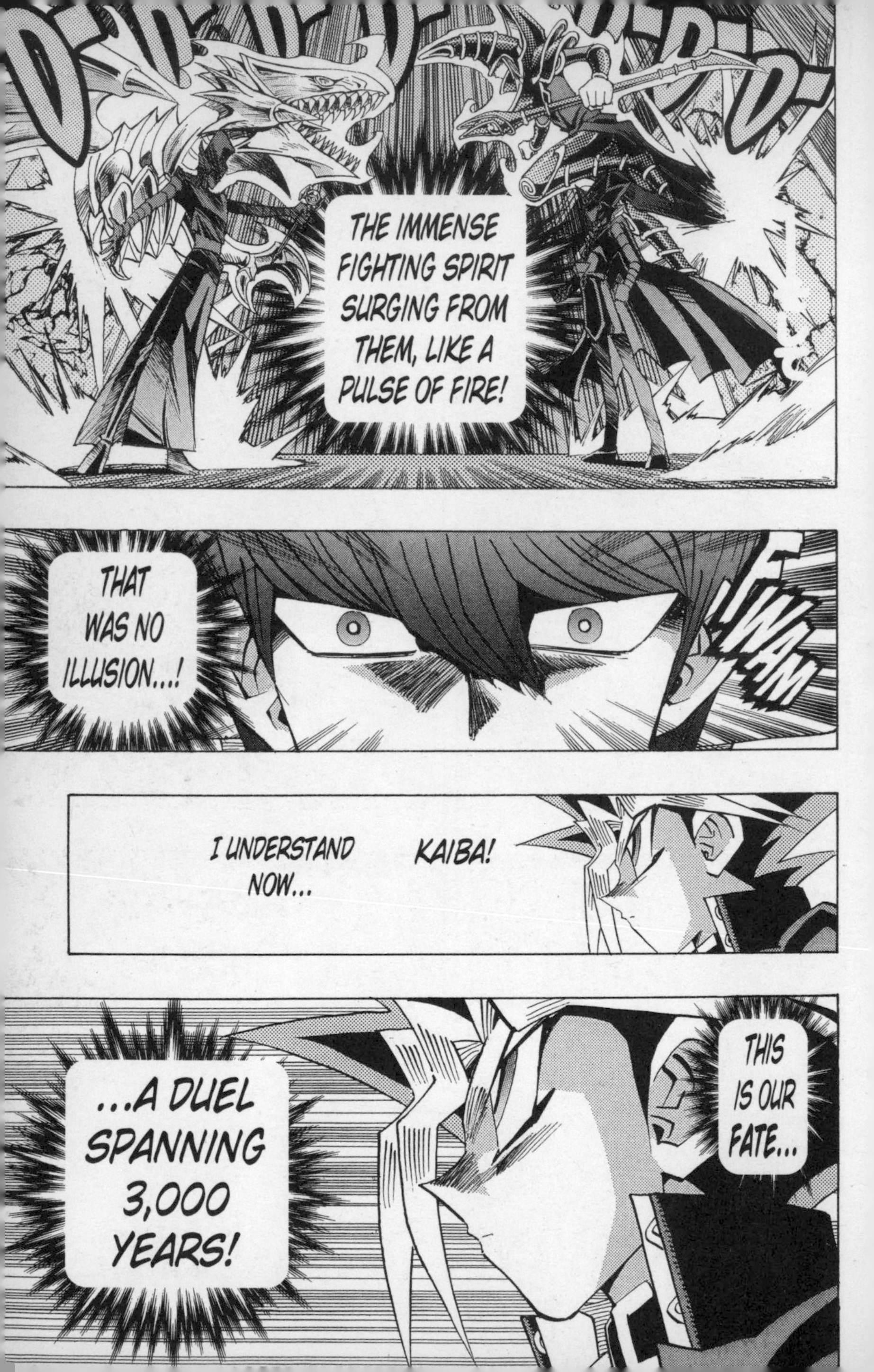
THE IMMENSE FIGHTING SPIRIT SURGING FROM THEM, LIKE A PULSE OF FIRE!
THAT WAS NO ILLUSION...!
I UNDERSTAND NOW...
KAIBA!
THIS IS OUR FATE...
...A DUEL SPANNING 3,000 YEARS!

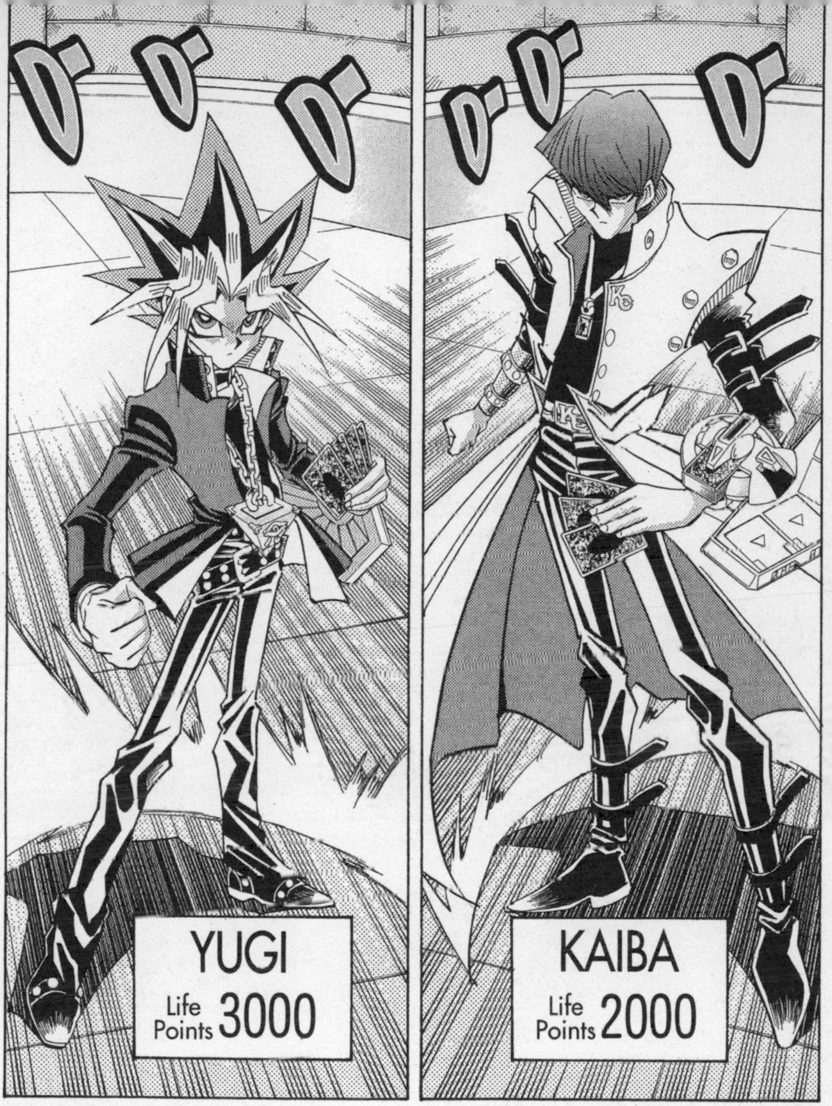
KAIBA
Life Points 2000
YUGI
Life Points 3000

DUEL 199:
THE SERVANTS SURPASS GOD

READ THIS WAY

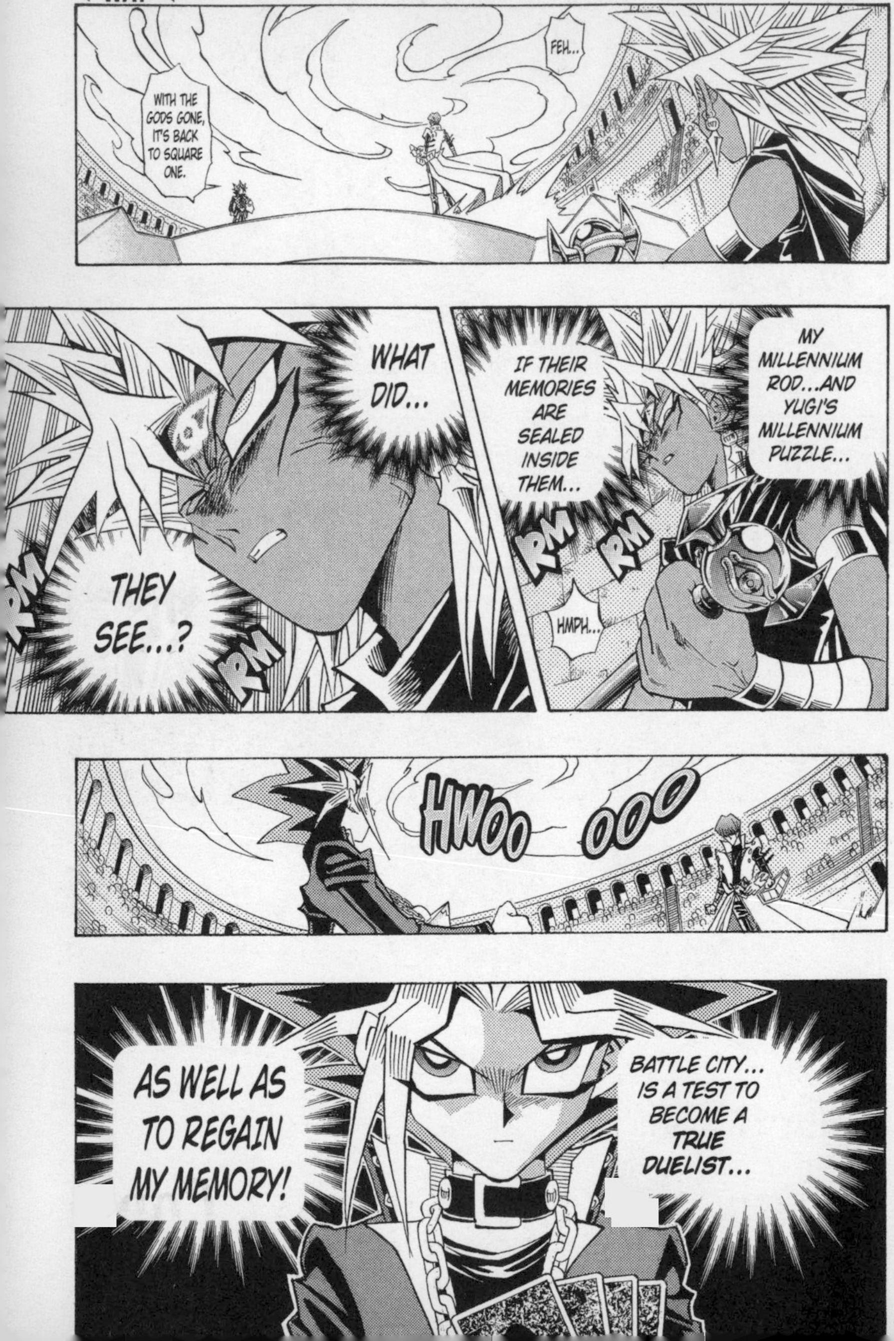
FEH...
WITH THE GODS GONE, IT'S BACK TO SQUARE ONE.
MY MILLENNIUM ROD...AND YUGI'S MILLENNIUM PUZZLE...
IF THEIR MEMORIES ARE SEALED INSIDE THEM...
RM
RM
HMPH...
WHAT DID...
THEY SEE...?
RM
RM
HWOO OOO
BATTLE CITY... IS A TEST TO BECOME A TRUE DUELIST...
AS WELL AS TO REGAIN MY MEMORY!

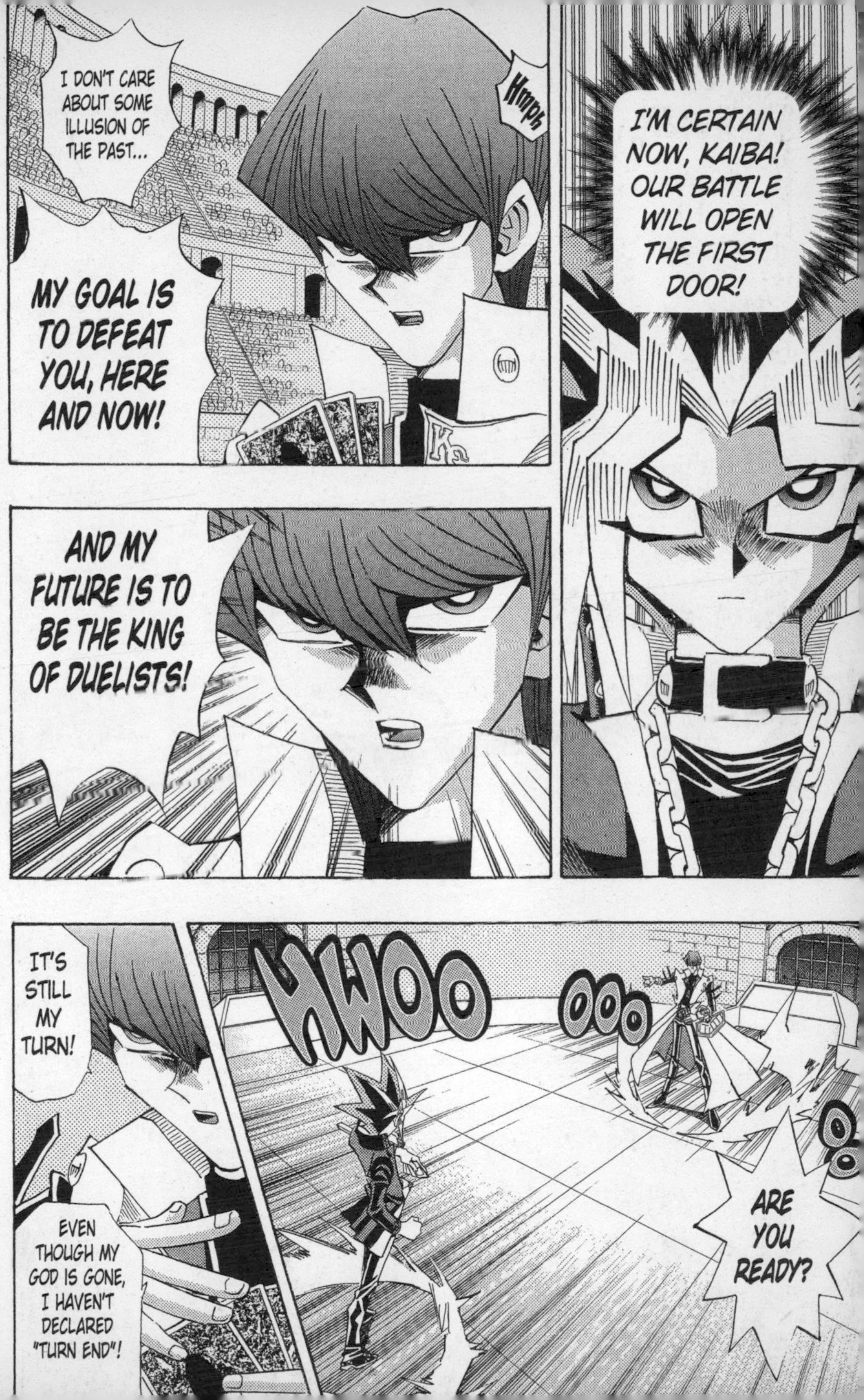
I'M CERTAIN NOW, KAIBA! OUR BATTLE WILL OPEN THE FIRST DOOR!
Hmph
I DON'T CARE ABOUT SOME ILLUSION OF THE PAST...
MY GOAL IS TO DEFEAT YOU, HERE AND NOW!
AND MY FUTURE IS TO BE THE KING OF DUELISTS!
HWOOOOO
ARE YOU READY?
IT'S STILL MY TURN!
EVEN THOUGH MY GOD IS GONE, I HAVEN'T DECLARED "TURN END"!

READ THIS WAY

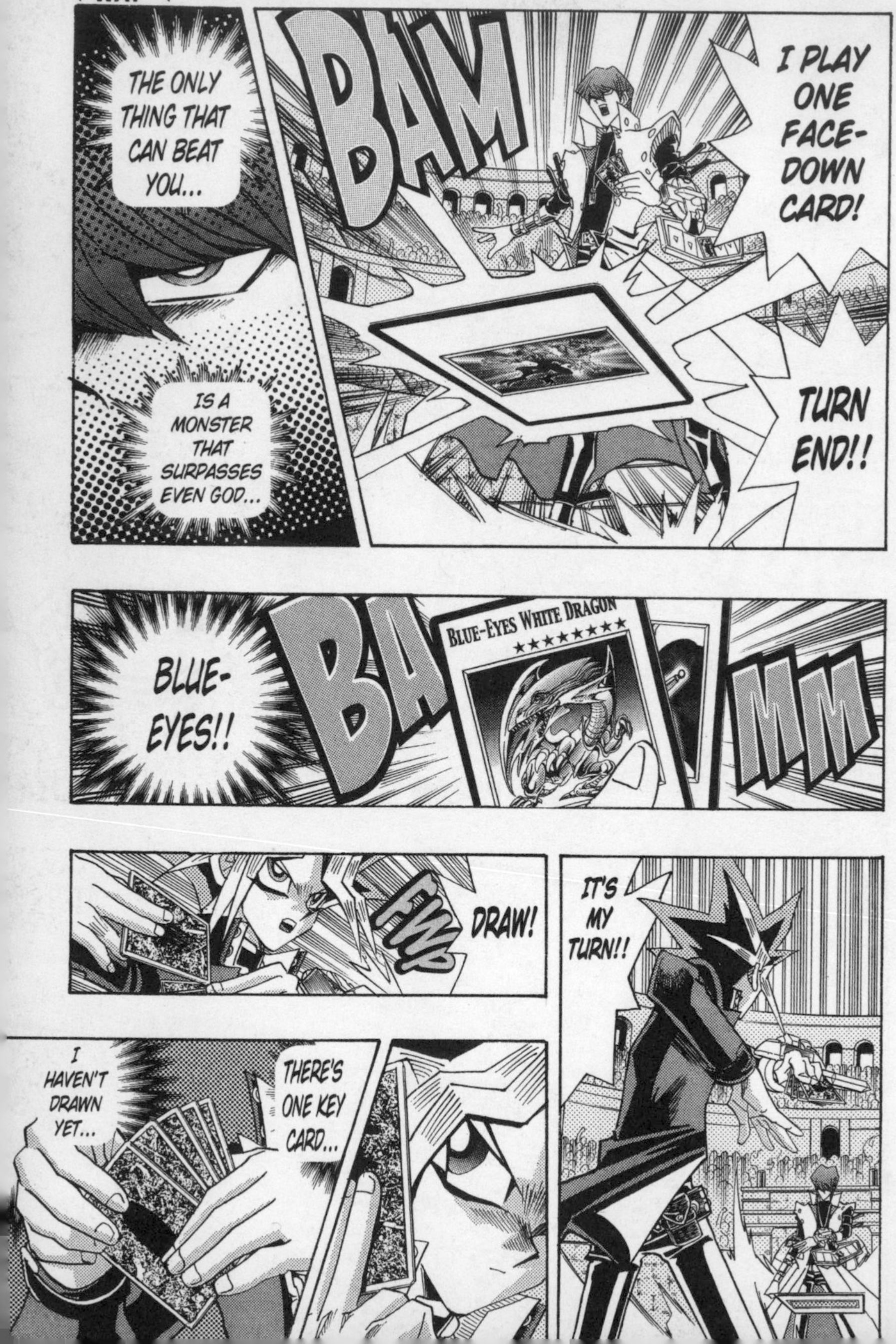
I PLAY ONE FACE-DOWN CARD!
BAM
TURN END!!
THE ONLY THING THAT CAN BEAT YOU...
IS A MONSTER THAT SURPASSES EVEN GOD...
BAMM
BLUE-EYES WHITE DRAGON
BLUE-EYES!!
IT'S MY TURN!!
DRAW!
FWP
THERE'S ONE KEY CARD...
I HAVEN'T DRAWN YET...

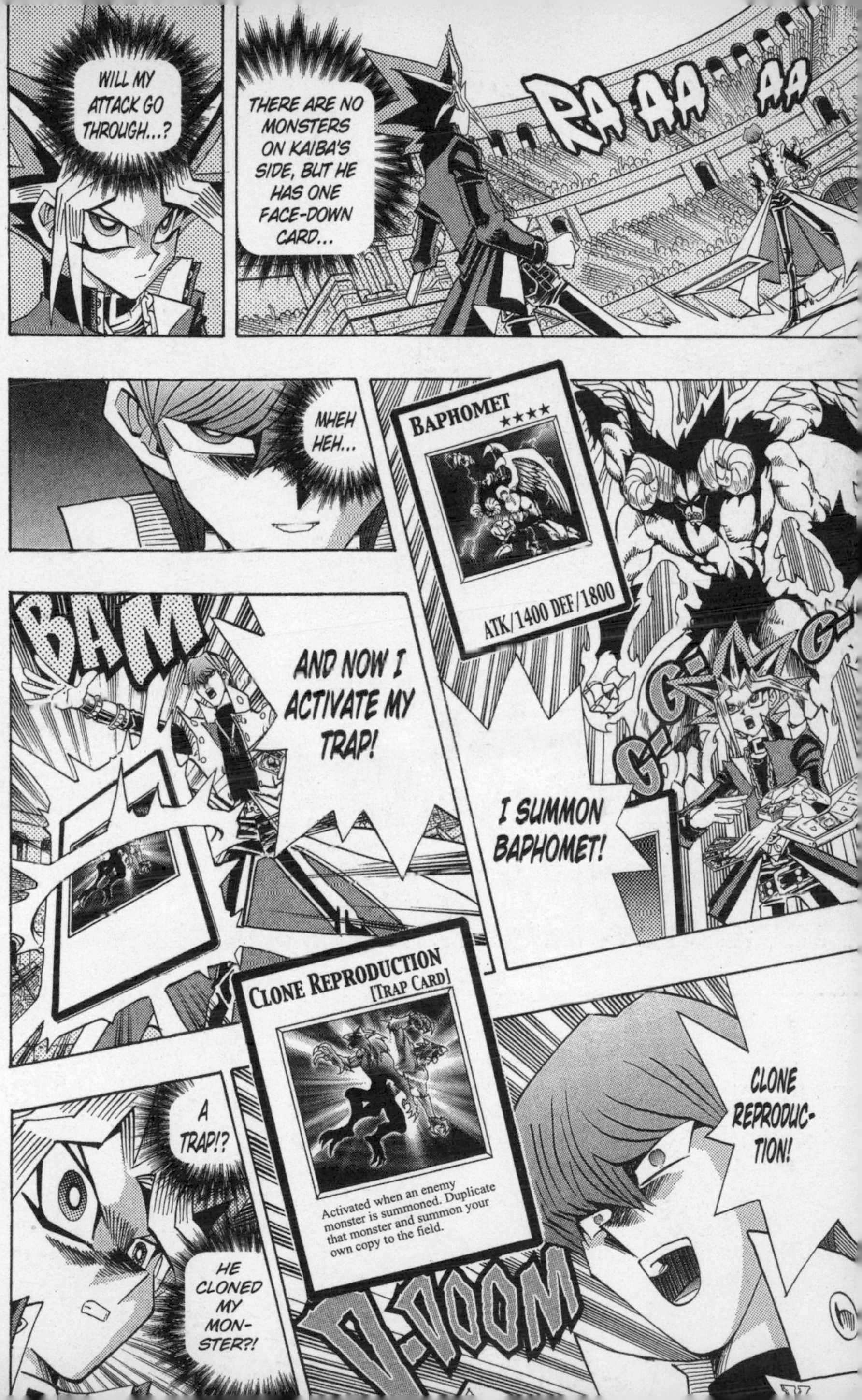
RAAAA AA
THERE ARE NO MONSTERS ON KAIBA'S SIDE, BUT HE HAS ONE FACE-DOWN CARD...
WILL MY ATTACK GO THROUGH...?
BAPHOMET ★★★★
ATK/1400 DEF/1800
G-G-G-G-G-
I SUMMON BAPHOMET!
MHEH HEH...
BAM
AND NOW I ACTIVATE MY TRAP!
CLONE REPRODUCTION!
CLONE REPRODUCTION
[TRAP CARD]
Activated when an enemy monster is summoned. Duplicate that monster and summon your own copy to the field.
D-DOOM
A TRAP!?
HE CLONED MY MONSTER?!

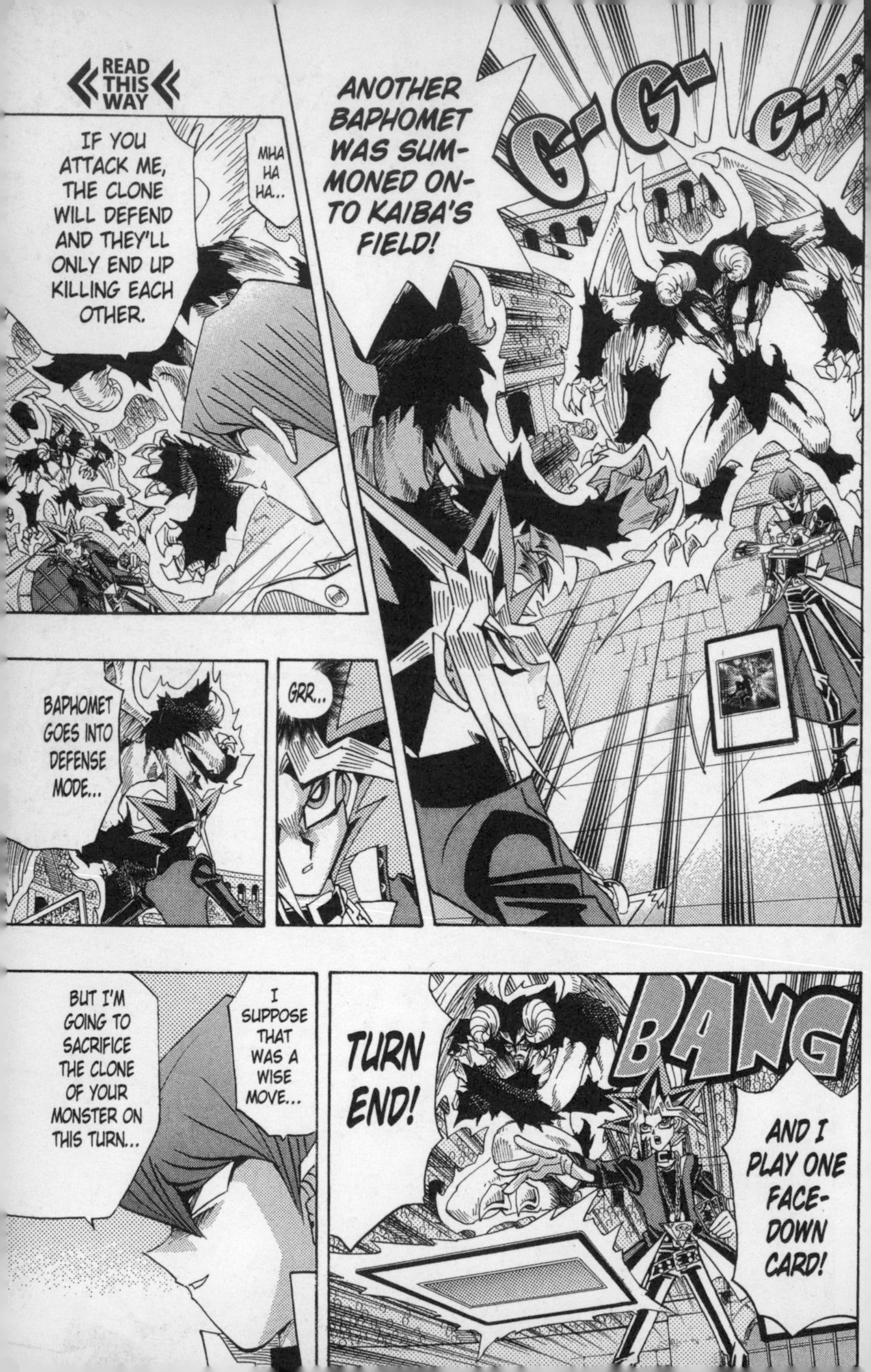
READ THIS WAY
G-G-G-
ANOTHER BAPHOMET WAS SUMMONED ONTO KAIBA'S FIELD!
MHA HA HA...
IF YOU ATTACK ME, THE CLONE WILL DEFEND AND THEY'LL ONLY END UP KILLING EACH OTHER.
GRR...
BAPHOMET GOES INTO DEFENSE MODE...
BANG
AND I PLAY ONE FACE-DOWN CARD!
TURN END!
I SUPPOSE THAT WAS A WISE MOVE...
BUT I'M GOING TO SACRIFICE THE CLONE OF YOUR MONSTER ON THIS TURN...

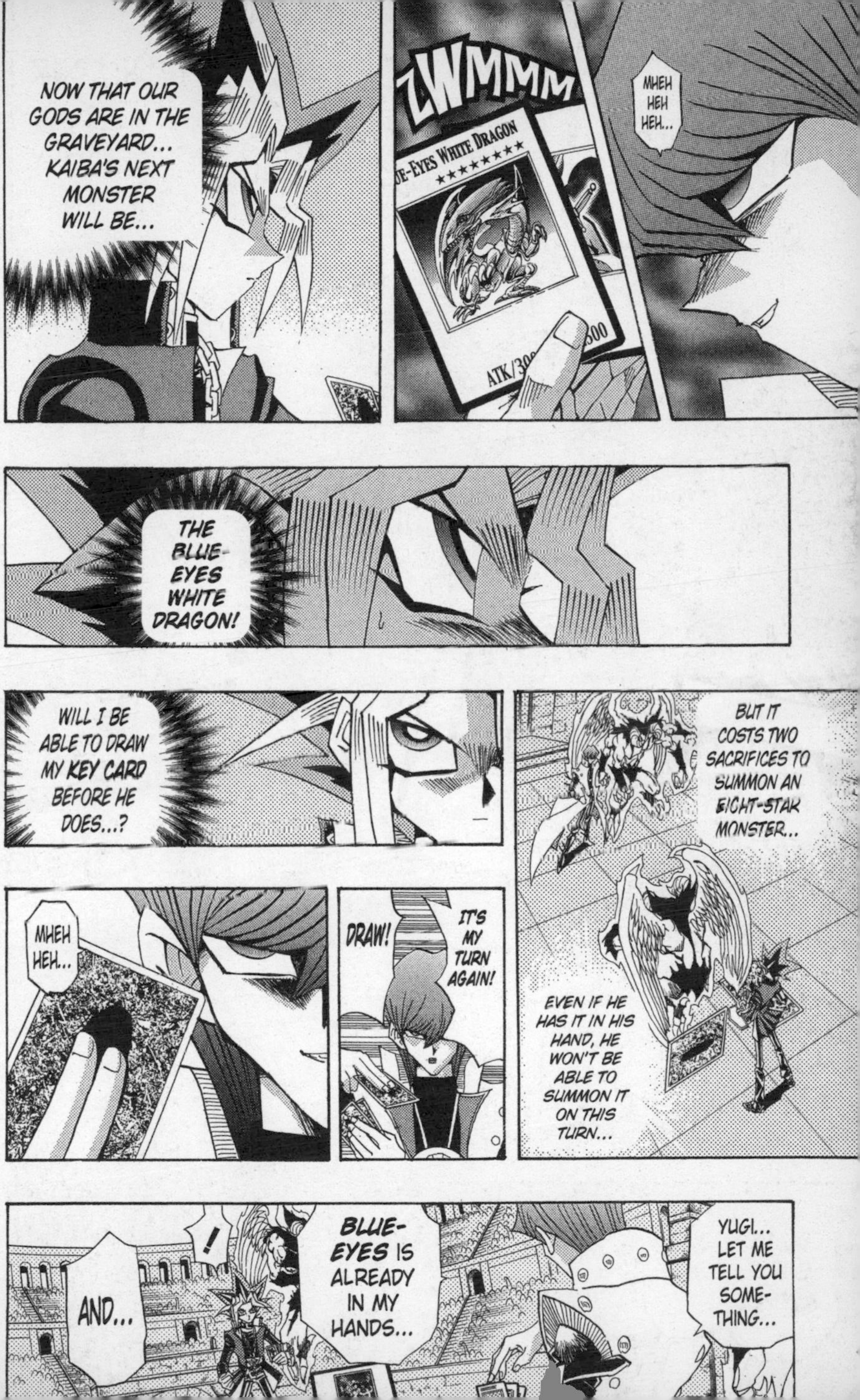
MHEH HEH HEH...
ZWMMM
NOW THAT OUR GODS ARE IN THE GRAVEYARD... KAIBA'S NEXT MONSTER WILL BE...
THE BLUE-EYES WHITE DRAGON!
BUT IT COSTS TWO SACRIFICES TO SUMMON AN EIGHT-STAR MONSTER...
EVEN IF HE HAS IT IN HIS HAND, HE WON'T BE ABLE TO SUMMON IT ON THIS TURN...
WILL I BE ABLE TO DRAW MY KEY CARD BEFORE HE DOES...?
IT'S MY TURN AGAIN!
DRAW!
MHEH HEH...
YUGI... LET ME TELL YOU SOME-THING...
BLUE-EYES IS ALREADY IN MY HANDS...
!
AND...

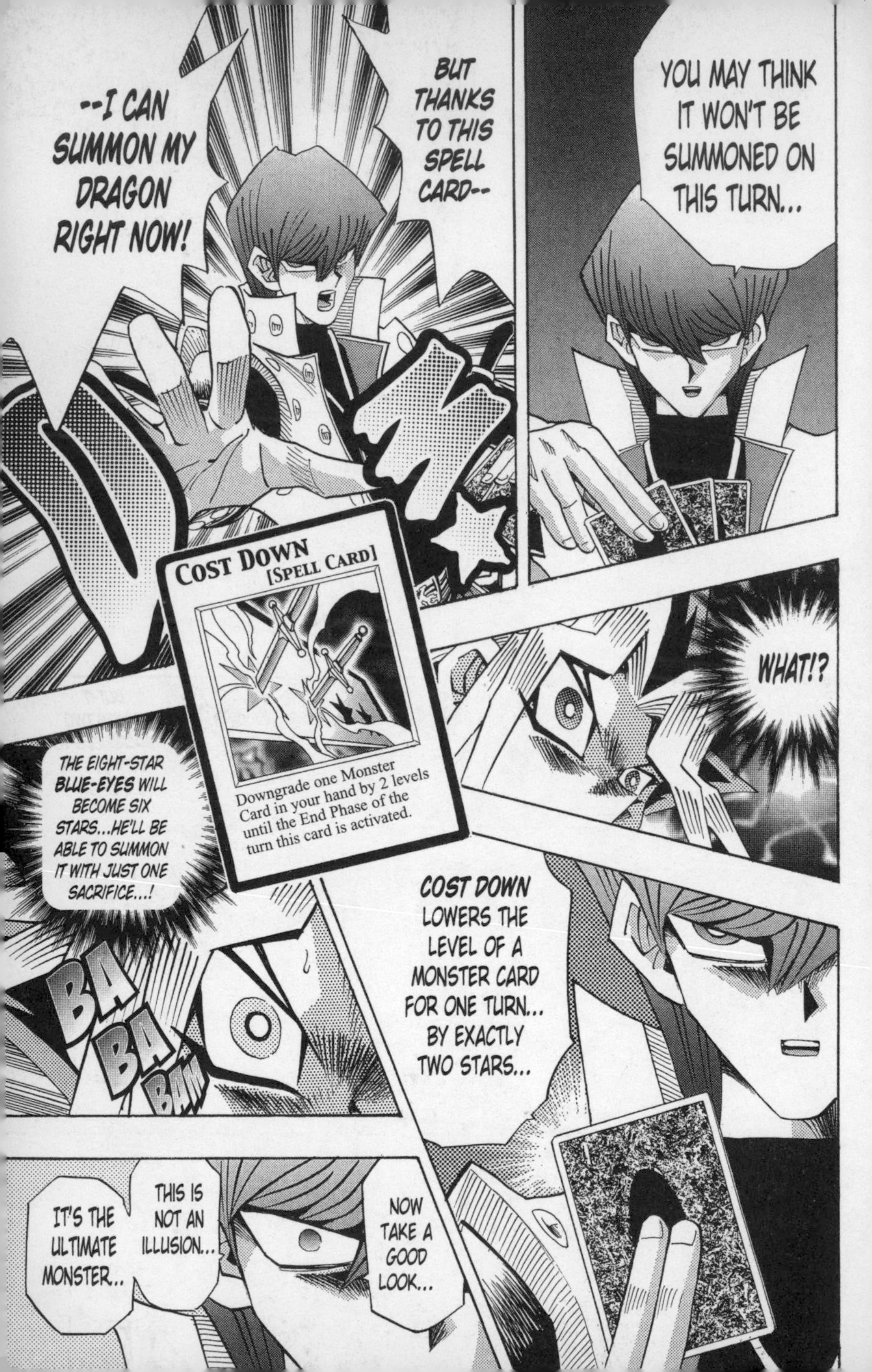
YOU MAY THINK IT WON'T BE SUMMONED ON THIS TURN...
BUT THANKS TO THIS SPELL CARD--
--I CAN SUMMON MY DRAGON RIGHT NOW!
COST DOWN [SPELL CARD]
Downgrade one Monster Card in your hand by 2 levels until the End Phase of the turn this card is activated.
WHAT!?
COST DOWN LOWERS THE LEVEL OF A MONSTER CARD FOR ONE TURN... BY EXACTLY TWO STARS...
THE EIGHT-STAR BLUE-EYES WILL BECOME SIX STARS...HE'LL BE ABLE TO SUMMON IT WITH JUST ONE SACRIFICE...!
BA BA BAM
NOW TAKE A GOOD LOOK...
THIS IS NOT AN ILLUSION...
IT'S THE ULTIMATE MONSTER..

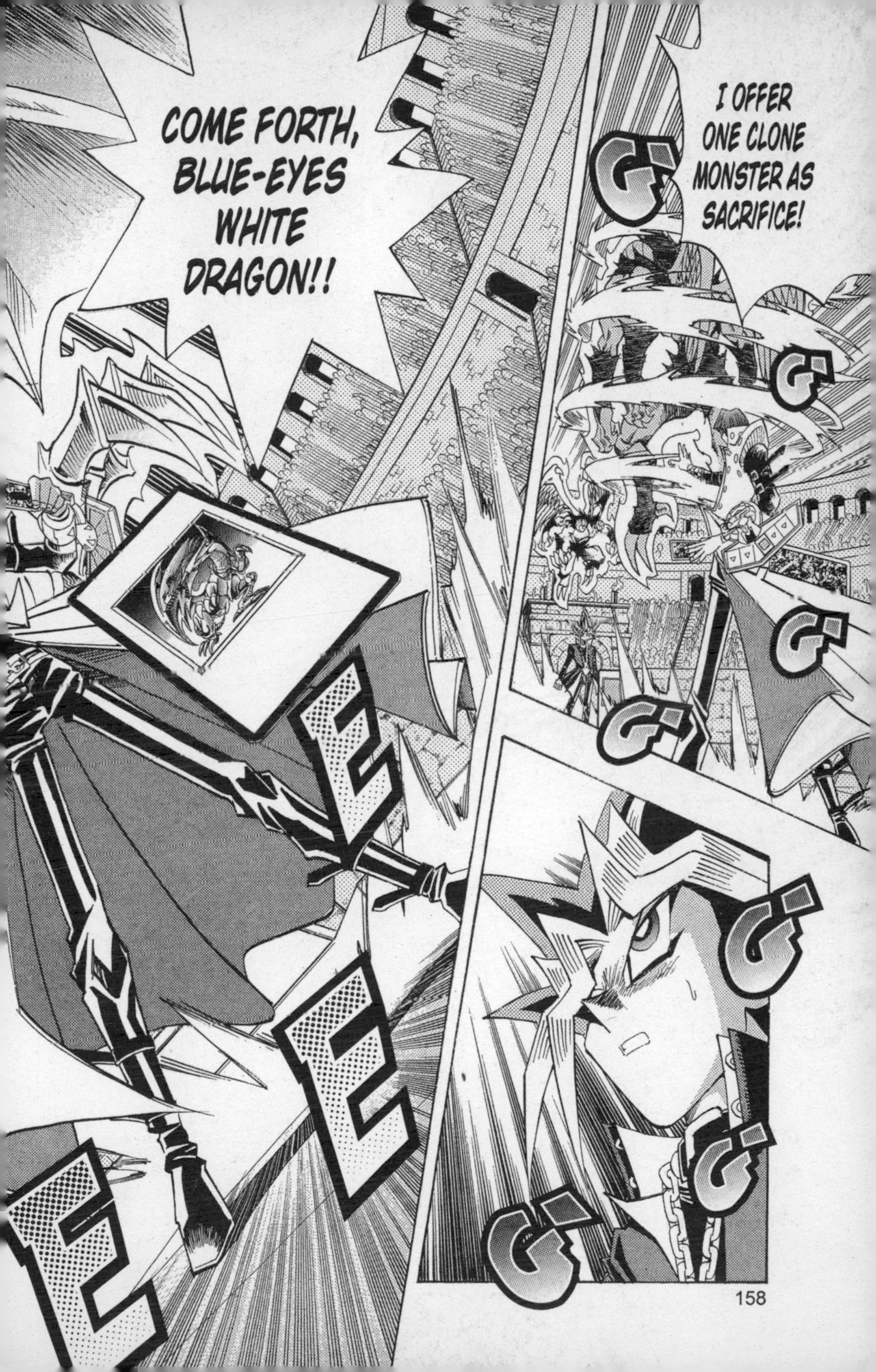
I OFFER ONE CLONE MONSTER AS SACRIFICE!
COME FORTH, BLUE-EYES WHITE DRAGON!!

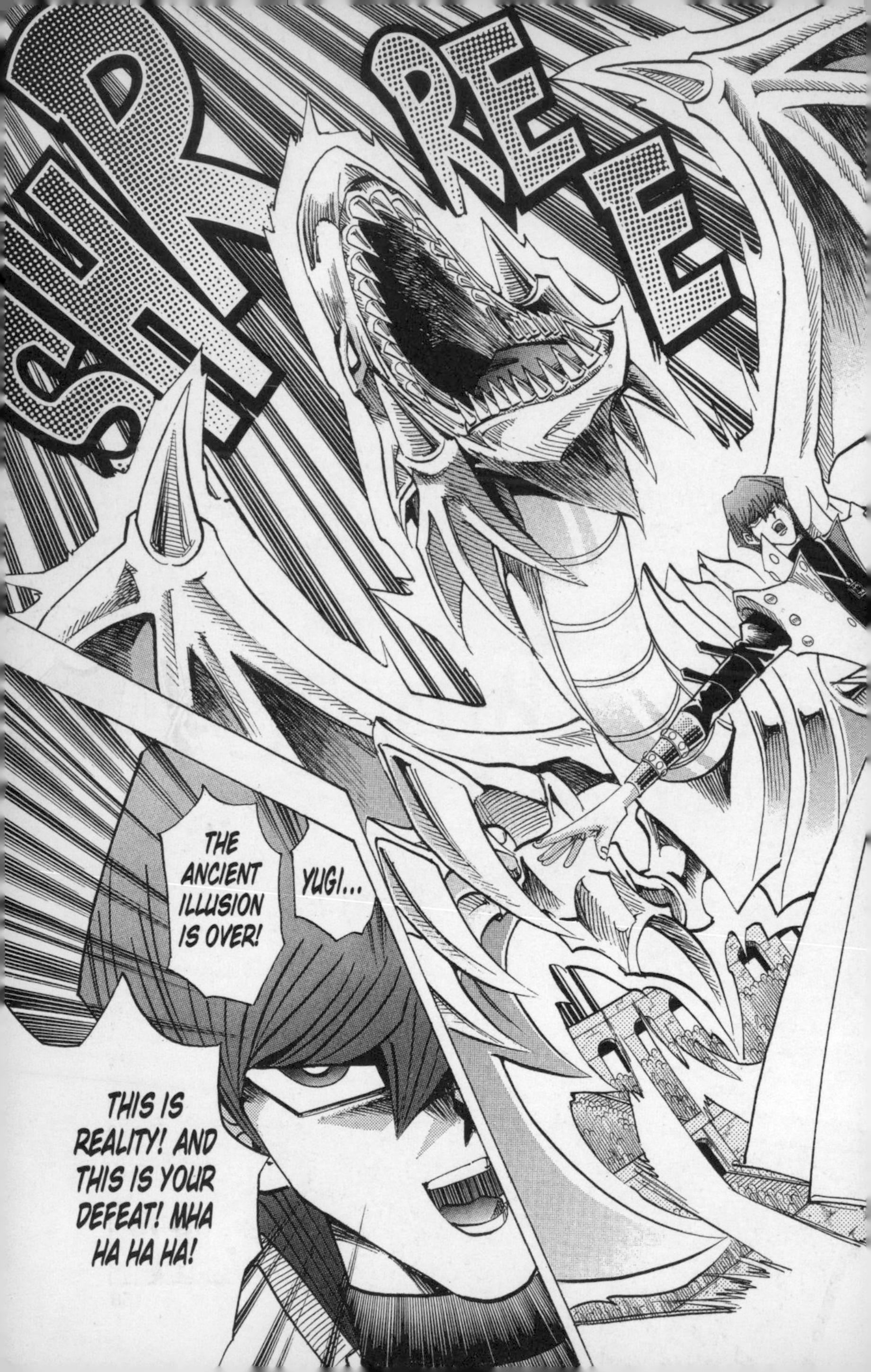
SHRREEE
YUGI...
THE ANCIENT ILLUSION IS OVER!
THIS IS REALITY! AND THIS IS YOUR DEFEAT! MHA HA HA HA!

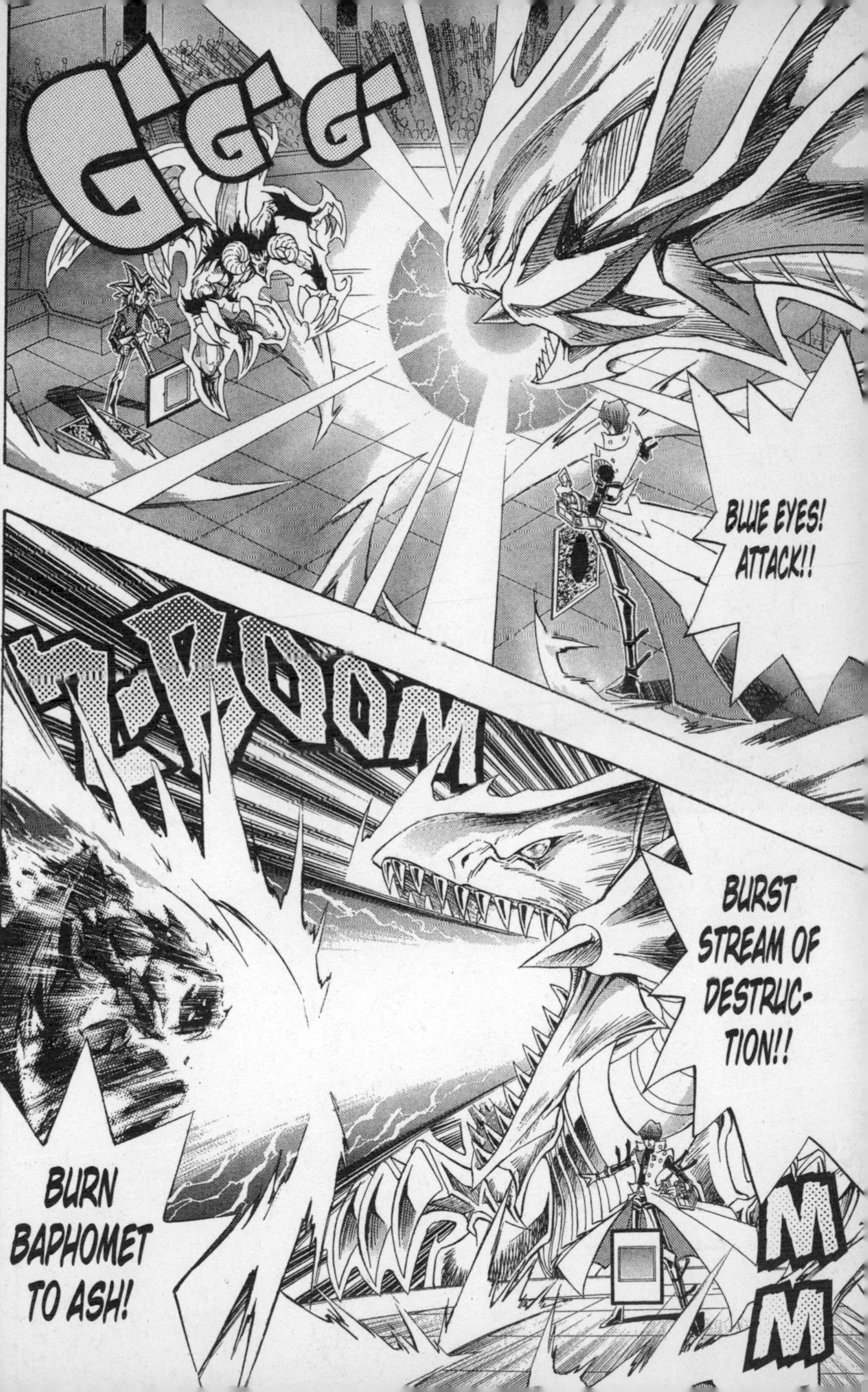
G G G
BLUE EYES! ATTACK!!
ZHOOM
BURST STREAM OF DESTRUC-TION!!
M M
BURN BAPHOMET TO ASH!

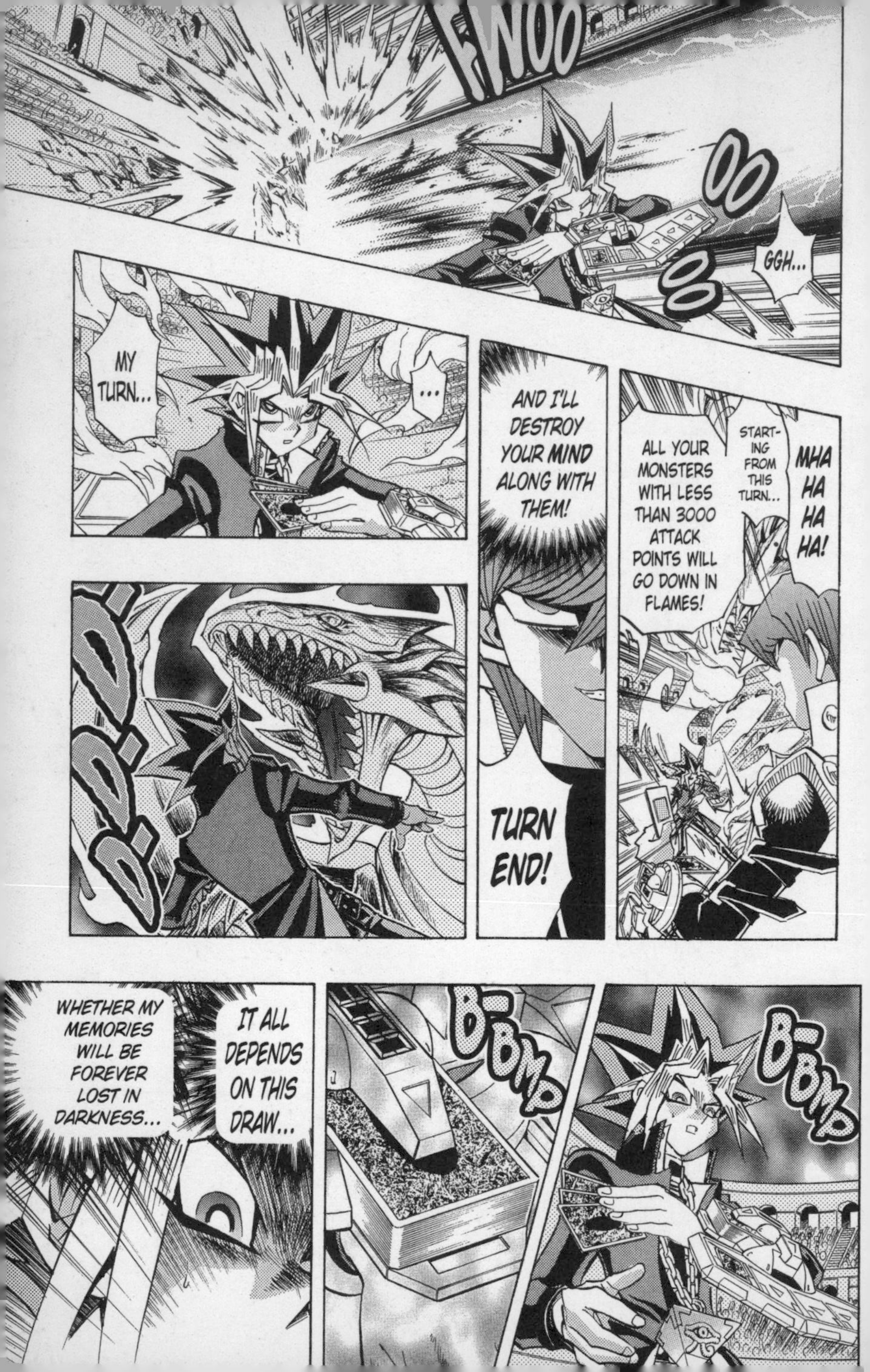
FWOO
OO
OO
GGH...
MHA HA HA HA!
STARTING FROM THIS TURN...
ALL YOUR MONSTERS WITH LESS THAN 3000 ATTACK POINTS WILL GO DOWN IN FLAMES!
AND I'LL DESTROY YOUR MIND ALONG WITH THEM!
TURN END!
...
MY TURN...
B-BOMP
B-BOMP
IT ALL DEPENDS ON THIS DRAW...
WHETHER MY MEMORIES WILL BE FOREVER LOST IN DARKNESS...

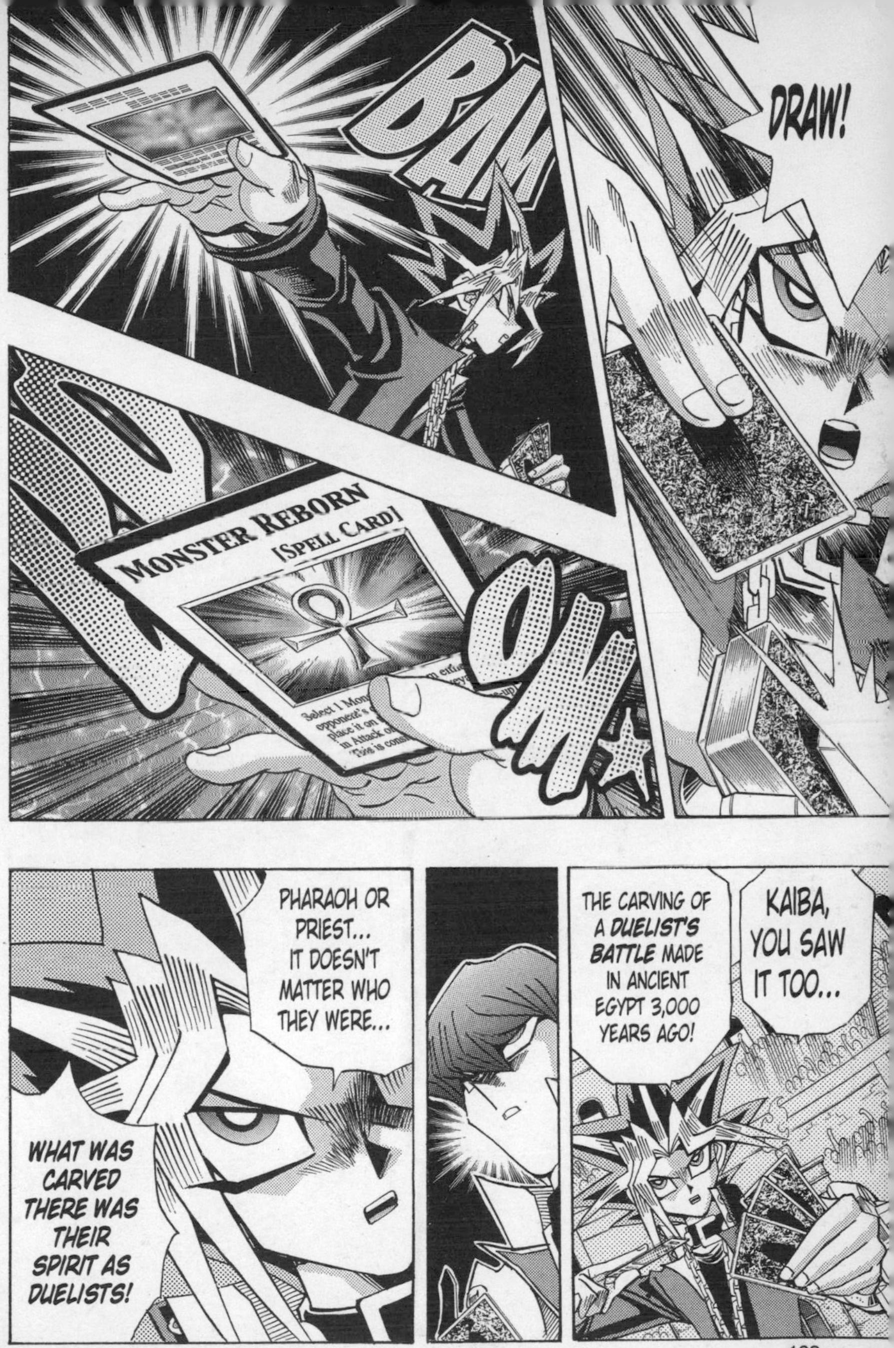
DRAW!
BAM
MONSTER REBORN
[SPELL CARD]
KAIBA, YOU SAW IT TOO...
THE CARVING OF A DUELIST'S BATTLE MADE IN ANCIENT EGYPT 3,000 YEARS AGO!
PHARAOH OR PRIEST... IT DOESN'T MATTER WHO THEY WERE...
WHAT WAS CARVED THERE WAS THEIR SPIRIT AS DUELISTS!

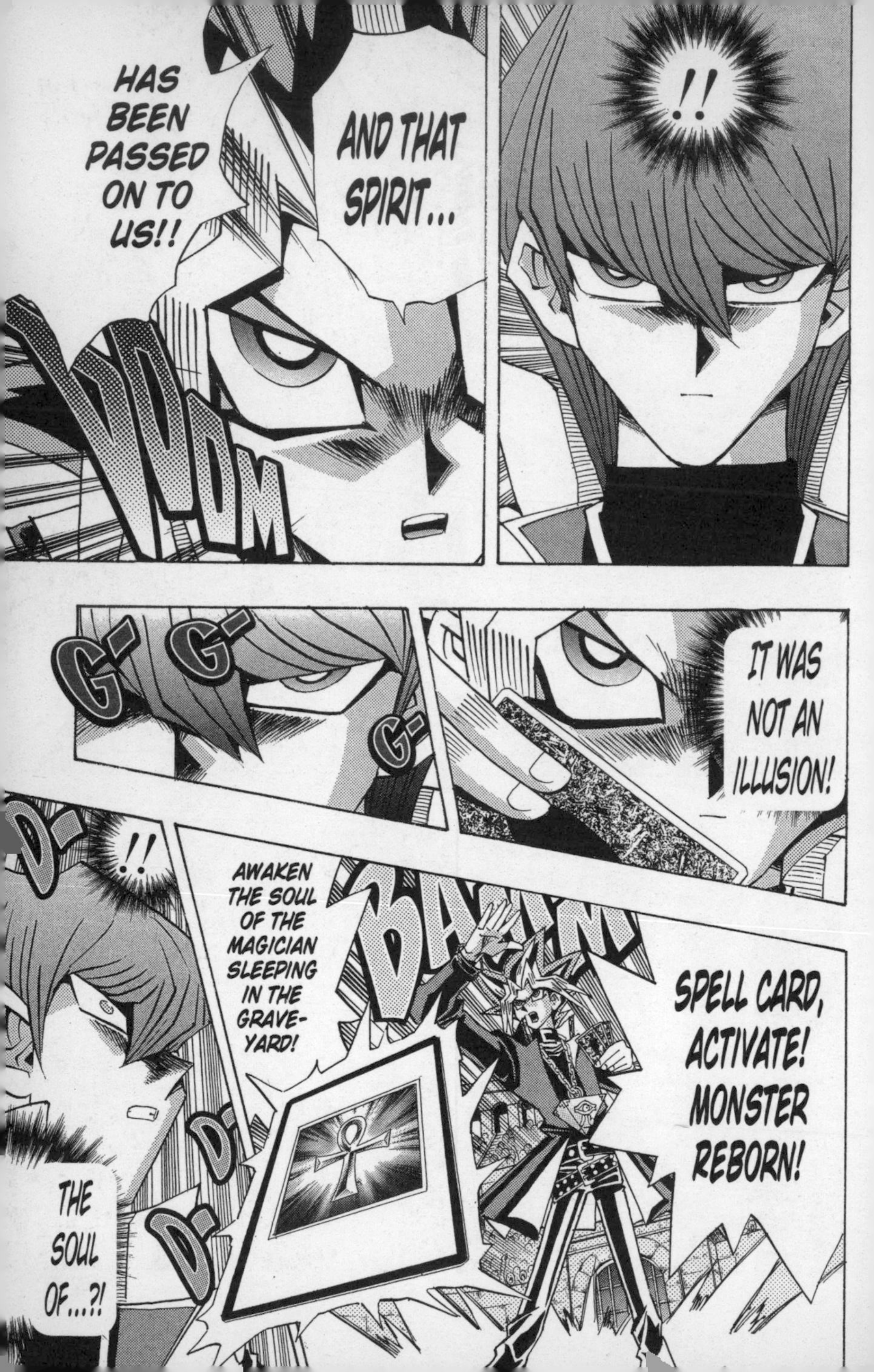
!!
AND THAT SPIRIT...
HAS BEEN PASSED ON TO US!!
IT WAS NOT AN ILLUSION!
G- G- G-
SPELL CARD, ACTIVATE! MONSTER REBORN!
AWAKEN THE SOUL OF THE MAGICIAN SLEEPING IN THE GRAVE-YARD!
!!
D- D- D-
THE SOUL OF...?!

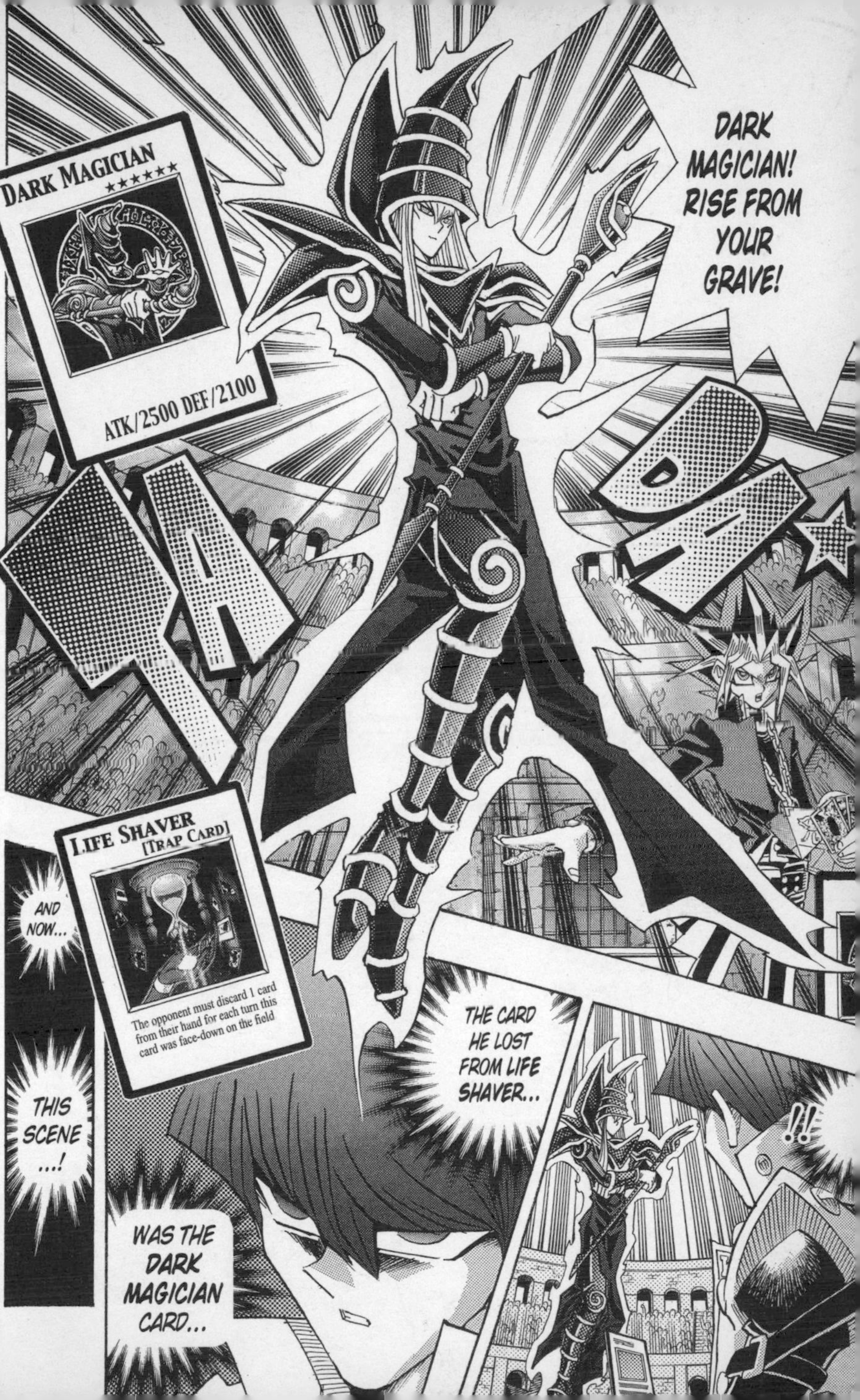
DARK MAGICIAN! RISE FROM YOUR GRAVE!
DARK MAGICIAN
ATK/2500 DEF/2100
!!
THE CARD HE LOST FROM LIFE SHAVER...
LIFE SHAVER [TRAP CARD]
The opponent must discard 1 card from their hand for each turn this card was face-down on the field
AND NOW...
THIS SCENE ...!
WAS THE DARK MAGICIAN CARD...

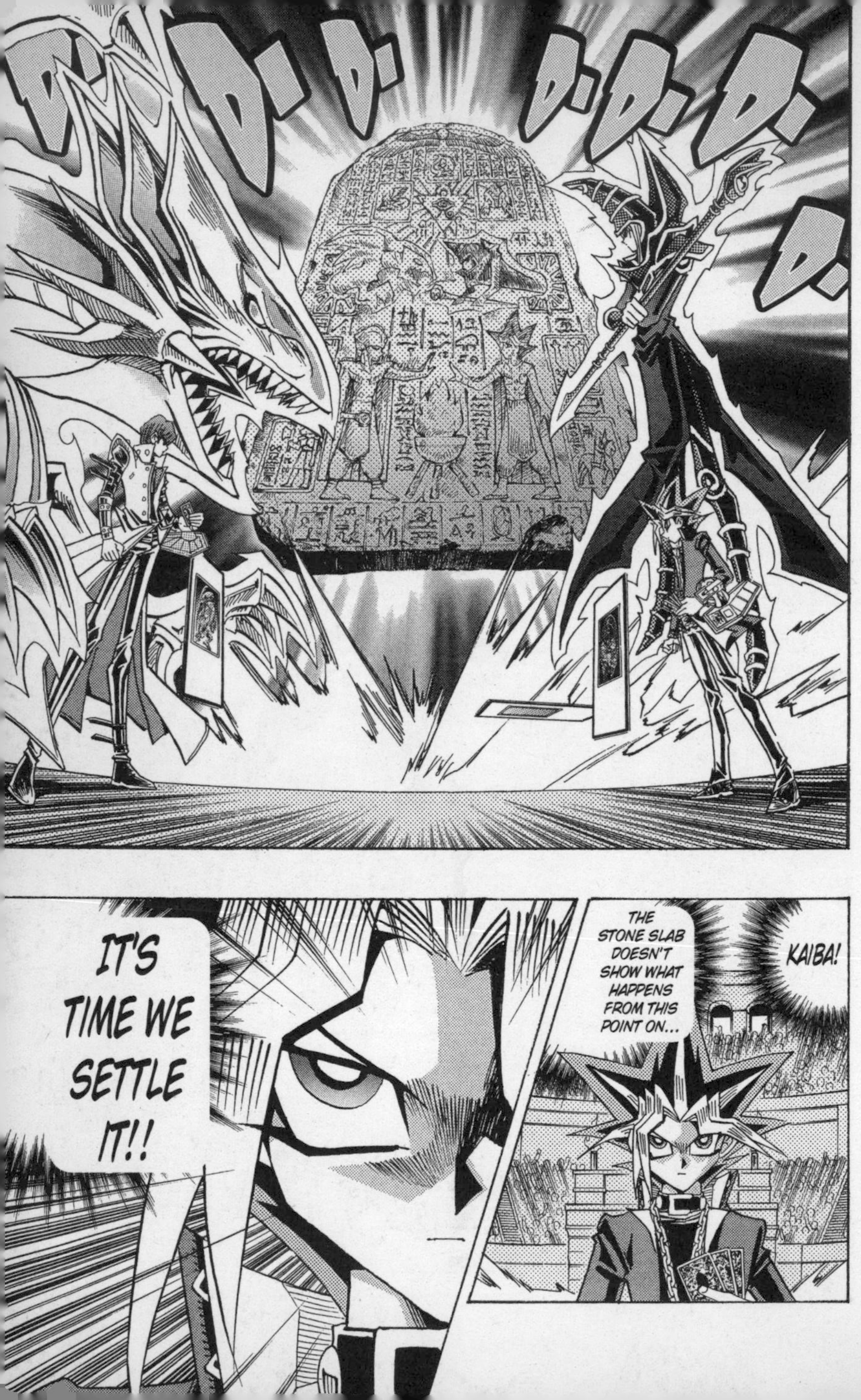
D· D· D· D· D· D· D·
KAIBA!
THE STONE SLAB DOESN'T SHOW WHAT HAPPENS FROM THIS POINT ON...
IT'S TIME WE SETTLE IT!!

Duel 200: Deck of Glass!

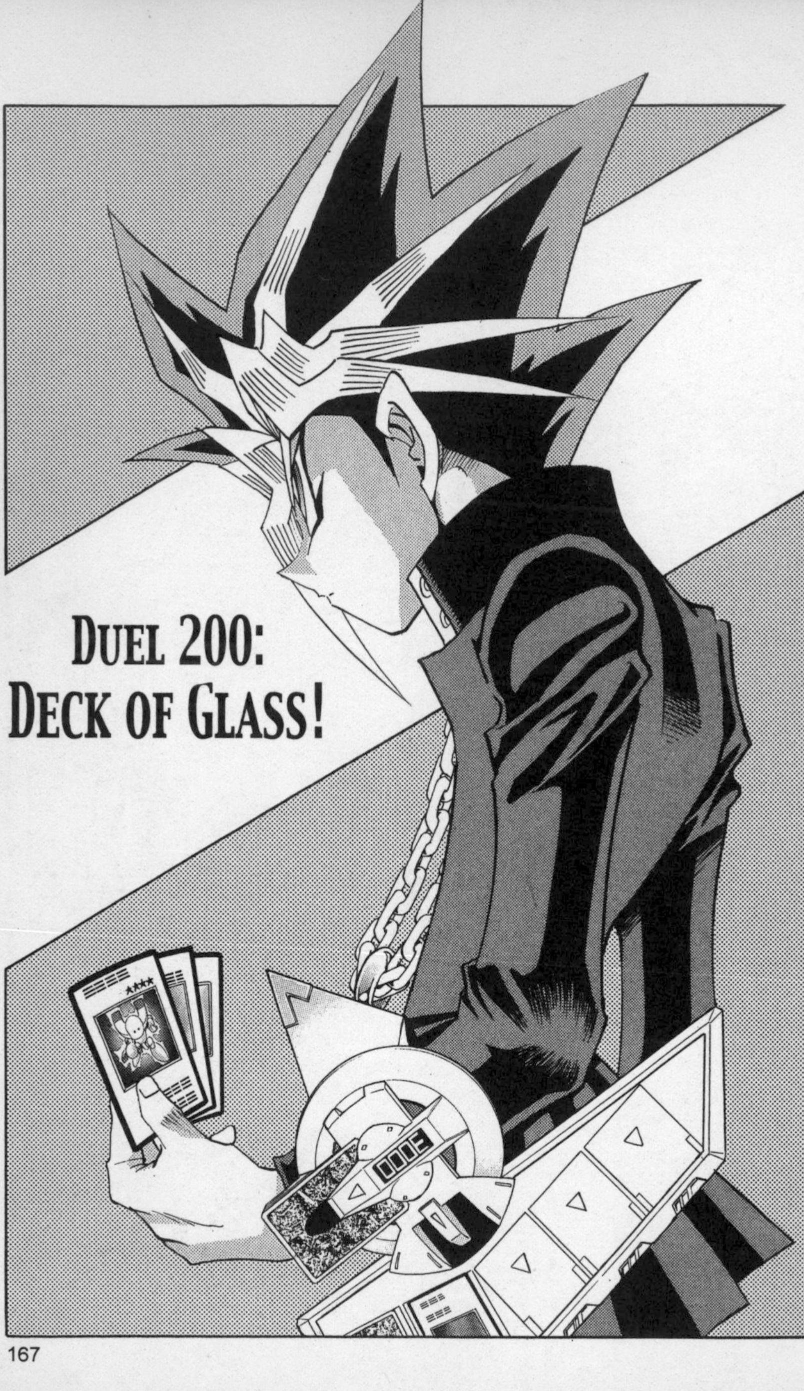

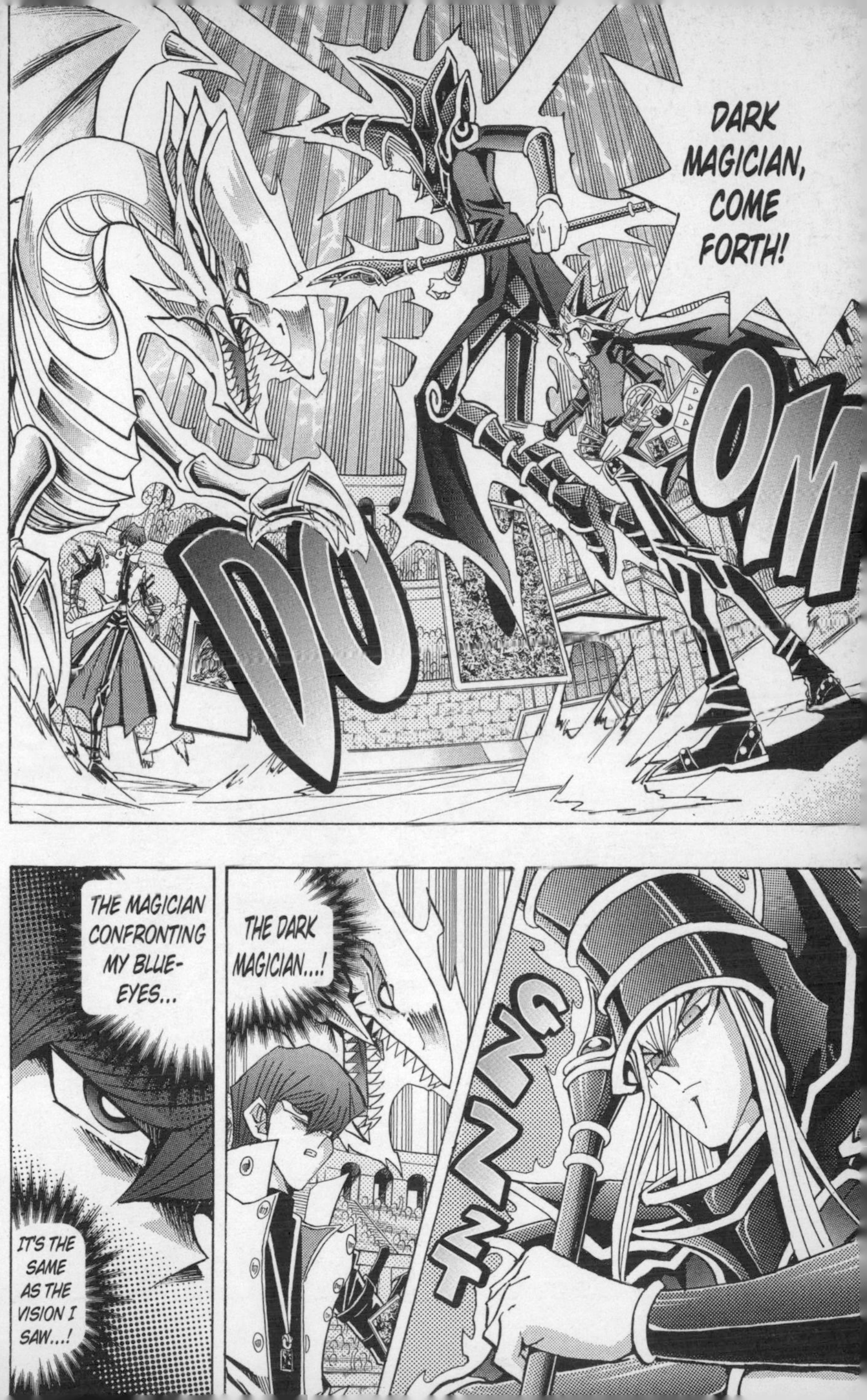
DARK MAGICIAN, COME FORTH!
DOOM
THE DARK MAGICIAN...!
THE MAGICIAN CONFRONTING MY BLUE-EYES...
IT'S THE SAME AS THE VISION I SAW...!

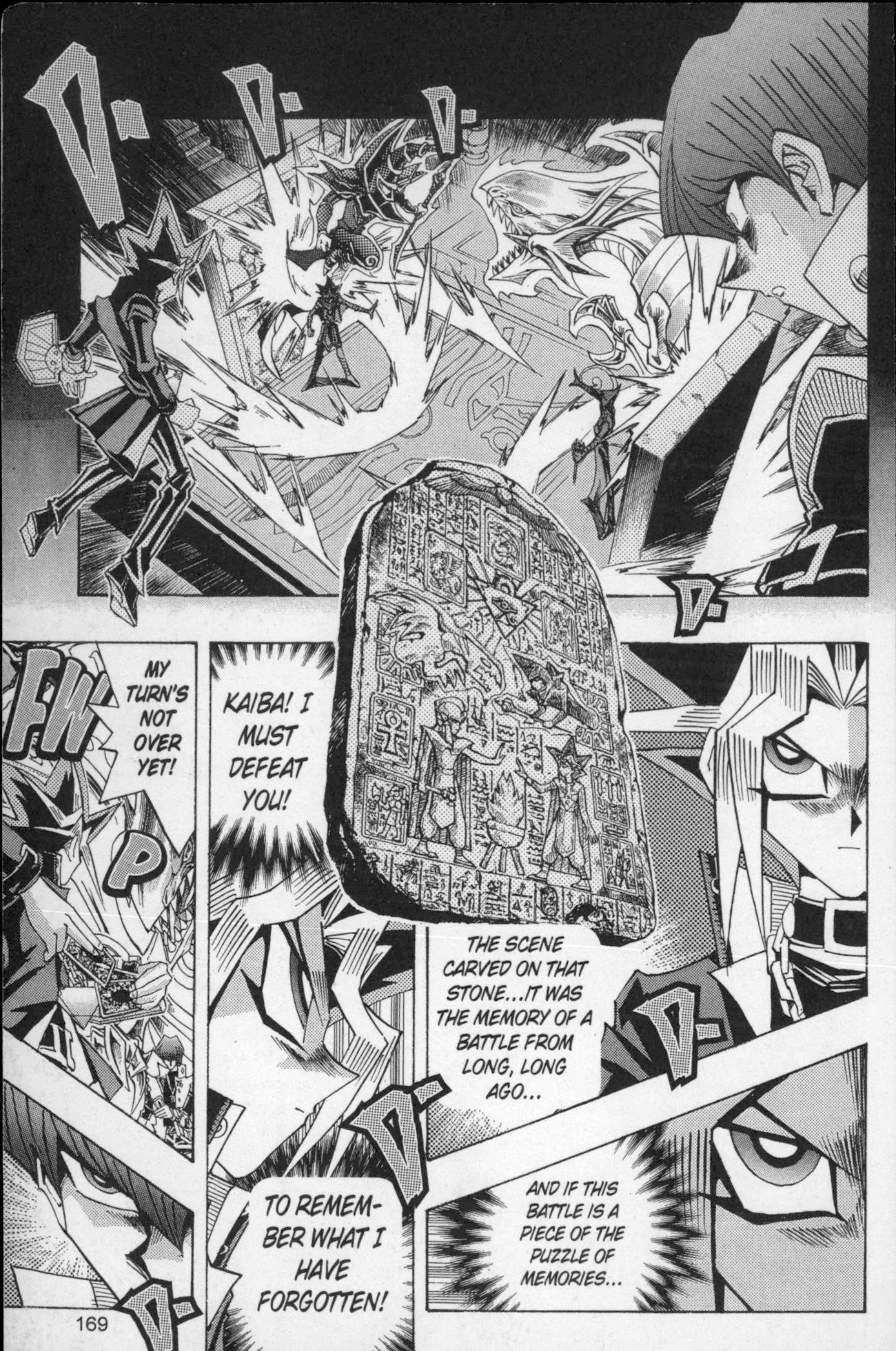
D- D- D- D-
D-
THE SCENE CARVED ON THAT STONE...IT WAS THE MEMORY OF A BATTLE FROM LONG, LONG AGO...
D-
KAIBA! I MUST DEFEAT YOU!
MY TURN'S NOT OVER YET!
FW
P
AND IF THIS BATTLE IS A PIECE OF THE PUZZLE OF MEMORIES...
D-
TO REMEM-BER WHAT I HAVE FORGOTTEN!
D-

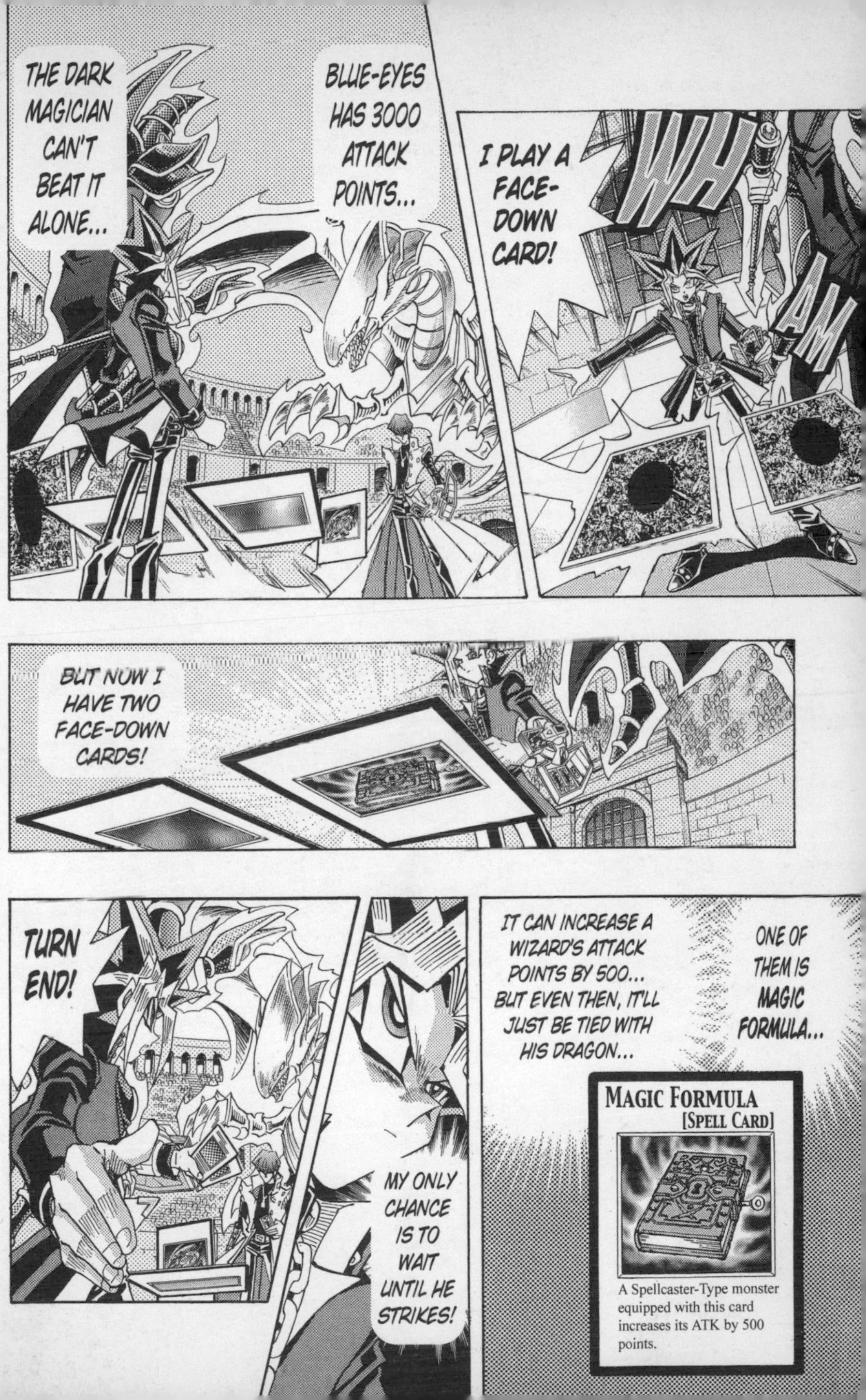
I PLAY A FACE-DOWN CARD!
WHAM
BLUE-EYES HAS 3000 ATTACK POINTS...
THE DARK MAGICIAN CAN'T BEAT IT ALONE...
BUT NOW I HAVE TWO FACE-DOWN CARDS!
ONE OF THEM IS MAGIC FORMULA...
IT CAN INCREASE A WIZARD'S ATTACK POINTS BY 500... BUT EVEN THEN, IT'LL JUST BE TIED WITH HIS DRAGON...
MAGIC FORMULA
[SPELL CARD]
A Spellcaster-Type monster equipped with this card increases its ATK by 500 points.
MY ONLY CHANCE IS TO WAIT UNTIL HE STRIKES!
TURN END!

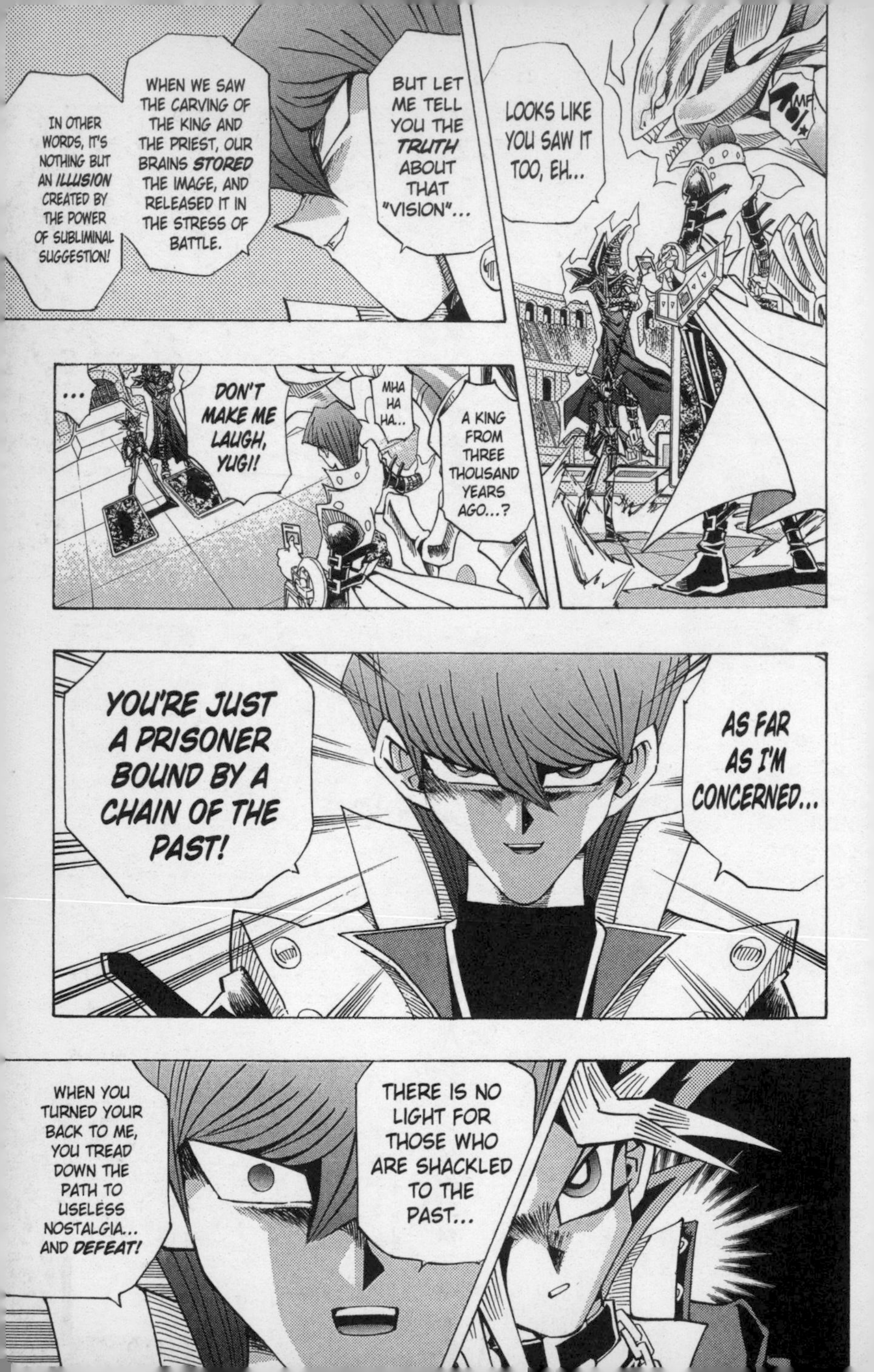
LOOKS LIKE YOU SAW IT TOO, EH...
BUT LET ME TELL YOU THE *TRUTH* ABOUT THAT "VISION"...
WHEN WE SAW THE CARVING OF THE KING AND THE PRIEST, OUR BRAINS *STORED* THE IMAGE, AND RELEASED IT IN THE STRESS OF BATTLE.
IN OTHER WORDS, IT'S NOTHING BUT AN *ILLUSION* CREATED BY THE POWER OF SUBLIMINAL SUGGESTION!
A KING FROM THREE THOUSAND YEARS AGO...?
MHA HA HA...
DON'T MAKE ME LAUGH, YUGI!
...
AS FAR AS I'M CONCERNED...
YOU'RE JUST A PRISONER BOUND BY A CHAIN OF THE PAST!
THERE IS NO LIGHT FOR THOSE WHO ARE SHACKLED TO THE PAST...
WHEN YOU TURNED YOUR BACK TO ME, YOU TREAD DOWN THE PATH TO USELESS NOSTALGIA... AND *DEFEAT!*

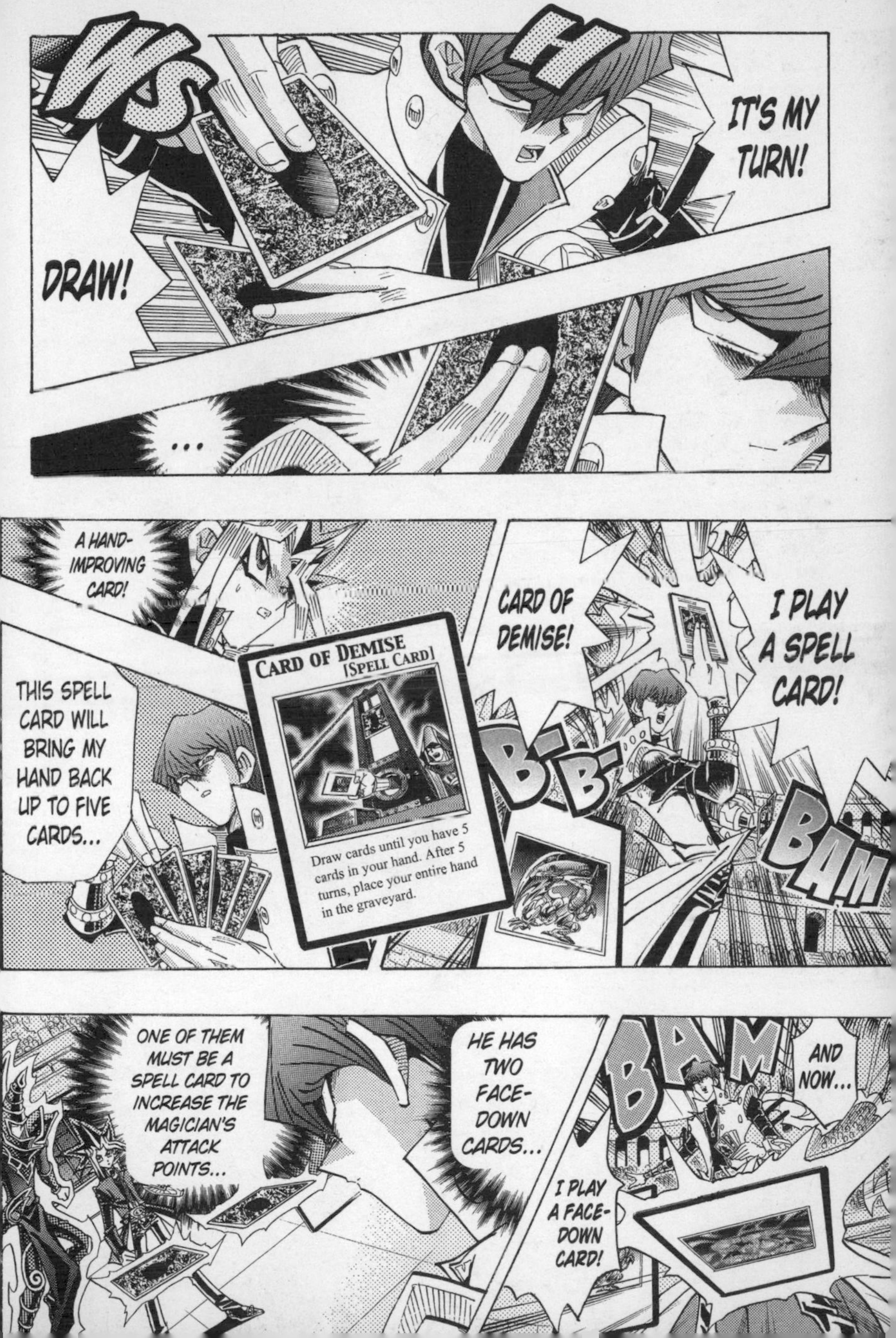
IT'S MY TURN!
DRAW!
...
I PLAY A SPELL CARD!
CARD OF DEMISE!
B-B-BAM
A HAND-IMPROVING CARD!
CARD OF DEMISE [SPELL CARD]
Draw cards until you have 5 cards in your hand. After 5 turns, place your entire hand in the graveyard.
THIS SPELL CARD WILL BRING MY HAND BACK UP TO FIVE CARDS...
AND NOW...
BAM
I PLAY A FACE-DOWN CARD!
HE HAS TWO FACE-DOWN CARDS...
ONE OF THEM MUST BE A SPELL CARD TO INCREASE THE MAGICIAN'S ATTACK POINTS...

READ THIS WAY

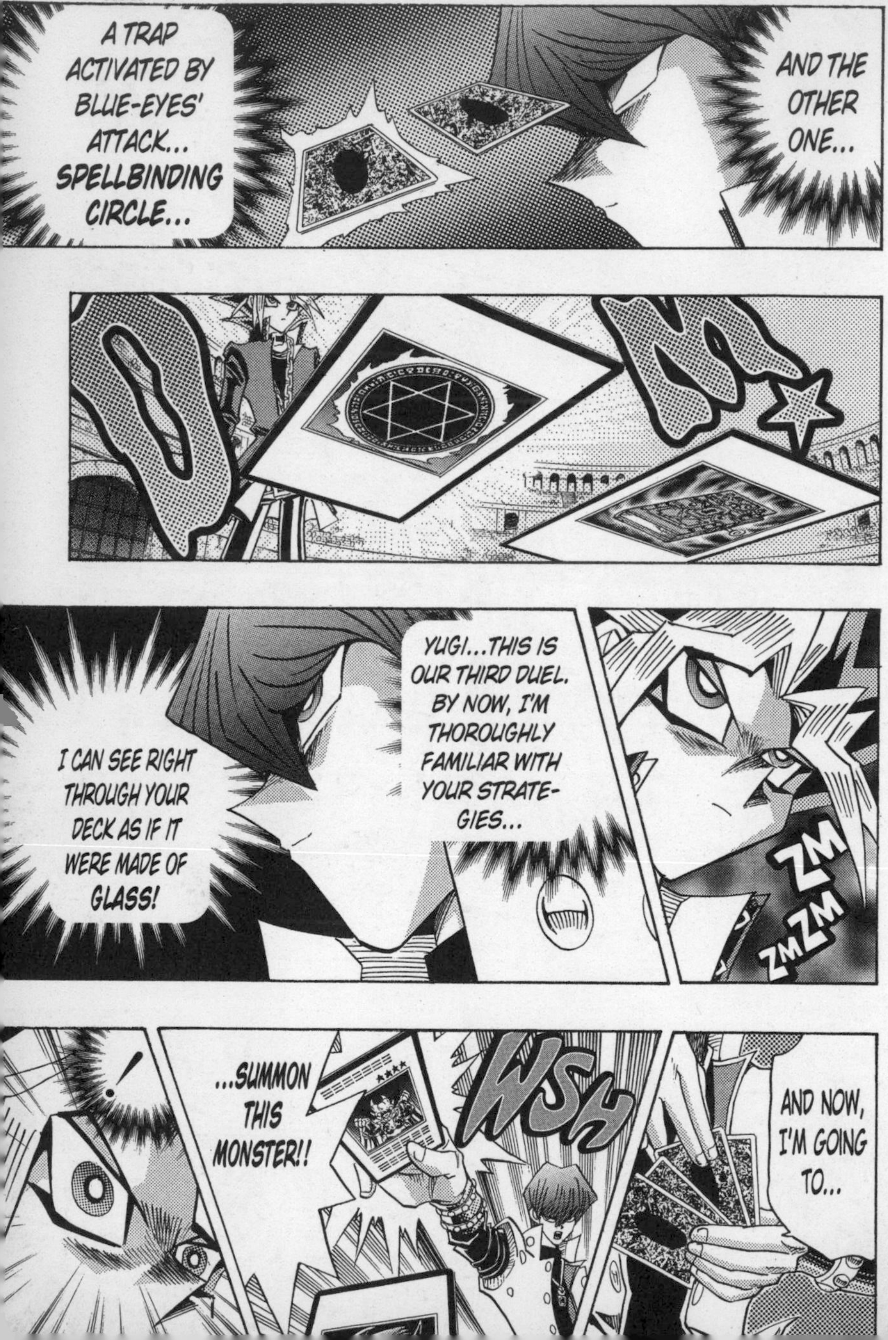
A TRAP ACTIVATED BY BLUE-EYES' ATTACK... SPELLBINDING CIRCLE...
AND THE OTHER ONE...
YUGI...THIS IS OUR THIRD DUEL. BY NOW, I'M THOROUGHLY FAMILIAR WITH YOUR STRATE-GIES...
ZM ZMZM
I CAN SEE RIGHT THROUGH YOUR DECK AS IF IT WERE MADE OF GLASS!
AND NOW, I'M GOING TO...
WSH
...SUMMON THIS MONSTER!!
!

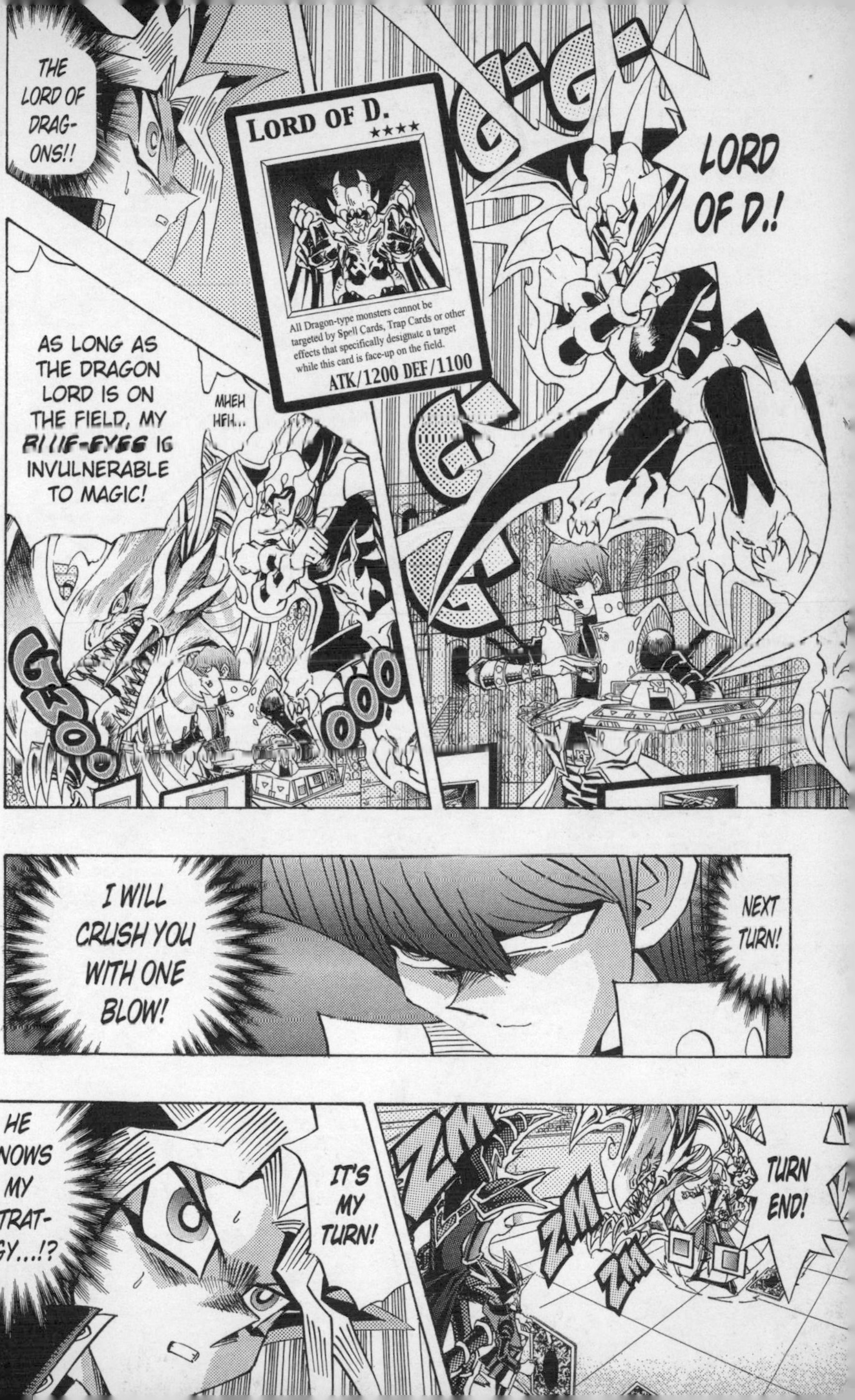
LORD OF D.!
LORD OF D. ★★★★
All Dragon-type monsters cannot be targeted by Spell Cards, Trap Cards or other effects that specifically designate a target while this card is face-up on the field.
ATK/1200 DEF/1100
THE LORD OF DRAG-ONS!!
MHEH HEH...
AS LONG AS THE DRAGON LORD IS ON THE FIELD, MY BLUE-EYES IS INVULNERABLE TO MAGIC!
GWOOOOO
NEXT TURN!
I WILL CRUSH YOU WITH ONE BLOW!
TURN END!
ZM ZM ZM
IT'S MY TURN!
HE KNOWS MY STRAT-EGY...!?

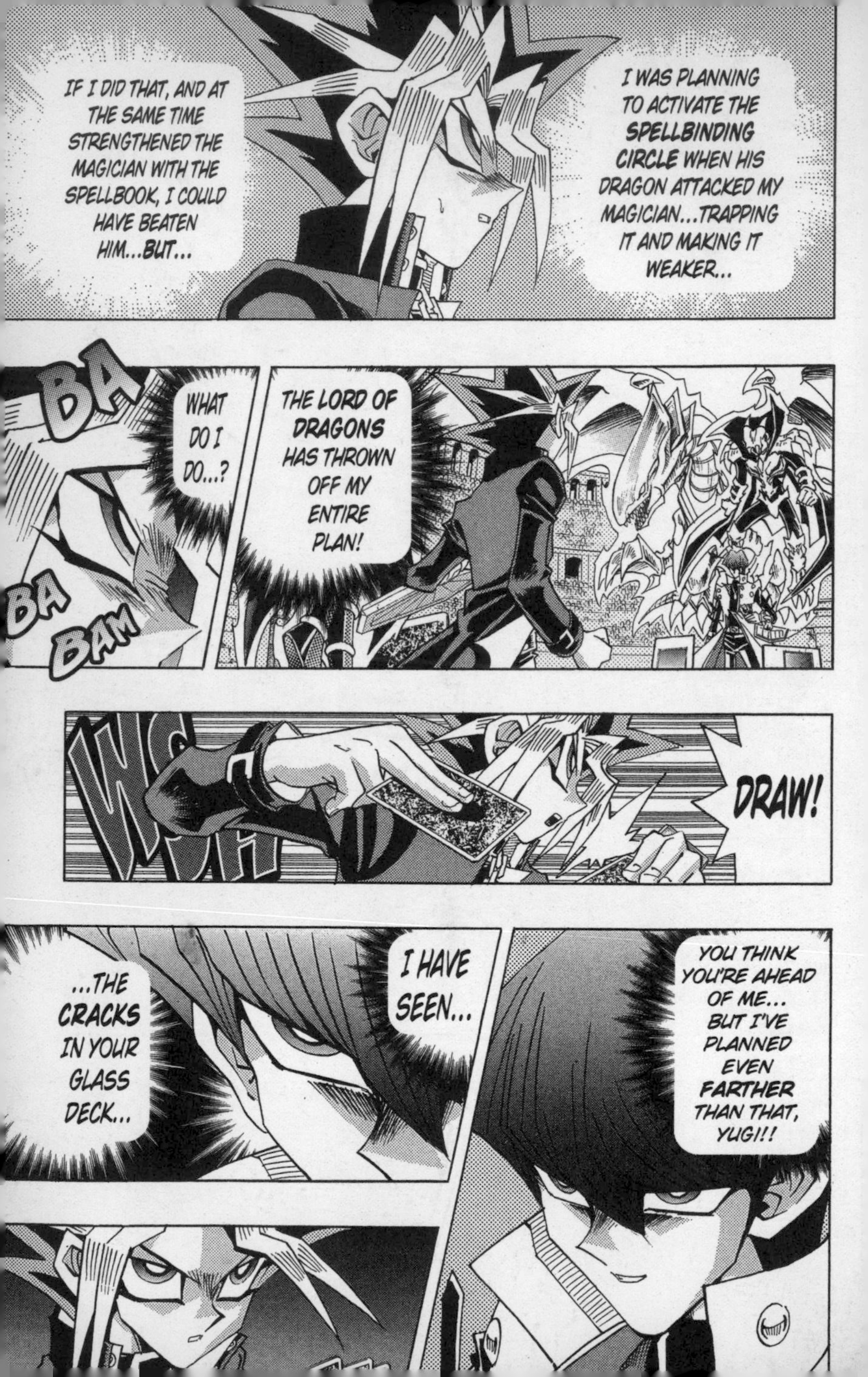

I WAS PLANNING TO ACTIVATE THE SPELLBINDING CIRCLE WHEN HIS DRAGON ATTACKED MY MAGICIAN...TRAPPING IT AND MAKING IT WEAKER...
IF I DID THAT, AND AT THE SAME TIME STRENGTHENED THE MAGICIAN WITH THE SPELLBOOK, I COULD HAVE BEATEN HIM...BUT...
THE LORD OF DRAGONS HAS THROWN OFF MY ENTIRE PLAN!
WHAT DO I DO...?
BA
BA
BAM
DRAW!
YOU THINK YOU'RE AHEAD OF ME... BUT I'VE PLANNED EVEN FARTHER THAN THAT, YUGI!!
I HAVE SEEN...
...THE CRACKS IN YOUR GLASS DECK...

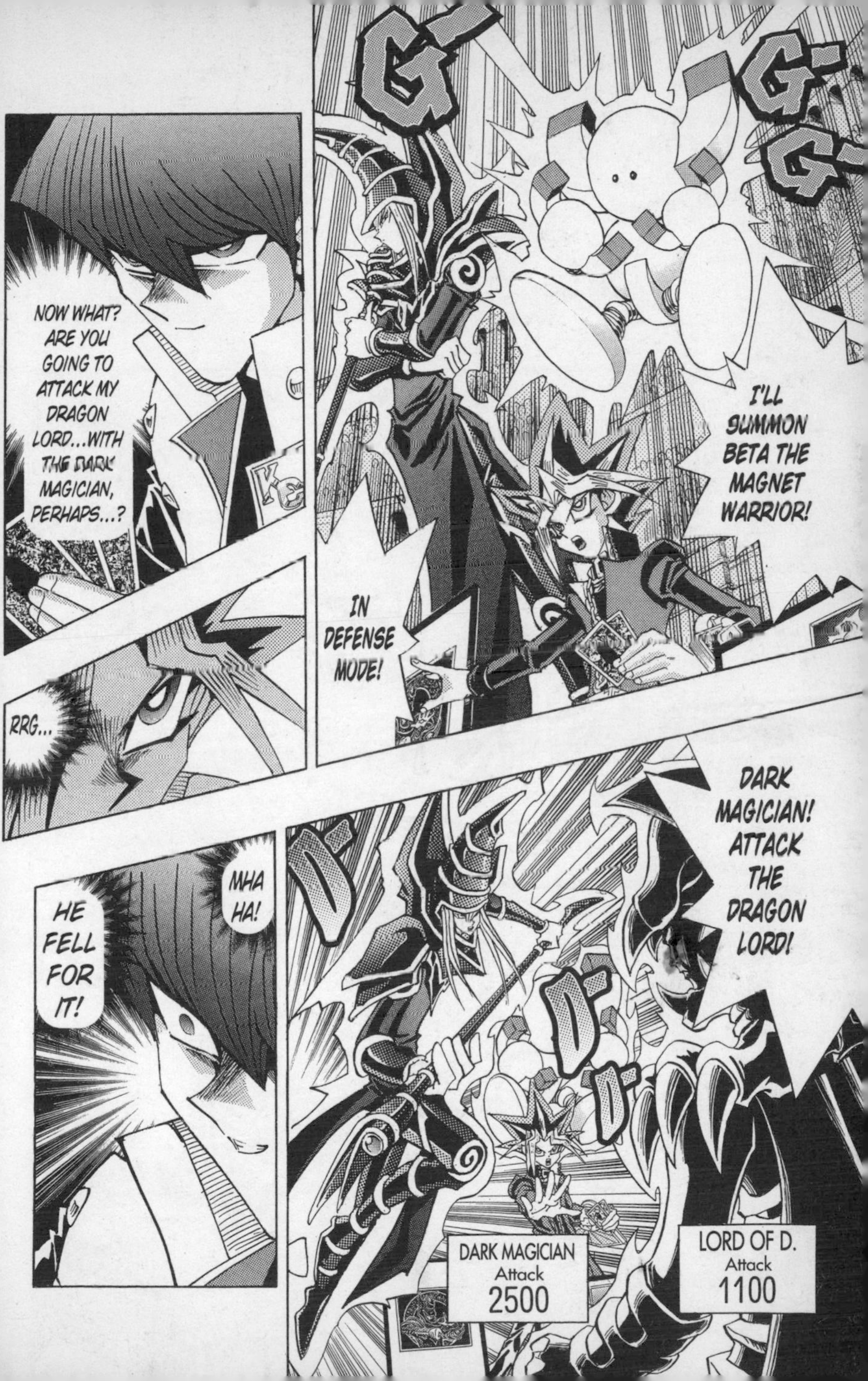
G-
G-G-
I'LL SUMMON BETA THE MAGNET WARRIOR!
IN DEFENSE MODE!
NOW WHAT? ARE YOU GOING TO ATTACK MY DRAGON LORD...WITH THE DARK MAGICIAN, PERHAPS...?
RRG...
DARK MAGICIAN! ATTACK THE DRAGON LORD!
D-D-D-D
LORD OF D.
Attack
1100
DARK MAGICIAN
Attack
2500
MHA HA!
HE FELL FOR IT!

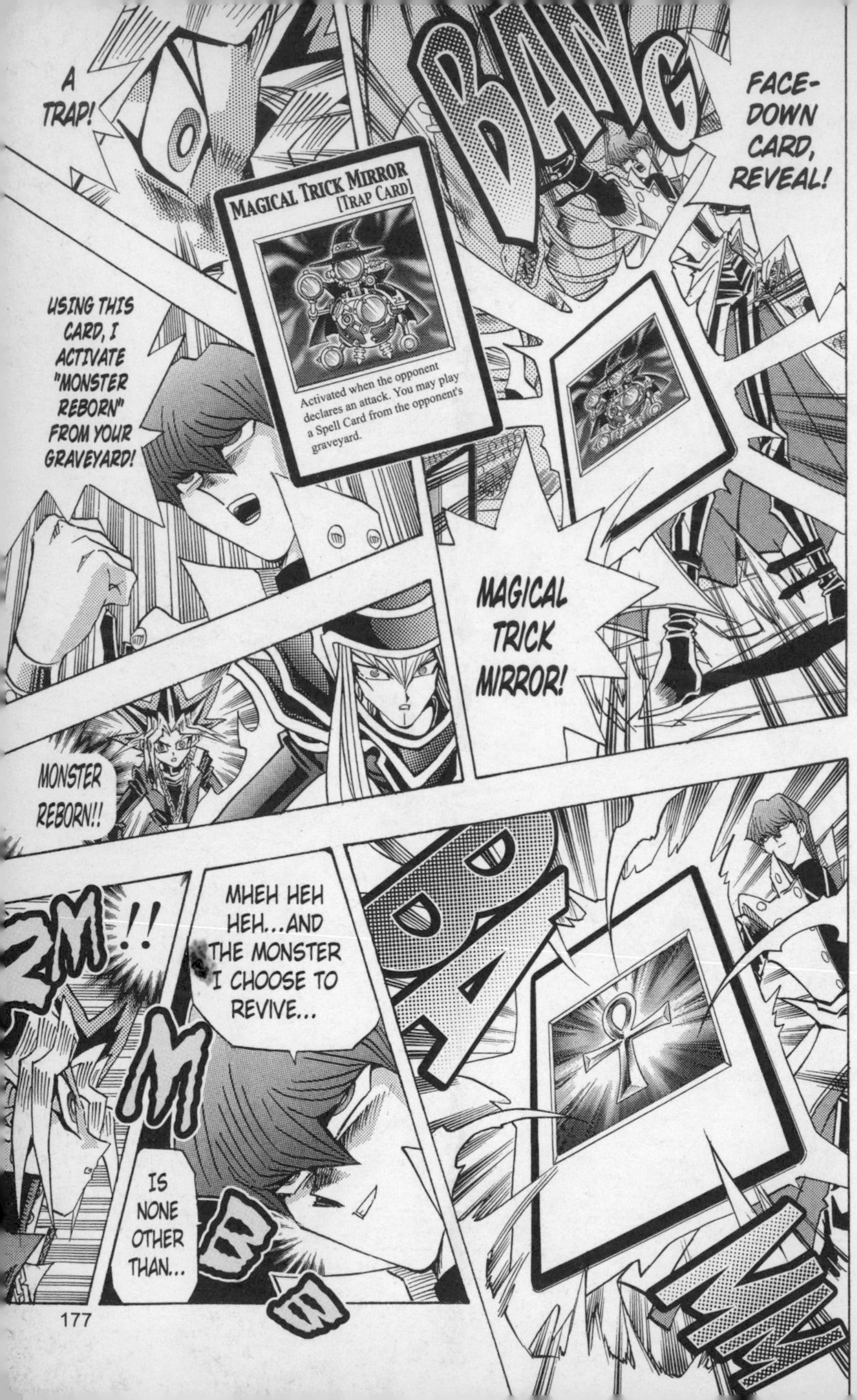
FACE-DOWN CARD, REVEAL!
BANG
A TRAP!
MAGICAL TRICK MIRROR
[TRAP CARD]
Activated when the opponent declares an attack. You may play a Spell Card from the opponent's graveyard.
MAGICAL TRICK MIRROR!
USING THIS CARD, I ACTIVATE "MONSTER REBORN" FROM YOUR GRAVEYARD!
MONSTER REBORN!!
MHEH HEH HEH...AND THE MONSTER I CHOOSE TO REVIVE...
IS NONE OTHER THAN...
!!

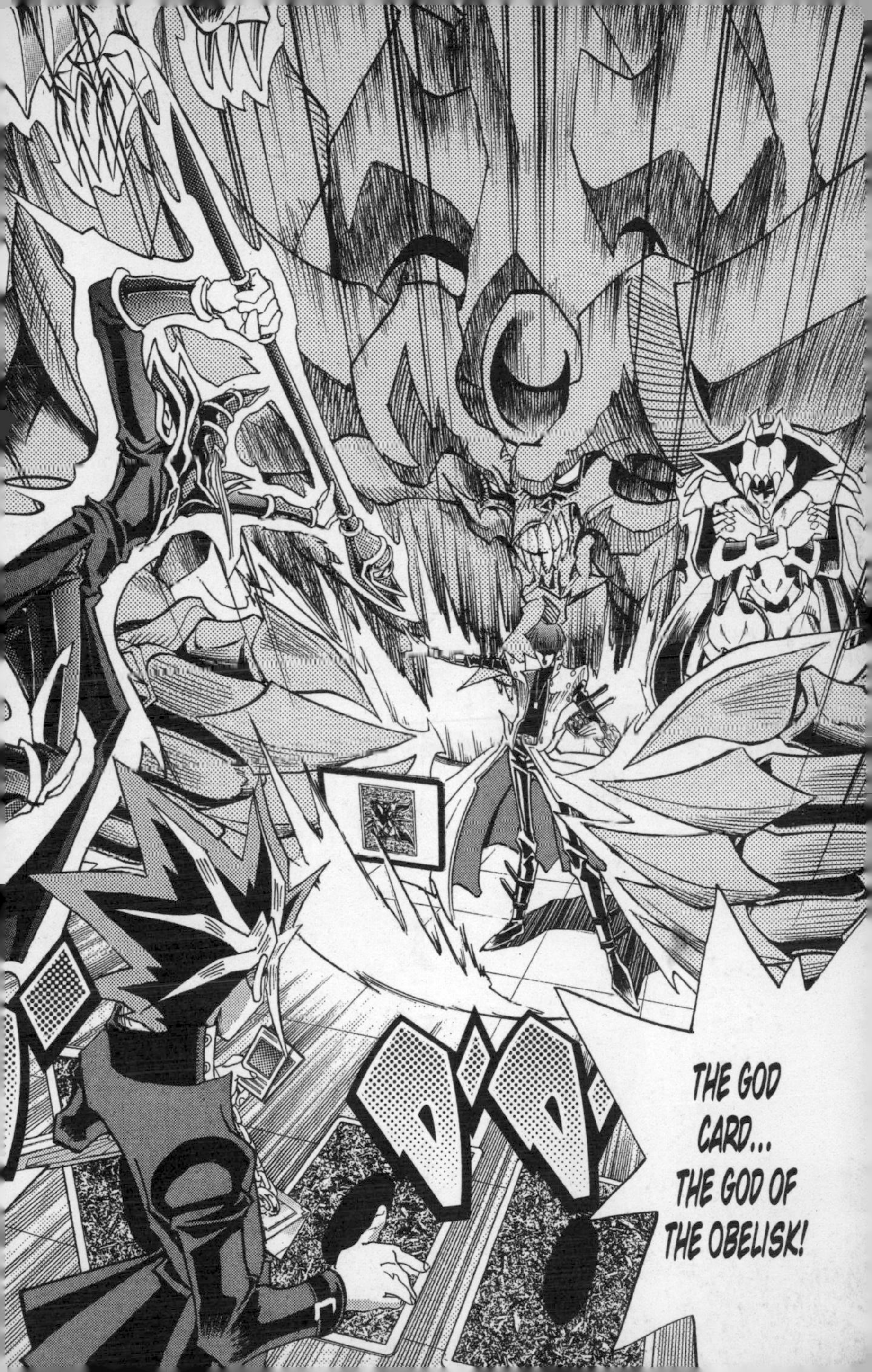
THE GOD CARD... THE GOD OF THE OBELISK!

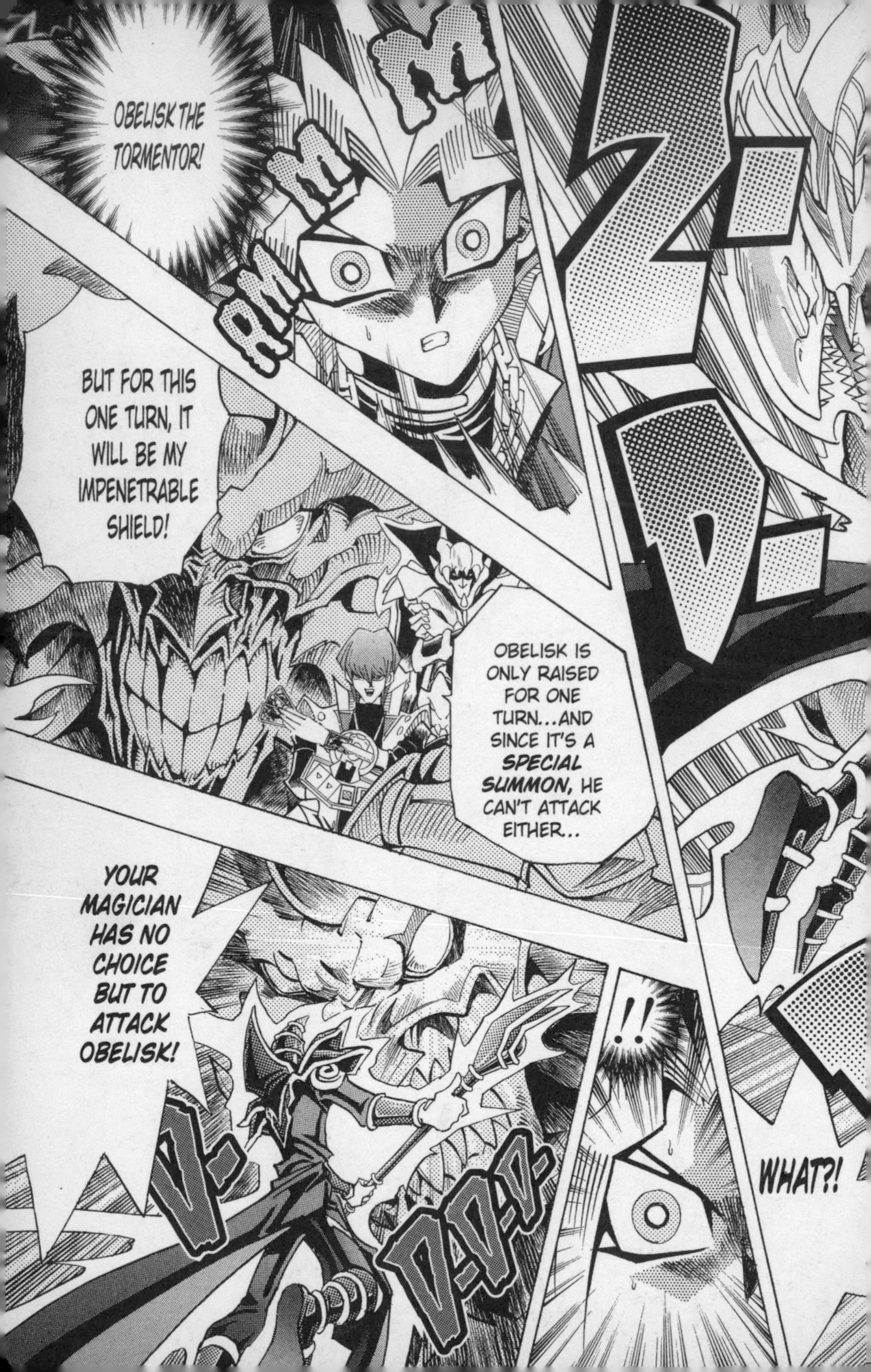
OBELISK THE TORMENTOR!
BUT FOR THIS ONE TURN, IT WILL BE MY IMPENETRABLE SHIELD!
OBELISK IS ONLY RAISED FOR ONE TURN...AND SINCE IT'S A SPECIAL SUMMON, HE CAN'T ATTACK EITHER...
YOUR MAGICIAN HAS NO CHOICE BUT TO ATTACK OBELISK!
!!
WHAT?!

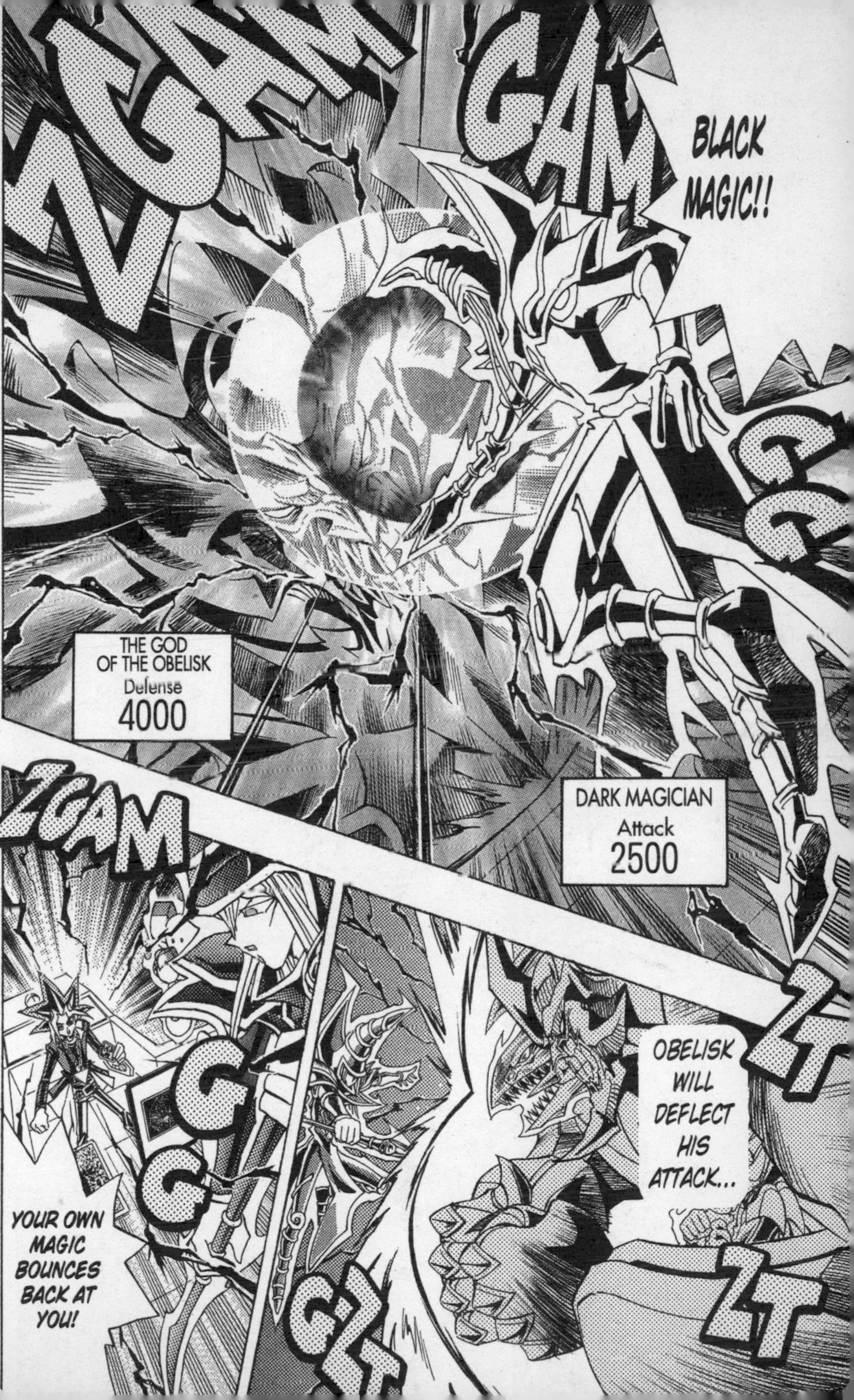
BLACK MAGIC!!
GAM
DARK MAGICIAN Attack 2500
THE GOD OF THE OBELISK Defense 4000
ZGAM
ZT
OBELISK WILL DEFLECT HIS ATTACK...
ZT
YOUR OWN MAGIC BOUNCES BACK AT YOU!

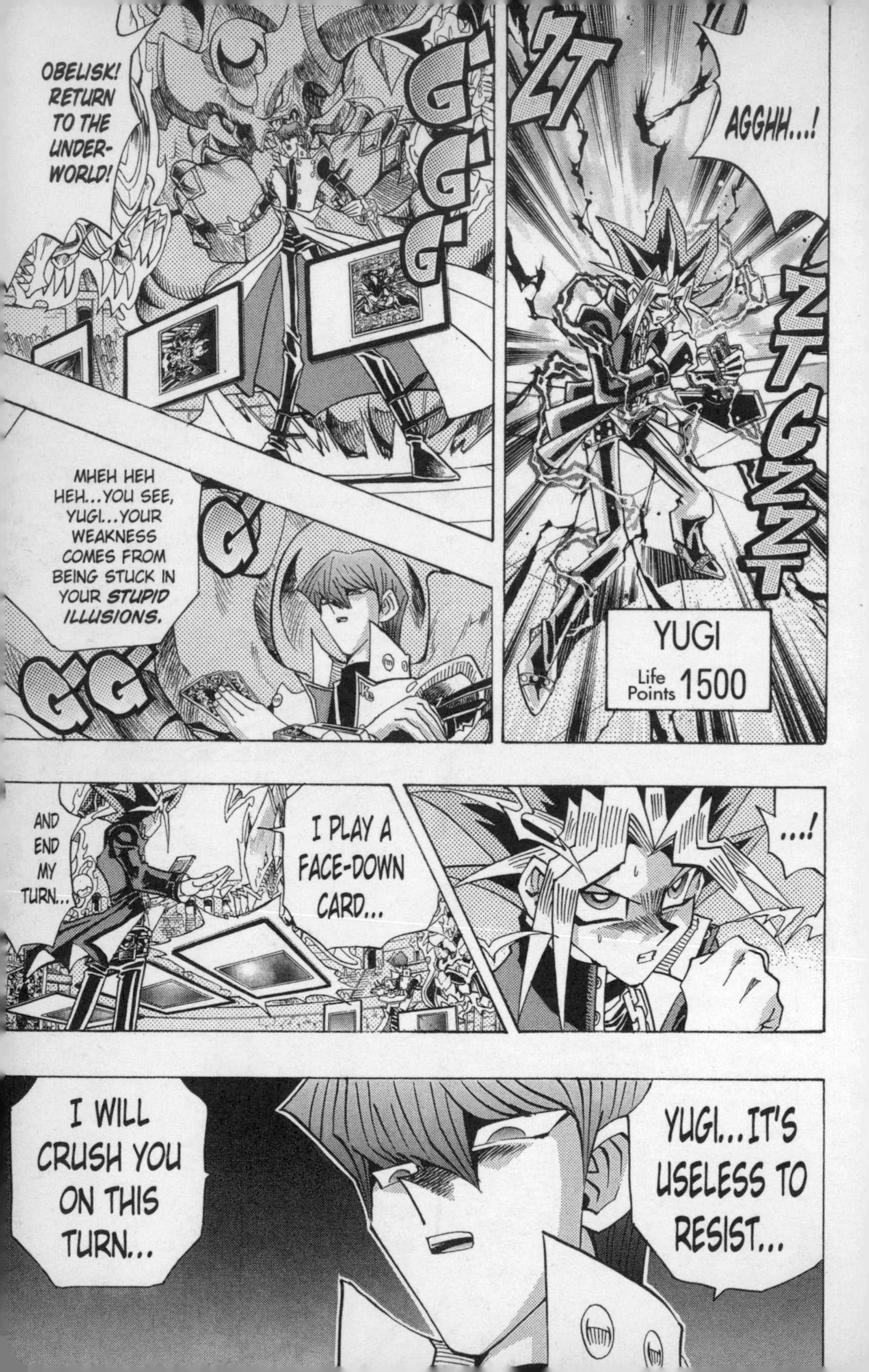
ZZT
AGGHH...!
ZZT GZZZT
YUGI
Life Points 1500
G G G
OBELISK! RETURN TO THE UNDER-WORLD!
G
MHEH HEH HEH...YOU SEE, YUGI...YOUR WEAKNESS COMES FROM BEING STUCK IN YOUR **STUPID ILLUSIONS.**
G G
...!
I PLAY A FACE-DOWN CARD...
AND END MY TURN...
YUGI...IT'S USELESS TO RESIST...
I WILL CRUSH YOU ON THIS TURN...

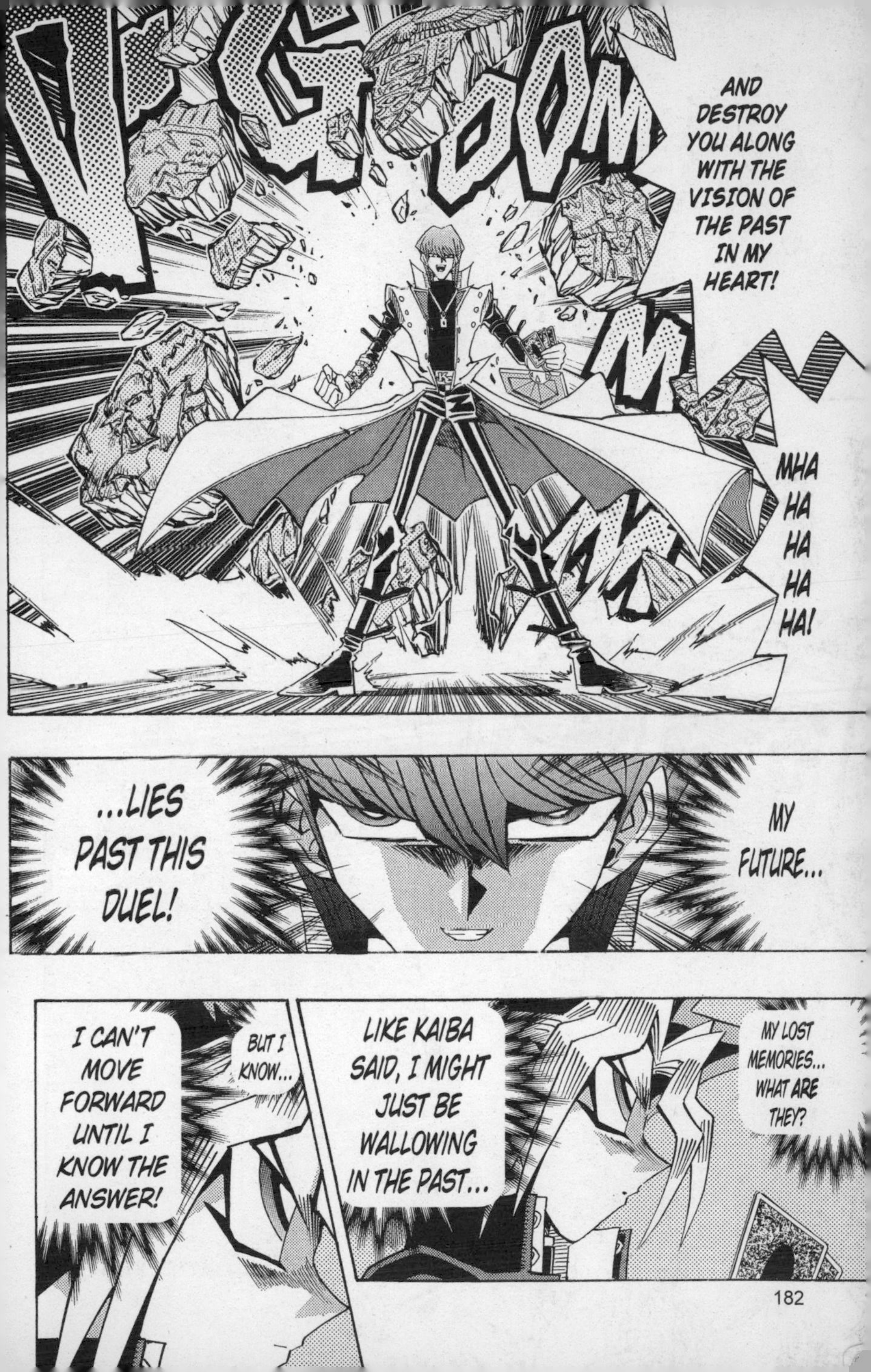
AND DESTROY YOU ALONG WITH THE VISION OF THE PAST IN MY HEART!
MHA HA HA HA HA!
MY FUTURE...
...LIES PAST THIS DUEL!
MY LOST MEMORIES... WHAT ARE THEY?
LIKE KAIBA SAID, I MIGHT JUST BE WALLOWING IN THE PAST...
BUT I KNOW...
I CAN'T MOVE FORWARD UNTIL I KNOW THE ANSWER!

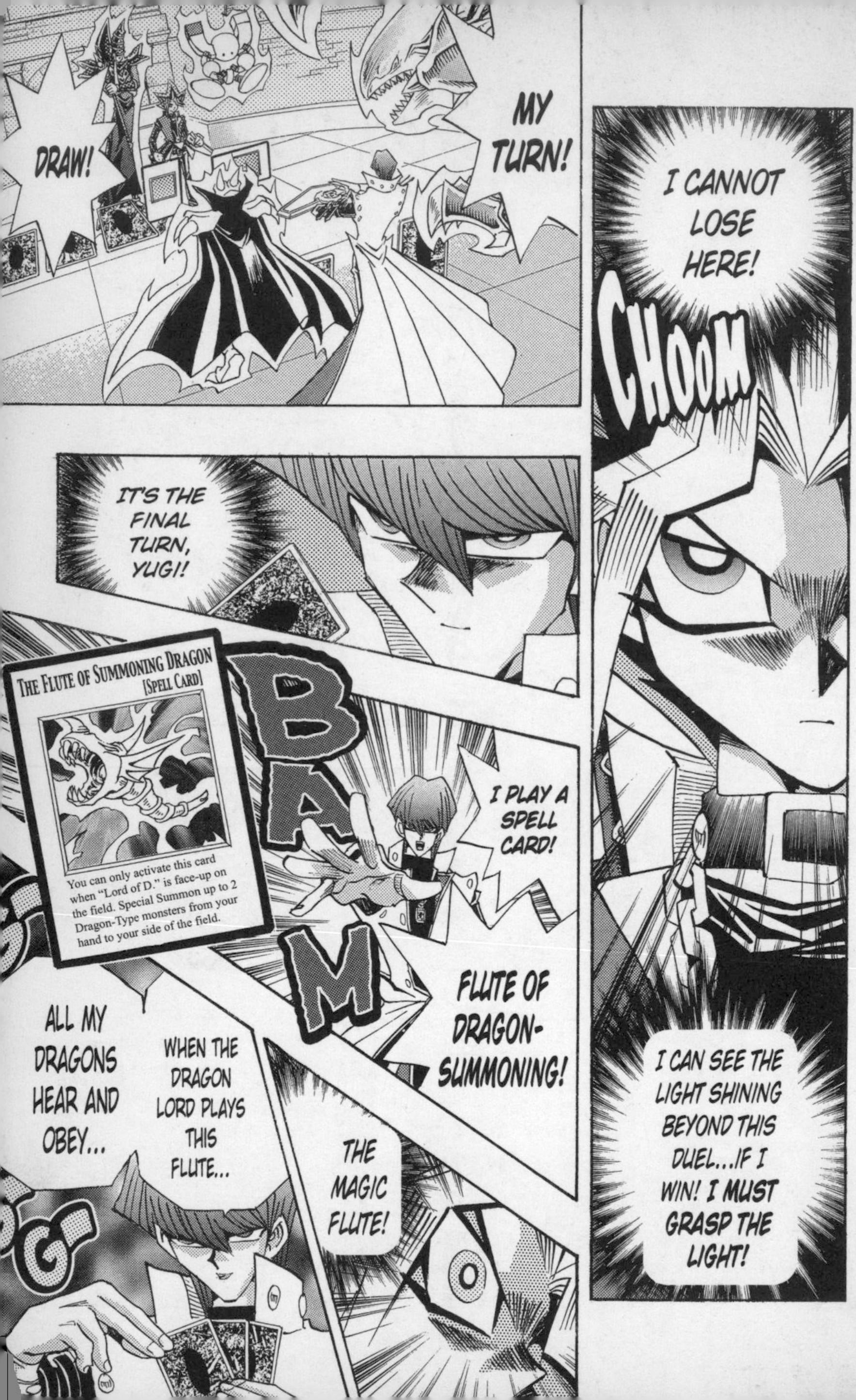
I CANNOT LOSE HERE!
CHOOM
I CAN SEE THE LIGHT SHINING BEYOND THIS DUEL...IF I WIN! I MUST GRASP THE LIGHT!
MY TURN!
DRAW!
IT'S THE FINAL TURN, YUGI!
I PLAY A SPELL CARD!
BAM
THE FLUTE OF SUMMONING DRAGON
[SPELL CARD]
You can only activate this card when "Lord of D." is face-up on the field. Special Summon up to 2 Dragon-Type monsters from your hand to your side of the field.
FLUTE OF DRAGON-SUMMONING!
THE MAGIC FLUTE!
WHEN THE DRAGON LORD PLAYS THIS FLUTE...
ALL MY DRAGONS HEAR AND OBEY...

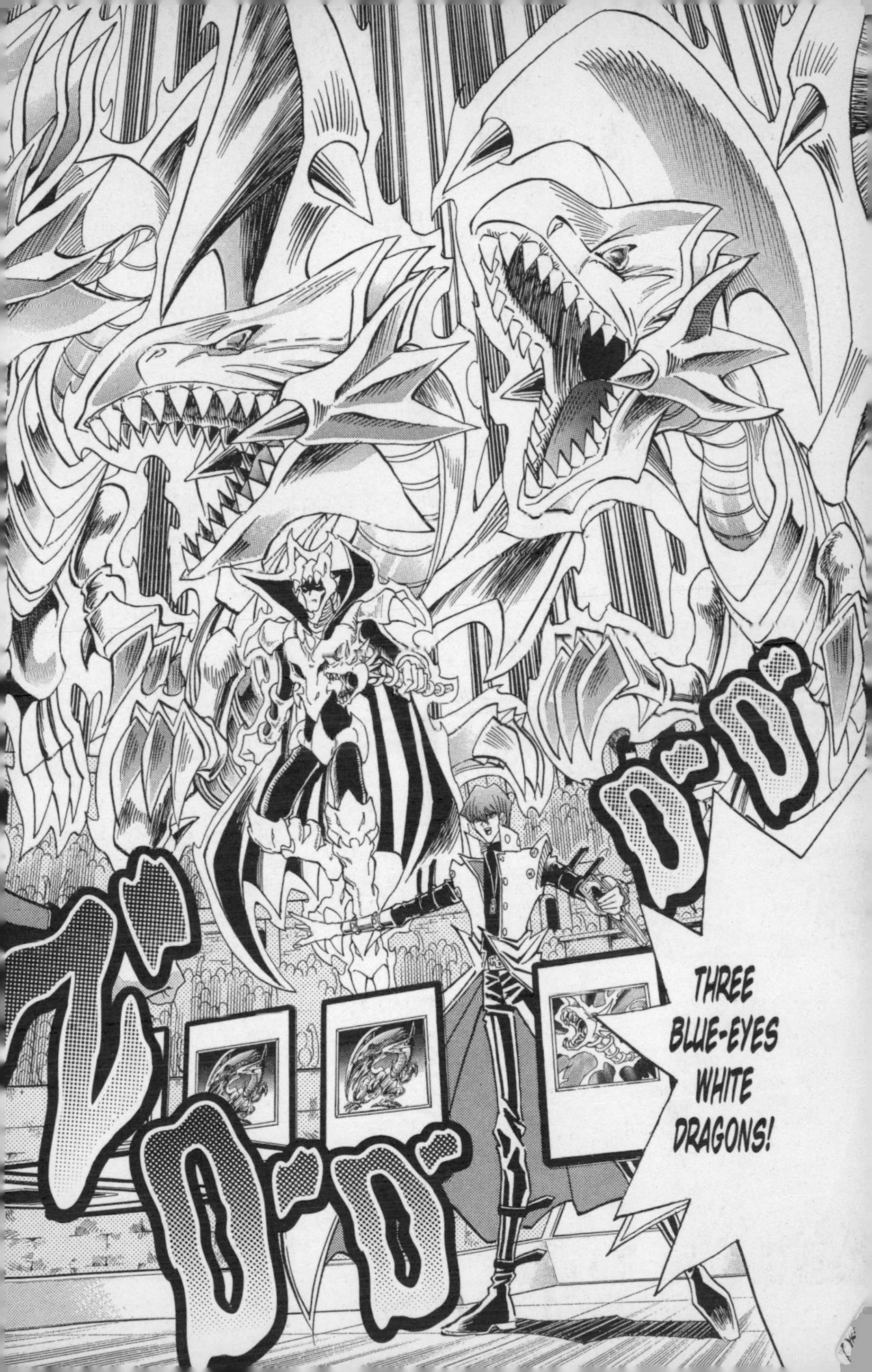
THREE BLUE-EYES WHITE DRAGONS!

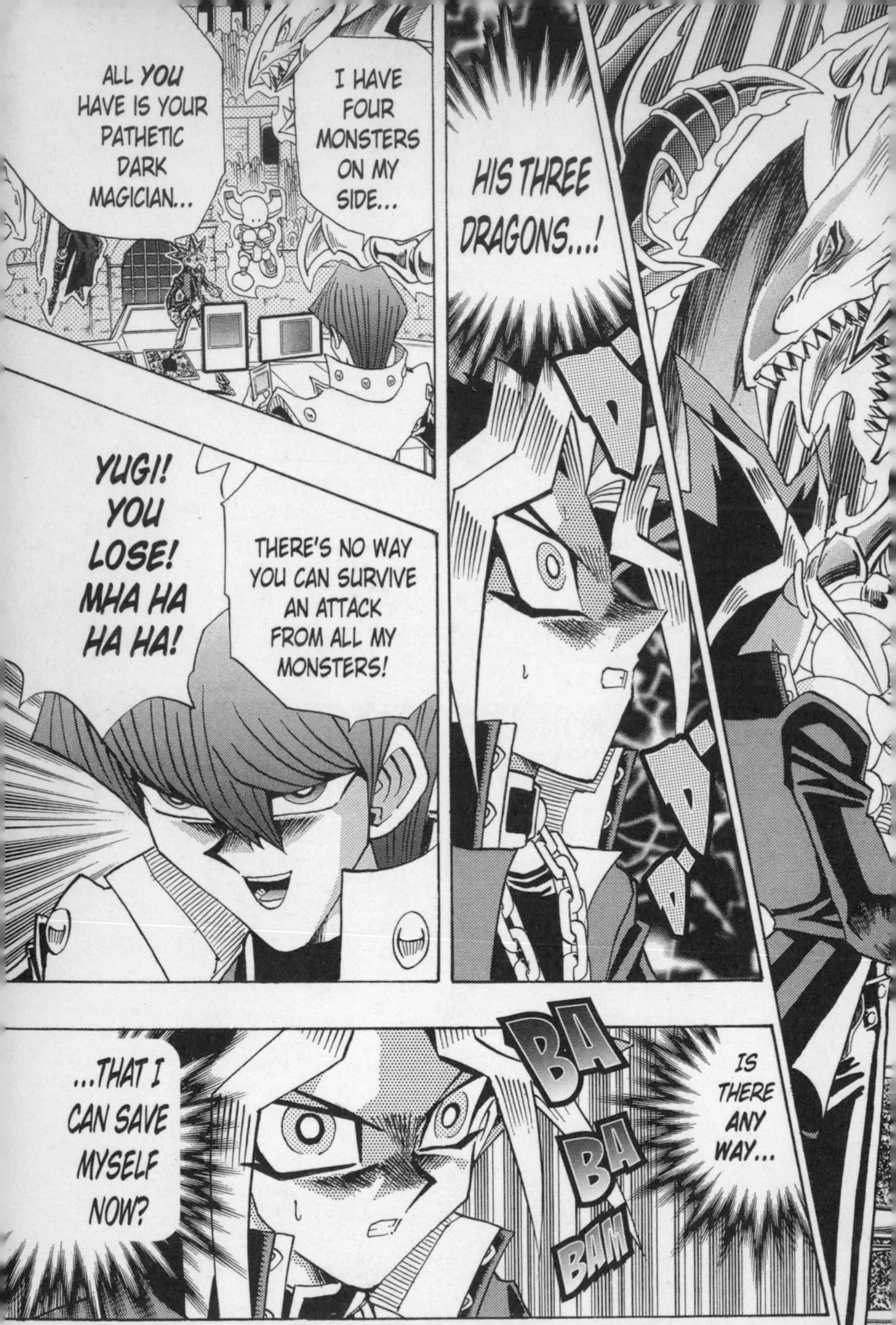
HIS THREE DRAGONS...!
I HAVE FOUR MONSTERS ON MY SIDE...
ALL YOU HAVE IS YOUR PATHETIC DARK MAGICIAN...
THERE'S NO WAY YOU CAN SURVIVE AN ATTACK FROM ALL MY MONSTERS!
YUGI! YOU LOSE! MHA HA HA HA!
IS THERE ANY WAY...
BA BA BAM
...THAT I CAN SAVE MYSELF NOW?

TO BE CONTINUED IN YU-GI-OH!: DUELIST VOL. 23!

MASTER OF THE CARDS

The "Duel Monsters" card game first appeared in volume two of the original **Yu-Gi-Oh!** graphic novel series, but it's in **Yu-Gi-Oh!: Duelist** (originally printed in Japan as volumes 8-31 of **Yu-Gi-Oh!**) that it gets really important. As many fans know, some of the card names are different between the English and Japanese versions. In case you play the game, or you're interested in playing, here's a rundown of some of the cards in this graphic novel. Some cards only appear in the **Yu-Gi-Oh!** video games, not in the actual trading card game.

FIRST APPEARANCE IN THIS VOLUME	JAPANESE CARD NAME	ENGLISH CARD NAME
p.25	*Obelisk no Kyoshinhei* (Obelisk the Giant God Soldier)	The God of the Obelisk (NOTE: Called "Obelisk the Tormentor" in the English anime and card game.)
p.25	*Osiris no Tenkûryû* (Osiris the Heaven Dragon)	Slifer the Sky Dragon
p.34	*Queen's Knight*	Queen's Knight
p.36	*X-Head Cannon*	X-Head Cannon
p.38	*Kuribo*	Kuriboh
p.39	*Cross Soul*	Soul Exchange
p.41	*Enemy Controller*	Enemy Controller

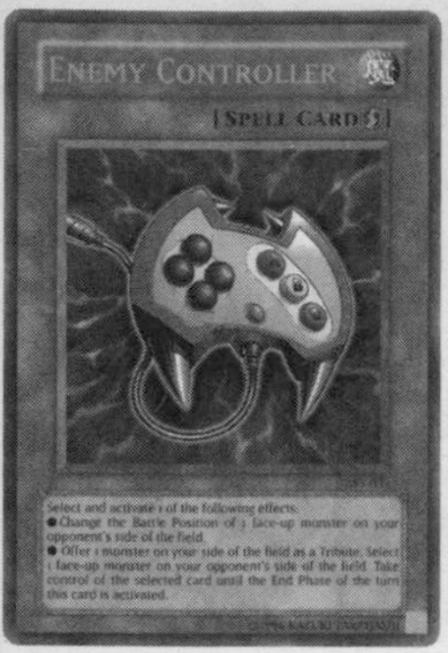
Enemy Controller
[Spell Card]
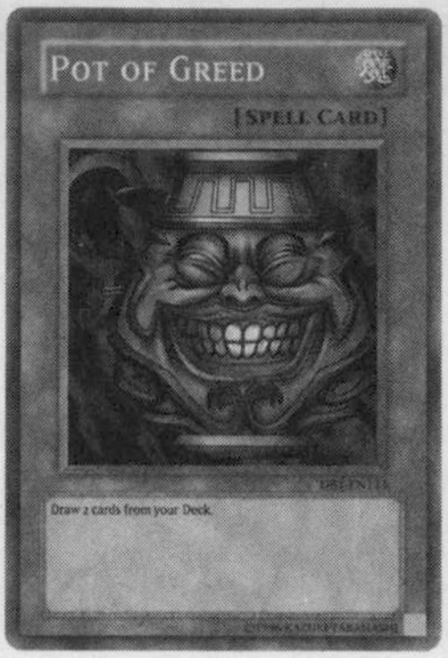
Pot of Greed
[Spell Card]
Draw 2 cards from your Deck.
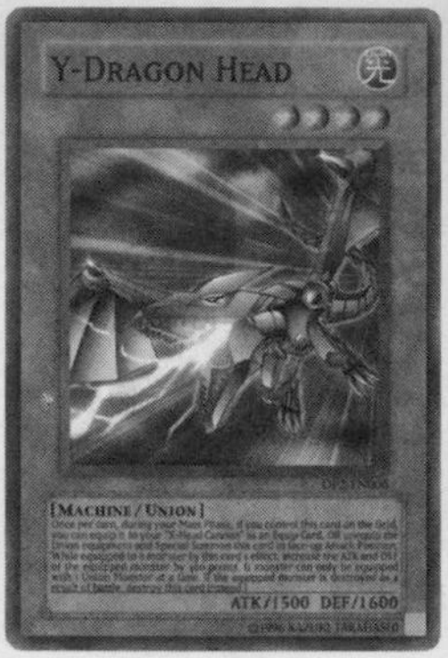
Y-Dragon Head
[Machine / Union]
ATK/1500 DEF/1600

FIRST APPEARANCE IN THIS VOLUME	JAPANESE CARD NAME	ENGLISH CARD NAME
p.43	*Hikari no Fûsatsuken* (Sealing Sword of Light)	Lightforce Sword
p.50	*Tensei no Fukujû* (Obedience to God's Voice/Heavenly Voice)	Voice of the Heavens (NOTE: Not a real game card. Called "Lullaby of Obedience" in the English anime.)
p.51	*Exchange*	Exchange
p.54	*Y-Dragon Head*	Y-Dragon Head
p.55	*XY-Dragon Cannon*	XY-Dragon Cannon
p.61	*Black Magician Girl*	Dark Magician Girl
p.70	*Kezuriyuku Inochi* (Life Shaver)	Life Shaver (NOTE: Not a real game card.)
p.72	*Big Shield Guardna*	Big Shield Guardna
p.75	*Z-Metal Caterpillar*	Z-Metal Tank
p.76	*XYZ-Dragon Cannon*	XYZ-Dragon Cannon
p.79	*Tamashii no Tsuna* (Soul Rope)	Soul Rope (NOTE: Not a real game card.)

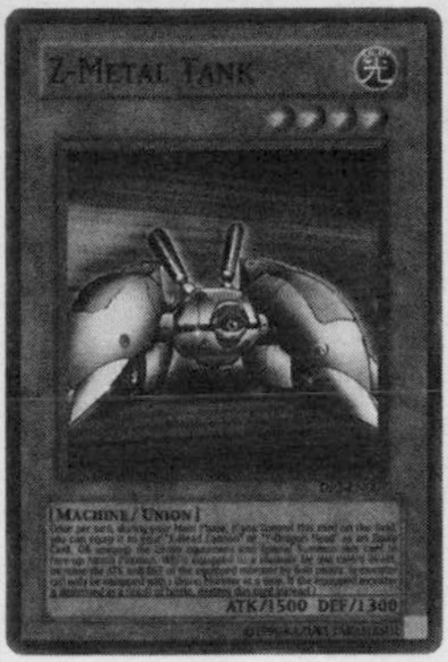
Z-METAL TANK
[MACHINE / UNION]
ATK/1500 DEF/1300
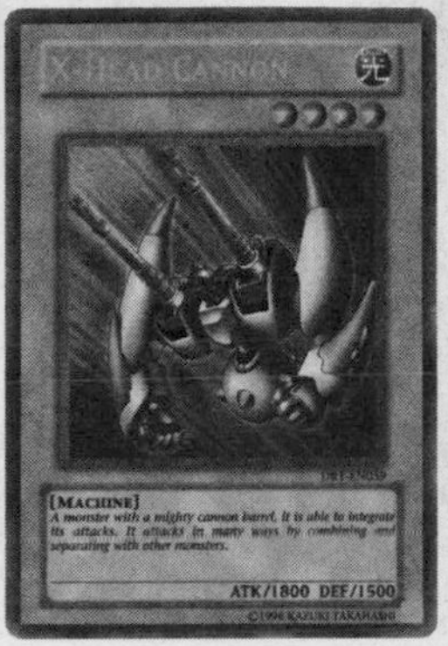
X-HEAD CANNON
[MACHINE]
A monster with a mighty cannon barrel. It is able to integrate its attacks. It attacks in many ways by combining and separating with other monsters.
ATK/1800 DEF/1500
©1996 KAZUKI TAKAHASHI
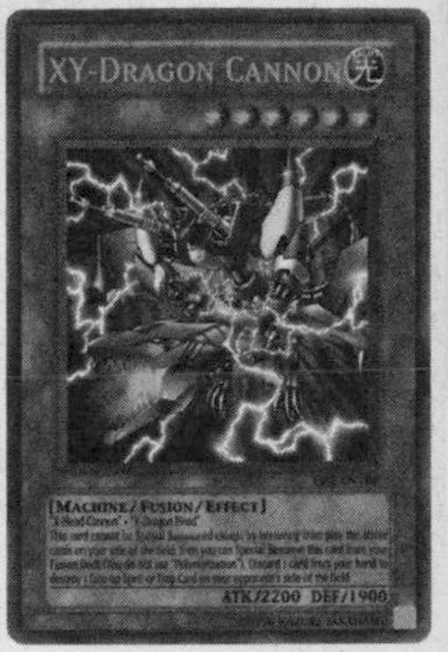
XY-DRAGON CANNON
[MACHINE / FUSION / EFFECT]
ATK/2200 DEF/1900

FIRST APPEARANCE IN THIS VOLUME	JAPANESE CARD NAME	ENGLISH CARD NAME
p.80	*King's Knight*	King's Knight
p.81	*Jack's Knight*	Jack's Knight
p.96	*Akûkan Busshitsu Tensô Sôchi* (Interdimensional Matter Teleportation Device)	Interdimensional Matter Transporter
p.120	*Gôyoku na Tsubo* (Pot of Greed)	Pot of Greed
p.153	*Clone Fukusei* (Clone Reproduction)	Clone Reproduction
p.153	*Blue Eyes White Dragon*	Blue Eyes White Dragon
p.154	*Baphomet*	Baphomet (NOTE: Called "Berfomet" in the English anime and card game.)
p.157	*Cost Down*	Cost Down
p.162	*Shisha Sosei* (Resurrection of the Dead)	Monster Reborn
p.164	*Black Magician*	Dark Magician
p.167	*Magnet Warrior Beta*	Beta the Magnet Warrior

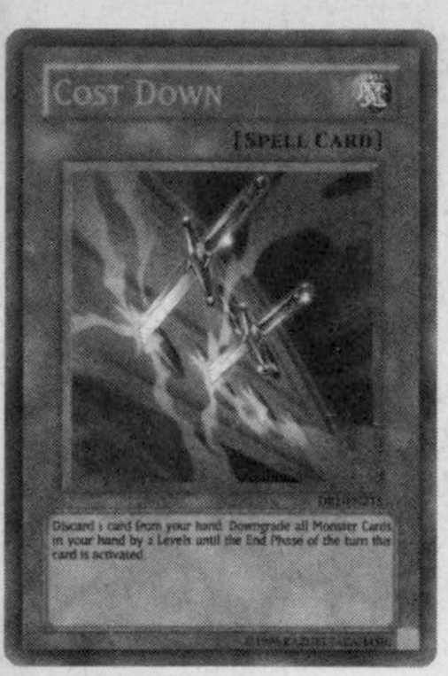
COST DOWN
[SPELL CARD]
Discard 1 card from your hand. Downgrade all Monster Cards in your hand by 2 Levels until the End Phase of the turn the card is activated.

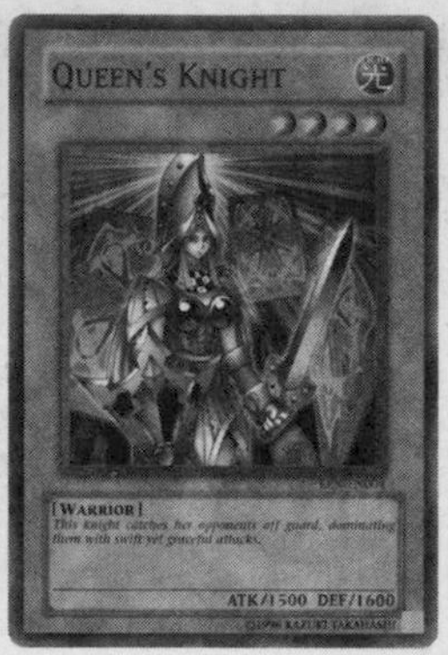
QUEEN'S KNIGHT
[WARRIOR]
ATK/1500 DEF/1600

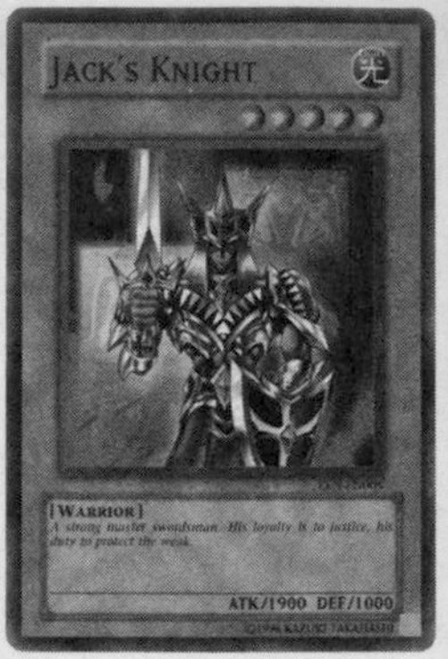
JACK'S KNIGHT
[WARRIOR]
ATK/1900 DEF/1000

FIRST APPEARANCE IN THIS VOLUME	JAPANESE CARD NAME	ENGLISH CARD NAME
p.170	*Majutsu no Jumonsho* (Spellbook of Sorcery)	Magic Formula
p.172	*Inochikezuri no Hôsatsu* (Precious Card of Slashing Life)	Card of Demise (NOTE: Not a real game card.)
p.173	*Rokubôsei no Jubaku* (Binding Curse of the Hexagram)	Spellbinding Circle
p.174	*Lord of Dragon*	Lord of D.
p.177	*Kikai Jikake no Magic Mirror* (Mechanical Magic Mirror)	Magical Trick Mirror (NOTE: Not a real game card.)
p.183	*Dragon wo Yobu Fue* (Dragon-Summoning Flute)	The Flute of Summoning Dragon

IN THE NEXT VOLUME...

Yugi and Kaiba's greatest battle reenacts itself...Blue-Eyes Ultimate Dragons vs. Dark Magician! One duelist will lose, and the other will go on to face god...the greatest Egyptian God Card, the Sun Dragon Ra! But can anyone defeat the ultimate God Card in the hands of its master, the mad Marik?

COMING OCTOBER 2007!

KAIBA
LIFE POINT
1900

YŪGI
LIFE POINT
1500

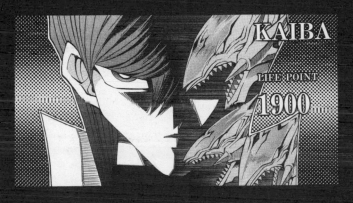

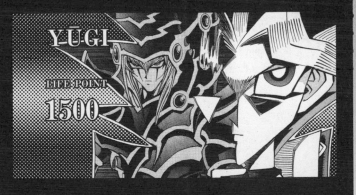

Save 50% off the ne...

SHONEN JUMP

THE WORLD'S MOST POPULAR MANGA™

SUBSCRIBE TODAY and SAVE 50% OFF the cover price PLUS enjoy all the benefits of the SHONEN JUMP SUBSCRIBER CLUB, exclusive online content & special gifts ONLY AVAILABLE to SUBSCRIBERS!

☑ **YES!** Please enter my 1 year subscription (12 issues) to *SHONEN JUMP* at the INCREDIBLY LOW SUBSCRIPTION RATE of $29.95 and sign me up for the SHONEN JUMP Subscriber Club!

Only $29⁹⁵!

NAME **CHASE BRANCH LIBRARY**

ADDRESS **31 W. SEVEN MILE RD.**

CITY **DETROIT, MI 48235**   STATE   ZIP

E-MAIL ADDRESS **78-8002**

☐ MY CHECK IS ENCLOSED   ☐ BILL ME LATER

CRED CARD: ☐ VISA   ☐ MASTERCARD

ACCOUNT #   EXP. DATE

SIGNATURE

CLIP AND MAIL TO ➡

SHONEN JUMP
Subscriptions Service Dept.
P.O. Box 515
Mount Morris, IL 61054-0515

JUN 2012

Make checks payable to: **SHONEN JUMP.**
Canada add US $12. No foreign orders. Allow 6-8 weeks fo...

P6SJGN   YU-GI-OH! © 1996 by Kazuki Takahashi / SHUEISHA Inc..